VERMONT CRIMES AND CRIMINAL PROCEDURE 2021

Title 13 of the Vermont Statutes, Current through April 1, 2021

Access the law at your fingertips. This 2021 edition of Vermont Crimes and Criminal Procedure provides the practitioner with a convenient copy to bring to court or the office. Look for other titles in our series such as Vermont Court Procedure.

ISBN: 9798737393601

Peter Edwards, Esq.
Vermont Legal Publishing, LLC

Table of Contents

Chapter 1: General Provisions

§ 1. Felonies and misdemeanors defined

Any other provision of law notwithstanding, any offense whose maximum term of imprisonment is more than two years, for life, or which may be punished by death is a felony. Any other offense is a misdemeanor. (Amended 1971, No. 199 (Adj. Sess.), § 1; 1973, No. 109, § 2, eff. 30 days from April 25, 1973.)

§ 2. Crimes committed partly outside State

A person who, with intent to commit a crime, does an act within this State in execution or part execution of such intent, which culminates in the commission of a crime either within or without this State, shall be punished for such crime in this State in the same manner as if the same had been committed entirely within this State. A crime committed by means of an electronic communication, including a telephonic communication, shall be considered to have been committed at either the place where the communication originated or the place where it was received. (Amended 1999, No. 124 (Adj. Sess.), § 1.)

§ 3. Accessory aiding commission of felony

A person who aids in the commission of a felony shall be punished as a principal. (Amended 1971, No. 199 (Adj. Sess.), § 2; 1973, No. 109, § 3, eff. 30 days from April 25, 1973.)

§ 4. Accessory before the fact

A person who is accessory before the fact by counseling, hiring, or otherwise procuring an offense to be committed may be informed against or indicted, tried, convicted, and punished as if he or she were a principal offender in the Criminal Division of the Superior Court in the unit where the principal might be prosecuted. (Amended 1973, No. 118, § 3, eff. Oct. 1, 1973; 1973, No. 193 (Adj. Sess.), § 3, eff. April 9, 1974; 2009, No. 154 (Adj. Sess.), § 94.)

§ 5. Accessory after the fact

A person not standing in the relation of husband, wife, parent, grandparent, child, grandchild, brother, or sister, by consanguinity or affinity, to an offender, who, after the commission of a felony, harbors, conceals, maintains, or assists such offender with intent that he or she shall avoid or escape arrest or punishment therefor, shall be imprisoned not more than seven years or fined not more than $1,000.00, or both. (Amended 1971, No. 199 (Adj. Sess.), § 15; 1981, No. 223 (Adj. Sess.), § 23.)

§ 6. Prosecution and venue

An accessory after the fact may be prosecuted, convicted, and punished whether the principal has or has not been previously convicted, or is or is not amenable to justice, in the Criminal Division of the Superior Court in the unit where such person became an accessory or where the principal offense is committed. (Amended 1973, No. 118, § 4, eff. Oct. 1, 1973; 1973, No. 193 (Adj. Sess.), § 3, eff. April 9, 1974; 2009, No. 154 (Adj. Sess.), § 95.)

§ 7. Inciting to felony

A person who endeavors to incite, procure, or hire another person to commit a felony, though a felony is not actually committed as a result of such inciting, hiring, or procuring, shall be imprisoned not more than five years or fined not more than $500.00, or both. (Amended 1971, No. 199 (Adj. Sess.), § 15; 1981, No. 223 (Adj. Sess.), § 23.)

§ 8. Compounding felony

A person having knowledge of the commission of a felony who takes money, or a gratuity or reward, or an engagement therefor, upon an agreement or understanding, expressed or implied, to compound or conceal such felony or not to prosecute therefor, or not to give evidence thereof, shall be imprisoned not more than 10 years or fined not more than $1,000.00, or both. (Amended 1971, No. 199 (Adj. Sess.), § 15; 1981, No. 223 (Adj. Sess.), § 23.)

§ 9. Attempts

(a) A person who attempts to commit an offense and does an act toward the commission thereof, but by reason of being interrupted or prevented fails in the execution of the same, shall be punished as herein provided unless other express provision is made by law for the punishment of the attempt. If the offense attempted to be committed is murder, aggravated murder, kidnapping, arson causing death, human trafficking, aggravated human trafficking, aggravated sexual assault, or sexual assault, a person shall be punished as the offense attempted to be committed is by law punishable.

(b) If the offense attempted to be committed is a felony other than those set forth in subsection (a) of this section, a person shall be punished by the less severe of the following punishments:

(1) imprisonment for not more than 10 years or fined not more than $10,000.00, or both; or

(2) as the offense attempted to be committed is by law punishable.

(c) If the offense attempted to be committed is a misdemeanor, a person shall be imprisoned or fined, or both, in an amount not to exceed one-half the maximum penalty for which the offense so attempted to be committed is by law punishable. (Amended 1971, No. 199 (Adj. Sess.) § 3; 1973, No. 109, § 4, eff. 30 days from April 25, 1973; 1993, No. 95, § 5; 2011, No. 55, § 5.)

§ 10. Punishment for attempt on indictment charging commission

Under an information or indictment charging the commission of a felony, according as the proof is, the jury may return a verdict that the respondent is not guilty of the principal offense, but is guilty of an attempt to commit the same, in the manner stated in section 9 of this title, or the court may allow the respondent to plead guilty of such an attempt. In either case, the court shall pass sentence accordingly.

§ 11. Habitual criminals

A person who, after having been three times convicted within this State of felonies or attempts to commit felonies, or under the law of any other state, government, or country, of crimes which, if committed within this State, would be felonious, commits a felony other than murder within this State, may be sentenced upon conviction of such fourth or subsequent offense to imprisonment up to and including life. (Amended 1971, No. 199 (Adj. Sess.), § 15; 1995, No. 50, § 1.)

§ 11a. Repealed. 2019, No. 77, § 6, eff. June 19, 2019.

§ 12. Criminal use of anesthetics

A person who administers, attempts to administer, or causes to be administered to a person, chloroform, sulphuric ether, or any anesthetic agent, with intent to commit a crime or offense, or who secretly commits or attempts to commit a crime or offense against a person or the property of one who is rendered insensible or unconscious or incapable of resistence by such anesthetic agent, shall be imprisoned for life or for not less than three years. (Amended 1971, No. 199 (Adj. Sess.), § 15.)

§ 13. Repealed. 1999, No. 4, § 7.

§ 14. Lesser included offenses

(a) Upon indictment or information for any offense, a person may be convicted of a lesser included offense if supported by the evidence. If requested by either party, the jury shall be informed of the lesser included offense if supported by the evidence. The court, on its own motion, may raise the issue of a lesser included offense at a jury charge conference.

(b) If requested by either party, or in his or her discretion, the judge in a court trial shall consider a lesser included offense if supported by the evidence. (Added 1997, No. 153 (Adj. Sess.), § 1.)

Chapter 3: Abortion

§§ 101-104. Repealed.

2013, No. 98 (Adj. Sess.), § 1, eff. March. 24, 2014.

Chapter 5: Adultery And Bigamy

§§ 201, 202. Repealed.

1981, No. 223 (Adj. Sess.), § 24.

§§ 203, 204. Repealed.

1979, No. 152 (Adj. Sess.).

§ 205. Intermarriage of or fornication by persons prohibited to marry

Persons between whom marriages are prohibited by the laws of this State who intermarry or commit fornication with each other shall be imprisoned not more than five years or fined not more than $1,000.00, or both. (Amended 1981, No. 223 (Adj. Sess.), § 16.)

§ 206. Bigamy

A person having a husband or wife living who marries another person, or continues to cohabit with such second husband or wife in this State, shall be imprisoned not more than five years. This section shall not extend to a person whose husband or wife has been continually beyond the sea, or out of the State for seven consecutive years, the party marrying again not knowing the other to be living within that time; or to a person whose former marriage has been avoided by divorce or sentence of nullity, or was contracted under the age of consent and not afterwards assented to. (Amended 1971, No. 199 (Adj. Sess.), § 15; 2009, No. 3, § 12a, eff. Sept. 1, 2009.)

§ 207. Proof of respondent's civil marriage

In prosecutions for crimes and penalties where it is necessary to prove the fact of the civil marriage of the respondent, acts of cohabitation by the respondent with the supposed husband or wife, and other acts, admissions, and declarations of the respondent tending to prove such marriage shall be admitted in evidence as competent testimony. (Amended 2009, No. 3, § 12a, eff. Sept. 1, 2009.)

§ 208. Alleging civil marriage in bigamy prosecution

In prosecutions for bigamy it shall be sufficient to allege in the information or indictment that, at the time of the second civil marriage, the respondent had a wife or husband living, without specifying the time or place of the former marriage or the name of the former husband or wife. (Amended 2009, No. 3, § 12a, eff. Sept. 1, 2009.)

Chapter 7: Advertisements

§ 301. Posting utility poles

A person who paints or posts a sign, advertisement, or notice on a telegraph, telephone, or electric light pole shall be fined $5.00 for each offense.

§ 302. Advertising littering streets and highways

A person who by himself, herself, servant, or agent, advertises an entertainment or occupation, by throwing posters, bills, or advertising sheets of any kind, loose in a public street or highway, shall be fined not more than $50.00 nor less than $5.00, with costs.

§ 303. Posting on private property

A person who advertises his or her wares or occupations, by painting or posting notice of the same on fences or other private property, or on rocks or other natural objects, without leave of the owner, shall be fined $10.00.

§§ 304-307. Repealed.

1979, No. 152 (Adj. Sess.).

Chapter 8: Humane And Proper Treatment Of Animals

Subchapter 1: Cruelty To Animals

§ 351. Definitions

As used in this chapter:

(1) "Animal" means all living sentient creatures, not human beings.

(2) "Secretary" means the Secretary of Agriculture, Food and Markets.

(3) "Horse" means the entire family of Equidae.

(4) "Humane officer" or "officer" means any law enforcement officer as defined in 23 V.S.A. § 4(11); auxiliary State Police officers; deputy game wardens; humane society officer, employee, or agent; animal control officer appointed by the legislative body of a municipality; local board of health officer or agent; or any officer authorized to serve criminal process.

(5) "Humane society" or "society for prevention of cruelty to animals" means the Vermont Humane Federation, Inc., or its successor, or any incorporated humane society that, through its agents, has the lawful authority to interfere with acts of cruelty to animals.

(6) "Local board of health" means the town or city health officer and the selectboard members or aldermen.

(7) "Necessary medical attention" shall include medical or surgical treatment for injury, disease, excessive parasitism, dehydration, malnutrition, pain, or impaired locomotive function.

(8) "Person" means any individual, firm, partnership, or corporation, or authorized agent or representative of a person, partnership, or corporation.

(9) "Sanitation" means the maintenance of clean conditions for indoor and outdoor enclosures to minimize health hazards, including periodic cleanings to remove excretions or other waste materials, dirt, and trash.

(10) "Torture" or "torment" means omission, neglect, or an act by an animal owner or other person, whereby physical pain, suffering, or death is caused or permitted to be caused to an animal.

(11) "Livestock" means cattle, bison, horses, sheep, goats, swine, Cervidae, ratites, and camelids.

(12) "Poultry" means meat and egg producing chickens, exhibition (fancy) chickens, turkeys, domestic ducks, geese, pheasants, chicken partridge, and cotarnix quail.

(13) "Livestock and poultry husbandry practices" means the raising, management and using of animals to provide humans with food, fiber, or transportation in a manner consistent with:

(A) husbandry practices recommended for the species by fully accredited agricultural colleges and the U.S. Department of Agriculture Extension Service;

(B) husbandry practices modified for the species to conform to the Vermont environment and terrain; and

(C) husbandry practices that minimize pain and suffering.

(14) "Agricultural or sporting association" means an organization or association determined by the Secretary.

(15) "Living space" means any cage, crate, or other structure used to confine an animal that serves as its principal, primary housing and that provides protection from the elements. Living space does not include a structure, such as a doghouse, in which an animal is not confined, or a cage, crate, or other structure in which the animal is temporarily confined.

(16) "Adequate food" means food that is not spoiled or contaminated and is of sufficient nutritional content to meet the normal daily requirements for the condition and size of the animal and the environment in which it is kept. An animal shall be fed or have food available at least once each day, unless a licensed veterinarian instructs otherwise or withholding food is in accordance with accepted veterinary practices or livestock and poultry husbandry practices.

(17) "Adequate water" means potable water that is either accessible to the animal at all times or is provided at suitable intervals for the species and in sufficient quantity for the health of the animal. In no event shall the interval when water is not provided exceed 24 hours. Snow or ice is not an adequate water source unless provided in accordance with livestock and poultry husbandry practices.

(18) [Repealed.]

(19) "Enclosure" means any structure, fence, device, or other barrier used to restrict an animal or animals to a limited amount of space.

(20) "Livestock guardian dog" means a purpose-bred dog that is:

(A) specifically trained to live with livestock without causing them harm while repelling predators;

(B) being used to live with and guard livestock; and

(C) acclimated to local weather conditions.

(21) "Sexual conduct" means:

(A) any act between a person and animal that involves contact between the mouth, sex organ, or anus of a person and the mouth, sex organ, or anus of an animal; or

(B) without a bona fide veterinary or animal husbandry purpose, the insertion, however slight, of any part of a person's body or of any instrument, apparatus, or other object into the vaginal or anal opening of an animal.

(22) "Adequate constructed shelter" means a well-drained and structurally sound building with a waterproof roof that is of sufficient size to provide a windbreak and protection from exposure to prevailing winds, rain, hail, sleet, snow, and sun and that provides enough space to accommodate at one time all livestock and animals comfortably. The building opening size and height shall, at a minimum, allow six inches of clearance above the largest animal's ears when the animal is standing in a normal position, and the clearance shall be maintained at that level even with manure and litter buildup.

(23) "Adequate natural shelter" means a natural structure or formation, which may include a stand of trees that:

(A) is a well-drained area of sufficient size to provide a windbreak and protection from exposure to prevailing winds, rain, hail, sleet, sun, and snow; and

(B) provides enough space to accommodate at one time all livestock or animals maintained out-of-doors in the area.

(24) "Adequate ventilation" means that ventilation in an enclosed or confined area shall be sufficient to control excessive ambient temperatures and humidity and to prevent the accumulation of toxic gases, such as ammonia. (Added 1989, No. 270 (Adj. Sess.), § 2; amended 1997, No. 130 (Adj. Sess.), § 4; 2003, No. 42, § 2, eff. May 27, 2003; 2003, No. 120 (Adj. Sess.), § 1; 2009, No. 121 (Adj. Sess.), § 4; 2013, No. 161 (Adj. Sess.), § 72; 2013, No. 162 (Adj. Sess.), § 1; 2017, No. 58, § 1; 2017, No. 62, § 10; 2019, No. 116 (Adj. Sess.), § 1.)

§ 351a. Purpose of subchapter

The purpose of this subchapter is to prevent cruelty to animals. In implementing this subchapter, enforcement officers are encouraged to educate the public on requirements of the subchapter and, when appropriate, to seek voluntary resolution of violations. (Added 1997, No. 130 (Adj. Sess.), § 5.)

§ 351b. Scope of subchapter

This subchapter shall not apply to:

(1) activities regulated by the Department of Fish and Wildlife pursuant to 10 V.S.A. Part 4, including the act of destroying feral swine in accordance with 10 V.S.A. § 4709(f);

(2) scientific research governed by accepted procedural standards subject to review by an institutional animal care and use committee;

(3) livestock and poultry husbandry practices for raising, management, and use of animals;

(4) veterinary medical or surgical procedures; and

(5) the killing of an animal as provided by 20 V.S.A. §§ 3809 and 3545. (Added 1997, No. 130 (Adj. Sess.), § 6; amended 2019, No. 129 (Adj. Sess.), § 22.)

§ 352. Cruelty to animals

A person commits the crime of cruelty to animals if the person:

(1) Intentionally kills or attempts to kill any animal belonging to another person without first obtaining legal authority or consent of the owner.

(2) Overworks, overloads, tortures, torments, abandons, administers poison to, cruelly harms or mutilates an animal or exposes a poison with intent that it be taken by an animal.

(3) Ties, tethers, or restrains an animal, either a pet or livestock, in a manner that is inhumane or is detrimental to its welfare. Livestock and poultry husbandry practices are exempted.

(4) Deprives an animal that a person owns, possesses, or acts as an agent for of adequate food, water, shelter, rest, sanitation, or necessary medical attention or transports an animal in overcrowded vehicles.

(5)(A) Owns, possesses, keeps, or trains an animal engaged in an exhibition of fighting; possesses, keeps, or trains any animal with intent that it be engaged in an exhibition of fighting; or permits any such act to be done on premises under his or her charge or control.

(B) Owns, possesses, ships, transports, delivers, or keeps a device, equipment, or implement for the purpose of training or conditioning an animal for participation in animal fighting or enhancing an animal's fighting capability.

(6) Acts as judge or spectator at events of animal fighting or bets or wagers on the outcome of such fight.

(7) As poundkeeper, officer, or agent of a humane society or as an owner or employee of an establishment for treatment, board, or care of an animal, knowingly receives, sells, transfers, or otherwise conveys an animal in his or her care for the purpose of research or vivisection.

(8) Intentionally torments or harasses an animal owned or engaged by a police department or public agency of the State or its political subdivisions or interferes with the lawful performance of a police animal.

(9) Knowingly sells, offers for sale, barters, or displays living baby chicks, ducklings, or other fowl that have been dyed, colored, or otherwise treated so as to impart to them an artificial color or fails to provide poultry with proper brooder facilities.

(10) Uses a live animal as bait or lure in a race, game, or contest or in training animals in a manner inconsistent with 10 V.S.A. Part 4 or the rules adopted thereunder.

(11)(A) Engages in sexual conduct with an animal.

(B) Possesses, sells, transfers, purchases, or otherwise obtains an animal with the intent that it be used for sexual conduct.

(C) Organizes, promotes, conducts, aids, abets, or participates in as an observer an act involving any sexual conduct with an animal.

(D) Causes, aids, or abets another person to engage in sexual conduct with an animal.

(E) Permits sexual conduct with an animal to be conducted on premises under his or her charge or control.

(F) Advertises, offers, or accepts the offer of an animal with the intent that it be subject to sexual conduct in this State. (Added 1989, No. 270 (Adj. Sess.), § 2; amended 1997, No. 130 (Adj. Sess.), § 7; 2003, No. 120 (Adj. Sess.), § 2; 2015, No. 53, § 1; 2017, No. 62, § 10; 2017, No. 112 (Adj. Sess.), § 1, eff. May 1, 2018.)

§ 352a. Aggravated cruelty to animals

A person commits the crime of aggravated cruelty to animals if the person:

(1) kills an animal by intentionally causing the animal undue pain or suffering;

(2) intentionally, maliciously, and without just cause tortures, mutilates, or cruelly beats an animal; or

(3) intentionally injures or kills an animal that is in the performance of official duties while under the supervision of a law enforcement officer. (Added 1997, No. 130 (Adj. Sess.), § 8; amended 2003, No. 120 (Adj. Sess.), § 3; 2015, No. 118 (Adj. Sess.), § 6.)

§ 352b. Rules; affirmative defense

(a) An enforcement officer implementing the provisions of section 352 or 352a of this title shall be guided by rules established by the Secretary.

(b) Except as provided in subsection (c) of this section, an affirmative defense to prosecution under section 352 or 352a of this title may be raised when:

(1) except for vivisection or research under subdivision 352(7) of this title, the defendant was a veterinarian whose conduct conformed to accepted veterinary practice for the area, or was a scientist whose conduct was a part of scientific research governed by accepted procedural standards subject to review by an institutional care and use committee;

(2) the defendant's conduct was designed to control or eliminate rodents, ants, or other common pests on the defendant's own property;

(3) the defendant was a person appropriately licensed to utilize pesticides under 6 V.S.A. chapter 87;

(4) the defendant humanely euthanized any animal as a representative of a duly organized humane society, animal shelter, or town pound according to rules of this subchapter, or as a veterinarian destroying animals under 20 V.S.A. chapter 193 or 20 V.S.A. §§ 3511 and 3513; or

(5) a State agency was implementing a rabies control program.

(c) An affirmative defense to a charge of abandonment under section 352 of this title shall not be recognized where a person abandons an animal at or near an animal shelter or veterinary clinic, farm, or other place of shelter, without making reasonable arrangements for the care of the animal.

(d) The authority to enforce this chapter shall not be construed in a manner inconsistent with the animal control or disease control eradication programs in Title 6, or 20 V.S.A. chapters 191, 193, 194, and 195 or the provisions of 10 V.S.A. Part 4, or the rules adopted thereunder. (Added 1997, No. 130 (Adj. Sess.), § 9; amended 2003, No. 42, § 2, eff. May 27, 2003.)

§ 353. Degree of offense; sentencing upon conviction

(a) Penalties.

(1) Except as provided in subdivision (3), (4), or (5) of this subsection, cruelty to animals under section 352 of this title shall be punishable by a sentence of imprisonment of not more than one year or a fine of not more than $2,000.00, or both. Second and subsequent convictions shall be punishable by a sentence of imprisonment of not more than two years or a fine of not more than $5,000.00, or both.

(2) Aggravated cruelty under section 352a of this title shall be punishable by a sentence of imprisonment of not more than five years or a fine of not more than $5,000.00, or both. Second and subsequent offenses shall be punishable by a sentence of imprisonment of not more than ten years or a fine of not more than $7,500.00, or both.

(3) An offense committed under subdivision 352(5) or (6) of this title shall be punishable by a sentence of imprisonment of not more than five years or a fine of not more than $5,000.00, or both.

(4)(A) Except as provided in subdivision (B) of this subdivision (4), a person found in violation of subdivision 352(3), (4), or (9) of this title pursuant to this subdivision shall be imprisoned not more than one year or fined not more than $2,000.00, or both. Second and subsequent convictions shall be punishable by a sentence of imprisonment of not more than two years or a fine of not more than $5,000.00, or both.

(B) In lieu of a criminal citation or arrest, a law enforcement officer may issue a civil citation to a person who violates subdivision 352(3), (4), or (9) of this title if the person has not been previously adjudicated in violation of this chapter. A person adjudicated in violation of subdivision 352(3), (4), or (9) of this title pursuant to this subdivision shall be assessed a civil penalty of not more than $500.00. At any time prior to the person admitting the violation and paying the assessed penalty, the State's Attorney may withdraw the complaint filed with the Judicial Bureau and file an information charging a violation of subdivision 352(3), (4), or (9) of this title in the Criminal Division of the Superior Court.

(C) Nothing in this subdivision shall be construed to require that a civil citation be issued prior to a criminal charge of violating subdivision 352(3), (4), or (9) of this title.

(5) A person who violates subdivision 352(1) of this title by intentionally killing or attempting to kill an animal belonging to another or subdivision 352(2) of this title by torturing, administering poison to, or cruelly harming or mutilating an animal shall be imprisoned not more than two years or fined not more than $5,000.00, or both.

(b) In addition to any other sentence the court may impose, the court may require a defendant convicted of a violation under section 352 or 352a of this title to:

(1) Forfeit any rights to the animal subjected to cruelty, and to any other animal, except livestock or poultry owned, possessed, or in the custody of the defendant.

(2) Repay the reasonable costs incurred by any person, municipality or agency for providing care for the animal prior to judgment. If the court does not order a defendant to pay all the applicable costs incurred or orders only partial payment, it shall state on the record the reasons for that action.

(3) Forfeit any future right to own, possess, or care for any animal for a period that the court deems appropriate.

(4) Participate in available animal cruelty prevention programs or educational programs, or both, or obtain psychiatric or psychological counseling, within a reasonable distance from the defendant's residence. If a juvenile is adjudicated delinquent under section 352 or 352a of this title, the court may order the juvenile to undergo a psychiatric or psychological evaluation and to participate in treatment that the court determines to be appropriate after due consideration of the evaluation. The court may impose the costs of such programs or counseling upon the defendant when appropriate.

(5) Permit periodic unannounced visits for a period up to one year by a humane officer to inspect the care and condition of any animal permitted by the court to remain in the care, custody, or possession of the defendant. Such period may be extended by the court upon motion made by the State.

(c) Upon an order of forfeiture of an animal under this section or section 354 of this title, the court shall order custody of the animal remanded to a humane society or other individual deemed appropriate by the court, for further disposition in accordance with accepted practices for humane treatment of animals. A transfer of rights under this section constitutes a transfer of ownership and shall not constitute or authorize any limitation upon the right of the humane society, individual, or other entity, to whom rights are granted to dispose of the animal. (Added 1989, No. 270 (Adj. Sess.), § 2; amended 1997, No. 130 (Adj. Sess.), § 10; 2003, No. 120 (Adj. Sess.), § 4; 2007, No. 51, § 20; 2009, No. 154, § 238; 2013, No. 67, § 12; 2017, No. 62, § 10; 2017, No. 112 (Adj. Sess.), § 1a, eff. May 1, 2018.)

§ 354. Enforcement; possession of abused animal; searches and seizures; forfeiture

(a) The Secretary of Agriculture, Food and Markets shall be consulted prior to any enforcement action brought pursuant to this chapter that involves livestock and poultry. Law enforcement may consult with the Secretary in person or by electronic means, and the Secretary shall assist law enforcement in determining whether the practice or animal condition, or both, represent acceptable livestock or poultry husbandry practices.

(b) Any humane officer as defined in section 351 of this title may enforce this chapter. As part of an enforcement action, a humane officer may seize an animal being cruelly treated in violation of this chapter.

(1) Voluntary surrender. A humane officer may accept animals voluntarily surrendered by the owner anytime during the cruelty investigation. The humane officer shall have a surrendered animal examined and assessed within 72 hours by a veterinarian licensed to practice in the State of Vermont.

(2) Search and seizure using a search warrant. A humane officer having probable cause to believe an animal is being subjected to cruel treatment in violation of this subchapter may apply for a search warrant pursuant to the Vermont Rules of Criminal Procedure to authorize the officer to enter the premises where the animal is kept and seize the animal. The application and affidavit for the search warrant shall be reviewed and authorized by an attorney for the State when sought by an officer other than an enforcement officer defined in 23 V.S.A. § 4(11). A veterinarian licensed to practice in Vermont must accompany the humane officer during the execution of the search warrant.

(3) Seizure without a search warrant. If the humane officer witnesses a situation in which the humane officer determines that an animal's life is in jeopardy and immediate action is required to protect the animal's health or safety, the officer may seize the animal without a warrant. The humane officer shall immediately take an animal seized under this subdivision to a licensed veterinarian for medical attention to stabilize the animal's condition and to assess the health of the animal.

(c) A humane officer shall provide suitable care at a reasonable cost for an animal seized under this section, and have a lien on the animal for all expenses incurred. A humane officer may arrange for the euthanasia of a severely injured, diseased, or suffering animal upon the recommendation of a licensed veterinarian. A humane officer may arrange for euthanasia of an animal seized under this section when the owner is unwilling or unable to provide necessary medical attention required while the animal is in custodial care or when the animal cannot be safely confined under standard housing conditions. An animal not destroyed by euthanasia shall be kept in custodial care and provided with necessary medical care until final disposition of the criminal charges except as provided in subsections (d) through (h) of this section. The custodial caregiver shall be responsible for maintaining the records applicable to all animals seized, including identification, residence, location, medical treatment, and disposition of the animals.

(d) If an animal is seized under this section, the State may institute a civil proceeding for forfeiture of the animal in the territorial unit of the Criminal Division of the Superior Court where the offense is alleged to have occurred. The proceeding shall be instituted by a motion for forfeiture if a criminal charge has been filed or a petition for forfeiture if no criminal charge has been filed, which shall be filed with the court and served upon the animal's owner. The civil forfeiture proceeding is intended to run independently from any criminal prosecution and shall not be delayed pending disposition of any criminal proceeding.

(e)(1) A preliminary hearing shall be held within 21 days of institution of the civil forfeiture proceeding. If the defendant requests a hearing on the merits, the court shall schedule a final hearing on the merits to be held within 21 days of the date of the preliminary hearing. Time limits under this subsection shall not be construed as jurisdictional.

(2) If the defendant fails to respond to the notice for preliminary hearing, the court shall enter a default judgment ordering the immediate forfeiture of the animal in accordance with the provisions of subsection 353(c) of this title. A motion to reopen a default judgment shall be filed in writing with the court no later than 30 days after entry of a default judgment. A default judgment shall not be reopened unless good cause is shown.

(f)(1) At the hearing on the motion for forfeiture, the State shall have the burden of establishing by clear and convincing evidence that the animal was subjected to cruelty, neglect, or abandonment in violation of section 352 or 352a of this title. The court shall make findings of fact and conclusions of law and shall issue a final order. If the State meets its burden of proof, the court shall order the immediate forfeiture of the animal in accordance with the provisions of subsection 353(c) of this title.

(2) Affidavits of law enforcement officers, humane officers, animal control officers, veterinarians, or expert witnesses of either party shall be admissible evidence that may be rebutted by witnesses called by either party. The affidavits shall be delivered to the other party at least five business days prior to the hearing. Upon request of the other party or the court, the party offering an affidavit shall make the affiant available by telephone at the hearing. The court may allow any witness to testify by telephone in lieu of a personal appearance and shall adopt rules with respect to such testimony.

(3) No testimony or other information presented by the defendant in connection with a forfeiture proceeding under this section or any information directly or indirectly derived from such testimony or other information may be used for any purpose, including impeachment and cross-examination, against the defendant in any criminal case, except a prosecution for perjury or giving a false statement.

(g)(1) If the defendant is convicted of criminal charges under this chapter or if an order of forfeiture is entered against an owner under this section, the defendant or owner shall be required to repay all reasonable costs incurred by the custodial caregiver for caring for the animal, including veterinary expenses. The Restitution Unit within the Center for Crime Victim Services is authorized to collect the funds owed by the defendant or owner on behalf of the custodial caregiver or a governmental agency that has contracted or paid for custodial care in the same manner as restitution is collected pursuant to section 7043 of this title. The restitution order shall include the information required under subdivision 7043(e)(2)(A) of this title. The court shall make findings with respect to the total amount of all costs incurred by the custodial caregiver.

(2)(A) If the defendant is acquitted of criminal charges under this chapter and a civil forfeiture proceeding under this section is not pending, an animal that has been taken into custodial care shall be returned to the defendant unless the State institutes a civil forfeiture proceeding under this section within seven business days of the acquittal.

(B) If the court rules in favor of the owner in a civil forfeiture proceeding under this section and criminal charges against the owner under this chapter are not pending, an animal that has been taken into custodial care shall be returned to the owner unless the State files criminal charges under this section within seven business days after the entry of final judgment.

(C) If an animal is returned to a defendant or owner under this subdivision, the defendant or owner shall not be responsible for the costs of caring for the animal.

(h) A forfeiture order issued under this section may be appealed as a matter of right to the Supreme Court. The order shall not be stayed pending appeal.

(i) The provisions of this section are in addition to and not in lieu of the provisions of section 353 of this title.

(j) It is unlawful for a person to interfere with a humane officer or the Secretary of Agriculture, Food and Markets engaged in official duties under this chapter. A person who violates this subsection shall be prosecuted under section 3001 of this title. (Added 1989, No. 270 (Adj. Sess.), § 2; amended 1997, No. 130 (Adj. Sess.), § 11; 2003, No. 42, § 2, eff. May 27, 2003; 2003, No. 120 (Adj. Sess.), § 5; 2009, No. 154, § 238; 2013, No. 201 (Adj. Sess.), § 1; 2015, No. 155 (Adj. Sess.), § 7; 2017, No. 11, § 24.)

§ 355. Interference with or cruelty to a guide dog

(a) As used in this section:

(1) "Custody" means the care, control, and maintenance of a dog.

(2) "Guide dog" means a dog, whose status is reasonably identifiable, individually trained to do work or perform tasks for the benefit of an individual with a disability for purposes of guiding an individual with impaired vision, alerting an individual with impaired hearing to the presence of people or sounds, assisting an individual during a seizure, pulling a wheelchair, retrieving items, providing physical support and assistance with balance and stability, and assisting with navigation.

(3) "Notice" means:

(A) a verbal or otherwise communicated warning regarding the behavior of another person and a request that the person stop the behavior; and

(B) a written confirmation submitted to the local law enforcement agency, either by the owner of the guide dog or another person on his or her behalf, which shall include a statement that the warning and request was given and the person's telephone number.

(b) No person shall recklessly injure or cause the death of a guide dog, or recklessly permit a dog he or she owns or has custody of to injure or cause the death of a guide dog. A person who violates this subsection shall be imprisoned not more than two years or fined not more than $3,000.00, or both.

(c) No person who has received notice or has knowledge that his or her behavior, or the behavior of a dog he or she owns or has custody of, is interfering with the use of a guide dog shall recklessly continue to interfere with the use of a guide dog, or recklessly allow the dog he or she owns or has custody of to continue to interfere with the use of a guide dog, by obstructing, intimidating, or otherwise jeopardizing the safety of the guide dog user or his or her guide dog. A person who violates this subsection shall be imprisoned not more than one year or fined not more than $1,000.00, or both.

(d) No person shall recklessly interfere with the use of a guide dog, or recklessly permit a dog he or she owns or has custody of to interfere with a guide dog, by obstructing, intimidating, or otherwise jeopardizing the safety of the guide dog user or his or her guide dog. A person who violates this subsection commits a civil offense and shall be:

(1) for a first offense, fined not more than $100.00;

(2) for a second or subsequent offense, fined not more than $250.00.

(e) A violation of subsection (d) of this section shall constitute notice as defined in subdivision (a)(3) of this section.

(f) As provided in section 7043 of this title, restitution shall be considered by the court in any sentencing under this section if the victim has suffered any material loss. Material loss for purposes of this section means uninsured:

(1) veterinary medical expenses;

(2) costs of temporary replacement assistance services, whether provided by a person or guide dog;

(3) replacement value of an equally trained guide dog without any differentiation for the age or experience of the dog;

(4) loss of wages; and

(5) costs and expenses incurred by the person as a result of the injury to the guide dog. (Added 2009, No. 121 (Adj. Sess.), § 1.)

§ 356. Humane officer required training

All humane officers as defined in subdivision 351(4) of this title shall complete a certification program on animal cruelty investigation training as developed and approved by the Animal Cruelty Investigation Advisory Board. (Added 2015, No. 155 (Adj. Sess.), § 6, eff. July 1, 2017.)

Subchapter 3: General Provisions

§ 361. Interference with domestic animals

(a) A person commits the crime of interference with domestic animals if the person confines or secretes a domestic animal owned by another, with the intention of concealing its identity or the identity of its owner. A person also commits the crime of interference with domestic animals if he or she conceals the fact that the animal is licensed by removing the collar, harness, or identification, or defaces a tattoo or brand tag from any licensed animal or other domestic animal owned by another.

(b) Interference with domestic animals shall be punishable by a sentence of imprisonment of not more than one year or a fine of not more than $2,000.00, or both. (Added 1989, No. 270 (Adj. Sess.), § 2.)

§ 362. Exposing poison on the land

A person who deposits any poison or substance poisonous to animals on his or her premises or on the premises or buildings of another, with the intent that it be taken by an animal, shall be in violation of subdivision 352(2) of this title. This section shall not apply to control of wild pests; protection of crops from insects, mice, and plant diseases; or the Department of Fish and Wildlife in control of destructive wild animals. (Added 1989, No. 270 (Adj. Sess.), § 2; amended 2003, No. 120 (Adj. Sess.), § 6; 2019, No. 77, § 7, eff. June 19, 2019.)

§ 363. Shooting birds for amusement

Except for the taking of game pursuant to Title 10, any person who keeps or uses any live bird for release to be shot for amusement or as a test of marksmanship or provides buildings, sheds, yards, rooms, fields, or other areas to be used for such shooting purposes, shall be in violation of subdivision 352(1) of this title. (Added 1989, No. 270 (Adj. Sess.), § 2; amended 2003, No. 120 (Adj. Sess.), § 7.)

§ 364. Animal fights

(a) A person who participates in a fighting exhibition of animals shall be in violation of subdivisions 352(5) and (6) of this title.

(b) Notwithstanding any provision of law to the contrary, in addition to seizure of fighting birds or animals involved in a fighting exhibition, a law enforcement officer or humane officer may seize:

(1) any equipment associated with that activity;

(2) any other personal property which is used to engage in a violation or further a violation of subdivisions 352(5) and (6) of this title; and

(3) monies, securities, or other things of value furnished or intended to be furnished by a person to engage in or further a violation of subdivisions 352(5) and (6) of this title.

(c) In addition to the imposition of a penalty under this chapter, conviction under this section shall result in forfeiture of all seized fighting animals, equipment, and other property subject to seizure under this section. The animals may be destroyed humanely or otherwise disposed of as directed by the court.

(d) Property subject to forfeiture under this subsection may be seized upon process issued by the court having jurisdiction over the property. Seizure without process may be made:

(1) incident to a lawful arrest;

(2) pursuant to a search warrant; or

(3) if there is probable cause to believe that the property was used or is intended to be used in violation of this section.

(e) Forfeiture proceedings instituted pursuant to the provisions of this section for property other than animals are subject to the procedures and requirements for forfeiture as set forth in 18 V.S.A. chapter 84, subchapter 2. (Added 1989, No. 270, (Adj. Sess.), § 2; amended 2015, No. 53, § 2.)

§ 365. Shelter of animals

(a) Adequate shelter. All livestock and animals that are to be predominantly maintained in an outdoor area shall be provided with adequate natural shelter or adequate constructed shelter to prevent direct exposure to the elements.

(b) Shelter for livestock.

(1) Livestock animals confined in enclosed areas shall be provided with adequate ventilation and shall have access to adequate exercise. Equines housed within a designated space continually, without access to a paddock, turn out, or other exercise area, shall be provided the opportunity for periodic exercise, either through free choice or through a forced work program, to maintain normal muscle tone and mass for the age, size, and condition of the animal or in accordance with accepted agricultural or veterinary practices. Nothing in this section shall control dairy herd housing facilities, either loose housing, comfort tie-stall, or stanchion lockups, or other housing under control of the Agency of Agriculture, Food and Markets. This subdivision shall not apply to any accepted housing or grazing practices for any livestock industry.

(2) Notwithstanding the provisions of subdivision (1) of this subsection, livestock may be temporarily confined in a space sufficient for them to stand and turn about freely, provided that they are exercised in accordance with livestock and poultry husbandry practices, and are provided sufficient food, water, shelter, and proper ventilation.

(3) A leash, rope, or chain used to restrict a livestock animal shall be affixed in a manner that prevents the livestock animal from becoming entangled or injured and shall permit the livestock animal access to adequate shelter, adequate food, and adequate water. This subdivision shall not apply to a livestock animal that is in transit or in the immediate control of a person.

(c) Minimum size of living space; dogs and cats.

(1) A dog shall be provided a minimum living space that is large enough to allow the dog, in a normal manner, to turn about freely, stand, sit, and lie down. A dog shall be presumed to have minimum living space if provided with floor space in the greater amount of the following:

(A) If the dog is:

(i) less than 33 pounds (15 kilograms), floor space of at least eight square feet;

(ii) 33 or more pounds (15 or more kilograms) up to and including 66 pounds (30 kilograms), floor space of at least 12 square feet; and

(iii) more than 66 pounds (30 kilograms), floor space of at least 24 square feet.

(B) Floor space in square footage calculated according to the following formula: floor space in square feet = (length of dog in inches + 6) × (length of dog in inches + 6) ÷ 144. The length of the dog in inches shall be measured from the tip of the nose of the dog to the base of its tail.

(2) The specifications required by subdivision (1) of this subsection shall be required for each dog, regardless of whether the dog is housed individually or with other animals.

(3)(A) A cat over the age of two months shall be provided a minimum living space that is large enough to allow the cat, in a normal manner, to turn about freely, stand, sit, and lie down. A cat shall be presumed to have minimum living space if provided with floor space of at least eight square feet and a primary structure of at least 24 inches in height. Floor space shall be calculated to include any raised resting platforms provided.

(B) The requirements of this subdivision (c)(3) shall apply to each cat regardless of whether the cat is housed individually or with other animals.

(4)(A) Each female dog with nursing puppies shall be provided the living space required under subdivision (1) of this subsection (c) plus sufficient additional floor space to allow for a whelping box and the litter, based on the size or the age of the puppies. When the puppies discontinue nursing, the living space requirements of subdivisions (1) and (2) of this subsection shall apply for all dogs housed in the same living space.

(B) Each female cat with nursing kittens shall be provided the living space required under subdivision (3) of this subsection (c) plus sufficient additional floor space to allow for a queening box and the litter, based on the size or the age of the kittens. When the kittens discontinue nursing, the living space requirements of subdivision (3) of this subsection shall apply for all cats housed in the same living space.

(5)(A) Females in heat (estrus) shall not be housed in the same primary living space or enclosure with intact males, except for breeding purposes.

(B) A dog or cat exhibiting a vicious or overly aggressive disposition shall be housed separately from other dogs or cats.

(6) All dogs or cats shall have access to adequate water and adequate food.

(d) Daily exercise; dogs or cats. A dog or cat confined in a living space shall be permitted outside the living space for an opportunity of at least one hour of daily exercise, unless otherwise modified or restricted by a licensed veterinarian. Separate space for exercise is not required if an animal's living space is at least three times larger than the minimum requirements set forth in subdivision (c)(1) of this section.

(e) Shelter for dogs maintained outdoors in enclosures.

(1) Except as provided in subdivision (2) of this subsection, a dog or dogs maintained outdoors in an enclosure shall be provided with one or more shelter structures. A shelter structure shall:

(A) Provide each dog housed in the structure sufficient space to, in a normal manner, turn about freely, stand, sit, and lie down.

(B) Be structurally sound and constructed of suitable, durable material.

(C) Be enclosed with sides, a roof, and a ground or floor surface that enables the dog to stay clean and dry.

(D) Have an entrance or portal large enough to allow each dog housed in the shelter unimpeded access to the structure, and the entrance or portal shall be constructed with a windbreak or rainbreak.

(E) Provide adequate protection from cold and heat, including protection from the direct rays of the sun and the direct effect of wind, rain, or snow. Shivering due to cold is evidence of inadequate shelter for any dog.

(2) A shelter structure is not required for a healthy livestock guardian dog that is maintained outdoors in an enclosure.

(3) If multiple dogs are maintained outdoors in an enclosure at one time:

(A) Each dog will be provided with an individual structure, or the structure or structures provided shall be cumulatively large enough to contain all of the dogs at one time.

(B) A shelter structure shall be accessible to each dog in the enclosure.

(4) The following categories of dogs shall not be maintained outdoors in an enclosure when the ambient temperature is below 50 degrees Fahrenheit:

(A) dogs that are not acclimated to the temperatures prevalent in the area or region where they are maintained;

(B) dogs that cannot tolerate the prevalent temperatures of the area without stress or discomfort; and

(C) sick or infirm dogs or dogs that cannot regulate their own body temperature.

(5) Metal barrels, cars, refrigerators, freezers, and similar objects shall not be used as a shelter structure for a dog maintained in an outdoor enclosure.

(6) In addition to the shelter structure, one or more separate outdoor areas of shade shall be provided, large enough to contain all the animals and protect them from the direct rays of the sun.

(f) Tethering of dog.

(1) Except as provided under subdivision (2) of this subsection, a dog predominantly maintained outdoors on a tether shall be on a tether that allows the dog to walk a distance in any one direction that is at least four times the length of the dog as measured from the tip of its nose to the base of its tail, and shall allow the dog access to the shelter.

(2)(A) A dog regularly used in training or participation in competitive or recreational sled dog activities and housed outdoors in close proximity with other dogs may, if necessary for the safety of the dog, be maintained on a tether that allows the dog to walk a distance in any one direction that is at least two times the length of the dog, as measured from the tip of its nose to the base of its tail. The tether shall be attached to the anchor at a central point, allowing the dog access to a 360 degree area.

(B) If a tethering method involves the use of a trolley and cable and allows the dog to move freely along the length of the cable, the tether shall be long enough to allow the dog to lie down within its shelter without discomfort.

(3) A tether used for any dog shall be attached to both the dog and the anchor using swivels or similar devices that prevent the tether from becoming entangled or twisted. The tether shall be attached to a well-fitted collar or harness on the dog. The tether shall be of a size and weight that will not cause discomfort to a tethered dog. A choke collar shall not be used as part of a tethering method.

(g), (h) [Repealed.]

(i) Violations. Failure to comply with this section shall be a violation of subdivision 352(3) or (4) of this title.

(j) [Repealed.] (Added 1989, No. 270 (Adj. Sess.), § 2; amended 1989, No. 256 (Adj. Sess.), § 10(a), eff. Jan. 1, 1991; 1997, No. 130 (Adj. Sess.), § 12; 2003, No. 120 (Adj. Sess.), § 8; 2017, No. 58, § 2; 2019, No. 116 (Adj. Sess.), § 2.)

§ 366. Prohibited use of animals

(a) No live animal shall be used as a fund-raising device or award in a contest, lottery, game, or promotion by any person or entity other than at an event recognized by an agricultural or sporting association. An alternative cash prize shall be offered. A person or entity shall not transfer or award an animal without reasonable assurance that the person receiving the animal will provide proper transportation and adequate care.

(b) No live fowl, turtles, or rabbits under eight weeks of age in lots of less than six shall be offered for sale or sold, displayed, or given away.

(c) No dog, puppy, cat, or kitten shall be offered for sale, sold, displayed, or given away on the side of any highway, as defined in 19 V.S.A. § 1, except by the owner or lessor of the abutting land. It shall be an affirmative defense under this subsection that a transaction involving a sale or giving away of a dog, puppy, cat, or kitten was previously arranged by the parties, and the sale or giving away on the side of the highway was only for the convenient transfer of the animal.

(d) A person who violates this section shall be subject to a fine of not more than $250.00. (Added 1989, No. 270 (Adj. Sess.), § 2; amended 1997, No. 130 (Adj. Sess.), § 13; 2001, No. 98 (Adj. Sess.), § 1, eff. May 8, 2002.)

Subchapter 5: Euthanasia

§ 371. Euthanizing animals

(a) Registered animal shelters may purchase, possess, and administer approved euthanasia solution to euthanize injured, sick, homeless, or unwanted pets and animals in accordance with the rules established by the Secretary of Agriculture, Food and Markets under 20 V.S.A. § 3913.

(b) No person shall euthanize animals for an animal shelter without first completing the certification training program under 20 V.S.A. § 3913, except a Vermont licensed veterinarian and a person in training under such program. (Added 1989, No. 270 (Adj. Sess.), § 2; amended 1993, No. 116 (Adj. Sess.), § 2, eff. March 23, 1994; 2003, No. 42, § 2, eff. May 27, 2003.)

Subchapter 7: Transportation Of Animals

§ 381. Transportation by railroad; rest and feeding

(a) A railroad company transporting animals shall not permit them to be confined in cars more than 28 consecutive hours, including the time they have been confined on connecting roads, without unloading them for rest, water, and feeding for at least five consecutive hours, unless prevented from so unloading by storm or other accidental causes. Animals unloaded shall be properly fed, watered, and sheltered during each rest by the owner, or fed, watered, and sheltered during each rest by the owner or person having custody of the animals. In case of default, the railroad company transporting the animal shall provide feed and watering at the owner's expense. In this case, the company shall have a lien upon the animals for food, care, and custody furnished.

(b) Violation of the 28-hour rule of this section is a violation of subdivision 352(4) of this title. (Added 1989, No. 270 (Adj. Sess.), § 2; amended 2003, No. 120 (Adj. Sess.), § 9.)

§ 382. Transportation by truck; rest and feeding

(a) No person shall confine or permit to be confined any animals being transported by truck under his or her orders or control for more than 18 consecutive hours without their removal from the truck for a rest period of not less than four hours. The animals shall be provided with feed and water during this period except when reasonable space, food, and water are provided in the vehicle. Reasonable space for animals and protection from the weather shall be provided in trucks employed commercially in the long distance transportation of animals.

(b) A person who violates a provision of this section shall be in violation of subdivision 352(4) of this title. (Added 1989, No. 270 (Adj. Sess.), § 2; amended 2003, No. 120 (Adj. Sess.), § 10.)

§ 383. Shipping of animals

(a) There shall be separation of livestock species, as defined in 6 V.S.A. § 761, when these animals are transported by either rail or truck.

(b) Failure to provide such separation shall be a violation of subdivisions 352(3) and (4) of this title. (Added 1989, No. 270 (Adj. Sess.), § 2; amended 1995, No. 39, § 3, eff. April 17, 1995; 2003, No. 120 (Adj. Sess.), § 11.)

§ 384. Preference of animals as freight

Any private or common carrier operating within this State shall yield to vehicles containing cattle, sheep, swine, equine, or other animals to allow continuous passage in preference to other freight. All vehicles and common carriers loaded with animals at any station shall take precedence over all other freight. (Added 1989, No. 270 (Adj. Sess.), § 2.)

§ 385. Transportation on the highway without title documents

(a) No person, except the owner of cattle being transported or a person acting under written authority of the owner, shall transport cattle on any public highway unless the person has in his or her possession a bill of sale or a memorandum signed by the owner of the cattle and containing the owner's address, the number, breed, and ear tag number of the cattle, and the name of the place to which the cattle are to be transported. Any person transporting such cattle shall, on demand, exhibit a bill of sale or memorandum to any State investigator, sheriff, deputy sheriff, constable, police officer, or State Police officer.

(b) Violation of this section shall be punishable by a sentence of imprisonment of not more than 60 days or a fine of not more than $1,000.00, or both. (Added 1989, No. 270 (Adj. Sess.), § 2.)

§ 386. Confinement of animals in vehicles

(a) A person shall not leave an animal unattended in a standing or parked motor vehicle in a manner that would endanger the health or safety of the animal.

(b) Any humane officer or member of a fire and rescue service may use reasonable force to remove any such animal from a motor vehicle. The officer so removing an animal shall deliver the animal to a humane society, veterinarian, or town or municipal pound. If the owner of the animal cannot be found, the officer shall place a written notice in the vehicle, bearing the name of the officer and the department and address where the animal may be claimed. The owner shall be liable for reasonable expenses, and a lien may be placed on the animal for these expenses. The officer may not be held liable for criminal or civil liability for any damage resulting from actions taken under subsection (a) of this section.

(c) Failure to comply with subsection (a) of this section is a violation of subdivision 352(3) of this title. (Added 1989, No. 270 (Adj. Sess.), § 2; amended 2003, No. 120 (Adj. Sess.), § 12.)

§ 387. Transportation of horses; vehicles

(a) Every vehicle utilized for the transportation of more than seven horses on the highway shall meet the following requirements:

(1) there shall be at least two doors for loading and unloading, which shall not be on the same side;

(2) loading ramps shall be provided if the vertical distance from the floor of the truck to the ground is greater than 15 inches;

(3) the interior compartment construction shall be of smooth material with no hazardous, sharp protrusions;

(4) there shall be sufficient openings to ensure adequacy of ventilation;

(5) partitions shall be placed in compartments having no stalls;

(6) doorways shall be of sufficient height to allow safe loading and unloading; and

(7) compartment height shall be sufficient to allow clearance of the poll and withers of each horse loaded.

(b) Vehicles under this section shall have no more than one tier in compartments carrying horses.

(c) The Secretary shall establish rules for compliance with the provisions of this subchapter.

(d) Failure to comply with this section, or the rules established thereunder, is a violation of subdivision 352(3) of this title. (Added 1989, No. 270 (Adj. Sess.), § 2; amended 2003, No. 42, § 2, eff. May 27, 2003; 2003, No. 120 (Adj. Sess.), § 13.)

Subchapter 9: Use Of Drugs In Animals In Livestock Competitions

§ 391. Definitions

In addition to those definitions set forth in section 351 of this title, the following words shall have the following definitions:

(1) "Animal pulling contest" means a pulling contest in which weights are pulled by animals for competitive purposes.

(2) "Secretary" means the Secretary of Agriculture, Food and Markets or a designee.

(3) "Competitive event" means pulling contests, trail rides, shows, and any other competition for premiums or prizes involving animals.

(4) "Drug" means those substances identified under 18 V.S.A. § 4051(5).

(5) "Owner" means any person, partnership, or corporation having title to animals in any competitive event.

(6) "Superintendent" means any individual designated to control animals during any livestock competition. (Added 1989, No. 270 (Adj. Sess.), § 2; amended 2003, No. 42, § 2, eff. May 27, 2003.)

§ 392. Administration of drugs; violation; rules

(a) No person shall administer internally or externally a drug that may affect or alter the normal performance of an animal entered in an animal pulling contest or competitive event. Any animal so treated shall be disqualified, and any award, premium, or trophy forfeited.

(b) The Secretary shall establish rules to implement the provisions of this subchapter. (Added 1989, No. 270 (Adj. Sess.), § 2; amended 2003, No. 42, § 2, eff. May 27, 2003.)

§ 393. Statement of ownership

A signed statement of ownership in the name of the handler, including a description of the animal, shall be submitted to the superintendent before the start of a competitive event or animal pulling contest. (Added 1989, No. 270 (Adj. Sess.), § 2.)

§ 394. Testing

(a) The Secretary may take specimens for drug testing of saliva, blood, or urine, or all three, from any animal entered in an animal pulling contest or a competitive event. If a drug is found in a chemical analysis of the saliva, urine, or blood, it shall be prima facie evidence that a drug has been administered. A proper chain of evidence shall be maintained.

(b) The Secretary may assess and retain a fee for the taking of a drug test sufficient to recoup the expense of the test procedure.

(c) Failure of an owner or handler to submit an animal for testing on request shall be treated under this chapter as if the presence of a drug were found in a test performed on the animal.

(d) Failure to provide adequate information or assistance in animal restraint for the Secretary to obtain an official sample shall be a violation of this section, subject to the penalty provision of section 397 of this title. (Added 1989, No. 270 (Adj. Sess.), § 2; amended 1993, No. 124 (Adj. Sess.), § 1; 2003, No. 42, § 2, eff. May 27, 2003.)

§ 395. Hearing; finding; order

Within 14 calendar days from the date test results are received by the Secretary, the Secretary shall notify the superintendent of the animal pulling contest or competitive event, and the animal's owner, of the results. If the presence of a drug is found in the test, the Secretary shall hold a hearing, at which the owner of the animal or a representative of the owner may appear and be heard. On the basis of all evidence presented, the Secretary shall issue a finding of whether the provisions of this subchapter have been violated. The Secretary shall make an appropriate order of whether the owner, the representative of the owner, or the animal shall be eligible to participate in future competitive events or animal pulling contests held in this State. (Added 1989, No. 270 (Adj. Sess.), § 2; amended 2003, No. 42, § 2, eff. May 27, 2003.)

§ 396. Appeal

Any person aggrieved by a finding and order or penalty of the Secretary under this subchapter may appeal to the Superior Court in the county in which the animal pulling contest or competitive event was held. (Added 1989, No. 270 (Adj. Sess.), § 2; amended 2003, No. 42, § 2, eff. May 27, 2003.)

§ 397. Administrative penalty

In addition to the forfeiture of any award, premium, or trophy otherwise due, and in addition to other penalties provided by law, a person violating this chapter may be assessed an administrative penalty in an amount not to exceed $1,000.00 by the Secretary. The Secretary shall utilize the provisions of 6 V.S.A. §§ 16 and 17 for purposes of assessing the penalty. (Added 1989, No. 270 (Adj. Sess.), § 2; amended 2003, No. 42, § 2, eff. May 27, 2003; 2019, No. 77, § 8, eff. June 19, 2019.)

§ 398. Loss of eligibility

Any person fined or convicted of administering an unlawful drug to animals entered in a competitive event or animal pulling contest held in another state shall be ineligible to compete in any animal pulling contest or competitive event in this State for a period not to exceed two years from the date of such fine or court conviction. (Added 1989, No. 270 (Adj. Sess.), § 2.)

§ 399. Abuse; disqualification

(a) Any person found rein-whipping or otherwise whipping a horse in an animal pulling contest under this subchapter shall be automatically disqualified, and be ineligible to receive any award, premium, or trophy. The light use of reins applied to the hindquarters may be permitted on entry to the pit and while the team is making its draw. The use of reins for other than guiding the animals at any other time is prohibited.

(b) Any person found face-whipping cattle in an animal pulling contest shall be automatically disqualified and ineligible to receive any award, premium, or trophy. If a goad stick is used in the contest, it must be made of wood, not taped, and not more than 3/4 inches in diameter.

(c) Excessive violation of either subsection (a) or (b) of this section shall be deemed a violation of subdivision 352(2) of this title. (Added 1989, No. 270 (Adj. Sess.), § 2; amended 2003, No. 120 (Adj. Sess.), § 14.)

§ 400. Alcohol breath test; disqualification

A superintendent may require that contestants or other participants at an animal pulling contest or competitive event pass a breathalyzer test for alcohol. The test shall be conducted by the State Police, sheriff, or local police before the contest or event occurs. Any person above a 0.10 percent concentration level shall be disqualified and barred from participation in any animal pulling contest or competitive event on the day of the test. (Added 1989, No. 270 (Adj. Sess.), § 2.)

Chapter 9: Animals

Subchapter 1: General Provisions

Subchapter 2: Societies For The Prevention Of Cruelty To Animals

Subchapter 3: Transportation Of Animals

Subchapter 4: Animal Stealing

Subchapter 5: Animal Pulling Contests

Chapter 11: Arson And Burning

§ 501. Arson causing death

A person who willfully and maliciously burns the building of another, or willfully and maliciously sets fire to a building owned in whole or in part by himself or herself, by means of which the life of a person is lost, shall be guilty of murder in the first degree.

§ 502. First degree arson

A person who willfully and maliciously sets fire to or burns or causes to be burned, or who willfully and maliciously aids, counsels, or procures the burning of any dwelling house, whether occupied, unoccupied, or vacant, or any kitchen, shop, barn, stable, or other outhouse that is parcel thereof, or belonging, or adjoining thereto, whether the property of himself or herself or of another, shall be guilty of arson in the first degree, and shall be imprisoned not more than 10 years nor less than two years or fined not more than $2,000.00, or both. (Amended 1971, No. 199 (Adj. Sess.), § 15; 1981, No. 223 (Adj. Sess.), § 23.)

§ 503. Second degree arson

A person who willfully and maliciously sets fire to or burns or causes to be burned, or who willfully and maliciously aids, counsels, or procures the burning of any building or structure of whatsoever class or character, whether the property of himself or herself or of another, not included or described in section 502 of this title, shall be guilty of arson in the second degree, and shall be imprisoned not more than five years nor less than one year or fined not more than $1,000.00, or both. (Amended 1971, No. 199 (Adj. Sess.), § 15; 1981, No. 223 (Adj. Sess.), § 23.)

§ 504. Third degree arson

A person who willfully and maliciously sets fire to or burns or causes to be burned, or who willfully and maliciously aids, counsels, or procures the burning of any personal property of whatsoever class or character, not less than $25.00 in value and the property of another person, shall be guilty of arson in the third degree, and shall be imprisoned not more than three years nor less than one year, or fined not more than $500.00, or both. (Amended 1971, No. 199 (Adj. Sess.), § 15; 1981, No. 223 (Adj. Sess.), § 23.)

§ 505. Fourth degree arson

A person who willfully and maliciously attempts to set fire to or willfully and maliciously attempts to burn or to aid, counsel, or procure the burning of any of the buildings or property mentioned in sections 502-504 of this title, or who willfully and maliciously commits any act preliminary thereto, or in furtherance thereof, shall be guilty of arson in the fourth degree, and shall be imprisoned not more than two years nor less than one year or fined not more than $500.00, or both. (Amended 1971, No. 199 (Adj. Sess.), § 15; 1981, No. 223 (Adj. Sess.), § 23.)

§ 506. Burning to defraud insurer

A person who willfully and with intent to injure or defraud the insurer sets fire to or burns or attempts so to do or who willfully and maliciously causes to be burned or who willfully and maliciously aids, counsels, or procures the burning of any building, structure, or personal property, of whatsoever class or character, whether the property of himself or herself or of another, which shall at the time be insured by any person, company, or corporation against loss or damage by fire, shall be imprisoned not more than five years nor less than one year or fined not more than $500.00, or both. (Amended 1971, No. 199 (Adj. Sess.), § 15; 1981, No. 223 (Adj. Sess.), § 23.)

§ 507. Burning forests

A person who willfully and maliciously sets on fire, or causes to be set on fire, woods or forest, so as to occasion injury to another person, shall be imprisoned not more than five years or fined not more than $500.00, or both. (Amended 1971, No. 199 (Adj. Sess.), § 15; 1981, No. 223 (Adj. Sess.), § 23.)

§ 508. Setting fires

A person who enters upon lands of another and sets a fire that causes damage shall be imprisoned not more than 60 days nor less than 30 days or fined not more than $100.00 nor less than $10.00, or both. The provisions of this section shall not affect the provisions of section 507 of this title. (Amended 1981, No. 223 (Adj. Sess.), § 23; 2019, No. 77, § 9.)

§ 509. Attempts

The placing or distributing of any inflammable, explosive, or combustible material or substance, or any device, in any building or property mentioned in sections 502-505 of this title in any arrangement or preparation with intent willfully and maliciously to set fire to or burn the same, or to procure the setting fire to or burning of the same shall, for the purposes of this chapter, constitute an attempt to burn such building or property.

Chapter 13: Assaults

§§ 601-607. Repealed. 1971, No. 222 (Adj. Sess.), § 7, eff. April 5, 1972.

§ 608. Assault and robbery

(a) A person who assaults another and robs, steals, or takes from his or her person or in his or her presence money or other property that may be the subject of larceny shall be imprisoned for not more than 10 years.

(b) A person who, being armed with a dangerous weapon, assaults another and robs, steals, or takes from his or her person or in his or her presence money or other property that may be the subject of larceny shall be imprisoned for not more than 15 years nor less than one year.

(c) If in the attempt or commission of an offense under subsection (a) or (b) of this section, a person causes bodily injury, such person shall be imprisoned for not more than 20 years nor less than one year. Any penalty imposed under this subsection shall be in lieu of any penalty imposed under subsection (a) or (b) of this section. (Added 1973, No. 73, eff. 30 days from April 14, 1973.)

Chapter 15: Barratry

§ 701. Penalty

A person who is a common barrator shall be fined not more than $50.00 and become bound with sufficient surety for his or her good behavior for not less than one year.

Chapter 17: Blasphemy And Defamation

§§ 801, 802. Repealed. 1979, No. 152 (Adj. Sess.).

Chapter 19: Breach Of The Peace; Disturbances

Subchapter 1: Riots

§ 901. Duties of officers

A Superior Court judge, sheriff, deputy sheriff, or constable having notice or knowledge of the unlawful, tumultuous, or riotous assemblage of three or more persons within his or her jurisdiction, among or as near as he or she can safely come to such rioters, shall command them in the name of the State of Vermont immediately and peaceably to disperse. If after such command the rioters do not disperse, such officer or magistrate and any other person as he or she commands to assist him or her shall apprehend and forthwith take them before a Criminal Division of a Superior Court. (Amended 1965, No. 194, § 10, operative February 1, 1967; 1973, No. 249 (Adj. Sess.), § 43, eff. April 9, 1974; 2009, No. 154 (Adj. Sess.), § 96.)

§ 902. Rioters refusing to disperse

Persons so unlawfully and riotously assembled who, after proclamation made, do not immediately disperse, and persons unlawfully and riotously assembled to the number of three or more who do an unlawful act against a man's person or property or against the public interest, and persons present at the place of an unlawful or riotous assemblage who, when commanded by a magistrate or officer to assist him or her or to leave the place of such riotous assemblage, fails so to do, shall each be imprisoned not more than six months or fined not more than $100.00, or both.

§ 903. Hindering officer

A person who, with force and arms, willfully and knowingly obstructs or in any manner hinders or hurts a person attempting to make proclamation against a riot, shall be punished as provided in section 902 of this title. Persons riotously assembled to whom proclamation would be made if the same were not hindered, who having knowledge of such hindrance do not immediately disperse, shall be imprisoned not more than six months or fined not more than $100.00, or both. (Amended 1981, No. 223 (Adj. Sess.), § 23.)

§ 904. Officer killing resisting rioter, not liable

Officers, and persons assisting them, in lawfully dispersing or apprehending such rioters, shall not be liable in a civil or criminal proceeding if a rioter, by reason of his or her resistance, is killed or injured.

§ 905. Rioters injuring building or vessel

Persons riotously assembled who destroy or injure a dwelling house or other building, steamboat, or vessel shall each be imprisoned not more than five years and fined not more than $1,000.00, or both, and be answerable to the person injured for the damages in a civil action. (Amended 1971, No. 199 (Adj. Sess.), § 15; 1981, No. 223 (Adj. Sess.), § 23.)

Subchapter 2: Labor And Employment Disturbances

§§ 931-933. Repealed. 1971, No. 222 (Adj. Sess.), § 7, eff. April 5, 1972.

Subchapter 3: Disturbing Religious Meetings

§§ 971-973. Repealed. 1971, No. 222 (Adj. Sess.), § 7, eff. April 5, 1972.

§§ 974-976. Repealed. 1959, No. 262, § 37, eff. June 11, 1959.

Subchapter 4: Other Disturbances Of The Peace

§ 1021. Definitions

(a) As used in this chapter:

(1) "Bodily injury" means physical pain, illness, or any impairment of physical condition.

(2) "Serious bodily injury" means:

(A) bodily injury that creates any of the following:

(i) a substantial risk of death;

(ii) a substantial loss or impairment of the function of any bodily member or organ;

(iii) a substantial impairment of health; or

(iv) substantial disfigurement; or

(B) strangulation by intentionally impeding normal breathing or circulation of the blood by applying pressure on the throat or neck or by blocking the nose or mouth of another person.

(3) "Deadly weapon" means any firearm, or other weapon, device, instrument, material, or substance, whether animate or inanimate that in the manner it is used or is intended to be used is known to be capable of producing death or serious bodily injury.

(b) As used in this subchapter, "course of conduct" means a pattern of conduct composed of two or more acts over a period of time, however short, evidencing a continuity of purpose. Constitutionally protected activity is not included within the meaning of "course of conduct." (Amended 1971, No. 222 (Adj. Sess.), § 1, eff. April 5, 1972; 1993, No. 95, § 3; 2005, No. 192 (Adj. Sess.), § 6, eff. May 26, 2006; 2013, No. 150 (Adj. Sess.), § 2; 2015, No. 162 (Adj. Sess.), § 4.)

§ 1022. Noise in the nighttime

A person who, between sunset and sunrise, disturbs and breaks the public peace by firing guns, blowing horns, or other unnecessary and offensive noise shall be fined not more than $50.00. However, this section shall not prevent a person employing workers, for the purpose of giving notice to his or her employees, from ringing bells or using whistles or gongs of such size and weight, in such manner, and at such hours as the selectboard members of the town, the aldermen of the city, or the trustees of the village may prescribe in writing.

§ 1023. Simple assault

(a) A person is guilty of simple assault if he or she:

(1) attempts to cause or purposely, knowingly, or recklessly causes bodily injury to another; or

(2) negligently causes bodily injury to another with a deadly weapon; or

(3) attempts by physical menace to put another in fear of imminent serious bodily injury.

(b) A person who is convicted of simple assault shall be imprisoned for not more than one year or fined not more than $1,000.00, or both, unless the offense is committed in a fight or scuffle entered into by mutual consent, in which case a person convicted of simple assault shall be imprisoned not more than 60 days or fined not more than $500.00, or both. (Amended 1971, No. 222 (Adj. Sess.), § 2, eff. April 5, 1972; 1981, No. 223 (Adj. Sess.), § 23.)

§ 1024. Aggravated assault

(a) A person is guilty of aggravated assault if the person:

(1) attempts to cause serious bodily injury to another, or causes such injury purposely, knowingly, or recklessly under circumstances manifesting extreme indifference to the value of human life;

(2) attempts to cause or purposely or knowingly causes bodily injury to another with a deadly weapon;

(3) for a purpose other than lawful medical or therapeutic treatment, the person intentionally causes stupor, unconsciousness, or other physical or mental impairment or injury to another person by administering to the other person without the other person's consent a drug, substance, or preparation capable of producing the intended harm;

(4) with intent to prevent a law enforcement officer from performing a lawful duty, the person causes physical injury to any person; or

(5) is armed with a deadly weapon and threatens to use the deadly weapon on another person.

(b) A person found guilty of violating a provision of subdivision (a)(1) or (2) of this section shall be imprisoned for not more than 15 years or fined not more than $10,000.00, or both.

(c) A person found guilty of violating a provision of subdivision (a)(3), (4), or (5) of this section shall be imprisoned for not more than five years or fined not more than $5,000.00, or both.

(d) Subdivision (a)(5) of this section shall not apply if the person threatened to use the deadly weapon:

(1) in the just and necessary defense of his or her own life or the life of his or her husband, wife, civil union partner, parent, child, brother, sister, guardian, or person under guardianship;

(2) in the suppression of a person attempting to commit murder, sexual assault, aggravated sexual assault, burglary, or robbery; or

(3) in the case of a civil or military officer lawfully called out to suppress a riot or rebellion, prevent or suppress an invasion, or assist in serving legal process, in suppressing opposition against him or her in the just and necessary discharge of his or her duty.

(e) Subsection (d) of this section shall not be construed to limit or infringe upon defenses granted at common law. (Amended 1971, No. 222 (Adj. Sess.), § 3, eff. April 5, 1972; 2005, No. 83, § 6; 2013, No. 96 (Adj. Sess.), § 50.)

§ 1025. Recklessly endangering another person

A person who recklessly engages in conduct which places or may place another person in danger of death or serious bodily injury shall be imprisoned for not more than one year or fined not more than $1,000.00 or both. Recklessness and danger shall be presumed where a person knowingly points a firearm at or in the direction of another, whether or not the actor believed the firearm to be loaded, and whether or not the firearm actually was loaded. (Amended 1971, No. 222 (Adj. Sess.), § 4, eff. April 5, 1972; 1999, No. 149 (Adj. Sess.), § 3.)

§ 1026. Disorderly conduct

(a) A person is guilty of disorderly conduct if he or she, with intent to cause public inconvenience or annoyance, or recklessly creates a risk thereof:

(1) engages in fighting or in violent, tumultuous, or threatening behavior;

(2) makes unreasonable noise;

(3) in a public place, uses abusive or obscene language;

(4) without lawful authority, disturbs any lawful assembly or meeting of persons; or

(5) obstructs vehicular or pedestrian traffic.

(b) A person who is convicted of disorderly conduct shall be imprisoned for not more than 60 days or fined not more than $500.00, or both. A person who is convicted of a second or subsequent offense under this section shall be imprisoned for not more than 120 days or fined not more than $1,000.00, or both. (Amended 1971, No. 222 (Adj. Sess.), § 5, eff. April 5, 1972; 2013, No. 150 (Adj. Sess.), § 3.)

§ 1026a. Aggravated disorderly conduct

(a) A person is guilty of aggravated disorderly conduct if he or she engages in a course of conduct directed at a specific person with the intent to cause the person inconvenience or annoyance, or to disturb the person's peace, quiet, or right of privacy and:

(1) engages in fighting or in violent, tumultuous, or threatening behavior;

(2) makes unreasonable noise;

(3) in a public place, uses abusive or obscene language; or

(4) threatens bodily injury or serious bodily injury, or threatens to commit a felony crime of violence as defined in section 11a of this title.

(b) A person who is convicted of aggravated disorderly conduct shall be imprisoned not more than 180 days or fined not more than $2,000.00, or both. (Added 2013, No. 150 (Adj. Sess.), § 4.)

§ 1027. Disturbing peace by use of telephone or other electronic communications

(a) A person who, with intent to terrify, intimidate, threaten, harass, or annoy, makes contact by means of a telephonic or other electronic communication with another and makes any request, suggestion, or proposal that is obscene, lewd, lascivious, or indecent; threatens to inflict injury or physical harm to the person or property of any person; or disturbs, or attempts to disturb, by repeated telephone calls or other electronic communications, whether or not conversation ensues, the peace, quiet, or right of privacy of any person at the place where the communication or communications are received shall be fined not more than $250.00 or be imprisoned not more than three months, or both. If the defendant has previously been convicted of a violation of this section or of an offense under the laws of another state or of the United States that would have been an offense under this section if committed in this State, the defendant shall be fined not more than $500.00 or imprisoned for not more than six months, or both.

(b) An intent to terrify, threaten, harass, or annoy may be inferred by the trier of fact from the use of obscene, lewd, lascivious, or indecent language or the making of a threat or statement or repeated telephone calls or other electronic communications as set forth in this section and any trial court may in its discretion include a statement to this effect in its jury charge.

(c) An offense committed by use of a telephone or other electronic communication device as set forth in this section shall be considered to have been committed at either the place where the telephone call or calls originated or at the place where the communication or communications or calls were received. (Added 1967, No. 171, § 1; amended 1999, No. 124 (Adj. Sess.), § 2; 2013, No. 150 (Adj. Sess.), § 5.)

§ 1028. Assault of protected professional; assault with bodily fluids

(a) A person convicted of a simple or aggravated assault against a protected professional as defined in subdivision (d)(1) of this section while the protected professional is performing a lawful duty, or with the intent to prevent the protected professional from performing his or her lawful duty, in addition to any other penalties imposed under sections 1023 and 1024 of this title, shall:

(1) for the first offense, be imprisoned not more than one year;

(2) for the second offense and subsequent offenses, be imprisoned not more than 10 years.

(b)(1) No person shall intentionally cause blood, vomitus, excrement, mucus, saliva, semen, or urine to come in contact with a protected professional while the person is performing a lawful duty.

(2) A person who violates this subsection shall be imprisoned not more than one year or fined not more than $1,000.00, or both.

(c) In imposing a sentence under this section, the court shall take into consideration whether the defendant was a patient at the time of the offense and had a psychiatric illness, the symptoms of which were exacerbated by the surrounding circumstances, irrespective of whether the illness constituted an affirmative defense to the charge.

(d) As used in this section:

(1) "Protected professional" shall mean a law enforcement officer; a firefighter; a health care worker; an employee, contractor, or grantee of the Department for Children and Families; or any emergency medical personnel as defined in 24 V.S.A. § 2651(6).

(2) "Health care facility" shall have the same meaning as defined in 18 V.S.A. § 9432(8).

(3) "Health care worker" means an employee of a health care facility or a licensed physician who is on the medical staff of a health care facility who provides direct care to patients or who is part of a team-response to a patient or visitor incident involving real or potential violence.

(e) This section shall not apply to an individual under 18 years of age residing in a residential rehabilitation facility. (Added 1973, No. 219 (Adj. Sess.), eff. 30 days from April 3, 1974; amended 1995, No. 146 (Adj. Sess.), § 1; 2007, No. 51, § 18; 2007, No. 198 (Adj. Sess.), § 1; 2011, No. 26, § 1, eff. May 12, 2011; 2015, No. 162 (Adj. Sess.), § 6.)

§ 1028a. Assault of correctional officer; assault with bodily fluids

(a) A person convicted of a simple or aggravated assault against an employee of the Department of Corrections whose official duties or job classification includes the supervision or monitoring of a person on parole, probation, or serving any sentence of incarceration whether inside or outside a correctional facility, and who was performing a lawful duty, in addition to any other penalties imposed under sections 1023 and 1024 of this title, shall:

(1) for the first offense, be imprisoned not more than one year; and

(2) for the second offense and subsequent offenses, be imprisoned not more than 10 years.

(b) No person shall intentionally cause blood, vomitus, excrement, mucus, saliva, semen, or urine to come in contact with:

(1) any person lawfully present in a correctional facility unless the person's presence within the facility requires the contact; or

(2) an employee of a correctional facility acting in the scope of employment unless the employee's scope of employment requires the contact.

(c) A person who violates subsection (b) of this section shall be imprisoned not more than two years or fined not more than $1,000.00, or both.

(d) A sentence imposed for a conviction of this section shall be served consecutively with and not concurrently with any other sentence. (Added 1997, No. 152 (Adj. Sess.), § 2; amended 2005, No. 63, § 25.)

§ 1029. Alcoholism, limitations, exceptions

(a) No political subdivision of the State may adopt or enforce a law or rule having the force of law that includes being found in an intoxicated condition as one of the elements of the offense giving rise to a criminal or civil penalty. No political subdivision may interpret or apply any law of general application to circumvent this provision.

(b) Nothing in this section affects any law or rule against operating a motor vehicle or other machinery under the influence of alcohol or possession or use of alcoholic beverages at stated times and places or by a particular class of persons.

(c) This section does not make intoxication or incapacitation as defined in 18 V.S.A. § 4802 an excuse or defense for any criminal act. Nothing contained herein shall change current law relative to insanity as a defense for any criminal act.

(d) This section does not relieve any person from civil liability for any injury to persons or property caused by that person while intoxicated or incapacitated. (Added 1977, No. 208 (Adj. Sess.), § 12; amended 2019, No. 167 (Adj. Sess.), § 12, eff. Oct. 7, 2020.)

§ 1030. Violation of an abuse prevention order, an order against stalking or sexual assault, or a protective order concerning contact with a child

(a) A person who intentionally commits an act prohibited by a court or who fails to perform an act ordered by a court, in violation of an abuse prevention order issued under 15 V.S.A. chapter 21 or 33 V.S.A. chapter 69, a protective order that concerns contact with a child and is issued under 33 V.S.A. chapter 51, or an order against stalking or sexual assault issued under 12 V.S.A. chapter 178, after the person has been served notice of the contents of the order as provided in those chapters; or in violation of a foreign abuse prevention order or an order against stalking or sexual assault issued by a court in any other state, federally recognized Indian tribe, territory or possession of the United States, the Commonwealth of Puerto Rico, or the District of Columbia shall be imprisoned not more than one year or fined not more than $5,000.00, or both.

(b) A person who is convicted of a second or subsequent offense under this section or is convicted of an offense under this section and has previously been convicted of domestic assault under section 1042 of this title, first degree aggravated domestic assault under section 1043 of this title, or second degree aggravated domestic assault under section 1044 of this title shall be imprisoned not more than three years or fined not more than $25,000.00, or both.

(c) Upon conviction under this section for a violation of an order issued under 15 V.S.A. chapter 21, the court shall, unless the circumstances indicate that it is not appropriate or not available, order the defendant to participate in domestic abuse counseling or a domestic abuse prevention program approved by the Department of Corrections. The defendant may at any time request the court to approve an alternative program. The defendant shall pay all or part of the costs of the counseling or program unless the court finds that the defendant is unable to do so.

(d) Upon conviction for a violation of an order issued under 12 V.S.A. chapter 178, the court may order the defendant to participate in mental health counseling or sex offender treatment approved by the Department of Corrections. The defendant shall pay all or part of the costs of the counseling unless the court finds that the defendant is unable to do so.

(e) Nothing in this section shall be construed to diminish the inherent authority of the courts to enforce their lawful orders through contempt proceedings.

(f) Prosecution for violation of an abuse prevention order or an order against stalking or sexual assault shall not bar prosecution for any other crime, including any crime that may have been committed at the time of the violation of the order. (Added 1989, No. 294 (Adj. Sess.), § 1; amended 1991, No. 180 (Adj. Sess.), § 4; 1995, No. 170 (Adj. Sess.), § 30, eff. May 15, 1996; 2005, No. 193 (Adj. Sess.), § 2, eff. Oct. 1, 2006; 2007, No. 174 (Adj. Sess.), § 4; 2007, No. 185 (Adj. Sess.), § 5; 2017, No. 44, § 3.)

§ 1031. Interference with access to emergency services

A person who, during or after the commission of a crime, willfully prevents or attempts to prevent a person from seeking or receiving emergency medical assistance, emergency assistance from a third party, or emergency assistance from law enforcement shall be imprisoned not more than one year or fined not more than $5,000.00, or both. (Added 2007, No. 174 (Adj. Sess.), § 7.)

§ 1032. Law enforcement use of prohibited restraint

(a) As used in this section:

(1) "Law enforcement officer" shall have the same meaning as in 20 V.S.A. § 2351a.

(2) "Prohibited restraint" means the use of any maneuver on a person that applies pressure to the neck, throat, windpipe, or carotid artery that may prevent or hinder breathing, reduce intake of air, or impede the flow of blood or oxygen to the brain.

(3) "Serious bodily injury" shall have the same meaning as in section 1021 of this title.

(b) A law enforcement officer acting in the officer's capacity as law enforcement who employs a prohibited restraint on a person that causes serious bodily injury to or death of the person shall be imprisoned for not more than 20 years or fined not more than $50,000.00, or both. (Added 2019, No. 147 (Adj. Sess.), § 6, eff. Oct. 1, 2020.)

Subchapter 6: Domestic Assaults

§ 1041. Definition

As used in this subchapter, "family or household members" means persons who are eligible for relief from abuse under 15 V.S.A. chapter 21. (Added 1993, No. 95, § 2.)

§ 1042. Domestic assault

Any person who attempts to cause or willfully or recklessly causes bodily injury to a family or household member or willfully causes a family or household member to fear imminent serious bodily injury shall be

imprisoned not more than 18 months or fined not more than $5,000.00, or both. (Added 1993, No. 95, §
2; 2007, No. 174 (Adj. Sess.), § 5.)

§ 1043. First degree aggravated domestic assault

(a) A person commits the crime of first degree aggravated domestic assault if the person:

(1) attempts to cause or willfully or recklessly causes serious bodily injury to a family or household member; or

(2) uses, attempts to use, or is armed with a deadly weapon and threatens to use the deadly weapon on a family or household member; or

(3) commits the crime of domestic assault and has been previously convicted of aggravated domestic assault.

(b) A person who commits the crime of first degree aggravated domestic assault shall be imprisoned not more than 15 years or fined not more than $25,000.00, or both.

(c) Conduct constituting the offense of first degree aggravated domestic assault under this section shall be considered a violent act for the purpose of determining bail. (Added 1993, No. 95, § 2.)

§ 1044. Second degree aggravated domestic assault

(a) A person commits the crime of second degree aggravated domestic assault if the person:

(1) Commits the crime of domestic assault and such conduct violates:

(A) specific conditions of a criminal court order in effect at the time of the offense imposed to protect that other person;

(B) a final abuse prevention order issued under 15 V.S.A. § 1103 or a similar order issued in another jurisdiction;

(C) a final order against stalking or sexual assault issued under 12 V.S.A. § 5133 or a similar order issued in another jurisdiction; or

(D) a final order against abuse of a vulnerable adult issued under 33 V.S.A. § 6935 or a similar order issued in another jurisdiction.

(2) Commits the crime of domestic assault; and

(A) has a prior conviction within the last 10 years for violating an abuse prevention order issued under section 1030 of this title; or

(B) has a prior conviction for domestic assault under section 1042 of this title or a prior conviction in another jurisdiction for an offense that, if committed within the State, would constitute a violation of section 1042 of this title.

(3) As used in this subsection:

(A) "Issued in another jurisdiction" means issued by a court in any other state; in a federally recognized Indian tribe, territory, or possession of the United States; in the Commonwealth of Puerto Rico; or in the District of Columbia.

(B) "Prior conviction in another jurisdiction" means a conviction issued by a court in any other state; in a federally recognized Indian tribe, territory, or possession of the United States; in the Commonwealth of Puerto Rico; or in the District of Columbia.

(b) A person who commits the crime of second degree aggravated domestic assault shall be imprisoned not more than five years or fined not more than $10,000.00, or both.

(c) Conduct constituting the offense of second degree aggravated domestic assault under this section shall be considered a violent act for the purpose of determining bail. (Added 1993, No. 95, § 2; amended 2007, No. 174 (Adj. Sess.), § 6; 2013, No. 17, § 11; 2019, No. 7, § 1, eff. April 23, 2019.)

§§ 1045, 1046. [Reserved.].

§ 1047. Offense committed within the presence of a child

When imposing sentence for an offense listed in this subchapter, the court may consider whether the offense was committed within the presence of a child. (Added 2007, No. 174 (Adj. Sess.), § 8.)

§ 1048. Removal of firearms

(a)(1) When a law enforcement officer arrests, cites, or obtains an arrest warrant for a person for domestic assault in violation of this subchapter, the officer may remove any firearm:

(A) that is contraband or will be used as evidence in a criminal proceeding; or

(B) that is in the immediate possession or control of the person being arrested or cited, in plain view of the officer at the scene of the alleged domestic assault, or discovered during a lawful search, including under exigent circumstances, if the removal is necessary for the protection of the officer, the alleged victim, the person being arrested or cited, or a family member of the alleged victim or of the person being arrested or cited.

(2) As used in this section, "family member" means any family member, a household member as defined in 15 V.S.A. § 1101(2), or a child of a family member or household member.

(b) A person cited for domestic assault shall be arraigned on the next business day after the citation is issued except for good cause shown. Unless the person is held without bail, the State's Attorney shall request conditions of release for a person cited or lodged for domestic assault.

(c)(1) At arraignment, the court shall issue a written order releasing any firearms removed pursuant to subdivision (a)(1)(B) of this section unless:

(A) the firearm is being or may be used as evidence in a pending criminal or civil proceeding;

(B) a court orders relinquishment of the firearm pursuant to 15 V.S.A. chapter 21 (abuse prevention) or any other provision of law consistent with 18 U.S.C. § 922(g)(8), in which case the weapon shall be stored pursuant to 20 V.S.A. § 2307;

(C) the person requesting the return is prohibited by law from possessing a firearm; or

(D) the court imposes a condition requiring the defendant not to possess a firearm.

(2) If the court under subdivision (1) of this subsection orders the release of a firearm removed under subdivision (a)(1)(B) of this section, the law enforcement agency in possession of the firearm shall make it available to the owner within three business days after receipt of the written order and in a manner consistent with federal law.

(d)(1) A law enforcement officer shall not be subject to civil or criminal liability for acts or omissions made in reliance on the provisions of this section. This section shall not be construed to create a legal duty to a victim or to any other person, and no action may be filed based upon a claim that a law enforcement officer removed or did not remove a firearm as authorized by this section.

(2) A law enforcement agency shall be immune from civil or criminal liability for any damage or deterioration of firearms removed, stored, or transported pursuant to this section. This subdivision shall not apply if the damage or deterioration occurred as a result of recklessness, gross negligence, or intentional misconduct by the law enforcement agency.

(3) This section shall not be construed to limit the authority of a law enforcement agency to take any necessary and appropriate action, including disciplinary action, regarding an officer's performance in connection with this section.

(e) This section shall not be construed:

(1) to prevent a court from prohibiting a person from possessing firearms under any other provision of law;

(2) to prevent a law enforcement officer from searching for and seizing firearms under any other provision of law; or

(3) to authorize a warrantless search under any circumstances other than those permitted by this section. (Added 2017, No. 92 (Adj. Sess.), § 1, eff. Sept. 1, 2018.)

Subchapter 5: Jurisdiction Of Justices

§ 1051 Repealed. 1971, No. 222 (Adj. Sess.), § 7, eff. April 5, 1972.

§ 1052. Repealed. 1959, No. 262, § 37, eff. June 11, 1959.

Subchapter 7: Stalking

§ 1061. Definitions

As used in this subchapter:

(1)(A) "Course of conduct" means two or more acts over a period of time, however short, in which a person follows, monitors, surveils, threatens, or makes threats about another person, or interferes with another person's property. This definition shall apply to acts conducted by the person directly or indirectly, and by any action, method, device, or means. Constitutionally protected activity is not included within the meaning of "course of conduct."

(B) As used in subdivision (A) of this subdivision (1), threaten shall not be construed to require an express or overt threat.

(2) "Emotional distress" means significant mental suffering or distress that may, but does not necessarily, require medical or other professional treatment or counseling.

(3) "Reasonable person" means a reasonable person in the victim's circumstances.

(4) "Stalk" means to engage purposefully in a course of conduct directed at a specific person that the person engaging in the conduct knows or should know would cause a reasonable person to fear for his or her safety or the safety of another or would cause a reasonable person substantial emotional distress. (Added 1993, No. 95, § 1; amended 1999, No. 124 (Adj. Sess.), § 3; 2005, No. 83, § 4; 2013, No. 150 (Adj. Sess.), § 1; 2015, No. 162 (Adj. Sess.), § 5.)

§ 1062. Stalking

Any person who intentionally stalks another person shall be imprisoned not more than two years or fined not more than $5,000.00, or both. (Added 1993, No. 95, § 1.)

§ 1063. Aggravated stalking

(a) A person commits the crime of aggravated stalking if the person intentionally stalks another person, and:

(1) such conduct violates a court order that prohibits stalking and is in effect at the time of the offense;

(2) has been previously convicted of stalking or aggravated stalking;

(3) has been previously convicted of an offense an element of which involves an act of violence against the same person;

(4) the person being stalked is under 16 years of age; or

(5) had a deadly weapon, as defined in section 1021 of this title, in his or her possession while engaged in the act of stalking.

(b) A person who commits the crime of aggravated stalking shall be imprisoned not more than five years or be fined not more than $25,000.00, or both.

(c) Conduct constituting the offense of aggravated stalking shall be considered a violent act for the purposes of determining bail. (Added 1993, No. 95, § 1; amended 2005, No. 83, § 5; 2015, No. 162 (Adj. Sess.), § 5.)

§ 1064. Defenses

In a prosecution under this subchapter, it shall not be a defense that the defendant was not provided actual notice that the course of conduct was unwanted. (Added 2015, No. 162 (Adj. Sess.), § 5.)

Chapter 21: Bribery

§ 1101. Bribing public officers or employees

(a) A person shall not, directly or indirectly, corruptly, give, offer, or promise to an executive, legislative, or judicial officer, or to any employee, appointee, or designee of any executive, legislative, or judicial officer, or to a person who is a candidate or applicant for an executive, legislative, or judicial office, a gift or gratuity:

(1) with intent to influence his or her finding, decision, report, or opinion in any matter within his or her official capacity or employment; or

(2) for or because of any finding, decision, report, or opinion in any matter within his or her official capacity or employment.

(b) A person who violates this section shall, if the gift or gratuity is less than $500.00 in value, be imprisoned not more than two years or fined not more than $5,000.00, or both. A person who violates this section shall, if the gift or gratuity is $500.00 or more in value, be imprisoned not more than five years or fined not more than $10,000.00, or both. (Amended 1971, No. 199 (Adj. Sess.), § 15; 1981, No. 223 (Adj. Sess.), § 23; 1987, No. 48, § 1.)

§ 1102. Public officers or employees accepting bribes

(a) An executive, legislative, or judicial officer, or any employee, appointee, or designee of such officer, or a person who is a candidate or applicant for an executive, legislative, or judicial office, shall not, directly or indirectly, corruptly, ask, demand, exact, solicit, accept, receive, or agree to receive a gift or gratuity, or a promise to make a gift or to do an act beneficial to himself or herself or another:

(1) with the understanding that he or she will be influenced thereby in any finding, decision, report, or opinion in any matter within his or her official capacity or employment; or

(2) for or because of any finding, decision, report, or opinion in any matter within his or her official capacity or employment.

(b) A person who violates this section shall, if the gift, gratuity, or benefit is less than $500.00 in value, be imprisoned not more than two years or fined not more than $5,000.00, or both. A person who violates this section shall, if the gift, gratuity, or benefit is $500.00 or more in value, be imprisoned not more than 10 years or fined not more than $10,000.00, or both. (Amended 1971, No. 199 (Adj. Sess.), § 15; 1981, No. 223 (Adj. Sess.), § 23; 1987, No. 48, § 2.)

§ 1103. Bribing triers of causes

A person who corrupts or attempts to corrupt a master, auditor, referee, commissioner, juror, or arbitrator by giving, offering, or promising a gift or gratuity, with intent to bias the opinion or influence the decision of such person, in relation to a cause or matter pending in the court or before an inquest, or for the decision of which such officer has been chosen or appointed, shall be imprisoned not more than five years or fined not more than $1,000.00, or both. (Amended 1971, No. 185 (Adj. Sess.), § 236, eff. March 29, 1972; 1971, No. 199 (Adj. Sess.), § 15; 1981, No. 223 (Adj. Sess.), § 23.)

§ 1104. Triers of causes accepting bribes

A person summoned as a juror, or chosen or appointed as a master, auditor, referee, commissioner, or arbitrator, who corruptly takes anything to give his or her verdict, award, or report, or corruptly receives a gift or gratuity from a party to an action, cause, or proceedings, for the trial or decision of which such juror was summoned, or for the hearing or determination of which such master, auditor, referee, commissioner, or arbitrator was chosen or appointed, shall be imprisoned not more than five years or fined not more than $1,000.00, or both. (Amended 1971, No. 185 (Adj. Sess.), § 236, eff. March 29, 1972; 1971, No. 199 (Adj. Sess.), § 15; 1981, No. 223 (Adj. Sess.), § 23.)

§ 1105. Public Utility Commission members or clerk not to accept pay except from State

If a member of the Public Utility Commission or the clerk of such Commission receives pay for any service from any party other than the State, or for neglect of any service, he or she shall be imprisoned not more than six months or fined not more than $1,000.00, or both. This section shall not be construed to prevent the clerk of such Commission from receiving the usual fees for copies of records or papers in his or her office. (Amended 1959, No. 329 (Adj. Sess.), § 39, eff. March 1, 1961; 1971, No. 199 (Adj. Sess.), § 15; 1981, No. 223 (Adj. Sess.), § 23.)

§ 1106. Kickbacks; purchasing supplies

(a) An officer or agent of, or person employed by the State or a county, municipality, supervisory union school district, or public institution in this State, who, being authorized to procure material, supplies, or other articles by purchase or contract, or to employ service or labor, shall not corruptly, directly or indirectly, ask, demand, exact, solicit, seek, accept, receive, or agree to receive for himself or herself or for another, any benefit from the person who makes such contract, furnishes such material, supplies, or other articles, or from a person who renders service or labor under such contract, nor shall a person give or offer corruptly such benefit.

(b) A person who violates this section shall, if the benefit has a value of less than $500.00, be imprisoned not more than two years or fined not more than $5,000.00, or both. A person who violates this section shall, if the benefit is $500.00 or more in value, be imprisoned not more than five years or fined not more than $10,000.00, or both. (Amended 1987, No. 48, § 3.)

§ 1107. Kickbacks; granting licenses

(a) An officer or agent of, or person employed by the State or a county, municipality, supervisory union school district, or public institution in this State, who, being authorized, individually or as a member of a board or commission or other governmental entity, to grant a license, permit, or other authorization or thing of value, shall not corruptly, directly or indirectly, ask, demand, exact, solicit, seek, accept, receive, or agree to receive for himself or herself or for another, any benefit from a person who applies for a license, permit, or other authorization or thing of value, nor shall a person corruptly give or offer such benefit.

(b) A person who violates this section shall, if the value of the benefit is less than $500.00, be imprisoned not more than two years or fined not more than $5,000.00, or both. A person who violates this section shall, if the value of the benefit is $500.00 or more, be imprisoned not more than five years or fined not more than $10,000.00, or both. (Added 1987, No. 48, § 4.)

§ 1108. Kickbacks; private corporations

(a) An officer or agent of, or person employed by a private corporation or business entity, who, being authorized to procure material, supplies, or other articles by purchase or contract, or to employ service or labor, shall not, directly or indirectly, solicit, ask, demand, exact, seek, accept, receive, or agree to receive, with intent that he or she will be influenced adversely to the interest of the employer or principal, any benefit from a person who makes such contract, furnishes such material, supplies, or other articles, or from a person who renders service or labor under such contract, nor shall a person give or offer such benefit.

(b) A person who violates this section shall, if the value of the benefit is less than $500.00, be imprisoned not more than two years or fined not more than $5,000.00, or both. A person who violates this section shall, if the value of the benefit is $500.00 or more, be imprisoned not more than five years or fined not more than $10,000.00, or both. (Added 1987, No. 48, § 5.)

Chapter 23: Burglary

§ 1201. Burglary

(a) A person is guilty of burglary if he or she enters any building or structure knowing that he or she is not licensed or privileged to do so, with the intent to commit a felony, petit larceny, simple assault, or unlawful mischief. This provision shall not apply to a licensed or privileged entry, or to an entry that takes place while the premises are open to the public, unless the person, with the intent to commit a crime specified in this subsection, surreptitiously remains in the building or structure after the license or privilege expires or after the premises no longer are open to the public.

(b) As used in this section:

(1) "Building," "premises," and "structure" shall, in addition to their common meanings, include and mean any portion of a building, structure, or premises that differs from one or more other portions of such building, structure, or premises with respect to license or privilege to enter, or to being open to the public.

(2) "Occupied dwelling" means a building used as a residence, either full time or part time, regardless of whether someone is actually present in the building at the time of entry.

(c)(1) A person convicted of burglary shall be imprisoned not more than 15 years or fined not more than $1,000.00, or both.

(2) A person convicted of burglary and who carries a dangerous or deadly weapon, openly or concealed, shall be imprisoned not more than 20 years or fined not more than $10,000.00, or both.

(3) A person convicted of burglary into an occupied dwelling:

(A) shall be imprisoned not more than 25 years or fined not more than $1,000.00, or both; or

(B) shall be imprisoned not more than 30 years or fined not more than $10,000.00, or both, if the person carried a dangerous or deadly weapon, openly or concealed, during commission of the offense.

(4) When imposing a sentence under this section, the court shall consider as an aggravating factor whether, during commission of the offense, the person entered the building when someone was actually present or used or threatened to use force against the occupant. (Amended 1971, No. 199 (Adj. Sess.), § 15; 1981, No. 223 (Adj. Sess.), § 2; 2013, No. 195 (Adj. Sess.), § 9.)

§§ 1202, 1203. Repealed. 1981, No. 223 (Adj. Sess.), § 24.

§ 1204. Making or having burglar's tools

A person who manufactures or knowingly has in his or her possession any engine, machine, tool, or implement, adapted and designed for cutting through, forcing or breaking open any building, room, vault, safe, or other depository, in order to steal therefrom money or other property, knowing the same to be adapted and designed for such purpose, with intent to use or employ the same therefor, shall be imprisoned not more than 20 years or fined not more than $10,000.00, or both. (Amended 1971, No. 199 (Adj. Sess.), § 15; 1981, No. 223 (Adj. Sess.), § 23.)

Chapter 25: Children And Persons Who Are Incompetent

§ 1301. Contributing to juvenile delinquency

A person who causes, encourages, or contributes to the delinquency of a minor shall be imprisoned not more than two years or fined not more than $2,000.00, or both. (Amended 1971, No. 199 (Adj. Sess.), § 4; 1995, No. 147 (Adj. Sess.), § 2.)

§ 1302. Repealed. 1973, No. 249 (Adj. Sess.), § 111, eff. April 9, 1974.

§ 1303. Abandonment or exposure of baby

(a) A person who abandons or exposes a child under the age of two years whereby the life or health of such child is endangered shall be imprisoned not more than 10 years or fined not more than $10,000.00, or both.

(b)(1) It is not a violation of this section if a person voluntarily delivers a child not more than 30 days of age to:

(A) An employee, staff member, or volunteer at a health care facility.

(B) An employee, staff member, or volunteer at a fire station, police station, place of worship, or an entity that is licensed or authorized in this State to place minors for adoption.

(C) A 911 emergency responder at a location where the responder and the person have agreed to transfer the child.

(2) A person voluntarily delivering a child under this subsection shall not be required to reveal any personally identifiable information, but may be offered the opportunity to provide information concerning the child's or family's medical history.

(3) A person or facility to whom a child is delivered pursuant to this subsection shall not be required to reveal the name of the person who delivered the child unless there is a reasonable suspicion that the child has been abused and shall be immune from civil or criminal liability for any action taken pursuant to this subsection.

(4) A person or facility to whom a child is delivered pursuant to this subsection shall:

(A) Take temporary custody of the child and ensure that he or she receives any necessary medical care.

(B) Provide notice that he, she, or it has taken temporary custody of the child to a local law enforcement agency or the Vermont State Police.

(C) Provide notice that he, she, or it has taken temporary custody of the child to the Department for Children and Families, which shall take custody of the child as soon as practicable.

(5) The Department for Children and Families shall develop and implement a public information program to increase public awareness about the provisions of the Baby Safe Haven Law, and shall report on the elements and status of the program by January 15, 2006, to the chairs of the Senate Committee on Health and Welfare and the House Committee on Human Services.

(6) Except as provided in subdivision (3) of this subsection, this subsection shall not be construed to limit or otherwise affect procedures under 33 V.S.A. chapter 53 regarding termination of parental rights and regarding children in need of care or supervision. (Amended 1971, No. 199 (Adj. Sess.), § 15; 2005, No. 124 (Adj. Sess.), § 3; 2007, No. 102 (Adj. Sess.), § 1.)

§ 1304. Cruelty to a child

(a) A person over 16 years of age, having the custody, charge, or care of a child, who willfully assaults, ill treats, neglects, or abandons or exposes such child, or causes or procures such child to be assaulted, ill-treated, neglected, abandoned, or exposed, in a manner to cause such child unnecessary suffering, or to endanger his or her health, shall be imprisoned not more than two years or fined not more than $500.00, or both.

(b)(1) If the child suffers death, or serious bodily injury as defined in subdivision 1021(2) of this title, or is subjected to sexual conduct as defined in subdivision 2821(2) of this title, the person shall be imprisoned not more than ten years or fined not more than $20,000.00, or both.

(2) It shall be an affirmative defense to a charge under this subsection (b), if proven by a preponderance of the evidence, that the defendant engaged in the conduct set forth in subsection (a) of this section because of a reasonable fear that he or she or another person would suffer death, bodily injury, or serious bodily injury as defined in section 1021 of this title, or sexual assault in violation of chapter 72 of this title.

(c) The provisions of this section do not limit or restrict the prosecution for other offenses arising out of the same conduct, nor shall it limit or restrict defenses available under common law. (Amended 1971, No. 199 (Adj. Sess.), § 15; 2015, No. 60, § 25.)

§ 1305. Cruelty by person having custody of another

A person having the custody, charge, care, or control of another person, who inflicts unnecessary cruelty upon such person, or unnecessarily and cruelly fails to provide such person with proper food, drink, shelter, or protection from the weather, or unnecessarily and cruelly neglects to properly care for such person, shall be imprisoned not more than one year or fined not more than $200.00, or both. (Amended 1971, No. 199 (Adj. Sess.), § 15.)

§ 1306. Mistreatment of persons with impaired cognitive function

A person who willfully and maliciously teases, plagues, annoys, angers, irritates, maltreats, worries, or excites a person with a developmental or psychiatric disability or impaired cognitive function shall be imprisoned not more than one year or fined not more than $100.00 nor less than $5.00, or both. (Amended 2013, No. 96 (Adj. Sess.), § 51.)

§ 1307. Repealed. 1973, No. 249 (Adj. Sess.), § 111, eff. April 9, 1974.

§§ 1308, 1309. Repealed. 1991, No. 70, § 5, eff. May 1, 1992.

§ 1310. Discarded ice boxes

(a) A person shall not have in his or her possession where it is accessible to children an ice box, refrigerator, freezer, or similar cabinet virtually airtight and large enough for a child to enter, which has been discarded from use, unless the door or fastener thereof has been removed so that a child who enters the same can escape.

(b) A person who violates subsection (a) of this section shall be fined not more than $100.00 or imprisoned not more than 30 days, or both.

§ 1311. Unlawful sheltering; aiding a runaway child

(a) As used in this section:

(1) "Child's residence" means:

(A) the residence of an unemancipated child's parent, foster parent, guardian, legal custodian, parent lawfully exercising parent-child contact, or other person having legal or physical responsibility for the child;

(B) the residence where a child has been placed by the child's parent, foster parent, guardian, legal custodian, parent lawfully exercising parent-child contact, or by the Department for Children and Families or any other agency or department of the State; or

(C) any other lawfully authorized place of abode.

(2) "Runaway child" means an unemancipated child under 18 years of age, voluntarily absent from the child's residence without the consent of his or her parent, foster parent, guardian, legal custodian, parent lawfully exercising parent-child contact, or other person having legal or physical responsibility for the child.

(3) "Shelter" means to provide a physical haven, home, or lodging.

(b) A person commits the crime of unlawfully sheltering or aiding a runaway child if the person:

(1) knowingly shelters a runaway child;

(2) intentionally aids, helps, or assists a child to become a runaway child; or

(3) knowingly takes, entices, or harbors a runaway child, with the intent of committing a criminal act involving the child or with the intent of enticing or forcing the child to commit a criminal act.

(c) Exempt from the prohibitions of this section are:

(1) a shelter, or the directors, agents, or employees of a shelter, designated by the Commissioner for Children and Families pursuant to 33 V.S.A. § 5304, provided that the requirements of 33 V.S.A. § 5303(b) are satisfied; and

(2) a person who has taken the child into custody pursuant to 33 V.S.A § 5251 or 5301.

(d) It is a defense to a prosecution under this section that the defendant acted reasonably and in good faith to protect the child from imminent physical, mental, or emotional harm.

(e) This section shall not apply unless the child's parent, foster parent, guardian, legal custodian, parent lawfully exercising parent-child contact, or other person having legal or physical responsibility for the child has reported the child's absence to a law enforcement agency.

(f) A law enforcement agency shall promptly notify the child's parent, foster parent, guardian, legal custodian, parent lawfully exercising parent-child contact, or other person having legal or physical responsibility for the child when a runaway child has been located.

(g) A person who is convicted of a first violation of this section:

(1) with respect to sheltering a runaway child, shall, except as provided in subsection (h) of this section, be imprisoned not more than 30 days or fined not more than $500.00, or both;

(2) with respect to aiding, helping or assisting a child to become a runaway child, shall, except as provided in subsection (h) of this section, be imprisoned not more than one year or fined not more than $5,000.00, or both.

(h) A person who is convicted of a second or subsequent violation of this section, or who violates this section by transporting the child out of the State of Vermont, or who violates subdivision (b)(3) of this section, shall be imprisoned not more than five years or fined not more than $10,000.00, or both. (Added 2001, No. 41, § 2; amended 2013, No. 131 (Adj. Sess.), § 105.)

Chapter 27: Reports Of Physical Abuse Of Children

§§ 1351-1356. Repealed. 1981, No. 207 (Adj. Sess.), § 3, eff. April 25, 1982.

Chapter 28: Abuse, Neglect, And Exploitation Of Vulnerable Adults

§ 1375. Definitions

As used in this chapter:

(1) "Bodily injury" means physical pain, illness, or any impairment of physical condition.

(2) "Caregiver" means:

(A) a person, agency, facility, or other organization with responsibility for providing subsistence, health, or other care to a vulnerable adult, who has assumed the responsibility voluntarily, by contract, or by an order of the court; or

(B) a person providing care, including health care, custodial care, personal care, mental health services, rehabilitative services, or any other kind of care that is required because of another's age or disability.

(3) "Lewd and lascivious conduct" means any lewd or lascivious act upon or with the body, or any part or member thereof, of a vulnerable adult, with the intent of arousing, appealing to, or gratifying the lust, passions, or sexual desires of the person or the vulnerable adult.

(4) "Neglect" means intentional or reckless failure or omission by a caregiver to:

(A)(i) provide care or arrange for goods, services, or living conditions necessary to maintain the health or safety of a vulnerable adult, including, but not limited to, food, clothing, medicine, shelter, supervision, and medical services, unless the caregiver is acting pursuant to the wishes of the vulnerable adult or his or her representative, or an advanced directive as defined in 18 V.S.A. chapter 111; or

(ii) make a reasonable effort, in accordance with the authority granted the caregiver, to protect a vulnerable adult from abuse, neglect, or exploitation by others.

(B) Neglect may be repeated conduct or a single incident that has resulted in or could be expected to result in physical or psychological harm, as a result of subdivisions (A)(i) or (ii) of this subdivision (4).

(5) "Serious bodily injury" shall have the same meaning as in subdivision 1021(2) of this title.

(6) "Sexual act" means conduct between persons consisting of contact between the penis and the vulva, the penis and the anus, the mouth and the penis, the mouth and the vulva, or any intrusion, however slight, by any part of a person's body or any object into the genital or anal opening of another.

(7) "Sexual activity" means a sexual act, other than appropriate health care or personal hygiene, or lewd and lascivious conduct.

(8) "Vulnerable adult" means any person 18 years of age or older who:

(A) is a resident of a facility required to be licensed under 33 V.S.A. chapter 71;

(B) is a resident of a psychiatric hospital or a psychiatric unit of a hospital;

(C) has been receiving personal care and services from an agency certified by the Vermont Department of Disabilities, Aging and Independent Living or from a person or organization that offers, provides, or arranges for personal care; or

(D) regardless of residence or whether any type of service is received, is impaired due to brain damage, infirmities of aging, or a physical, mental, or developmental disability that results in some impairment of the individual's ability to:

(i) provide for his or her own care without assistance, including the provision of food, shelter, clothing, health care, supervision, or management of finances; or

(ii) protect himself or herself from abuse, neglect, or exploitation. (Added 2005, No. 79, § 2; amended 2005, No. 192 (Adj. Sess.), § 7, eff. May 26, 2006.)

§ 1376. Abuse

(a) A person who engages in conduct with an intent or reckless disregard that the conduct is likely to cause unnecessary harm, unnecessary pain, or unnecessary suffering to a vulnerable adult shall be imprisoned not more than one year or fined not more than $1,000.00, or both.

(b) A person who commits an assault, as defined in section 1023 of this title, with actual or constructive knowledge that the victim is a vulnerable adult, shall be imprisoned for not more than two years or fined not more than $2,000.00, or both.

(c) A person who commits an aggravated assault as defined in subdivision 1024(a)(1) or (2) of this title with actual or constructive knowledge that the victim is a vulnerable adult shall be imprisoned not more than 20 years or fined not more than $10,000.00, or both. (Added 2005, No. 79, § 2.)

§ 1377. Abuse by unlawful restraint and unlawful confinement

(a) Except as provided in subsection (b) of this section, no person shall knowingly or recklessly:

(1) cause or threaten to cause unnecessary or unlawful confinement or unnecessary or unlawful restraint of a vulnerable adult; or

(2) administer or threaten to administer a drug, a substance, or electroconvulsive therapy to a vulnerable adult.

(b) This section shall not apply if the confinement, restraint, administration, or threat is:

(1) part of a legitimate and lawful medical or therapeutic treatment; or

(2) lawful and reasonably necessary to protect the safety of the vulnerable adult or others, provided that less intrusive alternatives have been attempted if doing so would be reasonable under the circumstances.

(c) A person who violates this section shall:

(1) be imprisoned not more than two years or fined not more than $10,000.00, or both.

(2) if the violation causes bodily injury, be imprisoned not more than three years or fined not more than $10,000.00, or both.

(3) if the violation causes serious bodily injury, be imprisoned not more than 15 years or fined not more than $10,000.00, or both. (Added 2005, No. 79, § 2.)

§ 1378. Neglect

(a) A caregiver who intentionally or recklessly neglects a vulnerable adult shall be imprisoned not more than 18 months or fined not more than $10,000.00, or both.

(b) A caregiver who violates subsection (a) of this section, and as a result of such neglect, serious bodily injury occurs to the vulnerable adult, shall be imprisoned not more than 15 years or fined not more than $10,000.00, or both. (Added 2005, No. 79, § 2.)

§ 1379. Sexual abuse

(a) A person who volunteers for or is paid by a caregiving facility or program shall not engage in any sexual activity with a vulnerable adult. It shall be an affirmative defense to a prosecution under this subsection that the sexual activity was consensual between the vulnerable adult and a caregiver who was hired, supervised, and directed by the vulnerable adult. A person who violates this subsection shall be imprisoned for not more than two years or fined not more than $10,000.00, or both.

(b) No person, whether or not the person has actual knowledge of the victim's vulnerable status, shall engage in sexual activity with a vulnerable adult if:

(1) the vulnerable adult does not consent to the sexual activity; or

(2) the person knows or should know that the vulnerable adult is incapable of resisting, declining, or consenting to the sexual activity due to his or her specific vulnerability or due to fear of retribution or hardship.

(c) A person who violates subsection (b) of this section shall be:

(1) imprisoned for not more than five years or fined not more than $10,000.00, or both, if the sexual activity involves lewd and lascivious conduct;

(2) imprisoned for not more than 20 years or fined not more than $10,000.00, or both, if the sexual activity involves a sexual act.

(d) A caregiver who violates subsection (b) of this section shall be:

(1) imprisoned for not more than seven years or fined not more than $10,000.00, or both, if the sexual activity involves lewd and lascivious conduct.

(2) imprisoned for not more than 25 years or fined not more than $10,000.00, or both, if the sexual activity involves a sexual act. (Added 2005, No. 79, § 2.)

§ 1380. Financial exploitation

(a) No person shall willfully use, withhold, transfer, or dispose of funds or property of a vulnerable adult, without or in excess of legal authority, for wrongful profit or advantage. No person shall willfully acquire possession or control of or an interest in funds or property of a vulnerable adult through the use of undue influence, harassment, duress, or fraud.

(b) A person who violates subsection (a) of this section, and exploits money, funds, or property of no more than $500.00 in value, shall be imprisoned not more than 18 months or fined not more than $10,000.00, or both.

(c) A person who violates subsection (a) of this section, and exploits money, funds, or property in excess of $500.00 in value, shall be imprisoned not more than 10 years or fined not more than $10,000.00, or both. (Added 2005, No. 79, § 2.)

§ 1381. Exploitation of services

Any person who willfully forces or compels a vulnerable adult against his or her will to perform services for the profit or advantage of another shall be imprisoned not more than two years or fined not more than $10,000.00, or both. (Added 2005, No. 79, § 2.)

§ 1382. Deferred sentence

Notwithstanding the limitation of subsection 7041(a) of this title, a court may, on the motion of a party or on its own motion, with or without the consent of the State's Attorney, defer sentencing for a misdemeanor violation of this chapter and place the defendant on probation upon such terms and conditions as it may require. (Added 2005, No. 79, § 2.)

§ 1383. Adult Abuse Registry

A person who is convicted of a crime under this chapter shall be placed on the Adult Abuse Registry. A deferred sentence is considered a conviction for purposes of the Adult Abuse Registry. (Added 2005, No. 79, § 2.)

§ 1384. Civil action; recovery by Attorney General

(a) The Attorney General may bring an action for damages on behalf of the State against a person or caregiver who, with reckless disregard or with knowledge, violates section 1376 (abuse of a vulnerable adult), 1377 (abuse by unlawful restraint or confinement), 1378 (neglect of a vulnerable adult), 1380 (financial exploitation), or 1381 (exploitation of services) of this title, in addition to any other remedies provided by law, not to exceed the following:

(1) $5,000.00 if no bodily injury results;

(2) $10,000.00 if bodily injury results;

(3) $20,000.00 if serious bodily injury results; and

(4) $50,000.00 if death results.

(b) In a civil action brought under this section, the defendant shall have a right to a jury trial.

(c) A good faith report of abuse, neglect, exploitation, or suspicion thereof pursuant to 33 V.S.A. § 6902 or federal law shall not alone be sufficient evidence that a person acted in reckless disregard for purposes of subsection (a) of this section. (Added 2011, No. 141 (Adj. Sess.), § 1.)

§ 1385. Civil investigation

(a)(1) If the Attorney General has reason to believe a person or caregiver has violated section 1376, 1377, 1378, 1380, or 1381 of this title or an administrative rule adopted pursuant to those sections, he or she may:

(A) examine or cause to be examined any books, records, papers, memoranda, and physical objects of whatever nature bearing upon each alleged violation;

(B) demand written responses under oath to questions bearing upon each alleged violation;

(C) require the attendance of such person or of any other person having knowledge on the premises in the county where such person resides or has a place of business or in Washington County if such person is a nonresident or has no place of business within the State; and

(D) take testimony and require proof material for his or her information and administer oaths or take acknowledgment in respect of any book, record, paper, or memorandum.

(2) The Attorney General shall serve notice of the time, place, and cause of such examination or attendance or notice of the cause of the demand for written responses at least ten days prior to the date of such examination, personally or by certified mail, upon such person at his or her principal place of business or, if such place is not known, to his or her last known address. Any book, record, paper, memorandum, or other information produced by any person pursuant to this section shall not, unless otherwise ordered by a court of this State for good cause shown, be disclosed to any person other than the authorized agent or representative of the Attorney General or another law enforcement officer engaged in legitimate law enforcement activities unless with the consent of the person producing the same. This subsection shall not apply to any criminal investigation or prosecution.

(b) A person upon whom a notice is served pursuant to this section shall comply with the terms thereof unless otherwise provided by the court order. Any person who, with intent to avoid, evade, or prevent compliance, in whole or in part, with any civil investigation under this section, removes from any place, conceals, withholds, or destroys, mutilates, alters, or by any other means falsifies any documentary material in the possession, custody, or control of any person subject of any such notice or mistakes or conceals any information shall be subject to a civil fine of not more than $5,000.00.

(c) If a person fails to comply with a notice served pursuant to subsection (b) of this section or if satisfactory copying or reproduction of any such material cannot be done and such person refuses to surrender such material, the Attorney General may file a petition with the Civil Division of the Superior Court for enforcement of this section. Whenever any petition is filed under this section, the court shall have jurisdiction to hear and determine the matter presented and to enter such orders as may be required to effectuate the provisions of this section. Failure to comply with an order issued pursuant to this section shall be punished as contempt. (Added 2011, No. 141 (Adj. Sess.), § 2.)

§ 1386. Employment agreements

In accordance with 21 V.S.A. § 306, it is the policy of the State of Vermont that no confidential employment separation agreement shall inhibit the disclosure to prospective employers and responsible licensing entities of factual information about a prospective employee's background that would lead a reasonable person to conclude that the prospective employee has engaged in conduct jeopardizing the safety of a vulnerable adult or minor. (Added 2018, No. 5 (Sp. Sess.), § 1, eff. June 19, 2018.)

Chapter 29: Conspiracy

§§ 1401-1403. Repealed. 1985, No. 183 (Adj. Sess.), § 9.

§ 1404. Conspiracy

(a) A person is guilty of conspiracy if, with the purpose that an offense listed in subsection (c) of this section be committed, that person agrees with one or more persons to commit or cause the commission of that offense, and at least two of the co-conspirators are persons who are neither law enforcement officials acting in official capacity nor persons acting in cooperation with a law enforcement official.

(b) No person shall be convicted of conspiracy unless a substantial overt act in furtherance of the conspiracy is alleged and proved to have been done by the defendant or by a co-conspirator, other than a law enforcement official acting in an official capacity or a person acting in cooperation with a law enforcement official, and subsequent to the defendant's entrance into the conspiracy. Speech alone may not constitute an overt act.

(c) This section applies only to a conspiracy to commit or cause the commission of one or more of the following offenses:

(1) murder in the first or second degree;

(2) arson under sections 501-504 and 506 of this title;

(3) sexual exploitation of children under sections 2822, 2823, and 2824 of this title;

(4) receiving stolen property under sections 2561-2564 of this title; or

(5) an offense involving the sale, delivery, manufacture, or cultivation of a regulated drug or an offense under:

(A) 18 V.S.A. § 4230(c), relating to trafficking in cannabis;

(B) 18 V.S.A. § 4231(c), relating to trafficking in cocaine;

(C) 18 V.S.A. § 4233(c), relating to trafficking in heroin;

(D) 18 V.S.A. § 4234(b)(3), relating to unlawful selling or dispensing of a depressant, stimulant, or narcotic drug, other than fentanyl, heroin, or cocaine;

(E) 18 V.S.A. § 4234a(c), relating to trafficking in methamphetamine; or

(F) 18 V.S.A. § 4233a(b), relating to trafficking in fentanyl. (Added 1985, No. 183 (Adj. Sess.), § 1; amended 1989, No. 100, § 14; 2003, No. 54, § 2; 2011, No. 121 (Adj. Sess.), § 2, eff. May 9, 2012; 2013, No. 34, § 8; 2017, No. 62, § 6.)

§ 1405. Testimony of co-conspirator

No person shall be convicted of conspiracy upon the testimony of a co-conspirator, unsupported by corroborating evidence. (Added 1985, No. 183 (Adj. Sess.), § 2.)

§ 1406. Defense

It is a defense to a prosecution under this chapter that the defendant renounced his or her criminal purpose by:

(1) conduct designed to prevent the commission of the crime agreed upon; or

(2) giving timely notice to a law enforcement official of the conspiracy and of the defendant's part in it; or

(3) making a timely, positive statement to one or more of the other parties to the agreement that the defendant will not participate in the crime. (Added 1985, No. 183 (Adj. Sess.), § 3.)

§ 1407. Jurisdiction

This chapter applies if:

(1) the defendant while in this State conspires with another in this State; or

(2) the defendant while in this State conspires with another who is outside this State; or

(3) the defendant while outside of this State conspires with another who is in this State; or

(4) the defendant while outside of this State conspires with another outside of this State and an overt act in furtherance of the conspiracy is committed within this State by any conspirator. (Added 1985, No. 183 (Adj. Sess.), § 4.)

§ 1408. Venue

A conspiracy may be prosecuted in the county or territorial unit in which any conspirator entered the conspiracy or in which an overt act was done in furtherance of the conspiracy. A court with jurisdiction over a conspiracy under this section also is a proper court for prosecution of any offense committed in furtherance of that conspiracy. (Added 1985, No. 183 (Adj. Sess.), § 5.)

§ 1409. Penalties

The penalty for conspiracy is the same as that authorized for the crime that is the object of the conspiracy. A sentence imposed under this section shall be concurrent with any sentence imposed for an offense which was an object of the conspiracy. (Added 1985, No. 183 (Adj. Sess.), § 6; amended 2011, No. 121 (Adj. Sess.), § 3, eff. May 9, 2012.)

Chapter 31: Discrimination

§§ 1451-1453. Repealed. 1987, No. 74, § 2(a).

§ 1454. Statement of purpose

The Legislature finds and declares that it is the right of every person to enjoy the public peace and that sense of security and tranquility afforded by the protection of the law, and that wrongful activities motivated by hatred toward particular classes or groups of persons invade that protection. It is not the intent of this chapter to interfere with the exercise of rights protected by the constitutions of this State or the United States and the Legislature recognizes the constitutional rights of every citizen to harbor and express beliefs on any subject and to associate with others who share similar beliefs. (Added 1989, No. 172 (Adj. Sess.), § 1, eff. May 12, 1990.)

§ 1455. Hate-motivated crimes

A person who commits, causes to be committed, or attempts to commit any crime and whose conduct is maliciously motivated by the victim's actual or perceived race, color, religion, national origin, sex, ancestry, age, service in the U.S. Armed Forces, disability as defined by 21 V.S.A. § 495d(5), sexual orientation, or gender identity shall be subject to the following penalties:

(1) If the maximum penalty for the underlying crime is one year or less, the penalty for a violation of this section shall be imprisonment for not more than two years or a fine of not more than $2,000.00, or both.

(2) If the maximum penalty for the underlying crime is more than one year but less than five years, the penalty for a violation of this section shall be imprisonment for not more than five years or a fine of not more than $10,000.00, or both.

(3) If the maximum penalty for the underlying crime is five years or more, the penalty for the underlying crime shall apply; however, the court shall consider the motivation of the defendant as a factor in sentencing. (Added 1989, No. 172 (Adj. Sess.), § 2, eff. May 12, 1990; amended 1999, No. 56, § 4; 2013, No. 96 (Adj. Sess.), § 53.)

§ 1456. Burning of cross or other religious symbol

Any person who intentionally and maliciously sets fire to, or burns, causes to be burned, or aids or procures the burning of a cross or a religious symbol, with the intention of terrorizing or harassing a particular person or persons, shall be subject to a term of imprisonment of not more than two years or a fine of not more than $5,000.00, or both. (Added 1989, No. 172 (Adj. Sess.), § 3, eff. May 12, 1990.)

§ 1457. Civil liability and enforcement

Independent of any criminal prosecution or the result thereof, any person suffering damage, loss, or injury as a result of conduct prohibited by section 1455 or 1456 of this title may bring an action for injunctive relief, compensatory and punitive damages, costs and reasonable attorney's fees, and other appropriate relief against any person who engaged in such conduct. (Added 1989, No. 172 (Adj. Sess.), § 4, eff. May 12, 1990; amended 1999, No. 56, § 1.)

Chapter 33: Injunctions Against Hate-motivated Crimes

§ 1458. Definitions

For purposes of this chapter only:

(1) "Complainant" means a person who has suffered damage as a result of a hate-motivated crime.

(2) "Damage" includes destruction or defacement of personal or real property, personal injury, or the receipt of threats of violence. "Threats of violence" means verbal, electronic, or written communication, or course of conduct, or a combination thereof, that causes reasonable fear of injury to the complainant or the complainant's property.

(3) A "hate-motivated crime" occurs whenever a person engages in conduct prohibited by chapter 31 of this title or section 1063 of this title that causes damage to the person at whom the conduct was directed.

(4) "Hate-motivated crime injunction" or "order" means an injunction or other order issued under this chapter.

(5) "Plaintiff" means the Attorney General or a complainant.

(6) "Protected category" includes race, color, religion, national origin, sex, ancestry, age, service in the U.S. Armed Forces, disability as defined by 21 V.S.A. § 495d(5), sexual orientation, gender identity, and perceived membership in any such group. (Added 1999, No. 56, § 3; amended 2013, No. 96 (Adj. Sess.), § 54.)

§ 1459. Commencement of action and hearing

(a) The Superior Court shall have jurisdiction over proceedings under this chapter. The Vermont Rules of Civil Procedure and the Vermont Rules of Evidence shall apply.

(b) Proceedings under this chapter may be commenced in the county in which the complainant or the defendant resides, or in the county in which the incident occurred.

(c) A plaintiff may seek a hate-motivated crime injunction by filing a complaint under this chapter.

(d) A preliminary hearing upon the complaint shall be scheduled as soon as reasonably possible in consideration of the safety of the complainant. (Added 1999, No. 56, § 3.)

§ 1460. Juvenile defendants

(a) The general public shall be excluded from hearings held in the Civil Division of the Superior Court under this chapter where the defendant is under the age of 16. Only the parties, their counsel, the complainant, witnesses, and other persons accompanying a party for the party's assistance, and such other persons as the court finds to have a proper interest in the case, or in the work of the court, may be admitted by the court. In such a case, there shall be no publicity given by any person to any proceedings under the authority of this chapter except with the consent of the defendant and his or her parent or guardian. The records in such a case shall be subject to the confidentiality provision of 33 V.S.A. § 5117. Upon its own motion or the motion of a party, the court may open the hearing for good cause shown, in consideration of relevant factors, including the likelihood that a court would make a determination that charges against the defendant with respect to the underlying crime on which the hate-motivated crime injunction is based should be heard in the Criminal Division of the Superior Court pursuant to 33 V.S.A. chapter 52.

(b) If the defendant is 16 to 17 years of age, the hearing shall be open to the general public. However, upon its own motion or the motion of a party, the court may close the hearing for good cause shown. If the court orders the hearing to be closed, the confidentiality provisions of subsection (a) of this section shall apply.

(c) If a hate-motivated crime injunction is issued under this section, the court shall give notice of the contents of the order to the complainant, and to any school personnel or other appropriate persons the court finds to have a proper interest in the case and whose knowledge of the contents of the order is reasonably necessary to ensure the defendant's compliance with the order, regardless of whether the proceedings were open or closed to the general public. (Added 1999, No. 56, § 3; amended 2009, No. 154, § 238; 2013, No. 131 (Adj. Sess.), § 106.)

§ 1461. Relief

(a) If the court finds by a preponderance of the evidence that the defendant has committed a hate-motivated crime against the complainant, or if the parties stipulate to an order, the court shall make such preliminary and final orders as it deems necessary to protect the complainant and the complainant's property and other appropriate persons who are in need of protection and such persons' property, including any of the following orders:

(1) an order to refrain from committing any crime against the complainant;

(2) an order restricting the defendant's ability to contact the complainant;

(3) an order prohibiting the defendant from coming within a fixed distance of the complainant, the complainant's residence or other designated locations where the complainant is likely to spend time;

(4) an order to refrain from committing a hate-motivated crime against the complainant, other appropriate persons who are in need of protection and members of any protected category.

(b) A preliminary order issued under this chapter shall remain in effect until a final order is issued or for a fixed period that the court deems appropriate, but in no event more than 120 days without a further order from the court. A final order shall be issued for a fixed period, but in no event more than two years without a further order from the court. The court may extend any order for such time as it deems necessary to protect the complainant, other appropriate persons who are in need of protection and members of any protected category. It shall not be necessary for the court to find that the defendant has committed a hate-motivated crime during the pendency of an order to extend the terms of the order; however, the court shall find that there is a reasonable basis for continued protection. The court may modify its order at any subsequent time upon motion by either party and a showing of good cause.

(c) Every preliminary or final order issued under this section shall bear the following language: VIOLATION OF THIS ORDER MAY BE PROSECUTED AS A CRIME PUNISHABLE BY A TERM OF IMPRISONMENT OR A FINE, OR BOTH, OR MAY BE PROSECUTED AS CRIMINAL CONTEMPT PUNISHABLE BY A TERM OF IMPRISONMENT OR A FINE, OR BOTH. (Added 1999, No. 56, § 3.)

§§ 1461-1467. Repealed. 1987, No. 234 (Adj. Sess.), § 3.

§ 1462. Service

Hate-motivated crime complaints, notices of hearing, and orders shall be served as soon as reasonably possible and in a manner that takes into consideration the safety of the complainant. (Added 1999, No. 56, § 3.)

§ 1463. Procedure

(a) Notwithstanding any law to the contrary, proceedings commenced under this chapter shall be in addition to any other available civil or criminal remedies.

(b) The Supreme Court shall establish procedures consistent with this chapter that provide prompt access to relief.

(c) Police departments, sheriffs' departments, and the State Police shall establish procedures for filing orders issued under this chapter and for making their personnel aware of the existence and contents of such orders.

(d) The court that issues an order under this chapter shall transmit a copy of the order to the Department of Public Safety relief from abuse database. (Added 1999, No. 56, § 3.)

§ 1464. Enforcement

(a) Law enforcement officers are authorized to enforce orders issued under this chapter. Enforcement may include making an arrest in accordance with the provisions of Rule 3 of the Vermont Rules of Criminal Procedure.

(b) A law enforcement officer may rely upon a copy of any order issued under this chapter which has been provided to the law enforcement officer by any source. (Added 1999, No. 56, § 3.)

§ 1465. Penalties

(a) Provided that notice was properly served, a person who violates a hate-motivated crime injunction issued under this chapter shall be imprisoned not more than one year or fined not more than $2,000.00, or both.

(b) A person who is convicted of a second or subsequent offense under this section shall be imprisoned not more than three years or fined not more than $10,000.00, or both.

(c) Nothing in this section shall be construed to diminish the inherent authority of the courts to enforce their lawful orders through contempt proceedings.

(d) Prosecution under this section shall not bar prosecution for any other crime, including any crime that may have been committed at the time of the violation of the hate-motivated crime injunction. (Added 1999, No. 56, § 3.)

§ 1466. Civil penalties

The Attorney General may seek the imposition of a civil penalty of not more than $5,000.00, plus costs and reasonable attorney's fees for each violation of section 1455 or 1456 of this title, including violations of any injunction issued pursuant to this chapter. (Added 1999, No. 56, § 3.)

Chapter 35: Escape

§ 1501. Escape and attempts to escape

(a) A person who, while in lawful custody:

(1) escapes or attempts to escape from any correctional facility or a local lockup shall be imprisoned for not more than 10 years or fined not more than $5,000.00, or both; or

(2) escapes or attempts to escape from an officer, if the person was in custody as a result of a felony, shall be imprisoned for not more than 10 years or fined not more than $5,000.00, or both; or if the person was in custody as a result of a misdemeanor, shall be imprisoned for not more than two years or fined not more than $1,000.00, or both.

(b)(1) A person shall not, while in lawful custody:

(A) fail to return from work release to the correctional facility at the specified time, or visits other than the specified place, as required by the order issued in accordance with 28 V.S.A. § 753;

(B) fail to return from furlough to the correctional facility at the specified time, or visits other than the specified place, as required by the order issued in accordance with 28 V.S.A. § 808(a)(1)-(5) or § 723;

(C) escape or attempt to escape while on release from a correctional facility to do work in the service of such facility or of the Department of Corrections in accordance with 28 V.S.A. § 758; or

(D) elope or attempt to elope from the Vermont Psychiatric Care Hospital or a participating hospital, when confined by court order pursuant to chapter 157 of this title, or when transferred there pursuant to 28 V.S.A. § 703 and while still serving a sentence.

(2) A person who violates this subsection shall be imprisoned for not more than five years or fined not more than $1,000.00, or both.

(3) If the person is on furlough status pursuant to 28 V.S.A. § 723, 808(e), or 808a, a violation of this subdivision (1) of this subsection requires a showing that the person intended to escape from furlough.

(c) All sentences imposed under subsection (a) of this section shall be consecutive to any term or sentence being served at the time of the offense.

(d) As used in this section:

(1) "No refusal system" means a system of hospitals and intensive residential recovery facilities under contract with the Department of Mental Health that provides high intensity services, in which the facilities shall admit any individual for care if the individual meets the eligibility criteria established by the Commissioner in contract.

(2) "Participating hospital" means a hospital under contract with the Department of Mental Health to participate in the no refusal system.

(3) [Repealed.] (Amended 1967, No. 317 (Adj. Sess.), eff. March 22, 1968; 1971, No. 199 (Adj. Sess.), § 15; 1973, No. 109, § 5; 1973, No. 206 (Adj. Sess.), § 1, eff. 30 days from April 3, 1974; 2011, No. 79 (Adj. Sess.), § 14, eff. April 4, 2012; 2015, No. 5, § 1, eff. April 9, 2015; 2019, No. 77, § 10; 2019, No. 148 (Adj. Sess.), § 18, eff. Jan. 1, 2021.)

§ 1502. Unlawfully aiding prisoners

(a) A person shall not:

(1) rescue or attempt to rescue a prisoner from a place in which a person is confined by authority of the State, or from an officer conveying one to any such place of confinement; or

(2) counsel or assist in breaking open or attempting to break open any such place of confinement; or

(3) directly or indirectly aid a prisoner in escaping or attempting to escape from any such place of confinement, or from an officer conveying one thereto, or from any officer or person who has the lawful custody of such prisoner; or

(4) other than a prisoner, directly or indirectly break open or attempt to break open any such place of confinement.

(b) A person who violates a provision of this section shall be imprisoned not more than five years or fined not more than $500.00. (Amended 1971, No. 199 (Adj. Sess.), § 15.)

§ 1503. Giving prisoner tools for escape; aiding escaped prisoner

A person who gives to a prisoner in any such place of confinement, or conveys therein, a tool, instrument, or weapon with intent to enable a prisoner to escape, whether such escape is effected or not; or who, not being a parent, child, wife, husband, brother, or sister of such prisoner, harbors, conceals, aids or comforts a prisoner who has escaped from any such place of confinement, knowing thereof, shall be punished as provided In section 1502 of this title. (Amended 1973, No. 201 (Adj. Sess.), § 1.)

§ 1504. Repealed. 2019, No. 77, § 12, eff. June 19, 2019.

§ 1505. Repealed. 1995, No. 147 (Adj. Sess.), § 6.

§ 1506. Officer aiding or voluntarily allowing escape

An officer or person employed in keeping, taking care of, or guarding the State prison or the prisoners therein, who aids or voluntarily suffers the escape of a prisoner, shall be imprisoned not more than 20 years. Jailers and officers, other than those employed in keeping, taking care of, or guarding the State prison or prisoners therein, who voluntarily suffer a prisoner in their custody, upon conviction or upon a criminal charge, to escape, shall be imprisoned not more than five years or fined not more than $1,000.00, or both. (Amended 1971, No. 199 (Adj. Sess.), § 15; 1981, No. 223 (Adj. Sess.), § 23.)

§ 1507. Repealed. 1977, No. 233 (Adj. Sess.), § 5a, eff. April 17, 1978.

Chapter 37: Explosives

§ 1601. Willful and malicious injuries caused by explosives

A person who willfully and maliciously, by the explosion of gunpowder or any other explosive substance, unlawfully destroys or injures a dwelling house, office, shop, or other building, or a ship, vessel, or a dam or reservoir for storing water, shall be imprisoned not more than 20 years or fined not more than $1,000.00, or both. (Amended 1971, No. 199 (Adj. Sess.), § 15; 1981, No. 223 (Adj. Sess.), § 23.)

§ 1602. Attempts

A person who willfully and maliciously throws into, against, or upon, or puts, places, or explodes, or causes to be exploded, in, upon, or near a dwelling house, office, shop, building, ship, vessel, or any dam or reservoir for storing water, gunpowder or other explosive substance, or a bombshell, torpedo, or other instrument filled or loaded with an explosive substance, with intent unlawfully to destroy or injure such dwelling house, office, shop, building, ship, vessel, or any dam or reservoir for storing water, or any person or property therein, shall be imprisoned not more than 10 years or fined not more than $500.00, or both. (Amended 1971, No. 199 (Adj. Sess.), § 15; 1981, No. 223 (Adj. Sess.), § 23.)

§ 1603. Definitions

For the purposes of this chapter:

(1) "Destructive device" means any:

(A) explosive, incendiary, or poison gas bomb; or

(B) explosive, incendiary, or poison gas grenade; or

(C) explosive, incendiary, or poison gas rocket having a propellant charge of more than four ounces; or

(D) explosive, incendiary, or poison gas missile having an explosive or incendiary charge of more than one-quarter ounce; or

(E) explosive, incendiary, or poison gas mine; or

(F) device that consists of or includes a breakable container including a flammable liquid or compound, and a wick composed of any material that, when ignited, is capable of igniting the flammable liquid or compound, and can be carried or thrown by one individual acting alone; or

(G) device similar to those devices enumerated in subdivisions (1) and (1)(A)-(E) of this section.

A destructive device does not include a firearm or ammunition therefor.

(2) "Explosive" means dynamite, or any explosive compound of which nitroglycerin forms a part, or fulminate in bulk or dry condition, or blasting caps, or detonating fuses, or blasting powder, or any other similar explosive. The term does not include a firearm or ammunition therefor or any components of ammunition for a firearm including primers, smokeless powder, or black gunpowder.

(3) "Hoax device" means any device so designed, assembled, fabricated, or manufactured as to convey the physical appearance of an explosive or incendiary bomb or the physical appearance of any of the

devices enumerated in subdivisions (1)(A)-(F) of this section that is lacking an explosive or incendiary charge. (Added 1971, No. 107, § 1, eff. 30 days from April 22, 1971; amended 1975, No. 222 (Adj. Sess.), § 3, eff. 30 days from April 7, 1976.)

§ 1604. Possession of destructive devices

A person who manufactures, possesses, stores, or transports a destructive device or a hoax device shall be imprisoned for not more than 10 years or fined not more than $5,000.00, or both. (Added 1971, No. 107, § 2, eff. 30 days from April 22, 1971; amended 1975, No. 222 (Adj. Sess.), § 2, eff. 30 days from April 7, 1976.)

§ 1605. Injuries caused by destructive devices

A person who purposely and maliciously uses a destructive device to injure a person or to damage or destroy the property of another shall be imprisoned for not more than 20 years or fined not more than $10,000.00, or both. (Added 1971, No. 107, § 3, eff. 30 days from April 22, 1971.)

§ 1606. Possession and use of explosives

A person who possesses, purchases, stores, uses, or transports an explosive without a license as provided in 20 V.S.A. chapter 177, subchapter 2, division 2 shall be imprisoned for not more than five years or fined not more than $1,000.00, or both. (Added 1971, No. 107, § 4, eff. 30 days from April 22, 1971.)

§ 1607. Sale of explosives

A person who gives, transfers, or sells an explosive to another who does not hold a license issued under 20 V.S.A. chapter 177, subchapter 2, division 2 shall be imprisoned for not more than five years or fined not more than $1,000.00, or both. (Added 1971, No. 107, § 5, eff. 30 days from April 22, 1971.)

§ 1608. Injuries caused by explosives

A person who purposely and maliciously uses an explosive to injure a person or to damage or destroy the property of another shall be imprisoned for not more than 20 years or fined not more than $10,000.00, or both. (Added 1971, No. 107, § 6, eff. 30 days from April 22, 1971.)

§ 1609. Record of sale

(a) A person may not give, transfer, or sell an explosive to another unless the purchaser exhibits a valid license issued under 20 V.S.A. chapter 177, subchapter 2, division 2.

(b) A person who gives, transfers, or sells an explosive to another shall record the name and address of the purchaser, the license number of the purchaser, the date of sale, the type and quantity of explosives sold, the serial or lot number of the explosives, if any, and the purpose for which the explosive is to be used on forms provided by the Commissioner of Public Safety. The purchaser holding a license shall keep a record of each purchase made and the disposition of the explosives, giving a full report without delay but in no event later than 24 hours after discovery of the loss or theft of any of such explosives to the Commissioner of Public Safety. The records shall be kept by the seller and the purchaser for a period of two years and shall be open to inspection by any law enforcement officer.

(c) A person who violates a provision of this section shall be imprisoned for not more than five years or fined not more than $1,000.00, or both. (Added 1971, No. 107, § 7, eff. 30 days from April 22, 1971.)

§ 1610. Purchase in contiguous states

Any person holding a valid license under 20 V.S.A. chapter 177, subchapter 2, division 2 may purchase explosives in any state contiguous to this State and transport them into this State, provided that he or she furnishes a record of each purchase to the Commissioner of Public Safety within 15 days of the transportation of the explosives into this State, and that he or she comply with both the laws applicable to the purchases in the contiguous state, and the pertinent statutes of the U.S. government. (Added 1971, No. 107, § 8, eff. 30 days from April 22, 1971.)

§ 1611. Exemptions

(a) Nothing contained in this chapter shall apply to the U.S. Armed Forces, the duly authorized militia of the State, the fire or police departments of this State, or to the State or any subdivision thereof.

(b) Nothing contained in this chapter shall apply to destructive devices or explosives while being transported upon vessels, motor vehicles, or railroad cars in conformity with the regulations adopted by the Interstate Commerce Commission.

(c) The provisions of section 1604 of this title do not apply to a person who holds a valid license issued under Title 18 of the United States Code, chapter 44, to manufacture, possess, use, store, or transport a destructive device provided he or she is complying with the terms of the license. (Added 1971, No. 107, § 9, eff. 30 days from April 22, 1971.)

§ 1612. Placing a hoax device

A person who willfully and maliciously puts, places, or installs a hoax device in any building, house, facility of public transport, vehicular conveyance, ship, boat, aircraft, dam or reservoir for storing water shall be imprisoned for not more than 10 years or fined not more than $5,000.00, or both. (Added 1975, No. 222 (Adj. Sess.), § 4, eff. 30 days from April 7, 1976.)

Chapter 39: Extortion And Threats

§ 1701. Definition and penalty

A person who maliciously threatens to accuse another of a crime or offense, or with an injury to his or her person or property, with intent to extort money or other pecuniary advantage, or with intent to compel the person so threatened to do an act against his or her will, shall be imprisoned not more than three years or fined not more than $500.00, or both. (Amended 1971, No. 199 (Adj. Sess.), § 15; 1973, No. 109, § 6; 1981, No. 223 (Adj. Sess.), § 23.)

§ 1702. Criminal threatening

(a) A person shall not by words or conduct knowingly:

(1) threaten another person; and

(2) as a result of the threat, place the other person in reasonable apprehension of death or serious bodily injury.

(b) A person who violates subsection (a) of this section shall be imprisoned not more than one year or fined not more than $1,000.00, or both.

(c) A person who violates subsection (a) of this section with the intent to prevent another person from reporting to the Department for Children and Families the suspected abuse or neglect of a child shall be imprisoned not more than two years or fined not more than $1,000.00, or both.

(d) As used in this section:

(1) "Serious bodily injury" shall have the same meaning as in section 1021 of this title.

(2) "Threat" and "threaten" shall not include constitutionally protected activity.

(e) Any person charged under this section who is under 18 years of age shall be adjudicated as a juvenile delinquent.

(f) It shall be an affirmative defense to a charge under this section that the person did not have the ability to carry out the threat. The burden shall be on the defendant to prove the affirmative defense by a preponderance of the evidence. (Added 2015, No. 162 (Adj. Sess.), § 6b.)

§ 1703. Domestic terrorism

(a) As used in this section:

(1) "Domestic terrorism" means engaging in or taking a substantial step to commit a violation of the criminal laws of this State with the intent to:

(A) cause death or serious bodily injury to multiple persons; or

(B) threaten any civilian population with mass destruction, mass killings, or kidnapping.

(2) "Serious bodily injury" shall have the same meaning as in section 1021 of this title.

(3) "Substantial step" means conduct that is strongly corroborative of the actor's intent to complete the commission of the offense.

(b) A person who willfully engages in an act of domestic terrorism shall be imprisoned for not more than 20 years or fined not more than $50,000.00, or both.

(c) It shall be an affirmative defense to a charge under this section that the actor abandoned his or her effort to commit the crime or otherwise prevented its commission under circumstances manifesting a complete and voluntary renunciation of his or her criminal purpose. (Added 2017, No. 135 (Adj. Sess.), § 2, eff. May 21, 2018.)

Chapter 41: False Alarms And Reports

§ 1751. False alarms to agencies of public safety

(a) A person who willfully or knowingly gives, or aids or abets in giving, by any means any false alarm of fire or other emergency to be transmitted to or within any organization, official or volunteer, for dealing with emergencies involving danger to life or property shall be imprisoned for not more than one year or fined not more than $1,000.00, or both.

(b) If bodily injury or death is sustained by any person as a result of a violation of this section, the person convicted of the violation in lieu of any penalty imposed by subsection (a) of this section shall be imprisoned for not more than five years or fined not more than $2,000.00, or both; however, this subsection shall not prevent the imposition of a greater fine or sentence against any person who is convicted of any degree of homicide, including manslaughter. (Added 1971, No. 169 (Adj. Sess.), § 1.)

§ 1752. Tampering with facilities

A person who willfully or knowingly tampers with, interferes with, or impairs any public fire alarm apparatus, wire, or associated equipment shall be imprisoned for not more than one year or fined not more than $1,000.00, or both. (Added 1971, No. 169 (Adj. Sess.), § 2.)

§ 1753. False public alarms

(a) A person who initiates or willfully circulates or transmits a report or warning of an impending bombing or other offense or catastrophe, knowing that the report or warning is false or baseless and that it is likely to cause evacuation of a building, place of assembly, or facility of public transport, or to cause public inconvenience or alarm, shall, for the first offense, be imprisoned for not more than two years or fined not more than $5,000.00, or both. For the second or subsequent offense, the person shall be imprisoned for not more than five years or fined not more than $10,000.00, or both. In addition, the court may order the person to perform community service. Any community service ordered under this section shall be supervised by the Department of Corrections.

(b) [Repealed.] (Added 1971, No. 169 (Adj. Sess.), § 3; amended 1997, No. 153 (Adj. Sess.), § 3; 1999, No. 113 (Adj. Sess.), § 20; 1999, No. 124 (Adj. Sess.), § 4; 2015, No. 147 (Adj. Sess.), § 11, eff. May 31, 2016.)

§ 1754. False reports to law enforcement authorities

(a) A person who knowingly gives false information to any law enforcement officer with purpose to implicate another or to deflect an investigation from the person or another person shall be imprisoned for not more than one year or fined not more than $1,000.00, or both.

(b) A person shall be imprisoned for not more than six months or fined not more than $500.00, or both, if the person:

(1) reports to law enforcement authorities an offense or other incident within their concern knowing that it did not occur; or

(2) pretends to furnish such authorities with information relating to an offense or incident when the person knows the person has no information relating to such offense or incident. (Added 1971, No. 169 (Adj. Sess.), § 4; amended 1981, No. 223 (Adj. Sess.), § 23; 2005, No. 149 (Adj. Sess.), § 1.)

Chapter 43: Forgery And Counterfeiting

§ 1801. Forgery and counterfeiting of papers, documents, etc.

A person who wittingly, falsely, and deceitfully makes, alters, forges, or counterfeits, or wittingly, falsely, or deceitfully causes to be made, altered, forged, or counterfeited, or procures, aids, or counsels the making, altering, forging, or counterfeiting, of a writ, process, public record, or any certificate, return, or attestation of a clerk of a court, public register, notary public, justice, or other public officer, in relation to a matter wherein such certificate, return, or attestation may be received as legal proof, or a charter, deed, or any evidence or muniment of title to property, will, terminal care document, testament, bond, or writing obligatory, letter of attorney, policy of insurance, bill of lading, bill of exchange, promissory note, or an order drawn on a person or corporation, or on a State, county, or town or school district treasurer, for money or other property, or an acquittance or discharge for money or other property, or an acceptance of a bill of exchange, or indorsement or assignment of a bill of exchange or promissory note, for the payment of money, or any accountable receipt for money, goods, or other property, or certificate of stock, with intent to injure, or defraud a person, shall be imprisoned not more than 10 years and fined not more than $1,000.00, or both. (Amended 1971, No. 199 (Adj. Sess.), § 15; 1981, No. 141 (Adj. Sess.), § 2, eff. April 8, 1982; 1981, No. 223 (Adj. Sess.), § 23.)

§ 1802. Uttering forged or counterfeited instrument

A person who utters and publishes as true a forged, altered, or counterfeited record, deed, instrument, or other writing mentioned in section 1801 of this title, knowing the same to be false, altered, forged, or counterfeited, with intent to injure or defraud a person, shall be imprisoned not more than 10 years and fined not more than $1,000.00, or both. (Amended 1971, No. 199 (Adj. Sess.), § 15; 1981, No. 223 (Adj. Sess.), § 23.)

§ 1803. Counterfeiting or altering peddler's license

A person who counterfeits a license to a peddler, or alters such license granted agreeably to the provisions of law, or utters and publishes as true a counterfeit or altered license, shall be imprisoned not more than ten years. (Amended 1971, No. 199 (Adj. Sess.), § 15.)

§ 1804. Counterfeiting paper money

A person who falsely makes, alters, forges, or counterfeits, or procures to be made, altered, forged, or counterfeited, or aids or assists in making, altering, forging, or counterfeiting, a note, or imitation of, or purporting to be a note issued by the United States, used as currency, or a bank bill or promissory note, or imitation of, or purporting to be a bank bill or promissory note, issued by a banking company incorporated by the Congress of the United States or by the legislature of a state of the United States or of another country, with intent to injure or defraud a person; and a person who utters, passes, or gives in payment, or offers to pass or give in payment, or procures to be offered, passed, or given in payment, or has in his or her possession with intent to offer, pass, or give in payment, such altered, forged, counterfeited, or imitated note, bank bill, or promissory note, knowing the same to be altered, forged, counterfeited, or imitated, shall be imprisoned not more than 14 years and fined not more than $1,000.00, or both. (Amended 1971, No. 199 (Adj. Sess.), § 15; 1981, No. 223 (Adj. Sess.), § 23.)

§ 1805. Counterfeiting scrip

A person who falsely makes, alters, forges, or counterfeits or procures to be made, altered, forged, or counterfeited, or aids or assists in making, altering, forging, or counterfeiting, any scrip or imitation purporting to be scrip issued, under the authorization of 11 V.S.A. chapter 5, with intent to injure or defraud, and a person who utters, passes, or gives in payment or offers to pass or give in payment or has in his or her possession with intent to offer, pass or give in payment, such altered, forged, counterfeited, or imitated scrip, knowing the same to be altered, forged, counterfeited, or imitated shall be punishable for forgery, notwithstanding any other penalty provided in 11 V.S.A. chapter 5.

§ 1806. Affixing false signature to obligation of corporation

A person who, with intent to pass the same as true, fraudulently affixes to an instrument or writing purporting to be a note, draft, or other evidence of debt issued by a corporation, a fictitious or pretended signature purporting to be the signature of an officer or agent of such corporation, though no such person may ever have been an officer or agent of such corporation nor such corporation ever have existed, shall be imprisoned not more than 14 years or fined not more than $1,000.00, or both. (Amended 1971, No. 199 (Adj. Sess.), § 15; 1981, No. 223 (Adj. Sess.), § 23.)

§ 1807. Making or repairing tools for counterfeit money

A person who engraves, makes, or mends, or begins to engrave, make, or mend, a plate, block, or press, or other tool, instrument, or implement, or makes or provides paper or other material adapted and designed for forging or making a false or counterfeit bank bill or promissory note, in the similitude of the bills or notes issued by the United States, or by a bank or banking company established and incorporated by the Congress of the United States, or by the legislature of this State or any of the United States or of any other country; and a person who has in his or her possession such plate or block engraved in any part, or a press or other tool, instrument, or implement, or paper or other material adapted and designed as aforesaid, with intent to use the same, or cause or permit the same to be used, in forging or making such false and counterfeit bank bills or notes, shall be imprisoned not more than 14 years and fined not more than $1,000.00, or both. (Amended 1971, No. 199 (Adj. Sess.), § 15; 1981, No. 223 (Adj. Sess.), § 23.)

§ 1808. Joining parts of several bills or instruments

A person who fraudulently unites different parts of several bank bills or other genuine instruments, so as to produce an additional bank bill or instrument, with intent to pass all of them as genuine, shall be imprisoned not more than 14 years and fined not more than $1,000.00, or both. (Amended 1971, No. 199 (Adj. Sess.), § 15; 1981, No. 223 (Adj. Sess.), § 23.)

§ 1809. Counterfeiting coin

A person who counterfeits gold or silver coin, current by law or usage in this State, or utters, passes, or gives in payment such counterfeit gold or silver coin, knowing the same to be false and counterfeit, with intent to injure or defraud a person, and a person who has in his possession false money or coin, counterfeited in the similitude of gold or silver coin, current as aforesaid, knowing the same to be false and counterfeit, with intent to utter or pass the same as true, or counsels, advises, or assists in counterfeiting, uttering, or passing such gold or silver coin, shall be imprisoned not more than 15 years and fined not more than $1,000.00, or both. (Amended 1971, No. 199 (Adj. Sess.), § 15; 1981, No. 223 (Adj. Sess.), § 23.)

§ 1810. Making or repairing tools for counterfeiting coin

A person who casts, stamps, engraves, makes, or mends, or knowingly has in his or her possession, a mould, pattern, die, puncheon, engine, press, or other tool or instrument adapted and designed for coining or making counterfeit coin in the similitude of gold or silver coin, current by law or usage in this State, with intent to use or employ the same or to cause or permit the same to be used or employed in coining or making such false or counterfeit coin, shall be imprisoned not more than 15 years and fined not more than $1,000.00, or both. (Amended 1971, No. 199 (Adj. Sess.), § 15; 1981, No. 223 (Adj. Sess.), § 23.)

§ 1811. Making imitation of gold or silver

A person who makes, mixes, or changes a metal in imitation of gold or silver, or teaches a person the art of making, mixing, or changing a metal in imitation of gold or silver, with intent that the same shall be used for coining, shall be imprisoned not more than 10 years and fined not more than $500.00, or both. (Amended 1971, No. 199 (Adj. Sess.), § 15; 1981, No. 223 (Adj. Sess.), § 23.)

§ 1812. Officers to make seizures

A district judge, sheriff, deputy sheriff, high bailiff, or constable within his or her jurisdiction shall seize forged, false, or counterfeited bank bills or notes or coin and the instruments or implements made or kept for the purpose of making, forging, changing, or counterfeiting gold or silver coin, bank bills, or notes, and deliver the same as soon as may be to the State's Attorney of such county, with the names of the persons from whom the same are taken. (Amended 1965, No. 194, § 10, operative February 1, 1967; 1973, No. 249 (Adj. Sess.), § 44, eff. April 9, 1974; 2017, No. 93 (Adj. Sess.), § 12.)

§ 1813. Making or uttering illicit money

If a person or corporation within the State, without authority of law, emits and utters a bill of credit, or makes, signs, draws, or indorses a bond, promissory writing or note, bill of exchange, order, or other paper to be used as and in lieu of money, such person or each member of such corporation assenting thereto shall be imprisoned not more than one year or fined not more than $600.00, or both. (Amended 1981, No. 223 (Adj. Sess.), § 23.)

§ 1814. Selling or passing illicit money

A person who sells, utters, or passes a bill of credit, bond, promissory writing or note, bill of exchange, order, or other paper, made, signed, drawn, or indorsed to be used as and in lieu of money, without authority from this State or some other state or country, knowing the same to have been made, signed, drawn, or indorsed for the purposes aforesaid, without such lawful authority, shall be fined not more than $1,000.00.

§ 1815. Description of paper forged or counterfeited

In a complaint, information, or indictment for forgery or counterfeiting, or for uttering and publishing as true an instrument, document, or paper which may be the subject of the offense of forgery or counterfeiting, it shall be sufficient to describe such instrument, document, or paper by the name or designation by which it is usually known or by the purport thereof, without setting forth a copy or facsimile or otherwise describing the same or its value. A misnaming of such instrument, document, or paper shall not affect the cause, provided, that as set forth, the same appears to be any one of the instruments, documents, or papers that is made a subject of the offense of forgery or counterfeiting.

§ 1816. Possession or use of credit card skimming devices and re-encoders

(a) A person who knowingly, wittingly, and with the intent to defraud possesses a scanning device, or who knowingly, wittingly, and with intent to defraud uses a scanning device to access, read, obtain, memorize, or store, temporarily or permanently, information encoded on the computer chip or magnetic strip of a payment card without the permission of the authorized user of the payment card shall be imprisoned not more than 10 years or fined not more than $10,000.00, or both.

(b) A person who knowingly, wittingly, and with the intent to defraud possesses a re-encoder, or who knowingly, wittingly, and with the intent to defraud uses a re-encoder to place encoded information on the computer chip or magnetic strip or stripe of a payment card or any electronic medium that allows an authorized transaction to occur without the permission of the authorized user of the payment card from which the information is being re-encoded shall be imprisoned not more than 10 years or fined not more than $10,000.00, or both.

(c) Any scanning device or re-encoder described in subsection (e) of this section allegedly possessed or used in violation of subsection (a) or (b) of this section shall be seized and upon conviction shall be forfeited. Upon forfeiture, any information on the scanning device or re-encoder shall be removed permanently.

(d) Any computer, computer system, computer network, or any software or data owned by the defendant that are used during the commission of any public offense described in this section or any computer owned by the defendant that is used as a repository for the storage of software or data illegally obtained in violation of this section shall be subject to forfeiture.

(e) For purposes of this section:

(1) "Payment card" means a credit card, debit card, or any other card that is issued to an authorized user and that allows the user to obtain, purchase, or receive goods, services, money, or anything else of value.

(2) "Re-encoder" means an electronic device that places encoded information from the computer chip or magnetic strip or stripe of a payment card onto the computer chip or magnetic strip or stripe of a different payment card or any electronic medium that allows an authorized transaction to occur.

(3) "Scanning device" means a scanner, reader, or any other electronic device that is used to access, read, scan, obtain, memorize, or store, temporarily or permanently, information encoded on the computer chip or magnetic strip or stripe of a payment card.

(f) Nothing in this section shall preclude prosecution under any other provision of law. (Added 2009, No. 116 (Adj. Sess.), § 3, eff. May 21, 2010.)

Chapter 45: Flags And Ensigns

Subchapter 1: Uniform Flag Law

§ 1901. Definition
The words flag, standard, color, ensign, or shield, as used in this subchapter, shall include any flag, standard, color, ensign, or shield, or copy, picture, or representation thereof, made of any substance or represented or produced thereon, and of any size, evidently purporting to be such flag, standard, color, ensign, or shield of the United States or of this State, or a copy, picture, or representation thereof.

§ 1902. Display
A person shall not, in any manner, for exhibition or display:

(1) Place or cause to be placed any word, figure, mark, picture, design, drawing, or advertisement of any nature upon any flag, standard, color, ensign, or shield of the United States or of this State, or authorized by any law of the United States or of this State;

(2) Expose to public view any such flag, standard, color, ensign, or shield upon which shall have been printed, painted, or otherwise produced, or to which shall have been attached, appended, affixed, or annexed any such word, figure, mark, picture, design, drawing, or advertisement; or

(3) Expose to public view for sale, manufacture, or otherwise, or sell, give or have in possession for sale, for gift, or for use for any purpose any substance, being an article of merchandise, or receptacle, or thing for holding or carrying merchandise, upon or to which shall have been produced or attached any such flag, standard, color, ensign, or shield, in order to advertise, call attention to, decorate, mark, or distinguish such article or substance.

§ 1903. Illegal acts

A person shall not publicly mutilate, deface, defile, defy, trample upon, or by word or act cast contempt upon any such flag, standard, color, ensign, or shield.

§ 1904. Construction

This subchapter shall not apply to any act permitted by the statutes of the United States, or of this State, or by the U.S. Army and Navy regulations, nor shall it apply to any printed or written document or production, stationery, ornament, picture, or jewelry whereon shall be depicted such flag, standard, color, ensign, or shield with no design or words thereon and disconnected with any advertisement. (Amended 1964, No. 23 (Sp. Sess.), eff. March 9, 1964; 1991, No. 222 (Adj. Sess.), § 1.)

§ 1904a. Use of State Seal and Coat of Arms

The State Seal and Coat of Arms may be used for commemorative medals or for public displays not connected with any advertising, provided that:

(1) the use does not imply State endorsement or approval when none has been given; and

(2) a sample of the medal or display is delivered to the Secretary of State prior to manufacture, distribution, or sale. (Added 1991, No. 222 (Adj. Sess.), § 2.)

§ 1905. Penalty

A person who violates any provision of this subchapter shall be imprisoned not more than one year or fined not more than $1,000.00, or both.

§ 1906. Uniform interpretation

This subchapter shall be so construed as to effectuate its general purpose and to make uniform the laws of the states which enact it.

Subchapter 2: Other Provisions

§ 1931. Repealed. 1979, No. 152 (Adj. Sess.).

Chapter 47: Frauds

§ 2001. False personation

A person who falsely personates or represents another, and in such assumed character receives money or other property intended to be delivered to the party so personated, with intent to convert the same to the person's own use, shall be imprisoned not more than 10 years or fined not more than $2,000.00, or both. (Amended 1971, No. 199 (Adj. Sess.), § 15; 2005, No. 156 (Adj. Sess.), § 1.)

§ 2002. False pretenses or tokens

A person who designedly by false pretenses or by privy or false token and with intent to defraud, obtains from another person money or other property, or a release or discharge of a debt or obligation, or the signature of a person to a written instrument, the false making whereof would be punishable as forgery, shall be imprisoned not more than 10 years or fined not more than $2,000.00, or both, if the money or property so obtained exceeds $900.00 in value. A person who violates this section shall be imprisoned for not more than one year or fined not more than $1,000.00, or both, if the money or property obtained in violation of this section is valued at $900.00 or less. (Amended 1971, No. 199 (Adj. Sess.), § 15; 1981, No. 223 (Adj. Sess.), § 23; 2005, No. 156 (Adj. Sess.), § 2.)

§ 2003. False tokens described

The use of a matured check, or other order for the payment of money, as a means of obtaining from another person money or other property, or a release or discharge of a debt or obligation, or the signature of a person to a written instrument the false making whereof would be punishable as forgery, such as is specified in section 2002 of this title, by a person who knows that the drawer thereof is not entitled to draw for the sum specified therein upon the drawee, is the use of a false token within the meaning of section 2002 of this title, although representation is not made in respect thereto.

§ 2004. Repealed. 1973, No. 249 (Adj. Sess.), § 111, eff. April 9, 1974.

§ 2005. False advertising

A person, firm, corporation, or association, or an agent or employee thereof, who, with intent to sell courses of instruction or to dispose of merchandise, real estate, securities, or service or to induce the public to enter into any obligations relating thereto, shall knowingly make, publish, circulate, or place before the public on radio or television or in a newspaper, magazine, or other publication or in form of a book, notice, circular, pamphlet, letter, handbill, poster, bill, sign, placard, card, label, or tag, or through an electronic communication, an advertisement, or statement regarding educational advantages, merchandise, real estate, securities or service, which advertisement or statement shall contain anything untrue, deceptive, or misleading, shall be fined not more than $1,000.00. (Amended 1967, No. 20, eff. March 3, 1967; 1999, No. 124 (Adj. Sess.), § 5.)

§ 2006. False statement as to financial ability

A person shall not knowingly make to a person, company, or corporation, or to a commercial agency, a false statement in writing signed by himself, herself, or by his or her direction, with intent that it shall be relied upon, respecting his or her financial condition, or the financial ability to pay of himself, herself, or other person, company, or corporation in which he or she is financially interested or by which he or she is employed as manager, secretary, or superintendent, for the purpose of procuring in any form the delivery of personal property, the payment of cash, the making of a loan or credit, the extension of a credit, the discount of an account receivable, or the making, acceptance, discount, sale, or indorsement of a bill of exchange or promissory note, for the benefit of himself, herself, or such other person, company, or corporation.

§ 2007. Receiving value upon false statement

Knowing that a false statement in writing has been made respecting the financial condition or means or ability to pay of himself, herself, or other person in whom he or she is financially interested or for whom he or she is acting, a person shall not procure, upon the faith thereof, for the benefit of himself, herself, or such other person, any of the things of benefit specified in section 2006 of this title.

§ 2008. False statement as to present validity of prior statement

Knowing that a statement in writing has been made respecting the financial condition or means or ability to pay of himself, herself, or other person in whom he or she is financially interested or for whom he or she is acting, a person shall not falsely represent on a later day, in writing, that such statement would be true if made on such later day, and thereby procure for the benefit of himself, herself, or such other person any of the things of benefit specified in section 2006 of this title.

§ 2009. Penalties

A person who violates a provision of sections 2006-2008 of this title shall be imprisoned not more than one year or fined not more than $1,000.00, or both.

§ 2010. Repealed. 1967, No. 202, § 6, eff. April 17, 1967.

§ 2011. Fraudulent use of badges

A person not entitled by the rules and regulations of the departments of the Grand Army of the Republic, the American Legion, Veterans of Foreign Wars of the United States, Sons of Veterans, Woman's Relief Corps, Ladies of the Grand Army of the Republic, Woman's Auxiliary of the American Legion, or of any patriotic, secret, or charitable society, who willfully wears a badge, button, or insignia of any such society or uses the same for any fraudulent purpose within the State, shall be imprisoned not more than 30 days or fined not more than $50.00, or both.

§ 2012. Misrepresenting livestock

(a) A person shall not make false or fraudulent representations for the purpose of obtaining a certificate of registration of an animal in a herd register or other register of a club, association, society, company, or corporation.

(b) A person shall not make false or fraudulent representations for the purpose of transfer of such certificate of registration.

(c) A person shall not fraudulently represent that an animal is a registered animal, or has been registered, with the intent that such representation shall be relied upon by another.

(d)(1) A "person" under this section is a person as defined in 1 V.S.A. § 128.

(2) A "registered animal" is an animal duly registered as a purebred in the official herd book or similar register of any recognized purebred registry association organized for the purpose of registering a particular breed of animals whose lineage has been established by registry records.

(3) An animal has been "registered" when it qualifies as a registered animal as defined in subdivision (2) of this subsection.

(e) A person who violates a provision of subsection (a), (b), or (c) of this section shall be fined not more than $300.00 and shall be liable civilly for damages. (Amended 1963, No. 81.)

§ 2013. Painting or disguising horses

A person who knowingly and designedly for the purpose of competing for a purse or premium offered by an agricultural society, corporation, or association within the State, enters or drives a horse or horse kind painted or disguised, or who for such purpose falsely and fraudulently represents a horse to be another from what it really is, or who for such purpose knowingly or designedly enters or drives a horse or horse kind in a class in which it is not entitled to be entered under the rules of such society, corporation, or association, shall be imprisoned not more than six months or fined not more than $500.00, or both. (Amended 1981, No. 223 (Adj. Sess.), § 23.)

§ 2014. Transferring chattel without notice of lien

A person who sells or disposes of personal property, or causes the same to be sold or disposed of by another, upon which there is a lien created by a previous attachment or conditional sale, or upon which he or she has previously given a bill of sale, without giving notice to the purchaser of such lien or bill of sale, with intent to defraud, shall be imprisoned not more than one year or fined not more than $200.00, or both. (Amended 1971, No. 199 (Adj. Sess.), § 15; 1981, No. 223 (Adj. Sess.), § 23.)

§ 2015. Transferring realty without notice of encumbrance

A person who knowingly and with intent to defraud sells, mortgages, or bonds real estate upon which there is an existing encumbrance, and receives a portion of the consideration of such sale or conveyance, without notifying the person taking such title or lien of such prior encumbrance, and embodying a description thereof in such subsequent conveyance, shall be imprisoned not more than three years or fined not more than $1,000.00, or both. (Amended 1971, No. 199 (Adj. Sess.), § 15.)

§ 2016. Signing or issuing false certificates of stock

A president or other officer or agent of a bank, railroad, manufacturing, or other corporation who willfully and designedly signs, with intent that it shall be issued or used, or causes to be issued or used, a false certificate or evidence of the ownership or transfer of shares of stock in such corporation, or a certificate or evidence of such ownership or transfer, that such officer has no authority to make or issue, shall be imprisoned not more than 10 years nor less than one year and fined not more than $1,000.00, or both. (Amended 1971, No. 199 (Adj. Sess.), § 15; 1981, No. 223 (Adj. Sess.), § 23.)

§ 2017. Repealed. 1979, No. 152 (Adj. Sess.).

§ 2018. Fraudulent use of slugs and tokens

A person who operates or causes to be operated, or attempts to operate or to cause to be operated, any automatic vending machine, slot machine, turnstile, coin-box telephone, or other receptacle designed to receive lawful coin of the United States in connection with the sale, use, or enjoyment of property, transportation, or other service, by means of a slug or any false, counterfeited, mutilated, or sweated coin or by any means, method, trick, or device whatsoever not lawfully authorized by the owner, lessee, or licensee of such machine, turnstile, coin-box telephone, or receptacle; or one who takes, obtains, or receives from or in connection with any automatic vending machine, slot machine, turnstile, coin-box telephone, or other receptacle designed to receive lawful coin of the United States in connection with the sale, use, or enjoyment of property or service, any goods, wares, merchandise, transportation, gas, electric current, article of value, or the use or enjoyment of any transportation or any telephone or telegraph facilities or service, or of any musical instrument, phonograph, or other property, without depositing in and surrendering to such machine, turnstile, coin-box telephone, or other receptacle lawful coin to the amount required therefor by the owner, lessee, or licensee of such machine, turnstile, coin-box telephone, or receptacle, shall be fined not more than $100.00 or be imprisoned for not more than 30 days, or both. (Amended 1971, No. 199 (Adj. Sess.), § 15.)

§ 2019. Manufacture and sale of devices for cheating

A person who manufactures for sale, advertises for sale, sells, offers for sale, or gives away any slug, device, or substance whatsoever, designed or calculated to be placed or deposited in any automatic vending machine, slot machine, turnstile, coin-box telephone, or other such receptacle, depository or contrivance, designed to receive lawful coin of the United States in connection with the sale, use, or enjoyment of property or service, with the intent or having cause to believe that such slug, device, or substance shall or will be used to cheat or defraud the person entitled to the contents of any such machine, turnstile, coin-box telephone, or other such receptacle, depository, or contrivance, shall be fined not more than $500.00 or be imprisoned for not more than one year, or both. (Amended 1971, No. 199 (Adj. Sess.), § 15.)

§ 2020. Repealed. 1959, No. 262, § 37, eff. June 11, 1959.

§ 2021. Telecommunications fraud and facilitation of telecommunications fraud

(a) Definitions. As used in this section:

(1) "Telecommunications device" means any type of instrument, device, machine, or equipment that is capable of transmitting or receiving interactive two-way electromagnetic communication, including voice, image, data, and information, or any part of such instrument, device, machine, or equipment, or any computer circuit, computer chip, electronic mechanism, or other component that is capable of facilitating the transmission or reception of any interactive two-way electromagnetic communication.

(2) "Telecommunications service" shall be the service provided by a telecommunications service provider as defined in subdivision (3) of this section.

(3) "Telecommunications service provider" means a person providing telecommunications service, companies operating a cable television system as defined in 30 V.S.A. § 501(2), and companies operating a satellite system.

(4) "Unlawful telecommunications device" means a telecommunications device, identification code, or computer code that, alone or in conjunction with any other item, is used or is intended to be used to commit telecommunications fraud or facilitation of telecommunications fraud.

(5) "Traffic" means to sell, buy, receive, distribute, exchange, offer, advertise, transfer, or dispose of an unlawful telecommunications device, related equipment, or plans or instructions for manufacturing or using such devices.

(6) "Electronic serial number reader" means a device that is capable of acquiring or facilitating the acquisition of an electronic serial number, mobile identification number, personal identification number, or any code or encoded or encrypted transmission useful in originating, facilitating, or transmitting telecommunications service without the consent of the telecommunications service provider.

(b) Telecommunications fraud. A person with intent to defraud commits the crime of telecommunications fraud by:

(1) charging telecommunications service to an existing telephone number, calling or credit card number, account number, or other identifying subscriber number; or

(2) charging telecommunications service to a false, inactive, counterfeit, or stolen telephone number, calling or credit card number, account number, or other identifying subscriber number; or

(3) obtaining telecommunications service using a false, altered, or stolen identification; or

(4) obtaining or attempting to obtain telecommunications service by the use of an unlawful telecommunications device.

(c) Penalties. A person who is convicted of telecommunications fraud shall:

(1) if the benefit has a value of less than $500.00, be imprisoned not more than two years or fined not more than $5,000.00, or both; or

(2) if the benefit is $500.00 or more in value, be imprisoned not more than five years or fined not more than $10,000.00, or both.

(d) Amounts involved in a violation of subsection (b) of this section under one course of conduct may be aggregated in determining the charge or the penalty for the offense.

(e) A person commits the crime of facilitation of telecommunications fraud who knowingly:

(1) possesses with intent to defraud, manufactures, or traffics in an unlawful telecommunications device or modifies, programs, or reprograms a telecommunications device designed, adapted, or that can be used:

(A) to commit a theft of telecommunications service; or

(B) to conceal with intent to defraud or to assist another to conceal with intent to defraud from any telecommunications service provider or governmental authority the existence or place of origin or destination of any telecommunications service; or

(2) manufactures or traffics in:

(A) plans or instructions for manufacturing or using an unlawful telecommunications device, except where the person manufactures or traffics in plans or instructions that are used for bona fide educational purposes exclusively; or

(B) material, data, computer facilities, computer software, computer hardware, reader, or other equipment knowing that the purchaser or a third person intends to use the material for the manufacture of an unlawful telecommunications device.

(f) Penalties. A person convicted of facilitation of telecommunications fraud shall:

(1) for a first offense, be imprisoned for not more than two years or fined not more than $5,000.00, or both; or

(2) for a second or subsequent offense, be imprisoned not more than five years or fined not more than $20,000.00, or both.

(g) Civil action. A person damaged as a result of a violation of this section may bring a civil action against the violator for damages and such other relief as the court deems appropriate. (1961, No. 86, §§ 1, 2; amended 1999, No. 35, § 2.)

§ 2022. Bad checks

A person who issues or passes a check or similar sight order for the payment of money, knowing that it will not be honored by the drawee, shall be imprisoned for not more than one year or fined not more than $1,000.00, or both. The court shall order restitution in the amount of the check or order, together with a service charge not to exceed $5.00, if it is established that the defendant has the ability to pay. For the purposes of this section, it may be inferred that the issuer knew that the check or order, other than a post-dated check or order, would not be paid if:

(1) the issuer had no account with the drawee at the time the check or order was issued; or

(2) the issuer had insufficient funds with the drawee at the time the check or order was issued or presented for payment, and

(A) the check or order was presented to the drawee for payment not more than 30 days after the date of issuance; and

(B) payment was refused by the drawee for reasons other than seizure or attachment of the issuer's funds by order of a court or authorized governmental agency; and

(C) the issuer or a person acting in his or her behalf failed to make full satisfaction of the amount of the check or order within 10 days after receiving notice of its dishonor by the drawee. (Added 1971, No. 254 (Adj. Sess.), § 3, eff. April 11, 1972; amended 1981, No. 232 (Adj. Sess.), § 1, eff. May 6, 1982.)

§ 2023. Simulating objects of antiquity or rarity

A person who, with the purpose of defrauding anyone or with the knowledge that he or she is facilitating a fraud to be perpetrated by anyone, makes or alters any object so that it appears to have value because of antiquity, rarity, source, or authorship that it does not possess shall be imprisoned for not more than one year or fined not more than $1,000.00, or both. (Added 1975, No. 109, § 3.)

§ 2024. Workers' compensation fraud; criminal penalties

Any person, including an employee, employer, medical case manager, health care provider, vocational rehabilitation provider, or workers' compensation insurance carrier, who knowingly and with intent to defraud makes a false statement or representation for the purpose of obtaining, affecting, or denying any benefit or payment under the provisions of 21 V.S.A. chapter 9 or the provisions of 8 V.S.A. Part 3, relating to insurance, either for herself or himself or for any other person, shall forfeit all benefits or payments obtained as a result of the false statement or representation and all or a portion of any right to compensation under the provisions of 21 V.S.A. chapter 9 as determined by the Commissioner and:

(1) for fraud involving $10,000.00 or more, be fined not more than $100,000.00 or imprisoned not more than three years, or both; and

(2) for fraud involving less than $10,000.00, be fined not more than $10,000.00 or imprisoned not more than two years, or both. (Added 1993, No. 225 (Adj. Sess.), § 23; amended 2003, No. 132 (Adj. Sess.), § 16, eff. May 26, 2004; 2009, No. 142 (Adj. Sess.), § 2.)

§ 2025. Employers without workers' compensation insurance; criminal sanction

Any employer who fails to comply with the provisions of 21 V.S.A. § 687 shall be fined not more than $2,500.00 or imprisoned for up to one year, or both. For the purposes of this section, the term employer includes the owner or operator of a business, the officers of a corporation, and the partners in a partnership. (Added 1997, No. 19, § 10.)

§ 2026. Installation of object in lieu of air bag

(a) No person shall knowingly install or reinstall or knowingly cause to be installed or reinstalled:

(1) an object in lieu of a vehicle air bag that was designed in accordance with the federal safety regulation for the make, model, and year of a vehicle; or

(2) an inoperable vehicle air bag, knowing the air bag is inoperable.

(b) A person who violates subsection (a) of this section shall be imprisoned for not more than three years or fined not more than $10,000.00, or both.

(c) A person who violates subsection (a) of this section, and serious bodily injury as defined in section 1021 of this title or death results, shall be imprisoned for not more than 15 years or fined not more than $10,000.00, or both. (Added 2001, No. 122 (Adj. Sess.), § 1.)

§ 2027. Sale or trade of motor vehicle with an inoperable air bag

(a) Any person selling or trading a motor vehicle who has actual knowledge that the motor vehicle's air bag is inoperable shall notify the buyer or the person acquiring the trade, in writing, that the air bag is inoperable.

(b) A person who violates subsection (a) of this section shall be subject to a fine of not more than $3,000.00. (Added 2001, No. 122 (Adj. Sess.), § 2.)

§ 2028. Fraudulent violations of joint fiduciary accounts

(a) No person shall intentionally violate 8 V.S.A. § 14212(b) or (e) while acting as a fiduciary on a joint fiduciary account.

(b) A person who violates this section, or misappropriates funds of $500.00 or less in violation of this section, shall be imprisoned not more than two years or fined not more than $10,000.00, or both.

(c) A person who misappropriates funds of more than $500.00 in violation of this section, or who is convicted of a second or subsequent violation of this section, shall be imprisoned not more than 10 years or fined not more than $10,000.00, or both. (Added 2001, No. 115 (Adj. Sess.), § 4, eff. May 28, 2002.)

§ 2029. Home improvement fraud

(a) As used in this section, "home improvement" includes the fixing, replacing, remodeling, removing, renovation, alteration, conversion, improvement, demolition, or rehabilitation of or addition to any building or land, or any portion thereof, that is used or designed to be used as a residence or dwelling unit. Home improvement shall include the construction, replacement, installation, paving, or improvement of driveways, roofs, and sidewalks, and the limbing, pruning, and removal of trees or shrubbery and other improvements to structures or upon land that is adjacent to a dwelling house.

(b) A person commits the offense of home improvement fraud when he or she enters into a contract or agreement, written or oral, for $500.00 or more, with an owner for home improvement, or into several contracts or agreements for $2,500.00 or more in the aggregate, with more than one owner for home improvement, and he or she knowingly:

(1)(A) fails to perform the contract or agreement, in whole or in part; and

(B) when the owner requests performance or a refund of payment made, the person fails to either:

(i) refund the payment; or

(ii) make and comply with a definite plan for completion of the work that is agreed to by the owner;

(2) misrepresents a material fact relating to the terms of the contract or agreement or to the condition of any portion of the property involved;

(3) uses or employs any unfair or deceptive act or practice in order to induce, encourage, or solicit such person to enter into any contract or agreement or to modify the terms of the original contract or agreement; or

(4) when there is a declared state of emergency, charges for goods or services related to the emergency a price that exceeds two times the average price for the goods or services and the increase is not attributable to the additional costs incurred in connection with providing those goods or services.

(c) Whenever a person is convicted of home improvement fraud or of fraudulent acts related to home improvement:

(1) the person shall notify the Office of Attorney General;

(2) the court shall notify the Office of the Attorney General; and

(3) the Office of Attorney General shall place the person's name on the Home Improvement Fraud Registry.

(d)(1) A person who violates subsection (b) of this section shall be imprisoned not more than two years or fined not more than $1,000.00, or both, if the loss to a single consumer is less than $1,000.00.

(2) A person who is convicted of a second or subsequent violation of subdivision (1) of this subsection shall be imprisoned not more than three years or fined not more than $5,000.00, or both.

(3) A person who violates subsection (b) of this section shall be imprisoned not more than three years or fined not more than $5,000.00, or both, if:

(A) the loss to a single consumer is $1,000.00 or more; or

(B) the loss to more than one consumer is $2,500.00 or more in the aggregate.

(4) A person who is convicted of a second or subsequent violation of subdivision (3) of this subsection shall be imprisoned not more than five years or fined not more than $10,000.00, or both.

(5) A person who violates subsection (c) or (e) of this section shall be imprisoned for not more than two years or fined not more than $1,000.00, or both.

(e) A person who is sentenced pursuant to subdivision (d)(2), (3), or (4) of this section, or convicted of fraudulent acts related to home improvement, may engage in home improvement activities for compensation only if:

(1) the work is for a company or individual engaged in home improvement activities, and the person first notifies the company or individual of the conviction and notifies the Office of Attorney General of the person's current address and telephone number; the name, address, and telephone number of the company or individual for whom the person is going to work; and the date on which the person will start working for the company or individual; or

(2) the person notifies the Office of Attorney General of the intent to engage in home improvement activities, and that the person has filed a surety bond or an irrevocable letter of credit with the Office in an amount of not less than $50,000.00, and pays on a regular basis all fees associated with maintaining such bond or letter of credit.

(f) The Office of Attorney General shall release the letter of credit at such time when:

(1) any claims against the person relating to home improvement fraud have been paid;

(2) there are no pending actions or claims against the person for home improvement fraud; and

(3) the person has not been engaged in home improvement activities for at least six years and has signed an affidavit so attesting.

(g) [Reserved.]

(h) [Repealed.] (Added 2003, No. 51, § 1; amended 2005, No. 103 (Adj. Sess.), § 3, eff. April 5, 2006; 2007, No. 211 (Adj. Sess.), § 1; 2015, No. 13, § 1, eff. May 1, 2015.)

§ 2030. Identity theft

(a) No person shall obtain, produce, possess, use, sell, give, or transfer personal identifying information belonging or pertaining to another person with intent to use the information to commit a misdemeanor or a felony.

(b) No person shall knowingly or recklessly obtain, produce, possess, use, sell, give, or transfer personal identifying information belonging or pertaining to another person without the consent of the other person and knowingly or recklessly facilitating the use of the information by a third person to commit a misdemeanor or a felony.

(c) For the purposes of this section, "personal identifying information" includes name, address, birth date, Social Security number, motor vehicle personal identification number, telephone number, financial services account number, savings account number, checking account number, credit card number, debit card number, picture, identification document or false identification document, electronic identification number, educational record, health care record, financial record, credit record, employment record, e-mail address, computer system password, or mother's maiden name, or similar personal number, record, or information.

(d) This section shall not apply when a person obtains the personal identifying information belonging or pertaining to another person to misrepresent the person's age for the sole purpose of obtaining alcoholic beverages, tobacco, or another privilege denied based on age.

(e) It shall be an affirmative defense to an action brought pursuant to this section, to be proven by a preponderance of the evidence, that the person had the consent of the person to whom the personal identifying information relates or pertains.

(f) A person who violates this section shall be imprisoned for not more than three years or fined not more $5,000.00, or both. A person who is convicted of a second or subsequent violation of this section involving a separate scheme shall be imprisoned for not more than 10 years or fined not more than $10,000.00, or both. (Added 2003, No. 155 (Adj. Sess.), § 4, eff. June 8, 2004.)

§ 2031. Insurance fraud

(a) Definitions. As used in this section:

(1) "Conceal" means to take affirmative action intended to prevent others from discovering information. Mere failure to disclose information does not constitute concealment.

(2) "Insurance policy" has the same meaning as in 8 V.S.A. § 4722(3) and includes a workers' compensation policy issued pursuant to 21 V.S.A. chapter 9.

(3) "Insurer" has the same meaning as in 8 V.S.A. § 4901(2) and includes a workers' compensation insurer pursuant to 21 V.S.A. chapter 9.

(b) Fraudulent insurance act. No person shall, with intent to defraud:

(1) present or cause to be presented a claim for payment or benefit, pursuant to any insurance policy, that contains false representations as to any material fact or which conceals a material fact; or

(2) present or cause to be presented any information that contains false representations as to any material fact or that conceals a material fact concerning the solicitation for sale of any insurance policy or purported insurance policy, an application for certificate of authority, or the financial condition of any insurer.

(c) Penalties. A person who violates subsection (b) of this section shall:

(1) if the benefit wrongfully obtained or the loss suffered by any person as a result of the violation has a value of less than $900.00, be imprisoned for not more than six months or fined not more than $5,000.00, or both; or

(2) if the benefit wrongfully obtained or the loss suffered by any person as a result of the violation has a value of more than $900.00, be imprisoned for not more than five years or fined not more than $10,000.00, or both; or

(3) for a second or subsequent offense, regardless of the value of the benefit wrongfully obtained, be imprisoned not more than five years or fined not more than $20,000.00, or both.

(d) Administrative action. Upon the conviction of a practitioner for a violation of subsection (b) of this section, the prosecutor shall inform the appropriate licensing authority. Any victim may notify the appropriate licensing authorities in this State and any other jurisdiction in which the practitioner is licensed of the conviction.

(e) This section shall not be construed to limit or restrict prosecution under any other applicable law.

(f) Immunity. No insurer or insurance professional acting in good faith and furnishing or disclosing information to the appropriate law enforcement official shall be subject to civil liability for libel, slander, or any other cause of action arising from the furnishing or disclosing of such information, except if the information is furnished solely to obtain an advantage in connection with a claim that will be, is being, or has been filed.

(g) The public policy of this State is that the standards of this section shall not apply or be introduced into evidence in any civil or administrative proceeding, whether to argue public policy, materiality, or for any other purpose. (Added 2005, No. 179 (Adj. Sess.), § 1, eff. July 1, 2006; amended 2007, No. 208 (Adj. Sess.), § 4.)

§ 2032. Sales suppression devices

(a) As used in this section:

(1) "Automated sales suppression device," also known as a "zapper," means a software program, carried on a memory stick or removable compact disc, accessed through an Internet link, or accessed through any other means, that falsifies transaction data, transaction reports, or any other electronic records of electronic cash registers and other point-of-sale systems.

(2) "Electronic cash register" means a device that keeps a register or supporting documents through the means of an electronic device or computer system designed to record transaction data for the purpose of computing, compiling, or processing retail sales transaction data in any manner.

(3) "Phantom-ware" means a hidden programming option, whether preinstalled or installed at a later time, embedded in the operating system of an electronic cash register or hardwired into the electronic cash register that:

(A) can be used to create a virtual second till; or

(B) may eliminate or manipulate transaction records.

(4) "Transaction data" include items purchased by a customer, the price for each item, a taxability determination for each item, a segregated tax amount for each of the taxed items, the amount of cash or credit tendered, the net amount returned to the customer in change, the date and time of the purchase, the name, address, and identification number of the vendor, and the receipt or invoice number of the transaction.

(5) "Transaction reports" means a report documenting, but not limited to, the sales, taxes collected, media totals, and discount voids at an electronic cash register that is printed on cash register tape at the end of a day or shift, or a report documenting every action at an electronic cash register that is stored electronically.

(b)(1) A person shall not knowingly sell, purchase, install, transfer, or possess an automated sales suppression device or phantom-ware.

(2) A person who violates subdivision (1) of this subsection shall be imprisoned for not less than one year and not more than five years and fined not more than $100,000.00, or both.

(c) A person who violates subdivision (b)(1) of this section shall be liable to the State for:

(1) all taxes, interest, and penalties due as the result of the person's use of an automated sales suppression device or phantom-ware; and

(2) all profits associated with the person's sale of an automated sales suppression device or phantom-ware.

(d) An automated sales suppression device or phantom-ware and any device containing such device or software shall be deemed contraband and shall be subject to seizure by the Commissioner of Taxes or by a law enforcement officer when directed to do so by the Commissioner of Taxes. (Added 2013, No. 13, § 1, eff. April 25, 2013.)

Chapter 49: Fraud In Commercial Transactions

Subchapter 1: Bills Of Lading

§ 2051. Issue of bill of lading for goods not received

An officer, agent, or servant or a carrier, who, with intent to defraud, issues or aids in issuing a bill of lading, knowing that all or any part of the goods for which the bill of lading is issued, has not been received by such carrier or by an agent of such carrier or by a connecting carrier or is not under the carrier's control at the time of issuing the bill of lading, shall be imprisoned not more than five years or fined not more than $5,000.00, or both. (Added 1966, No. 29 (Sp. Sess.), § 6.)

§ 2052. Issue of bill of lading containing false statement

An officer, agent, or servant of a carrier, who, with intent to defraud, issues or aids in issuing a bill of lading for goods knowing that it contains any false statement, shall be imprisoned not more than one year or fined not more than $1,000.00, or both. (Added 1966, No. 29 (Sp. Sess.), § 7.)

§ 2053. Issue of duplicate bills of lading not so marked

An officer, agent, or servant of a carrier, who, with intent to defraud, issues or aids in issuing a duplicate or additional negotiable bill of lading for goods in violation of 9A V.S.A. § 7- 402, knowing that a former negotiable bill of lading for the same goods or any part of them is outstanding and uncancelled, shall be imprisoned not more than five years or fined not more than $5,000.00, or both. (Added 1966, No. 29 (Sp. Sess.), § 8.)

§ 2054. Negotiation of bill of lading for goods subject to security interest

A person who ships goods to which he or she has not title or in which there is a security interest and who takes for such goods a negotiable bill of lading which he or she afterwards negotiates for value with intent to deceive and without disclosing his or her want of title or the existence of the security interest, shall be imprisoned not more than one year or fined not more than $1,000.00, or both. (Added 1966, No. 29 (Sp. Sess.), § 9.)

§ 2055. Negotiation of bill of lading when goods are not in carrier's possession

A person who, with intent to deceive, negotiates or transfers for value a bill of lading knowing that any or all of the goods that by the terms of the bill of lading appear to have been received for transportation by the carrier that issued the bill of lading, are not in the possession or control of the carrier or of a connecting carrier, without disclosing this fact, shall be imprisoned not more than five years or fined not more than $5,000.00, or both. (Added 1966, No. 29 (Sp. Sess.), § 10)

§ 2056. Inducing carrier to issue bill of lading when goods have not been received

A person who, with intent to defraud, secures the issue by a carrier of a bill of lading, knowing that at the time of issue, any or all of the goods described in the bill of lading as received for transportation have not been received by the carrier or an agent of the carrier or a connecting carrier or are not under the carrier's control, by inducing an officer, agent, or servant of the carrier falsely to believe that the goods have been received by the carrier or are under its control, shall be imprisoned not more than five years or fined not more than $5,000.00, or both. (Added 1966, No. 29 (Sp. Sess.), § 11.)

§ 2057. Issue of nonnegotiable bill of lading not so marked

A person who, with intent to defraud, issues or aids in issuing a nonnegotiable bill of lading without the words "not negotiable" placed plainly upon the face thereof, shall be imprisoned not more than five years or fined not more than $5,000.00, or both. (Added 1966, No. 29 (Sp. Sess.), § 12.)

Subchapter 2: Warehouse Receipts

§ 2061. Issue of warehouse receipt for goods not received

A warehouseman, or any officer, agent or servant of a warehouseman, who issues or aids in issuing a warehouse receipt knowing that the goods for which the warehouse receipt is issued, have not been actually received by the warehouseman, or are not under his or her actual control at the time of issuing the warehouse receipt, shall be imprisoned not more than five years or fined not more than $5,000.00, or both. (Added 1966, No. 29 (Sp. Sess.), § 13.)

§ 2062. Issue of warehouse receipt containing false statement

A warehouseman, or any officer, agent, or servant of a warehouseman, who fraudulently issues or aids in fraudulently issuing a warehouse receipt for goods knowing that it contains any false statement, shall be imprisoned not more than one year or fined not more than $1,000.00, or both. (Added 1966, No. 29 (Sp. Sess.), § 14.)

§ 2063. Issue of duplicate warehouse receipts not so marked

A warehouseman, or any officer, agent, or servant of a warehouseman, who issues or aids in issuing a duplicate or additional negotiable warehouse receipt for goods knowing that a former negotiable warehouse receipt for the same goods or any part of them is outstanding and uncancelled, without plainly placing upon the face thereof the word "Duplicate," except in the case of a lost or destroyed warehouse receipt after proceedings as provided for in 9 V.S.A. § 7- 601, shall be imprisoned not more than five years or fined not more than $5,000.00, or both. (Added 1966, No. 29 (Sp. Sess.), § 15.)

§ 2064. Issue for warehouseman's goods of warehouse receipts that do not state his or her ownership

Where there are deposited with or held by a warehouseman goods of which he or she is owner, either solely or jointly or in common with others, the warehouseman, or any of his or her officers, agents, or servants, who knowing this ownership, issues or aids in issuing a negotiable warehouse receipt for those goods that does not state that ownership, shall be imprisoned not more than one year or fined not more than $1,000.00, or both. (Added 1966, No. 29 (Sp. Sess.), § 16.)

§ 2065. Delivery of goods without obtaining negotiable warehouse receipt

A warehouseman, or any officer, agent, or servant of a warehouseman, who delivers goods out of the possession of the warehouseman, knowing that a negotiable warehouse receipt, the negotiation of which would transfer the right to the possession of such goods, is outstanding and uncancelled, without obtaining the possession of the warehouse receipt at or before the time of such delivery, except in the cases provided for in 9A V.S.A. §§ 7- 205, 7- 209 and 7- 601, shall be imprisoned not more than one year or fined not more than $1,000.00, or both. (Added 1966, No. 29 (Sp. Sess.), § 17.)

§ 2066. Negotiation of warehouse receipt for goods subject to a security interest

A person who deposits goods to which he or she has not title or in which there is a security interest, and who takes for the goods a negotiable warehouse receipt which he or she afterwards negotiates for value with intent to deceive and without disclosing his or her want of title or the existence of the security interest, shall be imprisoned not more than one year or fined not more than $1,000.00, or both. (Added 1966, No. 29 (Sp. Sess.), § 18.)

Subchapter 3: Security Agreements

§ 2071. Penalty for failure to discharge security agreement

When the condition of a security agreement has been fulfilled, within 30 days thereafter, the secured party shall cause the security agreement to be discharged of record. A person who neglects or refuses so to do shall be fined not more than $50.00 nor less than $5.00. (Added 1966, No. 29 (Sp. Sess.), § 19.)

§ 2072. Removal of collateral from the State

No person may, with intent to defraud or to deprive a secured party or debtor of his or her legal rights or remedies, remove collateral from the State, or conceal or aid in concealing it. (Added 1966, No. 29 (Sp. Sess.), § 20.)

§ 2073. Sale of collateral

A debtor shall not sell, pledge, or exchange collateral without the consent of the secured party in writing recorded in the office where the security agreement is recorded or upon the back of the security agreement, and, in either case, on the margin of the record thereof in the office where it is recorded. (Added 1966, No. 29 (Sp. Sess.), § 21.)

§ 2074. Prior security interest to be set forth in subsequent security agreement

A debtor shall not execute a second or subsequent security agreement covering collateral that is the subject of a previously existing security agreement made by the debtor unless the existence of the previous security agreement is set forth in the subsequent security agreement. (Added 1966, No. 29 (Sp. Sess.), § 22.)

§ 2075. Penalties

A person who violates section 2072, 2073, or 2074 of this title shall be fined not more than double the value of the collateral so wrongfully removed from the State, sold, concealed, pledged, mortgaged, or exchanged, and half the fine shall be paid to the party injured. (Added 1966, No. 29 (Sp. Sess.), § 23.)

§ 2076. Statutory construction

Statutes using the words "pledge," "mortgage," "conditional sale," "lien," "assignment," and like terms in referring to a security interest in personal property shall also apply to a corresponding type of security interest under 9A V.S.A. §§ 1- 101 et seq. and sections 2051-2057, 2061-2066, 2071-2076 of this title. (Added 1966, No. 29 (Sp. Sess.), § 24.)

Chapter 51: Gambling And Lotteries

Subchapter 1: Lotteries

§ 2101. Setting up, promoting, or aiding

Except as provided in section 2143 of this title, a person who sets up or promotes a lottery for money or other property, or disposes of money or property by a lottery, and a person aiding or concerned in so doing, or who knowingly allows premises owned or occupied by him or her or under his or her control to be used for that purpose, or by persons raffling or using a game of chance for money or property, shall be imprisoned not more than one year or fined not more than $10,000.00, or both, for the first offense and imprisoned not more than three years or fined not more than $10,000.00, or both, for each subsequent offense. (Amended 1993, No. 183 (Adj. Sess.), § 4.)

§ 2102. Disposing of property by way of chance

Except as provided in section 2143 of this title, a person who sells or disposes of property by way of chance or, as an inducement to the sale of property, gives the purchaser or any other person other property to be drawn by way of chance or lottery shall be imprisoned not more than one year or fined not more than $10,000.00, or both, for the first offense and imprisoned not more than three years or fined not more than $10,000.00, or both, for each subsequent offense. (Amended 1993, No. 183 (Adj. Sess.), § 5.)

§ 2102a. Affirmative defense

It shall be an affirmative defense to a charge under section 2101 or 2102 of this title that the person charged complied with the provisions of section 2143 of this title. (Added 1993, No. 183 (Adj. Sess.), § 6.)

§ 2103. Lottery tickets

(a) A person shall not:

(1) sell a lottery ticket or an interest therein, or a paper purporting to be a lottery ticket or an interest therein;

(2) open or keep an office, shop, or store for the purpose of selling or procuring a lottery ticket or paper or an interest therein;

(3) act as a broker or agent in buying, selling, or procuring to be bought or sold or disposed of in any way such ticket or interest therein, or in effecting or in endeavoring to effect a contract in regard thereto;

(4) set up, exhibit, or publish or cause to be set up, exhibited, or published within this state written, printed, or electronically communicated proposals to buy, sell, or procure such ticket or interest therein.

(b) A person violating a provision hereof shall be fined not more than $300.00.

(c) For purposes of this section, no internet service provider or provider of internet transport facilities shall be liable solely as a result of use of its facilities by a third party for a prohibited use without the provider's actual knowledge or express consent. (Amended 1999, No. 124 (Adj. Sess.), § 6.)

Subchapter 2: Wagering And Gambling

§ 2131. Repealed. 1961, No. 185, § 7.

§ 2132. Repealed. 1979, No. 152 (Adj. Sess.).

§ 2133. At gaming house

A person who plays at cards, dice, tables, or other game for money or other valuable in a common gaming or gambling house that is maintained for lucre and gain, shall be fined not more than $200.00 or imprisoned not more than 60 days, or both.

§ 2134. Keeping gambling instrument

A person who has or keeps on premises owned or occupied by him or her implements or other things used in gambling and permits persons resorting to such premises to use such implements or things for the purpose of gambling shall be imprisoned not more than six months nor less than 10 days or fined not more than $500.00 nor less than $10.00, or both.

§ 2135. Gambling machines- Sale, lease, or rental

(a) A person, corporation, copartnership, or association shall not lease, rent, let on shares, sell, expose for sale, or offer for sale:

(1) a machine, apparatus, or device, into which may be inserted a piece of money or other object, and from which, as a result of such insertion and the application of physical or mechanical or electrical force, may issue with or without gum or confection, a piece of money, or slug, or a token, or a check or memoranda calling for money, credit, or merchandise or property; or

(2) a coin or slot machine, pinball machine, racing machines, or other device of like character, wherein there enters any element of chance, whether the same be played for money, checks, credits, merchandise, or other thing representative of value; or

(3) a machine or device of any kind or nature by the use or operation of which there is an element of chance for the winning or losing of money or other things of value.

(b) The provisions of this chapter shall not apply to slot machines that were manufactured prior to 1954 and that are not operated for gambling purposes. (Amended 1985, No. 100 (Adj. Sess.), eff. Feb. 5, 1986.)

§ 2136. Possession

A person shall be punished as provided in section 2139 of this title who has in his or her possession, or under his or her control, or who permits to be placed, maintained, or kept in a place of public resort or in premises occupied by him or her, or under his or her management or control a machine, apparatus, or device as mentioned in section 2135 of this title.

§ 2137. Seizure; hearing

A sheriff, deputy sheriff, constable, or police officer shall seize without a warrant any machine or device described in sections 2134 and 2135 of this title, found in a place of public resort. A sheriff or other officer making such a seizure shall forthwith make a complaint under oath, subscribed by him or her, to a district judge in the county in which such seizure is made and shall summon the owner or occupant of the place in which such seizure is made to appear before such court and show cause why such machine should not be destroyed. (Amended 1965, No. 194, § 10, operative February 1, 1967; 1973, No. 249 (Adj. Sess.), § 45, eff. April 9, 1974.)

§ 2138. Destruction

If, upon hearing, it is found that such machine was seized in a place of public resort, or was seized in any place by reason of a search warrant lawfully issued, the same shall be ordered destroyed and all money or other contents thereof forfeited to the State. The court shall issue its warrant to carry such order into effect.

§ 2139. Penalties

An association, copartnership, corporation, or person who violates a provision of sections 2135-2138 of this title shall be fined not more than $100.00 or be imprisoned not more than six months, or both.

§ 2140. Repealed. 1973, No. 249 (Adj. Sess.), § 111, eff. April 9, 1974.

§ 2141. Winning or losing by gambling

A person who wins or loses money or other valuable thing by play or hazard at any game, or by betting on such play or hazard, or sharing in a stake wagered by others on such play or hazard, shall be fined not more than $200.00 nor less than $10.00.

§ 2142. Repealed. 1979, No. 152 (Adj. Sess.).

§ 2143. Nonprofit organizations

(a) Notwithstanding the provisions of this chapter, a nonprofit organization, as defined in 31 V.S.A. § 1201(5), may organize and execute, and an individual may participate in lotteries, raffles, or other games of chance for the purpose of raising funds to be used in charitable, religious, educational, and civic undertakings or used by fraternal organizations to provide direct support to charitable, religious, educational, or civic undertakings with which they are affiliated. Except as provided in subsection (d) of this section, gambling machines and other mechanical devices described in section 2135 of this title shall not be utilized under authority of this section.

(b) A nonprofit organization may, notwithstanding the provisions of Title 7, distribute or utilize alcoholic beverages as prizes, rewards, winnings in any lottery, raffle, or other game of chance.

(c) A person shall not conduct a bingo game in which the numbers picked are communicated electronically or by satellite to players at another location.

(d) Casino events shall be limited as follows:

(1) A location may be the site of no more than:

(A) one casino event in any calendar quarter; or

(B) three casino events in any calendar year, as long as there are at least 15 days between each event.

(2) A location that is owned by a nonprofit, as defined in 31 V.S.A. § 1201(5), may be the site of no more than two casino events in any calendar month as long as there are at least 10 days between each event.

(3) A nonprofit organization, as defined in 31 V.S.A. § 1201(5), may organize and execute no more than one casino event in any calendar month.

(4) As used in this subsection, "casino event" means an event held during any 24-hour period at which any game of chance is conducted except those prohibited by subdivision 2135(a)(1) or (2) of this title. A "casino event" shall not include a fair, bazaar, field days, agricultural exposition, or similar event that utilizes a wheel of fortune, chuck-a-luck, or other such games commonly conducted at such events, or break-open tickets, bingo, a lottery, or a raffle.

(e) Games of chance shall be limited as follows:

(1) All proceeds raised by a game of chance shall be used exclusively for charitable, religious, educational, and civic undertakings after deducting:

(A) reasonable expenses, as determined by fair market value, of purchasing or renting materials and equipment used for the game of chance, of printing advertisements, and of the direct purchase of advertising through established media, such as newspapers, radio, and television; and

(B) reasonable expenses, as determined by fair market value, for rent for the premises on which the game of chance is executed and repairs and upkeep to the premises for nonprofit organizations having ownership in premises; and

(C) prizes awarded to players as limited in subdivision (4) of this subsection (e); and

(D) payments to persons as limited in subdivision (2) of this subsection (e).

(2) A nonprofit organization that organizes and executes a game of chance shall not pay any person, and no person shall receive, any fee, commission, wage, salary, reward, tip, donation, or other compensation in excess of $2,000.00 in any calendar year for organizing or executing games of chance or for working at the site of a game of chance. Refreshments or meals provided to a volunteer while working at the site shall not be considered compensation. Notwithstanding the provisions of this subdivision, a nonprofit organization that organizes and executes games of chance may pay not more than $15,000.00 in any calendar year, in the aggregate, to all persons for organizing, executing, or working at a game of chance.

In calculating the limitations on payments to persons contained in this subdivision, only that portion of a person's compensation attributable to gaming shall be considered.

(3) A nonprofit organization shall not permit any person who has not attained the age of majority to organize or execute a game of chance. A person who has not reached the age of majority may work performing services at a game of chance that are not related to the execution of the game of chance.

(4) A nonprofit organization may offer a prize worth not more than $400.00 in value for a single game of chance, except that the nonprofit organization may offer a prize worth not more than $1,000.00 in value for one game per day, a prize worth not more than $5,000.00 in value for one game per calendar month and a prize of a motor vehicle, firearm, motorcycle, or watercraft worth not more than $50,000.00 for one game per calendar year. A nonprofit organization may exceed the above prize limitations on four days per calendar year, if the days are at least 20 days apart and the total prize money offered for all games executed on the day does not exceed $50,000.00.

(5) A nonprofit organization shall not permit a person who organizes, executes, or works at a game of chance to play in any game of chance organized or executed by that nonprofit on the same day.

(6) A nonprofit organization shall not organize and execute games of chance on more than two days in any calendar week, nor shall games of chance be organized and executed at any location on more than two days in any calendar week, except that:

(A) Casino events may be conducted only as permitted under subsection (d) of this section.

(B) Break-open tickets may be purchased and distributed only as provided in 31 V.S.A. chapter 23.

(C) A nonprofit organization may organize and execute games of chance on three consecutive days not more than twice in any calendar year as long as there are at least 90 days between each event.

(D) Agricultural fairs that are registered with the Agency of Agriculture, Food and Markets may organize and execute games of chance for not more than 12 consecutive days during the fair once each calendar year.

(E) A nonprofit organization may organize and execute games of chance at a location used by another nonprofit organization that results in the location being used on more than two days a week if all the nonprofit organizations using the location were in existence as of January 1, 1994, and are not affiliated with each other or under common control.

(7) A nonprofit organization shall not knowingly permit any person who has been convicted of a crime, within the last 10 years, under the laws of this State or of any other state, government, or country that, if committed in this State, would be a felony criminal offense to organize or execute a game of chance. No person who has been convicted of such a crime shall organize or execute a game of chance.

(f) A nonprofit organization that organizes and executes a game of chance under subsection (a) of this section shall file financial reports with the Commissioner of Taxes as follows:

(1) For a nonprofit organization that is required to file federal tax forms 990 or 990T, or both, copies of those forms within 30 days of the filing date required by the Internal Revenue Service.

(2) For a nonprofit organization that has raised more than $10,000.00 during the preceding year from organizing and executing games of chance and is not required to file federal tax forms 990 or 990T, a financial report for the preceding year, by June 15 of each year, that contains all the following information:

(A) an itemized list of all expenditures made for purchasing or renting materials and equipment used for games of chance and of printing advertisements, and of the direct purchase of advertising through established media, such as newspapers, radio, and television;

(B) an itemized list of all expenditures made to all persons for organizing, executing, or working at a game of chance and made for rent for premises on which games of chance are executed;

(C) the amount of all prizes awarded;

(D) an itemized list of all disbursements for charitable, religious, educational, and civic undertakings; and

(E) an itemized list of all funds raised from organizing and executing games of chance.

(3) For a nonprofit organization that is required to withhold Vermont income taxes from gambling winnings pursuant to 32 V.S.A. § 5841(a), a financial report describing the amounts withheld, within 30 days of the filing date required by the Internal Revenue Service or by June 15 of each year, as applicable.

(4) If the required financial report is not filed within 30 days after the report is due or does not contain the information required by this subsection, the Commissioner of Taxes may bring an action in Superior Court against the nonprofit organization for injunctive relief to restrain the organization and execution of games of chance by that organization. The State shall not be required to demonstrate immediate and irreparable injury in order to be granted injunctive relief.

(g) The Commissioner of Taxes shall design the financial forms required by subsection (f) of this section and make them available on request.

(h) The Commissioner of Taxes shall provide the financial reports required by subsection (f) of this section to the Attorney General upon request, notwithstanding the provisions of 32 V.S.A. § 3102.

(i) A person who intentionally violates subsection (a) of this section shall be fined not more than $500.00.

(j) A person who intentionally violates subsection (c), (d), (e), or (f) of this section shall be fined not more than $10,000.00 for the first offense and fined not more than $100,000.00 or imprisoned not more than three years, or both, for each subsequent offense.

(k) A nonprofit organization that organizes and executes a game of chance under subsection (a) of this section shall permit its members to examine the financial books and records relating to gambling activities of the organization at any reasonable time and, upon request, shall provide photocopies of these records to its members at cost. (Added 1973, No. 215 (Adj. Sess.), § 2, eff. April 3, 1974; amended 1975, No. 41, § 1, eff. April 15, 1975; 1991, No. 267 (Adj. Sess.), § 1; 1993, No. 183 (Adj. Sess.),§§ 1-3; 1993, No. 221 (Adj. Sess.), §§ 33, 34; 2009, No. 16, § 1, eff. May 12, 2009; 2015, No. 57, § 38, eff. June 11, 2015; 2017, No. 73, § 12, eff. Sept. 1, 2017; 2017, No. 83, § 165.)

§ 2143a. Political parties

Notwithstanding the provisions of this chapter, a political party, organized under 17 V.S.A. chapter 45, may organize and execute, and an individual may participate in, raffles, the proceeds of which are to be used in undertakings consistent with the purpose of political parties. (Added 1983, No. 136 (Adj. Sess.).)

§ 2143b. Contests and sweepstakes

Notwithstanding the provisions of this chapter, a person may organize, execute, or participate in a contest or game of chance, including a sweepstakes, provided that persons who enter the contest or game of chance are not required to venture money or other valuable things. The cost of mailing an entry shall not be considered a venture of money or other valuable things. This section shall not be construed to prohibit a person from organizing, executing, or participating in a contest that is not a contest of chance. (Added 1989, No. 7; amended 2013, No. 9, § 2.)

Subchapter 3: Bookmaking; Pool Selling; Racing Offenses

§ 2151. Bookmaking; pool selling; off-track wagers

(a) A person shall not:

(1) engage in bookmaking or pool selling, except deer pools or other pools in which all of the monies paid by the participants, as an entry fee or otherwise, are paid out to either the winning participants based on the result of the pool or to a nonprofit organization or event as described in 31 V.S.A. § 1201(5) where the funds are to be used as described in that subdivision, or both;

(2) keep or occupy, for any period of time, any place or enclosure of any kind, with any material for recording any wager, or any purported wager, or selling pools, except as provided in subdivision (1) of this subsection, upon the result of any contest, lot, chance, unknown or contingent event, whether actual or purported;

(3) receive, hold, or forward, or purport or pretend to receive, hold, or forward, in any manner, any money, thing, or consideration of value, or the equivalent or memorandum thereof, wagered, or to be wagered, or offered for the purpose of being wagered, upon such result;

(4) record or register, at any time or place, any wager upon such result;

(5) permit any place or enclosure that the person owns, leases, or occupies to be used or occupied for any purpose or in any manner prohibited by subdivision (1), (2), (3), or (4) of this section; or

(6) with the exception of pools as provided in subdivision (1) of this subsection, lay, make, offer, or accept any wager, upon such result or contest of skill, speed, or power of endurance of human or beast, or between humans, beasts, or mechanical apparatus.

(b) Notwithstanding any provision to the contrary, a public retail establishment, including a holder of a second-class license issued under Title 7, may sell raffle tickets on the retail premises for a nonprofit organization that has organized the raffle, provided the raffle is conducted in accordance with section 2143 of this title and that no person is compensated for expenses, as outlined in subdivision 2143(e)(1)(B) of this title. (Added 1961, No. 185, § 1; amended 1983, No. 43, § 2; 1999, No. 33, § 1; 2019, No. 128 (Adj. Sess.), § 16.)

§ 2152. Penalty

A person who violates a provision of section 2151 of this title shall be fined not more than $250.00 or imprisoned not more than six months, or both, for the first offense and fined not more than $2,000.00 or imprisoned not more than five years, or both, for a subsequent offense. When a person has been convicted in any state of a felony or of a violation of a statute prohibiting bookmaking, his or her conviction under this section shall be considered a subsequent offense. (Added 1961, No. 185, § 2; amended 1971, No. 199 (Adj. Sess.), § 15.)

§ 2153. Prohibition on dog and horse race betting

A person shall not hold, conduct, operate, or simulcast a pari-mutuel dog race or pari-mutuel horse race for public exhibition. (Added 1961, No. 185, § 3; amended 1973, No. 233 (Adj. Sess.), § 12; 2019, No. 14, § 44, eff. April 30, 2019; 2019, No. 128 (Adj. Sess.), § 17.)

§ 2154. Repealed. 2019, No. 128 (Adj. Sess.), § 18.

§ 2155. Penalty

A person who violates a provision of section 2153 of this title shall be fined not more than $5,000.00 or imprisoned not more than two years, or both. (Added 1961, No. 185, § 5; amended 1971, No. 199 (Adj. Sess.), § 15; 1981, No. 223 (Adj. Sess.), § 23.)

§ 2156. Repealed. 2019, No. 128 (Adj. Sess.), § 19.

Subchapter 4: Stock Gambling

§ 2171. "Bucket shops"

A person or corporation shall not keep or cause to be kept a "bucket shop," office, store, or other place in which it is conducted or permitted the pretended buying or selling of stock or bonds of a corporation, or petroleum, cotton, grain, provisions, pork, or other produce, either on margins or otherwise, without any intention of receiving and paying for the property so bought, or of delivering the property so sold; or in which is conducted or permitted the pretended buying or selling of such property on margins; or when the party buying or offering to buy such property does not intend actually to receive the same if purchased, or the person selling such property to deliver it if sold.

§ 2172. Evidence

If stocks or bonds are in any manner quoted in such places, or the word "corporation," "association," or "company," or an abbreviation thereof, used therein and therewith, it shall be prima facie evidence that such stocks or bonds are the stocks or bonds of then going corporations. If such stocks or bonds, or such petroleum, cotton, grain, provisions, pork, or other produce are not actually received when purchased or actually delivered when sold, it shall be prima facie evidence that:

(1) such property was sold or purchased without any intention of receiving it or paying for or delivering it;

(2) such property was bought or sold on margins; and

(3) the parties buying or offering to buy or selling such property did not intend actually to receive or deliver the same.

§ 2173. Penalties

A person or corporation, whether acting individually, or as a member, officer, agent, or employee of a corporation, who violates a provision of section 2171 of this title shall be fined not more than $1,000.00 nor less than $200.00. A person who is guilty of a second offense, in addition to the penalty above prescribed, shall be imprisoned six months and, if a corporation, shall be liable to forfeit its charter. The continuance of such establishment after a first conviction shall be deemed a second offense. (Amended 1971, No. 199 (Adj. Sess.), § 15.)

§ 2174. What constitutes offense; accessories

The offense shall be complete against a person or corporation pretending or offering to sell or to buy, as provided in sections 2171 and 2172 of this title, whether the offer to sell or buy is accepted or not. A person or corporation communicating, receiving, exhibiting, or displaying in any manner such offer so to buy or sell or any statements or quotations of the prices of such property, with a view to such transaction, shall be deemed an accessory and shall be punished as provided in section 2173 of this title.

§ 2175. Commission merchants to furnish statement of contract

A person or corporation doing business as a commission merchant or broker shall furnish, on demand, to a customer or principal for whom such person or corporation has executed an order for the actual purchase or sale of any of the commodities mentioned in sections 2171 and 2172 of this title, either for immediate or future delivery, a written statement containing the names of the parties from whom such property was bought, or to whom sold, the time when, place where, and price at which the same was bought or sold. If such person or corporation refuses promptly to furnish such statement upon reasonable demand, such refusal shall be prima facie evidence that such property was not bought or sold in a legitimate manner.

§ 2176. Liability of landlords

A person who knowingly permits any of the illegal acts mentioned in sections 2171-2175 of this title in a building, booth, or erection of which he or she has the care or possession shall be fined not more than $1,000.00 nor less than $500.00. A penalty so adjudged shall be a lien upon the premises on or in which such unlawful acts are carried on or permitted.

§ 2177. Restraint by injunction; costs

When a prosecution is commenced for the violation of a provision of sections 2171, 2173, 2174, or 2176 of this title, the State's Attorney may petition the presiding judge of the Superior Court to enjoin the carrying on of such unlawful business in the place where the complaint, information, or indictment charges that it has been conducted. Such presiding judge shall hear and determine such petition in the manner provided by law and the rules of civil procedure for the determination of causes and may, if the allegations therein are sustained, permanently enjoin the person, firm, or corporation shown to have kept or caused to have been kept such place, from conducting such prohibited business therein. The Superior Court or presiding judge may, upon petition therefor in such proceedings, issue a temporary injunction to effect, during the pendency of the petition, the closing of such place against such unlawful business. The costs of the proceedings authorized by this section shall be taxed against the defendant in case the State prevails. (Amended 1971, No. 185 (Adj. Sess.), § 236, eff. March 29, 1972; 1973, No. 193 (Adj. Sess.), § 3, eff. April 9, 1974.)

Chapter 53: Homicide

§ 2301. Murder-degrees defined

Murder committed by means of poison, or by lying in wait, or by willful, deliberate, and premeditated killing, or committed in perpetrating or attempting to perpetrate arson, sexual assault, aggravated sexual assault, kidnapping, robbery, or burglary shall be murder in the first degree. All other kinds of murder shall be murder in the second degree. (Amended 1983, No. 23, § 1; 2018, No. 8 (Sp. Sess.), § 12, eff. June 28, 2018.)

§ 2302. Determination of degree

The jury by whom a person is tried for murder, if it finds such person guilty thereof, shall state in its verdict whether it is murder in the first or in the second degree. If such person is convicted on confession in open court, the court, by examination of witnesses, shall determine the degree of the crime and give sentence accordingly.

§ 2303. Penalties for first and second degree murder

(a)(1) The punishment for murder in the first degree shall be imprisonment for:

(A) a minimum term of not less than 35 years and a maximum term of life; or

(B) life without the possibility of parole.

(2) The punishment for murder in the second degree shall be imprisonment for:

(A) a minimum term of not less than 20 years and a maximum term of life; or

(B) life without the possibility of parole.

(3) Notwithstanding any other provision of law, this subsection shall apply only if the murder was committed on or after the effective date of this act.

(b) The punishment for murder in the first degree shall be imprisonment for life and for a minimum term of 35 years unless a jury finds that there are aggravating or mitigating factors which justify a different minimum term. If the jury finds that the aggravating factors outweigh any mitigating factors, the court may set a minimum term longer than 35 years, up to and including life without parole. If the jury finds that the mitigating factors outweigh any aggravating factors, the court may set a minimum term at less than 35 years but not less than 15 years.

(c) The punishment for murder in the second degree shall be imprisonment for life and for a minimum term of 20 years unless a jury finds that there are aggravating or mitigating factors which justify a different minimum term. If the jury finds that the aggravating factors outweigh any mitigating factors, the court may set a minimum term longer than 20 years, up to and including life without parole. If the jury finds that the mitigating factors outweigh any aggravating factors, the court may set a minimum term at less than 20 years but not less than 10 years.

(d)(1)(A) Before the court sentences a defendant for first or second degree murder, a jury shall consider the aggravating and mitigating factors set forth in subsections (e) and (f) of this section. The court shall allow the parties to present evidence and argument concerning the aggravating and mitigating factors and may empanel a new jury to consider them or conduct the hearing before the same jury that considered the guilt of the defendant.

(B) The parties shall file notice of intent to present evidence regarding specific aggravating and mitigating factors about which the parties have knowledge not less than 60 days before the hearing. A party may not present evidence on the presence of that aggravating or mitigating factor unless notice has been provided as required by this subdivision.

(C) The jury shall make findings concerning aggravating and mitigating factors and determine whether the aggravating factors outweigh the mitigating factors or the mitigating factors outweigh the aggravating factors. The findings shall be based on the evidence on the criminal charges presented to the jury at the sentencing hearing and at the trial.

(D) The burden shall be on the State to prove beyond a reasonable doubt the presence of aggravating factors or the absence of mitigating factors and to prove beyond a reasonable doubt that the aggravating factors outweigh the mitigating factors.

(2) After the jury renders a verdict on the aggravating and mitigating factors, the court shall allow the parties to present arguments concerning sentencing recommendations. The court shall make written findings of fact summarizing the offense and the defendant's participation in it. The findings shall be based on the evidence taken at trial, the evidence presented on aggravating and mitigating factors at the sentencing hearing, and information from the presentence report. The court shall impose a sentence consistent with subsection (b) or (c) of this subsection and with the jury's findings concerning aggravating and mitigating factors.

(e) Aggravating factors shall include the following:

(1) The murder was committed while the defendant was in custody under sentence of imprisonment.

(2) The defendant was previously convicted of a felony involving the use of violence to a person.

(3) The murder was committed while the defendant was engaged in the commission of, or in an attempt to commit, or in immediate flight after committing a felony.

(4) The victim of the murder was particularly weak, vulnerable, or helpless.

(5) The murder was particularly severe, brutal, or cruel.

(6) The murder involved multiple victims.

(7) The murder was random, predatory, or arbitrary in nature.

(8) Any other factor that the State offers in support of a greater minimum sentence.

(f) Mitigating factors shall include the following:

(1) The defendant had no significant history of prior criminal activity before sentencing.

(2) The defendant was suffering from a mental or physical disability or condition that significantly reduced his or her culpability for the murder.

(3) The defendant was an accomplice in the murder committed by another person and his or her participation was relatively minor.

(4) The defendant, because of youth or old age, lacked substantial judgment in committing the murder.

(5) The defendant acted under duress, coercion, threat, or compulsion insufficient to constitute a defense but which significantly affected his or her conduct.

(6) The victim was a participant in the defendant's conduct or consented to it.

(7) Any other factor that the defendant offers in support of a lesser minimum sentence.

(g) Subsections (b)-(f) of this section shall apply only if the murder was committed before the effective date of this act, and:

(1) the defendant was not sentenced before the effective date of this act; or

(2) the defendant's sentence was stricken and remanded for resentencing pursuant to the Vermont Supreme Court's decision in State v. Provost, 2005 VT 134 (2005). (Amended 1965, No. 30; 1971, No. 199, § 15; 1979, No. 175 (Adj. Sess.), § 1, eff. April 29, 1980; 1981, No. 223 (Adj. Sess.) § 20; 1987, No. 60, § 2, eff. May 16, 1987; 2005, No. 119 (Adj. Sess.), § 2, eff. May 1, 2006.)

§ 2304. Manslaughter- Penalties

A person who commits manslaughter shall be fined not more than $3,000.00 or imprisoned for not less than one year nor more than 15 years, or both. (Amended 1971, No. 199 (Adj. Sess.), § 15; 1981, No. 205 (Adj. Sess.), § 3.)

[Section 2305 effective until July 1, 2021; see also section 2305 effective July 1, 2021 .]

§ 2305. Justifiable homicide

If a person kills or wounds another under any of the circumstances enumerated below, he or she shall be guiltless:

(1) in the just and necessary defense of his or her own life or the life of his or her husband, wife, parent, child, brother, sister, master, mistress, servant, guardian, or ward; or

(2) in the suppression of a person attempting to commit murder, sexual assault, aggravated sexual assault, burglary, or robbery, with force or violence; or

(3) in the case of a civil officer; or a military officer or private soldier when lawfully called out to suppress riot or rebellion, or to prevent or suppress invasion, or to assist in serving legal process, in suppressing opposition against him or her in the just and necessary discharge of his or her duty. (Amended 1983, No. 23, § 2.)

[Section 2305 effective July 1, 2021; see also section 2305 effective until July 1, 2021 .]

§ 2305. Justifiable homicide

If a person kills or wounds another under any of the circumstances enumerated below, he or she shall be guiltless:

(1) in the just and necessary defense of the person's own life or the life of the person's spouse, parent, child, sibling, guardian, or ward; or

(2) in the forceful or violent suppression of a person attempting to commit murder, sexual assault, aggravated sexual assault, burglary, or robbery; or

(3) in the case of a law enforcement officer as defined in 20 V.S.A. § 2351(a) using force in compliance with 20 V.S.A. § 2368(b)(2), (4), and (5) or deadly force in compliance with 20 V.S.A. § 2368(c)(1)-(4). (Amended 1983, No. 23, § 2; 2019, No. 165 (Adj. Sess.), § 2, eff. July 1, 2021.)

§ 2306. Poisoning food, drink, medicine, or water

A person who mingles poison with food, drink, or medicine with intent to injure another person or who, with a like intent, willfully poisons a spring, well, or reservoir of water shall be imprisoned not more than 20 years. (Amended 1971, No. 199 (Adj. Sess.), § 15; 1981, No. 223 (Adj. Sess.), § 3.)

§ 2307. Repealed. 1995, No. 170 (Adj. Sess.), § 32, eff. May 15, 1996.

§ 2308. False testimony with intent to cause death

A person who willfully and corruptly bears false testimony with intent to take away the life of a person and thereby causes the life of such person to be taken shall be guilty of murder in the first degree.

§ 2309. Repealed. 1973, No. 118, § 25, eff. Oct. 1, 1973.

§ 2310. Conviction of lesser offense

(a) Upon indictment or information for an offense under this chapter, a person may be convicted of a lesser included offense, as the case may be, upon the proofs.

(b) The time limitation created by subsection 4501(b) of this title for the crime of manslaughter shall not bar a conviction under this section. (Amended 1987, No. 60, § 4, eff. May 16, 1987; 1995, No. 27, § 2.)

§ 2311. Aggravated murder defined

(a) A person is guilty of aggravated murder if he or she commits a first or second degree murder, as defined in section 2301 of this title, and at the time of his or her actions, one or more of the following circumstances was in fact present:

(1) The murder was committed while the defendant was in custody under sentence for murder or aggravated murder.

(2) The defendant had, prior to commencement of the trial for aggravated murder, been convicted of another aggravated murder or murder in any jurisdiction in the United States and territories.

(3) At the time of the murder, the defendant also committed another murder.

(4) At the time of the murder, the defendant knowingly created a great risk of death to another person or persons.

(5) The murder was committed for the purpose of avoiding or preventing lawful arrest by a law enforcement officer of any person, or effecting an escape by any person from lawful custody of a law enforcement officer.

(6) The murder was committed by a person hired for such purpose in return for anything of value. Both the person hired and the person hiring him or her are guilty of aggravated murder.

(7) The victim of the murder was known by the person to be a firefighter, a member of emergency medical personnel as defined in 24 V.S.A. § 2651(6), a person employed in any capacity in or about a correctional facility, or a law enforcement officer, and was performing his or her official duties.

(8) The murder was committed in perpetrating or attempting to perpetrate sexual assault or aggravated sexual assault.

(b) In a prosecution for aggravated murder, the State shall allege and prove beyond a reasonable doubt one or more of the circumstances enumerated in subsection (a) of this section.

(c) The punishment for aggravated murder shall be imprisonment for life and for no lesser term. The court shall not place on probation or suspend or defer the sentence of any person convicted of aggravated murder. A person sentenced under this section shall not be eligible for parole during the term of imprisonment imposed herein and shall not be eligible for work-release or noncustodial furlough except when serious medical services make custodial furlough inappropriate. (Added 1987, No. 60, § 1, eff. May 16, 1987; amended 2019, No. 16, § 1, eff. May 6, 2019.)

Chapter 55: Kidnapping

§§ 2401-2403. Repealed. 1989, No. 293 (Adj. Sess.), § 8.

§ 2404. Definitions

As used in this chapter:

(1) "Lawful custodian" means a parent, guardian, or other person responsible by authority of law for the care, custody, or control of another.

(2) "Relative" means a parent, stepparent, ancestor, descendant, sibling, uncle, or aunt, including a relative of the same degree through civil marriage or adoption.

(3) "Restrain" means to restrict substantially the movement of another person without the person's consent or other lawful authority by:

(A) removing the restrained person from the person's residence or place of business, or from a hospital or school; or

(B) moving the restrained person a substantial distance from the place where the restriction on the person's movement commenced; or

(C) confining the restrained person for a substantial period either in the place where the restriction commences or in a place to which the person has been moved.

(4) A restraint is "without consent" if it is accomplished:

(A) by acquiescence of the restrained person, if the restrained person is under 16 years of age and the restrained person's lawful custodian has not acquiesced in the movement or confinement; or

(B) by force, threat, or deception. (Added 1989, No. 293 (Adj. Sess.), § 3; amended 2009, No. 3, § 12a.)

§ 2405. Kidnapping

(a) A person commits the crime of kidnapping if the person:

(1) knowingly restrains another person with the intent to:

(A) hold the restrained person for ransom or reward; or

(B) use the restrained person as a shield or hostage; or

(C) inflict bodily injury upon the restrained person or place the restrained person or a third person in fear that any person will be subjected to bodily injury; or

(D) sexually assault the restrained person or place the restrained person or a third person in fear that any person will be sexually assaulted; or

(E) facilitate the commission of another crime or flight thereafter; or

(2) not being a relative of a person under the age of 16, knowingly restrains that person, without the consent of the person's custodian, with the intent to keep the person from his or her lawful custodian for a substantial period.

(b) Kidnapping is punishable by a maximum sentence of life imprisonment or a fine of not more than $50,000.00, or both. It is, however, an affirmative defense which reduces the penalty to imprisonment for not more than 30 years or a fine of not more than $50,000.00, or both, that the defendant voluntarily caused the release of the victim alive in a safe place before arraignment without having caused serious bodily injury to the victim. (Added 1989, No. 293 (Adj. Sess.), § 3.)

§ 2406. Unlawful restraint in the second degree

(a) A person commits the crime of unlawful restraint in the second degree if the person:

(1) not being a relative of a person under the age of 18, knowingly takes, entices, or harbors that person, without the consent of the person's custodian, knowing that he or she has no right to do so; or

(2) knowingly takes or entices from lawful custody or harbors any person who is mentally incompetent, or other person entrusted by authority of law to the custody of another person or an institution, without the consent of the person or institution, knowing that he or she has no right to do so; or

(3) knowingly restrains another person.

(b) It is a defense to a prosecution under this section that the defendant acted reasonably and in good faith to protect the person from imminent physical or emotional danger.

(c) Unlawful restraint in the second degree is punishable by imprisonment for not more than five years or a fine of not more than $25,000.00, or both. (Added 1989, No. 293 (Adj. Sess.), § 3; amended 2001, No. 41, § 4; 2013, No. 96 (Adj. Sess.), § 56.)

§ 2407. Unlawful restraint in the first degree

(a) A person commits the crime of unlawful restraint in the first degree if that person:

(1) knowingly restrains another person under circumstances exposing that person to a risk of serious bodily injury; or

(2) holds another person in a condition of involuntary servitude.

(b) Unlawful restraint in the first degree is punishable by imprisonment for not more than 15 years or a fine of not more than $50,000.00, or both. (Added 1989, No. 293 (Adj. Sess.), § 3.)

Chapter 56: Custodial Interference

§ 2451. Custodial interference

(a) A person commits custodial interference by taking, enticing, or keeping a child from the child's lawful custodian, knowingly, without a legal right to do so, when the person is a relative of the child and the child is less than 18 years old.

(b) A person who commits custodial interference shall be imprisoned not more than five years or fined not more than $5,000.00, or both.

(c) It shall be a defense to a charge of keeping a child from the child's lawful custodian that the person charged with the offense was acting in good faith to protect the child from real and imminent physical danger. Evidence of good faith shall include the filing of a nonfrivolous petition documenting that danger and seeking to modify the custodial decree in a Vermont court of competent jurisdiction. This petition must be filed within three business days of the termination of visitation rights. This defense shall not be available if the person charged with the offense has left the State with the child. (Added 1979, No. 149 (Adj. Sess.), § 1, eff. April 24, 1980; amended 2017, No. 11, § 25.)

Chapter 57: Larceny And Embezzlement

Subchapter 1: Larceny

§ 2501. Grand larceny

A person who steals from the actual or constructive possession of another, other than from his or her person, money, goods, chattels, bank notes, bonds, promissory notes, bills of exchange or other bills, orders, or certificates, or a book of accounts for or concerning money, or goods due or to become due or to be delivered, or a deed or writing containing a conveyance of land, or any other valuable contract in force, or a receipt, release or defeasance, writ, process, or public record, shall be imprisoned not more than 10 years or fined not more than $5,000.00, or both, if the money or other property stolen exceeds $900.00 in value. (Amended 1971, No. 199 (Adj. Sess.), § 15; 1981, No. 223 (Adj. Sess.), § 5; 2005, No. 156 (Adj. Sess.), § 3.)

§ 2502. Petit larceny

For offenses mentioned in section 2501 of this title where the money or other property stolen does not exceed $900.00 in value, the court may sentence the person convicted to imprisonment for not more than one year or to pay a fine of not more than $1,000.00, or both. (Amended 1965, No. 195, § 10, operative February 1, 1967; 1973, No. 193 (Adj. Sess.), § 3, eff. April 9, 1974; 1973, No. 249 (Adj. Sess.), § 46, eff. April 9, 1974; 1981, No. 223 (Adj. Sess.), § 6; 2005, No. 156 (Adj. Sess.), § 4; 2009, No. 154 (Adj. Sess.), § 97.)

§ 2503. Larceny from the person

A person who steals or attempts to steal from the person and custody of another, property, the subject of larceny, shall be imprisoned not more than 10 years or fined not more than $500.00, or both. (Amended 1971, No. 199 (Adj. Sess.), § 15.)

§ 2504. Taking parcel of realty

A person who by a trespass with intent to steal, takes and carries away anything of value that is parcel of the realty, or annexed thereto, and the property of another against his or her will, shall be imprisoned not more than 10 years or fined not more than $500.00, or both. (Amended 1971, No. 199 (Adj. Sess.), § 15.)

§ 2505. Unauthorized use of boats or aircraft

A person who, without the consent of the owner, takes, uses, operates, or removes, or causes to be taken, used, operated, or removed from a wharf, pier, anchorage, airfield, hanger, boathouse, or other building or from any place or locality on a private or public enclosure or space, a boat, other water-borne craft, or aircraft used for the transportation of persons or property upon water, or in the air, and operates, drives, uses, or causes the same to be operated, driven, or used for his or her own profit, pleasure, use, or purpose, shall be imprisoned not more than one year or fined not more than $500.00, or both. This section shall not be construed to limit or restrict prosecutions for grand larceny.

§ 2506. Disposition of property upon arrest for larceny or robbery

The officer who arrests a person charged as principal or accessory in robbery or larceny shall secure, if to be found, the property alleged to be stolen, and shall be answerable for the same, and shall annex a schedule thereof to his or her return. Upon conviction of the offender, the property shall be restored to the owner.

§ 2507. Larceny conviction in burglary or robbery prosecution

A person arraigned and tried for burglary or robbery may be convicted of larceny, if the jury finds that offense proved.

§ 2508. Conviction of attempted larceny

If, upon trial of a person for the offense of stealing from the person and custody of another, the evidence is not, in the opinion of the jury, sufficient to prove that offense, it may, upon sufficient evidence, convict such person of an attempt to commit such offense.

§ 2509. Pleading and proof of money stolen

(a) In a complaint, information or indictment for larceny, in which it is necessary to make an averment as to money, bank bills, or promissory notes, issued or purporting to be issued by an incorporated bank or banking institution or currency authorized to be circulated and circulating as money, it shall be sufficient to describe such money, bank bills, bank notes, or currency, simply as money, without specifying any particular coin, bank bill, bank note, or currency.

(b) So far as regards the description of property, such allegation shall be sustained by proof of any amount of coin or of any bank bill, bank note, or piece of currency, although the particular species of coin of which such amount was composed or the particular nature of such bank bill, bank note, or currency, is not proved.

Subchapter 2: Embezzlement

§ 2531. Embezzlement generally

(a) An officer, agent, bailee for hire, clerk, or servant of a banking association or an incorporated company, or a clerk, agent, bailee for hire, officer, or servant of a private person, partnership, trades union, joint stock company, unincorporated association, fraternal or benevolent association, except apprentices and other persons under the age of 16 years, who embezzles or fraudulently converts to his or her own use, or takes or secretes with intent to embezzle or fraudulently convert to his or her own use, money or other property that comes into his or her possession or is under his or her care by virtue of such employment, notwithstanding he or she may have an interest in such money or property, shall be guilty of embezzlement.

(b) If the money or property embezzled does not exceed $100.00 in value, the person shall be imprisoned not more than one year or fined not more than $1,000.00, or both. If the money or property embezzled exceeds $100.00 in value, the person shall be imprisoned not more than 10 years or fined not more than $10,000.00, or both. (Amended 1971, No. 199 (Adj. Sess.), § 15; amended 2013, No. 61, § 2.)

§ 2532. Officer or servant of incorporated bank

A cashier or other officer, agent, or servant of an incorporated bank who embezzles or fraudulently converts to his or her own use bullion, money, notes, bills, obligations, or securities or other effects or property belonging to and in the possession of such bank or belonging to any person and deposited therein, shall be guilty of larceny and shall be imprisoned not more than 10 years or fined not more than $1,000.00, or both. (Amended 1971, No. 199 (Adj. Sess.), § 15; 1981, No. 223 (Adj. Sess.), § 23.)

§ 2533. Receiver or trustee

A receiver or trustee appointed by the court in any litigation in this State, who embezzles or fraudulently converts to his or her own use any money or other property in his or her hands as such receiver or trustee, shall be guilty of larceny and shall be imprisoned not more than 10 years or fined not more than $1,000.00, or both. (Amended 1971, No. 199 (Adj. Sess.), § 15, 1981, No. 223 (Adj. Sess.), § 23.)

§ 2534. Executor or administrator

An executor or administrator who embezzles or fraudulently converts to his or her own use, money, obligations, securities, or other effects or property belonging to the estate of which he or she is executor or administrator, shall be guilty of larceny and shall be imprisoned not more than 10 years or fined not more than $1,000.00, or both. (Amended 1971, No. 199 (Adj. Sess.), § 15; 1981, No. 223 (Adj. Sess.), § 23.)

§ 2535. Guardian

A guardian who embezzles or fraudulently converts to his or her own use, money, obligations, securities, or other effects or property belonging to the person under guardianship or the estate of the person under guardianship, shall be guilty of larceny and shall be imprisoned not more than 10 years or fined not more than $1,000.00, or both. (Amended 1971, No. 199 (Adj. Sess.), § 15; 1981, No. 223 (Adj. Sess.), § 23; 2019, No. 77, § 14, eff. June 19, 2019.)

§ 2536. Carrier

A carrier or other person to whom money, goods, or other property, the subject of larceny, is delivered to be carried for hire, or a person entrusted with such property, who embezzles or fraudulently converts to his or her own use, or secretes with intent to embezzle or fraudulently convert to his or her own use such money, goods, or property before its delivery at the place at which, or to the person to whom, they were to be delivered, shall be imprisoned not more than 10 years or fined not more than $500.00, or both. (Amended 1971, No. 199 (Adj. Sess.), § 15.)

§ 2537. Person holding property in official capacity or belonging to the State or a municipality

A State, county, town, or municipal officer or other person who in his or her official capacity receives, collects, controls, or holds money, obligations, securities, or other property, who embezzles or fraudulently converts to his or her own use any of such money, obligations, securities, or other property, or a person who embezzles or fraudulently converts to his or her own use money or other property belonging to the State or to a county or municipality, or a municipal corporation, or a special purpose district, shall be guilty of larceny and shall be imprisoned not more than 10 years or fined not more than $1,000.00, or both. (Amended 1971, No. 199 (Adj. Sess.), § 15; 1981, No. 223 (Adj. Sess.), § 23; 2007, No. 169 (Adj. Sess.), § 1.)

§ 2538. School funds

A person entrusted with the charge of money, land, or other property belonging to a town or school district for the use of schools, who embezzles, misapplies, or conceals the same or any part thereof shall be liable to be removed from his or her trust and shall forfeit to such town or district double the amount so embezzled, misapplied, or concealed, to be recovered in a civil action on this statute, in the name of such town or district, with costs.

§ 2539. Pleading and proof of money embezzled and time of offense

(a) In prosecutions for embezzling, fraudulently converting to one's own use, or taking and secreting with intent so to embezzle or fraudulently convert, the bullion, money, notes, bank notes, checks, drafts, bills of exchange, obligations, or other securities for money, of a person, bank, corporation, or partnership, by a cashier or other officer, clerk, agent, or servant, it shall be sufficient to allege generally in the indictment an embezzlement, fraudulent conversion, or taking with such intent, of money to a certain amount, without specifying the particulars thereof.

(b) At the trial, evidence may be given of any such embezzlement, fraudulent conversion, or taking with such intent committed within six months next before the time stated in the indictment. It shall be sufficient to maintain the charge in the indictment and shall not be deemed a variance if it is proved that bullion, money, notes, bank notes, checks, drafts, bills of exchange, or other securities for money of such person, bank, corporation, or partnership, of whatever amount, were fraudulently embezzled, converted, or taken with such intent by the respondent within such period of six months.

Subchapter 3: Receiving Stolen Property

§ 2561. Penalty for receiving stolen property; venue

(a) A person who is a dealer in property who buys, receives, sells, possesses unless with the intent to restore to the owner, or aids in the concealment of property, knowing or believing the property to be stolen, shall be punished the same as for the stealing of such property.

(b) A person who buys, receives, sells, possesses unless with the intent to restore to the owner, or aids in the concealment of stolen property, knowing the same to be stolen, shall be punished the same as for the stealing of such property.

(c) A buyer, receiver, seller, possessor, or concealer under subsection (a) or (b) of this section may be prosecuted and punished in the Criminal Division of the Superior Court in the unit where the person stealing the property might be prosecuted, although such property is bought, received, or concealed in another county or unit. (Amended 1973, No. 118, § 5, eff. Oct. 1, 1973; 1973, No. 193 (Adj. Sess.), § 3, eff. April 9, 1974; 1981, No. 223 (Adj. Sess.), § 7; 1985, No. 183 (Adj. Sess.), § 7; 2009, No. 154 (Adj. Sess.), § 98.)

§ 2562. Joinder of counts for larceny and receiving stolen property

In a complaint, information, or indictment for larceny against one or more persons, counts may be added for buying, receiving, selling, possessing unless with the intent to restore to the owner, or aiding in the concealment of property stolen or a part thereof, knowing the same to be stolen. In such cause, the prosecutor shall not be put to his or her election, but upon one or more of the counts, the jury may convict or acquit one or more of the defendants, according to the proofs. (Amended 1981, No. 223 (Adj. Sess.), § 8.)

§ 2563. Conviction of one or more joint respondents

On trial of two or more persons upon complaint, information, or indictment, for jointly buying, receiving, selling, possessing unless with the intent to restore to the owner, or aiding in the concealment of stolen property, knowing the same to be stolen, if it is proved that one or more of the persons separately bought, received, sold, possessed unless with the intent to restore to the owner, or aided in the concealment of any such property, the jury may convict such of the persons as are proved to have bought, received, sold, possessed, or aided in the concealment of any part of such property, knowing the same to have been stolen. (Amended 1981, No. 223 (Adj. Sess.), § 9.)

§ 2564. Conviction of person who stole property not required

In a prosecution for buying, receiving, selling, possessing unless with the intent to restore to the owner, or aiding in the concealment of money or other property known to have been stolen, it shall not be necessary to aver nor on trial to prove that the person who stole the property has been convicted. (Amended 1981, No. 223 (Adj. Sess.), § 10.)

Subchapter 4: Shoplifting

§§ 2571, 2572. Repealed. 1977, No. 227 (Adj. Sess.), § 3, eff. April 17, 1978.

§ 2573. Definitions

As used in this chapter:

(1) "Retail value" means the merchant's indicated price of the merchandise at the time of the theft.

(2) "Merchandise" means any items of tangible personal property displayed, held, stored, or offered for sale.

(3) "Merchant" means an owner or manager of any retail mercantile establishment, or any person or persons in a supervisory capacity or security officer authorized in writing by the owner or manager to make requests or detentions under this subchapter.

(4) "Premises of a retail mercantile establishment" includes the retail mercantile establishment, any common use areas in shopping centers, and all parking areas set aside by a merchant or on behalf of a merchant for the parking of vehicles for the convenience of the patrons of the retail mercantile establishment.

(5) "Reasonable force" means only that minimum amount of force necessary to detain the person who the merchant has reasonable cause to believe has committed the offense of retail theft.

(6) "Retail mercantile establishment" means any place where merchandise is displayed or offered for sale to the public, including storage areas on the premises of such an establishment. (Added 1977, No. 227 (Adj. Sess.), § 1, eff. April 17, 1978; 1993, No. 165 (Adj. Sess.), § 2.)

§ 2574. Right of merchant to request merchandise to be kept in view

A merchant has the right to request in a reasonable manner any person at his or her retail mercantile establishment to place and keep in full view any merchandise that the person has removed from its place of display, for any purpose. Notice of this request shall be conspicuously posted by the merchant in said retail mercantile establishment. (Added 1977, No. 227 (Adj. Sess.), § 1, eff. April 17, 1978.)

§ 2575. Offense of retail theft

A person commits the offense of retail theft when the person, with intent of depriving a merchant wrongfully of the lawful possession of merchandise, money, or credit:

(1) takes and carries away or causes to be taken and carried away or aids and abets the carrying away of, any merchandise from a retail mercantile establishment without paying the retail value of the merchandise; or

(2) alters, transfers, or removes or causes to be altered, transferred, or removed or aids and abets the alteration, transfer, or removal of any label, price tag, indicia of value, or any other markings affixed to any merchandise in a retail mercantile establishment and purchases the merchandise for less than its retail value; or

(3) transfers or causes to be transferred or aids and abets in the transfer of any merchandise in a retail mercantile establishment from one container or location to another container or location and purchases the merchandise for less than its retail value; or

(4) alters, transfers, counterfeits, or reproduces a retail sales receipt or a Universal Product Code (UPC) label or possesses an altered, counterfeit, or reproduced retail sales receipt or UPC label; or

(5) possesses 15 or more altered, counterfeit, or reproduced retail sales receipts or UPC labels or possesses a device that is designed to alter, counterfeit, or reproduce retail sales receipts or UPC labels; or

(6) manufactures, sells, offers for sale, distributes, or knowingly possesses a laminated or coated bag intended to shield merchandise from detection by an electronic or magnetic theft detector; or

(7) manufactures, sells, offers for sale, distributes, or knowingly possesses any tool or device designed to allow or capable of allowing the deactivation or removal from any merchandise of any theft detection device without the permission of the merchant or the person owning or lawfully holding the merchandise. (Added 1977, No. 227 (Adj. Sess.), § 1; amended 2005, No. 157 (Adj. Sess.), § 1.)

§ 2576. Detention

(a) Any merchant who has reasonable cause to believe that a person has committed or attempted to commit retail theft may detain the person on or in the immediate vicinity of the premises of a retail mercantile establishment, affording the person the opportunity to be detained in a place out of public view if available, in a reasonable manner that may include the use of reasonable force and for a reasonable length of time for any of the following purposes:

(1) to request and verify identification;

(2) to make reasonable inquiry as to whether the person has in his or her possession unpurchased merchandise and, if unpurchased, to recover the merchandise;

(3) to inform a law enforcement officer of the detention of the person and surrender that person to the custody of a law enforcement officer; and

(4) in the case of a minor, to inform a law enforcement officer, and, if known or determined, the parent or parents, guardian, or other person having supervision of the minor of his or her detention and to surrender custody of the minor to the law enforcement officer, parent, guardian, or other person.

(b) Any person detained under subdivision (a)(3) or (4) of this section shall, if a telephone is available, have the right to make one local telephone call of reasonable duration. The merchant shall advise the person detained of this right. (Added 1977, No. 227 (Adj. Sess.), § 1, eff. April 17, 1978.)

§ 2577. Penalty

(a) A person convicted of the offense of retail theft of merchandise having a retail value not in excess of $900.00 shall be punished by a fine of not more than $500.00 or imprisonment for not more than six months, or both.

(b) A person convicted of the offense of retail theft of merchandise having a retail value in excess of $900.00 shall be punished by a fine of not more than $1,000.00 or imprisonment for not more than 10 years, or both.

(c) Notwithstanding the provisions of subsections (a) and (b) of this section, a person convicted of retail theft pursuant to:

(1) Subdivision 2575(4) of this title shall be imprisoned not more than two years or fined not more than $1,000.00, or both.

(2) Subdivision 2575(5), (6), or (7) of this title shall be imprisoned for not more than 10 years or fined not more than $5,000.00, or both. (Added 1977, No. 227 (Adj. Sess.), § 1, eff. April 17, 1978; amended 2005, No. 156 (Adj. Sess.), § 5; 2005, No. 157 (Adj. Sess.), § 2.)

§ 2578. Restitution

(a) A sentencing court may order reasonable restitution where merchandise stolen is not recovered or is recovered in damaged condition. Damages shall be calculated based on retail value.

(b) Restitution may be ordered in addition to any other penalties imposed.

(c) Restitution shall be supervised by the Department of Corrections. (Added 1977, No. 227 (Adj. Sess.), § 1, eff. April 17, 1978.)

§ 2579. Civil recovery for retail theft

(a) Any person over the age of 16 years or any emancipated minor who commits the offense of retail theft against a retail mercantile establishment in violation of section 2575 of this title shall be civilly liable to the retail mercantile establishment in an amount consisting of:

(1) damages equal to the retail price of the merchandise if the item is not returned in a merchantable condition; and

(2) a civil penalty of two times the retail price of the merchandise, to be not less than $25.00 and not more than $300.00.

(b) The fact that an action may be brought against an individual as provided in this section shall not limit the right of a retail mercantile establishment to demand, in writing, that a person who is liable for damages and penalties under this section remit the damages and penalties prior to the commencement of any legal action.

(c) If the person to whom a demand is made complies with the demand, that person shall incur no further civil liability for that specific act of retail theft.

(d) Any demand made under this section shall be accompanied by a copy of this law.

(e) A criminal prosecution under section 2575 of this title is not a prerequisite to the applicability of this section and such a criminal prosecution shall not bar an action under this section. An action under this section shall not bar a criminal prosecution under section 2575 of this title.

(f) The provisions of this section shall not be construed to prohibit or limit any other cause of action that a retail mercantile establishment may have against a person who unlawfully takes merchandise from a retail mercantile establishment, except as provided in subsection (c) of this section.

(g) Any testimony or statements by the defendant or any evidence derived from an attempt to reach a civil settlement or from a civil proceeding brought under this section shall be inadmissible in any other court proceeding relating to such retail theft.

(h) If a retail mercantile establishment files suit to recover damages and penalties pursuant to subsection (a) of this section and the mercantile establishment fails to appear at a hearing in such proceedings without excuse from the court, the court shall dismiss the suit with prejudice and award costs to the defendant.

(i) A person who knowingly uses the provisions of this section to demand or extract money from a person who is not legally obligated to pay a penalty shall be imprisoned not more than one year or fined not more than $1,000.00, or both. (Added 1993, No. 165 (Adj. Sess.), § 1.)

Subchapter 5: Theft Of Services

§ 2581. Definitions

As used in this subchapter:

(1) "Services" includes labor, professional service, transportation, public services not provided for in section 2021 of this title, accommodation in hotels, restaurants, or elsewhere, admission to exhibitions, or amusements or recreational facilities, use of vehicles or other movable property.

(2) "Movable property" means property the location of which can be changed, including things growing on, affixed to, or found in land, and documents although the rights represented thereby have no physical location.

(3) "Obtain" means:

(A) in relation to property, to bring about a transfer or purported transfer of a legal interest in the property, whether to the obtainer or another; or

(B) in relation to labor or service, to secure performance thereof. (Added 1967, No. 202, § 1, eff. April 17, 1967; amended 1973, No. 199 (Adj. Sess.), § 1; 1999, No. 35, § 3.)

§ 2582. Theft of services

(a) A person who purposely obtains services that he or she knows are available only for compensation, by deception or threat, or by false token or other means to avoid payment for the service shall if the services exceed $900.00 in value be imprisoned for not more than 10 years or fined not more than $5,000.00, or both. Otherwise, a person who violates a provision of this subsection shall be imprisoned for not more than one year or fined not more than $1,000.00, or both. Where compensation for service is ordinarily paid immediately upon the rendering of such service, as in the case of hotels, restaurants, and transportation, refusal to pay or absconding without payment or offer to pay gives rise to a rebuttable presumption that the service was obtained by deception as to intention to pay.

(b) A person who, having control over the disposition of services of others, to which he or she is not entitled, knowingly diverts such services to the person's own benefit or to the benefit of another not entitled thereto shall if the services exceed $900.00 in value be imprisoned for not more than 10 years or fined not more than $5,000.00, or both. Otherwise a person who violates a provision of this subsection shall be imprisoned for not more than one year or fined not more than $1,000.00, or both. (Added 1967, No. 202, § 2, eff. April 17, 1967; amended 1973, No. 199 (Adj. Sess.), § 2; 2005, No. 156 (Adj. Sess.), § 6.)

§§ 2583, 2584. Repealed. 1973, No. 199 (Adj. Sess.), § 3.

§ 2585. Hotel lien

(a) A hotel shall have a lien for the reasonable value of any service furnished or for the amount of any accommodation extended by cashing drafts, checks, or otherwise to a person upon all baggage and other property belonging to or under the control of such person and in or on the premises of such hotel and may retain possession of such property until the same are paid.

(b) The hotel may enforce the lien by sale as provided in 9 V.S.A. §§ 1952 and 1953. The owner of such property subject to hotel lien who desires to question the reasonableness of such charges shall have the rights provided in 9 V.S.A. § 1954. (Added 1967, No. 202, § 5, eff. April 17, 1967.)

Subchapter 6: Theft Of Rented Property

§ 2591. Theft of rented property

(a) A person who converts to his or her own use any personal property, other than a motor vehicle leased or rented pursuant to a written agreement that has been entrusted to the person under an agreement in writing that provides for the delivery of that personal property to a particular person or place or at a particular time, abandons it, or refuses or neglects to deliver it to the person or place and at the time specified in the written agreement, or who destroys, secretes, appropriates, converts, sells, or attempts to sell all or any part of it, or who removes or permits or causes it to be removed from this State, without the consent of its owner, shall be:

(1) if the value of the property involved is $900.00 or less, imprisoned not more than six months or fined not more than $500.00, or both;

(2) if the property involved exceeds $900.00 in value:

(A) imprisoned for not more than two years or fined not more than $1,000.00, or both; or

(B) imprisoned for not more than five years or fined not more than $5,000.00 if the person has been previously convicted of a violation of this subdivision (a)(2) of this section.

(b) All written agreements for the rental of personal property shall bear a statement in bold face type in the following form:

NOTICE

FAILURE TO RETURN THE RENTAL PROPERTY WITHIN 72 HOURS AFTER DELIVERY TO YOU OF NOTICE TO RETURN, OR WITHIN 15 DAYS AFTER THIS AGREEMENT HAS EXPIRED OR THE PRESENTING OF FALSE, FICTITIOUS OR MISLEADING IDENTIFICATION MAY BE CONSIDERED AS EVIDENCE OF AN INTENTION TO COMMIT LARCENY.

(Added 1969, No. 165 (Adj. Sess.); amended 1971, No. 199 (Adj. Sess.), § 15; 1995, No. 181 (Adj. Sess.), § 24; 2005, No. 156 (Adj. Sess.), § 7.)

§ 2592. Failure to return a rented or leased motor vehicle

(a) A person commits the offense of failure to return a rented or leased motor vehicle if the person:

(1) rents or leases a motor vehicle, as defined in 23 V.S.A. § 4(21), pursuant to an agreement in writing that provides for the return of the vehicle to a particular place at a particular time;

(2) intentionally and without good cause fails to return the vehicle to that place within 72 hours after the time and date specified;

(3) does not give notice to the person from whom the vehicle was rented or leased that he or she will not be able to return the vehicle on the date and time stated in the agreement and does not obtain an extension of the date and time on which the vehicle will be returned; and

(4) when the person rented or leased the vehicle, the person was provided the following notice in boldface type:

NOTICE

THE FAILURE TO RETURN A RENTED OR LEASED MOTOR VEHICLE WITHIN 72 HOURS AFTER THE DATE AND TIME SPECIFIED IN THE WRITTEN AGREEMENT WITHOUT EXTENDING THE DATE AND TIME IS A CRIME UNDER VERMONT LAW (13 V.S.A. § 2592) AND MAY RESULT IN A CRIMINAL PENALTY OF UP TO FIVE YEARS IMPRISONMENT OR A $5,000.00 FINE, OR BOTH.

(b) A person who violates this section shall be imprisoned for not more than three years or fined not more than $3,000.00, or both. If the person has been previously convicted of a violation of this section, the person shall be imprisoned not more than five years or fined not more than $5,000.00, or both. (Added 1995, No. 181 (Adj. Sess.), § 25.)

Chapter 59: Lewdness And Prostitution

Subchapter 1: Lewd And Indecent Conduct

§ 2601. Lewd and lascivious conduct

A person guilty of open and gross lewdness and lascivious behavior shall be imprisoned not more than five years or fined not more than $300.00, or both. (Amended 1981, No. 223 (Adj. Sess.), § 23.)

§ 2601a. Prohibited conduct

(a) No person shall engage in open and gross lewdness.

(b) A person who violates this section shall:

(1) be imprisoned not more than one year or fined not more than $300.00, or both, for a first offense; and

(2) be imprisoned not more than two years or fined not more than $1,000.00, or both, for a second or subsequent offense. (Added 2017, No. 44, § 1.)

§ 2602. Lewd or lascivious conduct with child

(a)(1) No person shall willfully and lewdly commit any lewd or lascivious act upon or with the body, or any part or member thereof, of a child under the age of 16 years, with the intent of arousing, appealing to, or gratifying the lust, passions, or sexual desires of such person or of such child.

(2) This section shall not apply if the person is less than 19 years old, the child is at least 15 years old, and the conduct is consensual.

(b) A person who violates subsection (a) of this section shall be:

(1) For a first offense, imprisoned not less than two years and not more than 15 years, and, in addition, may be fined not more than $5,000.00, or both.

(2) For a second offense, imprisoned not less than five years and a maximum term of life, and, in addition, may be fined not more than $25,000.00, or both.

(3) For a third or subsequent offense, imprisoned not less than 10 years and a maximum term of life, and, in addition, may be fined not more than $25,000.00, or both.

(c)(1) Except as provided in subdivision (2) of this subsection, a sentence ordered pursuant to subdivision (b)(2) of this section shall include at least a five-year term of imprisonment and a sentence ordered pursuant to subdivision (b)(3) of this section shall include at least a 10-year term of imprisonment. The five-year and 10-year terms of imprisonment required by this subdivision shall be served and may not be suspended, deferred, or served as a supervised sentence. The defendant shall not be eligible for probation, parole, furlough, or any other type of early release until the expiration of the five-year or 10-year term of imprisonment.

(2) The court may depart downwardly from the five-year and 10-year terms of imprisonment required by subdivisions (b)(2) and (3) of this section and impose a lesser term of incarceration if the court makes written findings on the record that the downward departure will serve the interests of justice and public safety.

(d) A person convicted of violating subdivision (b)(2) or (3) of this section shall be sentenced under section 3271 of this title.

(e) Any prior conviction for sexual assault or aggravated sexual assault shall be considered a prior offense for purposes of sentencing enhancement. This section shall not apply to a person who was convicted of sexual assault committed when the person was younger than 19 years of age and which involved consensual sex with a child at least 15 years of age.

(f) Conduct constituting the offense of lewd and lascivious conduct with a child under this section shall be considered a violent act for the purpose of determining bail under chapter 229 of this title. (Amended 1971, No. 199 (Adj. Sess.), § 15; 1995, No. 50, § 4; 2005, No. 79, § 9; 2005, No. 192 (Adj. Sess.), § 8, eff. May 26, 2006; 2007, No. 174 (Adj. Sess.), § 9; 2015, No. 43, § 1.)

§ 2603. Repealed. 1977, No. 51, § 2.

§ 2604. Repealed. 1959, No. 262, § 37, eff. June 11, 1959.

§ 2605. Voyeurism

(a) As used in this section:

(1) "Bona fide private investigator or bona fide security guard" means an individual lawfully providing services, whether licensed or unlicensed, pursuant to 26 V.S.A. §§ 3151 and 3151a.

(2) "Female breast" means any portion of the female breast below the top of the areola.

(3) "Circumstances in which a person has a reasonable expectation of privacy" means circumstances in which a reasonable person would believe that his or her intimate areas would not be visible to the public, regardless of whether that person is in a public or private area. This definition includes

circumstances in which a person knowingly disrobes in front of another, but does not expect nor give consent for the other person to photograph, film, or record his or her intimate areas.

(4) "Intimate areas" means the naked or undergarment-clad genitals, pubic area, buttocks, or female breast of a person.

(5) "Place where a person has a reasonable expectation of privacy" means:

(A) a place in which a reasonable person would believe that he or she could disrobe in privacy, without his or her undressing being viewed by another; or

(B) a place in which a reasonable person would expect to be safe from unwanted intrusion or surveillance.

(6) "Sexual conduct" shall have the same meaning as in section 2821 of this title.

(7) "Surveillance" means secret observation of the activities of another person for the purpose of spying upon and invading the privacy of the person.

(8) "View" means the intentional looking upon another person for more than a brief period of time, in other than a casual or cursory manner, with the unaided eye or a device designed or intended to improve visual acuity.

(b) No person shall intentionally view, photograph, film, or record in any format:

(1) the intimate areas of another person without that person's knowledge and consent while the person being viewed, photographed, filmed, or recorded is in a place where he or she would have a reasonable expectation of privacy; or

(2) the intimate areas of another person without that person's knowledge and consent and under circumstances in which the person has a reasonable expectation of privacy.

(c) No person shall display or disclose to a third party any image recorded in violation of subsection (b), (d), or (e) of this section.

(d) No person shall intentionally conduct surveillance or intentionally photograph, film, or record in any format a person without that person's knowledge and consent while the person being surveilled, photographed, filmed, or recorded is in a place where he or she would have a reasonable expectation of privacy within a home or residence. Bona fide private investigators and bona fide security guards engaged in otherwise lawful activities within the scope of their employment are exempt from this subsection.

(e) No person shall intentionally photograph, film, or record in any format a person without that person's knowledge and consent while that person is in a place where a person has a reasonable expectation of privacy and that person is engaged in sexual conduct.

(f) This section shall apply to a person who intentionally views, photographs, films, or records the intimate areas of a person as part of a security or theft prevention policy or program at a place of business.

(g) This section shall not apply to:

(1) a law enforcement officer conducting official law enforcement activities in accordance with State and federal law; or

(2) official activities of the Department of Corrections, a law enforcement agency, the Agency of Human Services, or a court for security purposes or during the investigation of alleged misconduct by a person in the custody of the Department of Corrections, a law enforcement agency, the Agency of Human Services, or a court.

(h) This section is not intended to infringe upon the freedom of the press to gather and disseminate news as guaranteed by the First Amendment to the Constitution of the United States.

(i) It shall be an affirmative defense to a violation of subsection (b) of this section that the defendant was a bona fide private investigator or bona fide security guard conducting surveillance in the ordinary course of business, and the violation was unintentional and incidental to otherwise legal surveillance. However, an unintentional and incidental violation of subsection (b) of this section shall not be a defense to a violation of subsection (c).

(j) For a first offense, a person who violates subsection (b), (d), or (e) of this section shall be imprisoned not more than two years or fined not more than $1,000.00, or both. For a second or subsequent offense, a person who violates subsection (b), (d), or (e) of this section shall be imprisoned not more than three years or fined not more than $5,000.00, or both. A person who violates subsection (c) of this section shall be imprisoned not more than five years or fined not more than $5,000.00, or both. (Added 2005, No. 83, § 2; amended 2009, No. 111 (Adj. Sess.), § 1; 2015, No. 62, § 1.)

§ 2606. Disclosure of sexually explicit images without consent

(a) As used in this section:

(1) "Disclose" includes transfer, publish, distribute, exhibit, or reproduce.

(2) "Harm" means physical injury, financial injury, or serious emotional distress.

(3) "Nude" means any one or more of the following uncovered parts of the human body:

(A) genitals;

(B) pubic area;

(C) anus; or

(D) post-pubescent female nipple.

(4) "Sexual conduct" shall have the same meaning as in section 2821 of this title.

(5) "Visual image" includes a photograph, film, videotape, recording, or digital reproduction.

(b)(1) A person violates this section if he or she knowingly discloses a visual image of an identifiable person who is nude or who is engaged in sexual conduct, without his or her consent, with the intent to harm, harass, intimidate, threaten, or coerce the person depicted, and the disclosure would cause a reasonable person to suffer harm. A person may be identifiable from the image itself or information offered in connection with the image. Consent to recording of the visual image does not, by itself, constitute consent for disclosure of the image. A person who violates this subdivision (1) shall be imprisoned not more than two years or fined not more than $2,000.00, or both.

(2) A person who violates subdivision (1) of this subsection with the intent of disclosing the image for financial profit shall be imprisoned not more than five years or fined not more than $10,000.00, or both.

(c) A person who maintains an Internet website, online service, online application, or mobile application that contains a visual image of an identifiable person who is nude or who is engaged in sexual conduct shall not solicit or accept a fee or other consideration to remove, delete, correct, modify, or refrain from posting or disclosing the visual image if requested by the depicted person.

(d) This section shall not apply to:

(1) Images involving voluntary nudity or sexual conduct in public or commercial settings or in a place where a person does not have a reasonable expectation of privacy.

(2) Disclosures made in the public interest, including the reporting of unlawful conduct, or lawful and common practices of law enforcement, criminal reporting, corrections, legal proceedings, or medical treatment.

(3) Disclosures of materials that constitute a matter of public concern.

(4) Interactive computer services, as defined in 47 U.S.C. § 230(f)(2), or information services or telecommunications services, as defined in 47 U.S.C. § 153, for content solely provided by another person. This subdivision shall not preclude other remedies available at law.

(e)(1) A plaintiff shall have a private cause of action against a defendant who knowingly discloses, without the plaintiff's consent, an identifiable visual image of the plaintiff while he or she is nude or engaged in sexual conduct and the disclosure causes the plaintiff harm.

(2) In addition to any other relief available at law, the court may order equitable relief, including a temporary restraining order, a preliminary injunction, or a permanent injunction ordering the defendant to cease display or disclosure of the image. The court may grant injunctive relief maintaining the confidentiality of a plaintiff using a pseudonym. (Added 2015, No. 62, § 2.)

Subchapter 2: Prostitution

§ 2631. Definitions

As used in this section:

(1) The term "prostitution" shall be construed to include the offering or receiving of the body for sexual intercourse for hire and shall also be construed to include the offering or receiving of the body for indiscriminate sexual intercourse without hire.

(2) The term "lewdness" shall be construed to mean open and gross lewdness.

(3) The term "assignation" shall be construed to include the making of an appointment or engagement for prostitution or lewdness as defined in this section.

§ 2632. Prostitution

(a) A person shall not:

(1) occupy a place, structure, building, or conveyance for the purpose of prostitution, lewdness, or assignation;

(2) knowingly permit a place, structure, building, or conveyance owned by the person or under the person's control to be used for the purpose of prostitution, lewdness, or assignation;

(3) receive or offer, or agree to receive, a person into a place, structure, building, or conveyance for the purpose of prostitution, lewdness, or assignation;

(4) permit a person to remain in a place, structure, building, or conveyance for the purpose of prostitution, lewdness, or assignation;

(5) direct, take or transport, or offer or agree to take or transport a person to a place, structure, building, or conveyance or to any other person knowingly, or with reasonable cause to know that the purpose of such directing, taking, or transporting is prostitution, lewdness, or assignation;

(6) procure or solicit or offer to procure or solicit a person for the purpose of prostitution, lewdness, or assignation;

(7) reside in, enter or remain in a place, structure, or building or enter or remain in a conveyance for the purpose of prostitution, lewdness, or assignation;

(8) engage in prostitution, lewdness, or assignation; or

(9) aid or abet prostitution, lewdness, or assignation, by any means whatsoever.

(b) A person who violates a provision of subsection (a) of this section shall be fined not more than $100.00 or may be imprisoned not more than one year. For a second offense such person shall be imprisoned for not more than three years. (Amended 2001, No. 49, § 14; 2017, No. 44, § 2.)

§ 2633. Repealed. 1973, No. 201 (Adj. Sess.), § 12.

§ 2634. Terms of probation

Probation or parole shall be granted or ordered in the case of a person infected with a venereal disease only on such terms and conditions as shall ensure medical treatment therefor and prevent the spread of such disease.

§ 2635. Slave traffic

(a) A person shall not:

(1) induce, entice, or procure a person to come into the State or to go from the State for the purpose of prostitution or for any immoral purpose or to enter a house of prostitution in the State;

(2) willfully or knowingly aid such person in obtaining transportation to or within the State for such purposes;

(3) place a person in the charge or custody of another person for immoral purposes or in a house of prostitution;

(4) induce, entice, procure, or compel such person to reside in a house of prostitution; or

(5) induce, entice, procure, or compel such person to live a life of prostitution.

(b) A person violating a provision hereof shall be imprisoned not more than 10 years nor less than one year or fined not more than $2,000.00 nor less than $200.00, or both. (Amended 1971, No. 199 (Adj. Sess.), § 15; 2001, No. 49, § 15; 2019, No. 131 (Adj. Sess.), § 48.)

§ 2635a. Repealed. 2011, No. 55, § 17(c).

§ 2636. Unlawful procurement

(a) A person shall not:

(1) induce, entice, procure, or compel a person, for the purpose of prostitution or for any other immoral purposes, to enter a house of prostitution;

(2) receive money or other valuable consideration for or on account of placing a person in a house of prostitution;

(3) pay money or other valuable consideration to procure a person for the purpose of placing such person for immoral purposes in a house of prostitution, with or without the person's consent; or

(4) knowingly receive money or other valuable thing for or on account of procuring or placing a person in a house of prostitution for immoral purposes, with or without the person's consent.

(b) A person violating a provision hereof shall be punished as provided in section 2635 of this title. (Amended 2001, No. 49, § 16, eff. June 12, 2001.)

§ 2637. Appropriating or levying upon earnings of prostitute

(a) A person shall not:

(1) hold, detain, or restrain a person in a house of prostitution for the purpose of compelling such person, directly or indirectly, by the person's voluntary or involuntary service or labor, to pay, liquidate, or cancel a debt, dues, or obligations incurred or claimed to have been incurred in such house of prostitution; or

(2) accept, receive, levy, or appropriate money or other valuable thing from the proceeds or earnings of a person engaged in prostitution.

(b) An acceptance, receipt, levy, or appropriation of such money or valuable thing shall be presumptive evidence of lack of consideration.

(c) A person who violates a provision of this section shall be punished as provided in section 2635 of this title. (Amended 2001, No. 49, § 17.)

Chapter 60: Human Trafficking

Subchapter 1: Criminal Acts

§ 2651. Definitions

As used in this subchapter:

(1) "Blackmail" means the extortion of money, labor, commercial sexual activity, or anything of value from a person through use of a threat to expose a secret or publicize an asserted fact, whether true or false, that would tend to subject the person to hatred, contempt, ridicule, or prosecution.

(2) "Coercion" means:

(A) threat of serious harm, including physical or financial harm, to or physical restraint against any person;

(B) any scheme, plan, or pattern intended to cause a person to believe that failure to perform an act would result in serious bodily or financial harm to or physical restraint of any person;

(C) the abuse or threatened abuse of law or the legal process;

(D) withholding, destroying, or confiscating any actual or purported passport, immigration document, or any other government identification document of another person;

(E) providing a drug, including alcohol, to another person with the intent to impair the person's judgment or maintain a state of chemical dependence;

(F) wrongfully taking, obtaining, or withholding any property of another person;

(G) blackmail;

(H) asserting control over the finances of another person;

(I) debt bondage; or

(J) withholding or threatening to withhold food or medication.

(3) "Commercial sex act" means any sexual act, sexual conduct, or sexually explicit performance on account of which anything of value is promised to, given to, or received by any person.

(4) "Debt bondage" means a condition or arrangement in which a person requires that a debtor or another person under the control of a debtor perform labor, services, sexual acts, sexual conduct, or a sexually explicit performance in order to retire, repay, or service a real or purported debt that the person has caused with the intent to defraud the debtor.

(5) "Family member" means a spouse, child, sibling, parent, next of kin, domestic partner, or legal guardian of a victim.

(6) "Human trafficking" means:

(A) to subject a person to a violation of section 2652 of this title; or

(B) "severe form of trafficking" as defined by 22 U.S.C. § 7105.

(7) "Labor servitude" means labor or services performed or provided by a person that are induced or maintained through force, fraud, or coercion. "Labor servitude" shall not include labor or services performed by a family member of a person who is engaged in the business of farming as defined in 10 V.S.A. § 6001(22) unless force, fraud, or coercion is used.

(8) "Serious bodily injury" shall have the same meaning as in subdivision 1021(2) of this title.

(9) "Sexual act" shall have the same meaning as in subdivision 3251(1) of this title.

(10) "Sexual conduct" shall have the same meaning as in subdivision 2821(2) of this title.

(11) "Sexually explicit performance" means a public, live, photographed, recorded, or videotaped act or show that:

(A) depicts a sexual act or sexual conduct;

(B) is intended to arouse, satisfy the sexual desires of, or appeal to the prurient interests of patrons or viewers; and

(C) lacks literary, artistic, political, or scientific value.

(12) "Venture" means any group of two or more individuals associated in fact, whether or not a legal entity.

(13) "Victim of human trafficking" means a victim of a violation of section 2652 of this title. (Added 2011, No. 55, § 2; amended 2013, No. 197 (Adj. Sess.), § 3; 2015, No. 133 (Adj. Sess.), § 1.)

§ 2652. Human trafficking
(a) No person shall knowingly:

(1) recruit, entice, harbor, transport, provide, or obtain by any means a person under the age of 18 for the purpose of having the person engage in a commercial sex act;

(2) recruit, entice, harbor, transport, provide, or obtain a person through force, fraud, or coercion for the purpose of having the person engage in a commercial sex act;

(3) compel a person through force, fraud, or coercion to engage in a commercial sex act;

(4) benefit financially or by receiving anything of value from participation in a venture, knowing that force, fraud, or coercion was or will be used to compel any person to engage in a commercial sex act as part of the venture;

(5) subject a person to labor servitude;

(6) recruit, entice, harbor, transport, provide, or obtain a person for the purpose of subjecting the person to labor servitude; or

(7) benefit financially or by receiving anything of value from participation in a venture, knowing that a person will be subject to labor servitude as part of the venture.

(b) A person who violates subsection (a) of this section shall be imprisoned for a term up to and including life or fined not more than $500,000.00, or both.

(c)(1)(A) A person who is a victim of sex trafficking in violation of subdivisions 2652(a)(1)-(4) of this title shall not be found in violation of or be the subject of a delinquency petition based on chapter 59 (lewdness and prostitution) or 63 (obscenity) of this title for any conduct committed as a victim of sex trafficking.

(B) Notwithstanding any other provision of law, a person under the age of 18 shall be immune from prosecution in the Criminal Division of the Superior Court for a violation of section 2632 of this title (prohibited acts; prostitution), but may be treated as a juvenile under 33 V.S.A. chapter 52 or referred to the Department for Children and Families for treatment under 33 V.S.A. chapter 53.

(2) If a person who is a victim of sex trafficking in violation of subdivisions 2652(a)(1)-(4) of this title is prosecuted for any offense or is the subject of any delinquency petition other than a violation of chapter 59 (lewdness and prostitution) or 63 (obscenity) of this title that arises out of the sex trafficking or benefits the sex trafficker, the person may raise as an affirmative defense that he or she committed the offense as a result of force, fraud, or coercion by a sex trafficker.

(d) In a prosecution for a violation of this section, the victim's alleged consent to the human trafficking is immaterial and shall not be admitted.

(e) If a person who is a victim of human trafficking is under 18 years of age at the time of the offense, the State may treat the person as the subject of a child in need of care or supervision proceeding. (Added 2011, No. 55, § 2.)

§ 2653. Aggravated human trafficking

(a) A person commits the crime of aggravated human trafficking if the person commits human trafficking in violation of section 2652 of this title under any of the following circumstances:

(1) the offense involves a victim of human trafficking who is a child under the age of 18;

(2) the person has previously been convicted of a violation of section 2652 of this title;

(3) the victim of human trafficking suffers serious bodily injury or death; or

(4) the actor commits the crime of human trafficking under circumstances that constitute the crime of sexual assault as defined in section 3252 of this title, aggravated sexual assault as defined in section 3253 of this title, or aggravated sexual assault of a child as defined in section 3253a of this title.

(b) A person who violates this section shall be imprisoned not less than 20 years and a maximum term of life or fined not more than $100,000.00, or both.

(c) The provisions of this section do not limit or restrict the prosecution for murder or manslaughter. (Added 2011, No. 55, § 2.)

§ 2654. Patronizing or facilitating human trafficking

(a) No person shall knowingly:

(1) permit a place, structure, or building owned by the person or under the person's control to be used for the purpose of human trafficking;

(2) receive or offer or agree to receive or offer a person into a place, structure, or building for the purpose of human trafficking; or

(3) permit a person to remain in a place, structure, building, or conveyance for the purpose of human trafficking.

(b) A person who violates this section shall be imprisoned not more than five years or fined not more than $100,000.00, or both. (Added 2011, No. 55, § 2.)

§ 2655. Solicitation

(a) No person shall knowingly solicit a commercial sex act from a victim of human trafficking.

(b) A person who violates this section shall be imprisoned not more than five years or fined not more than $100,000.00, or both. (Added 2011, No. 55, § 2.)

§ 2656. Human trafficking by a business entity; dissolution

If a business entity, including a corporation, partnership, association, or any other legal entity, is convicted of violating this chapter, the Attorney General may commence a proceeding in the Civil Division of the Superior Court to dissolve the entity pursuant to 11A V.S.A. §§ 14.30-14.33. (Added 2011, No. 55, § 2.)

§ 2657. Restitution

(a) A person convicted of a violation of this subchapter shall be ordered to pay restitution to the victim pursuant to section 7043 of this title.

(b) If the victim of human trafficking to whom restitution has been ordered dies before restitution is paid, any restitution ordered shall be paid to the victim's heir or legal representative, provided that the heir or legal representative has not benefited in any way from the trafficking.

(c) The return of the victim of human trafficking to his or her home country or other absence of the victim from the jurisdiction shall not limit the victim's right to receive restitution pursuant to this section. (Added 2011, No. 55, § 2.)

§ 2658. Motion to vacate by victim of human trafficking

(a) As used in this section:

(1) "Qualifying crime" means a criminal offense in this State that is not listed in 33 V.S.A. § 5204(a).

(2) "Victim of human trafficking" means:

(A) a victim of a violation of section 2652 or 2653 of this title; or

(B) a victim of a severe form of trafficking" as defined by 22 U.S.C. § 7102(14)(federal Trafficking Victims Protection Act).

(b) A person convicted of a qualifying crime may file a motion to vacate the conviction if it was obtained as a result of the person having been a victim of human trafficking. The motion shall be in writing, describe the supporting evidence with particularity, and include copies of any documents showing that the moving party is entitled to relief under this section.

(c) The court shall hold a hearing on the motion, provided that the court may dismiss a motion without a hearing if the court finds that the motion fails to assert a claim for which relief may be granted.

(d)(1) The court shall grant the motion if it finds by a preponderance of the evidence that:

(A) the moving party was convicted of a qualifying crime; and

(B) the conviction was obtained as a result of the moving party's having been a victim of human trafficking.

(2) If the motion is granted, the court shall vacate the conviction, strike the adjudication of guilt, and expunge the record of the criminal proceedings. The court shall issue an order to expunge, or redact the moving party's name from, all records and files related to the moving party's arrest, citation, investigation, charge, adjudication of guilt, criminal proceedings, and probation for the offense.

(e) Official documentation of a person's status as a victim of human trafficking provided by a federal, state, or local government agency shall create a presumption that the person's conviction was obtained as a result of having been a victim of human trafficking. Such documentation shall not be required to grant a motion under this section. (Added 2011, No. 94 (Adj. Sess.), § 1; amended 2019, No. 32, § 1.)

Subchapter 2: Resource Guide Posting; Private Cause Of Action For Victims; Victim Protection

§ 2661. Resource guide posting

(a) A notice offering help to victims of human trafficking shall be accessible on the official website of the Vermont Department of Labor and may be posted in a prominent and accessible location in workplaces.

(b) The notice should provide contact information for at least one local law enforcement agency and provide information regarding the National Human Trafficking Resource Center (NHTRC) hotline as follows:

"If you or someone you know is being forced to engage in any activity and cannot leave - whether it is commercial sex, housework, farm work, or any other activity - call the toll-free National Human Trafficking Resource Center Hotline at 1-888-373-7888 to access help and services. The toll-free hotline is:

• Available 24 hours a day, 7 days a week

• Operated by a nonprofit, nongovernmental organization

• Anonymous and confidential

• Accessible in 170 languages

• Able to provide help, referral to services, training, and general information."

(c) The notice described in this section should be made available in English, Spanish, and, if requested by an employer, another language.

(d) The Vermont Department of Labor shall develop and implement an education plan to raise awareness among Vermont employers about the problem of human trafficking, about the hotline described in this section, and about other resources that may be available to employers, employees, and potential victims of human trafficking. On or before January 15, 2013, the Department shall report to the House and Senate Committees on Judiciary, the House Committee on Human Services, and the Senate Committee on Health and Welfare on the progress achieved in developing and implementing the notice requirement and education plan required by this section. (Added 2011, No. 55, § 2.)

§ 2662. Private cause of action

(a) A victim of human trafficking may bring an action against the offender in the Civil Division of the Superior Court for damages, injunctive relief, punitive damages in the case of a willful violation, and reasonable costs and attorney's fees. Actual damages may include any loss for which restitution is available under section 2657 of this chapter.

(b) If the victim is deceased or otherwise unable to represent himself or herself, the victim may be represented by a legal guardian, family member, or other representative appointed by the court, provided that the legal guardian, family member, or other representative appointed by the court has not benefited in any way from the trafficking.

(c) In a civil action brought under this section, the victim's alleged consent to the human trafficking is immaterial and shall not be admitted. (Added 2011, No. 55, § 2.)

§ 2663. Classification of victims; immigration assistance

(a) Classification of victims of human trafficking. As soon as practicable after the initial encounter with a person who reasonably appears to a law enforcement agency, a State's Attorneys' office, or the Office of the Attorney General to be a victim of human trafficking, such agency or office shall:

(1) Notify the Victim's Compensation Program at the Center for Crime Victim Services that such person may be eligible for services under this chapter.

(2) Make a preliminary assessment of whether such victim or possible victim of human trafficking appears to meet the criteria for certification as a victim of a severe form of trafficking in persons as defined in 22 U.S.C. § 7105 (Trafficking Victims Protection Act) or appears to be otherwise eligible for any federal, state, or local benefits and services. If it is determined that the victim appears to meet such criteria, the agency or office shall report the finding to the victim and shall refer the victim to services available, including legal service providers. If the possible victim is under the age of 18 or is a vulnerable adult, the agency or office shall also notify the Family Services Division of the Department for Children and Families or the Office of Adult Protective Services in the Department of Disabilities, Aging, and Independent Living.

(b) Law enforcement assistance with respect to immigration. After the agency or office makes a preliminary assessment pursuant to subdivision (a)(2) of this section that a victim of human trafficking or a possible victim of human trafficking appears to meet the criteria for certification as a victim of a severe form of trafficking in persons, as defined in 22 U.S.C. § 7105 and upon the request of such victim, the agency or office shall provide the victim of human trafficking with a completed and executed U.S. citizenship and immigration service (USCIS) form I-914 supplement B declaration of law enforcement officer for victim of human trafficking in persons or a USCIS form I-918, supplement B, U nonimmigrant status certification, or both. These endorsements shall be completed by the certifying officer in accordance with the forms' instructions and applicable rules and regulations. The victim of human trafficking may choose which form to have the certifying officer complete. (Added 2011, No. 55, § 2.)

Chapter 61: Maiming

§ 2701. Definition of and penalty for maiming

Any person with malicious intent to maim or disfigure, who shall cut out or maim the tongue, put out or destroy an eye, cut or tear off an ear, cut, slit, or mutilate the nose or lip, or cut or disable a limb or member of another person, and any person privy to such intent who shall be present aiding in the commission of such offense shall be imprisoned for life or for not less than seven years. (Amended 1971, No. 199 (Adj. Sess.), § 15.)

Chapter 63: Obscenity

§ 2801. Definitions

As used in this act:

(1) "Minor" means any person less than 18 years old.

(2) "Nudity" means the showing of the human male or female genitals, pubic area or buttocks with less than a full opaque covering, or the showing of the female breast with less than a fully opaque covering of any portion thereof below the top of the nipple, or the depiction of covered male genitals in a discernably turgid state.

(3) "Sexual conduct" means acts of masturbation, homosexuality, sexual intercourse, or physical contact with a person's clothed or unclothed genitals, pubic area, buttocks or, if such person be a female, breast.

(4) "Sexual excitement" means the condition of human male or female genitals when in a state of sexual stimulation or arousal.

(5) "Sado-masochistic abuse" means flagellation or torture by or upon a person clad in undergarments, a mask or bizarre costume, or the condition of being fettered, bound or otherwise physically restrained on the part of one so clothed.

(6) "Harmful to minors" means that quality of any description or representation, in whatever form, of nudity, sexual conduct, sexual excitement, or sado-masochistic abuse, when it:

(A) Predominantly appeals to the prurient, shameful, or morbid interest of minors; and

(B) Is patently offensive to prevailing standards in the adult community in the State of Vermont as a whole with respect to what is suitable material for minors; and

(C) Is taken as a whole, lacks serious literary, artistic, political, or scientific value, for minors.

(7) "Advertising purposes" means purposes of propagandizing in connection with the commercial sale of a product or type of product, the commercial offering of a service, or the commercial exhibition of an entertainment.

(8) "Displays publicly" means the exposing, placing, posting, exhibiting, or in any fashion displaying in any location, whether public or private, an item in such a manner that it may be readily seen and its content or character distinguished by normal unaided vision viewing it from a street, highway, sidewalk, or lobby of a building that has unrestricted access by the public. (Amended 1967, No. 340 (Adj. Sess.), § 1, eff. March 23, 1968; 1973, No. 204 (Adj. Sess.), §§ 1, 2.)

§ 2802. Disseminating indecent material to a minor in the presence of the minor

(a) No person may, with knowledge of its character and content, sell, lend, distribute, or give away to a minor:

(1) any picture, photograph, drawing, sculpture, motion picture film, or similar visual representation or image, including any such representation or image which is stored electronically, of a person or portion of the human body which depicts nudity, sexual conduct, or sado-masochistic abuse and which is harmful to minors; or

(2) any book, pamphlet, magazine, printed matter however reproduced, or sound recording which contains any matter enumerated in subdivision (1) of this subsection, or explicit and detailed verbal descriptions or narrative accounts of sexual excitement, sexual conduct, or sado-masochistic abuse and which, taken as a whole, is harmful to minors.

(b) No person may, with knowledge of the character and content of a motion picture, show, or other presentation which, in whole or in part, depicts nudity, sexual conduct, or sado-masochistic abuse, and which is harmful to minors:

(1) exhibit such a motion picture, show, or other presentation to a minor; or

(2) sell or give away to a minor an admission ticket or pass to premises whereon there is exhibited or to be exhibited such a motion picture, show, or other presentation; or

(3) admit a minor to premises whereon there is exhibited or to be exhibited such a motion picture, show, or other presentation.

(c) This section shall apply only to acts occurring in the presence of the minor. (Amended 1967, No. 340 (Adj. Sess.), § 2, eff. March 23, 1968; 1999, No. 124 (Adj. Sess.), § 7; 2001, No. 41, § 7.)

§ 2802a. Disseminating indecent material to a minor outside the presence of the minor

(a) No person may, with knowledge of its character and content, and with actual knowledge that the recipient is a minor, sell, lend, distribute, or give away:

(1) any picture, photograph, drawing, sculpture, motion picture film, or similar visual representation or image, including any such representation or image which is communicated, transmitted, or stored electronically, of a person or portion of the human body which depicts nudity, sexual conduct, or sado-masochistic abuse and which is harmful to minors; or

(2) any book, pamphlet, magazine, printed matter, however reproduced, or sound recording which contains any matter enumerated in subdivision (1) of this subsection, or explicit and detailed verbal descriptions or narrative accounts of sexual excitement, sexual conduct, or sado-masochistic abuse and which, taken as a whole, is harmful to minors.

(b) No person may, with actual knowledge that the recipient or viewer is a minor, and with knowledge of the character and content of a motion picture, show or other presentation, including any such motion picture, show, or presentation which is communicated, transmitted, or stored electronically, which, in whole or in part, depicts nudity, sexual conduct, or sado-masochistic abuse, and which is harmful to minors:

(1) exhibit such a motion picture, show, or other presentation to a minor; or

(2) sell or give away to a minor an admission ticket or pass to premises whereon there is exhibited or to be exhibited such a motion picture, show, or other presentation.

(c) This section shall only apply to acts occurring outside the presence of the minor. (Added 2001, No. 41, § 8.)

§ 2802b. Minor electronically disseminating indecent material to another person

(a)(1) No minor shall knowingly and voluntarily and without threat or coercion use a computer or electronic communication device to transmit an indecent visual depiction of himself or herself to another person.

(2) No person shall possess a visual depiction transmitted to the person in violation of subdivision (1) of this subsection. It shall not be a violation of this subdivision if the person took reasonable steps, whether successful or not, to destroy or eliminate the visual depiction.

(b) Penalties; minors.

(1) Except as provided in subdivision (3) of this subsection, a minor who violates subsection (a) of this section shall be adjudicated delinquent. An action brought under this subdivision (1) shall be filed in family court and treated as a juvenile proceeding pursuant to 33 V.S.A. chapter 52, and may be referred to the juvenile diversion program of the district in which the action is filed.

(2) A minor who violates subsection (a) of this section and who has not previously been adjudicated in violation of that section shall not be prosecuted under chapter 64 of this title (sexual exploitation of children), and shall not be subject to the requirements of chapter 167, subchapter 3 of this title (sex offender registration).

(3) A minor who violates subsection (a) of this section who has previously been adjudicated in violation of that section may be adjudicated in family court as under subdivision (b)(1) of this section or prosecuted in district court under chapter 64 of this title (sexual exploitation of children), but shall not be subject to the requirements of chapter 167, subchapter 3 of this title (sex offender registration).

(4) Notwithstanding any other provision of law, the records of a minor who is adjudicated delinquent under this section shall be expunged when the minor reaches 18 years of age.

(c) Penalties; adults. A person 18 years of age or older who violates subdivision (a)(2) of this section shall be fined not more than $300.00 or imprisoned for not more than six months, or both.

(d) This section shall not be construed to prohibit a prosecution under section 1027 (disturbing the peace by use of telephone or electronic communication), 2601 (lewd and lascivious conduct), 2605 (voyeurism), or 2632 (prohibited acts) of this title, or any other applicable provision of law. (Added 2009, No. 58, § 4.)

§ 2803. Distribution of indecent material

No person may hire, employ, or permit a minor to sell, lend, distribute, or give away material, the sale, lending, distribution, or giving away of which to minors is prohibited by section 2802 of this title. (Amended 1967, No. 340 (Adj. Sess.), § 3.)

§ 2804. Exhibition of motion pictures

No person may, with knowledge of the character and content, exhibit a motion picture, show, or other presentation, harmful to minors as defined in subdivision 2801(6) of this title, which in whole or part depicts nudity and sexual conduct, as defined in section 2801, such that it may be viewed by minors from public property or private property not under the control of the person exhibiting the motion picture, show, or other presentation. (Added 1971, No. 192 (Adj. Sess.); amended 1977, No. 262 (Adj. Sess.), eff. April 19, 1978.)

§ 2804a. Publicly displaying sex or nudity for advertising purposes

No person may knowingly, publicly display nudity or sex for advertising purposes. A violation of this section occurs if a person:

(1) displays publicly or causes to be displayed publicly for advertising purposes a picture, photograph, drawing, sculpture, or other visual representation or image, including any such representation or image which is communicated, transmitted, or stored electronically, of a person or portion of the human body that depicts nudity, sado-masochistic abuse, sexual conduct, or sexual excitement, which is harmful to minors, or any page, poster, or other written or printed matter bearing such representation or a verbal description or narrative account of such items or activities; or

(2) permits any public display described in this section on premises owned, rented, or operated by him or her; or

(3) for advertising purposes, purchases space in any newspaper, magazine, or other circular, printed in this State, in order to insert any article or advertisement which contains material harmful to minors. (Added 1973, No. 204 (Adj. Sess.), § 3; amended 1999, No. 124 (Adj. Sess.), § 8.)

§ 2804b. Displaying obscene materials to minors

A person commits the crime of displaying obscene materials to minors if, being the owner, operator, or manager of a business or acting in a managerial capacity, he or she knowingly or recklessly permits a minor who is not accompanied by his or her parent or lawful guardian to enter or remain on the premises, if in that part of the premises where the minor is so permitted to be, there is visibly displayed:

(1) any picture, photograph, drawing, sculpture or other visual representation or image of a person or portion of the human body that depicts nudity, sexual conduct, sexual excitement, or sado-masochistic abuse which is harmful to minors; or

(2) any book, magazine, paperback, pamphlet, or other written or printed matter, however reproduced, that pictorially reveals a person or portion of the human body, depicts nudity, sexual conduct, sexual excitement, or sado-masochistic abuse, which is harmful to minors. (Added 1973, No. 204 (Adj. Sess.), § 4.)

§ 2805. Presumption and defense

(a) A person who engages in conduct prohibited by section 2802, 2802a, 2803, 2804, 2804a, or 2804b of this title is presumed to do so with knowledge of the character and content of the material, or the motion picture, show, or presentation exhibited or to be exhibited.

(b) In any prosecution arising under section 2802, 2802a, 2803, or 2804 of this title, it is an affirmative defense:

(1) that the minor as to whom the offense is alleged to have been committed exhibited to the accused a draft card, driver's license, birth certificate, or other official or apparently official document purporting to establish that the minor was 18 years of age or older; or

(2) that the defendant was in a parental or guardianship relationship with the minor; or that the minor was accompanied by a parent or legal guardian; or

(3) that the defendant was a bona fide school, museum, or public library, or was a person acting in the course of employment as an employee or official of such organization or of a retail outlet affiliated with and serving the educational purpose of such organization.

(c) In any prosecution arising out of sections 2804a and 2804b of this title, it shall be an affirmative defense for the defendant to prove:

(1) that the public display, even though in connection with a commercial venture, was primarily for literary, political, scientific, or artistic purposes; or

(2) that the public display was exhibited by a bona fide art, antique, or similar gallery or exhibition, and visible in a normal display setting; or

(3) that the defendant was a bona fide school, museum, or public library, or was a person acting in the course of employment as an employee or official of such organization or of a retail outlet affiliated with and serving the educational purpose of such organization. (Amended 1967, No. 340 (Adj. Sess.), § 4, eff. March 23, 1968; 1973, No. 204 (Adj. Sess.), § 5; 2001, No. 41, § 9.)

§ 2806. Severability

If any part or provision of this section or its application to any person or circumstances is for any reason adjudged invalid or unconstitutional by a court of competent jurisdiction, that judgment shall be limited in its effect to the facts involved in the controversy in which that judgment shall have been rendered and shall not affect the validity of the remainder of this section or its application to other persons and circumstances; and the Legislature declares that it would have enacted this section without the invalid part, provision, or application had that invalidity been apparent. (Amended 1967, No. 340 (Adj. Sess.), § 5.)

§ 2807. Penalty

A person who violates any provision of section 2802, 2802a, 2803, 2804, 2804a, or 2804b of this title shall be imprisoned not more than one year or fined not more than $1,000.00, or both. (Added 1967, No. 340 (Adj. Sess.), § 6; amended 1973, No. 204 (Adj. Sess.), § 6; 2001, No. 41, § 10.)

§ 2808. Uniformity

The provisions of this chapter shall be applicable and uniform throughout the State and all political subdivisions and municipalities therein, and no local authority shall enact any ordinances, rules, or regulations in conflict with the provisions thereof. (Added 1973, No. 204 (Adj. Sess.), § 7.)

§ 2809. Civil action prerequisite for criminal prosecution

Where evidence of conduct prohibited under subdivision 2802(a)(2) of this title consists entirely of written matter in a book or other publication however reproduced, a criminal prosecution may be commenced only after violation of a final injunction prohibiting such conduct. (Added 1973, No. 204 (Adj. Sess.), § 8.)

§ 2810. Commencement of civil action

(a) Whenever a prosecuting officer within this State has cause to believe that any person is engaging in or is about to engage in this State in conduct prohibited by this chapter, he or she may institute a civil action in the Superior Court in the county wherein such act is believed to be taking place or about to take place seeking a declaratory judgment that the material involved is in fact harmful to minors and seeking an injunction against the prohibited conduct.

(b) Any person who has or is about to disseminate, exhibit, publicly display, or display to minors the material involved in such a proceeding may, as a matter or right, intervene in the proceedings and shall thereupon have all of the rights of a party and shall be bound by a determination in the proceeding.

(c) The provisions of the Vermont Rules of Civil Procedure shall apply to a proceeding hereunder except as otherwise provided or inconsistent with this chapter.

(d) Upon the issuance of a search warrant pursuant hereto by a judge of a Superior Court of this State, a single copy of the material purportedly harmful to minors may be seized to secure and preserve evidence for civil and criminal proceedings under this chapter, subject to the following procedures:

(1) If only a single copy of such material is available within the jurisdiction, the defendant shall provide a duplicate to or make that copy available for duplication by the prosecuting officer during such period when the material is not on sale or exhibition.

(2) If only a single copy is available in the jurisdiction and circumstances prevent its duplication as provided for in subdivision (1) of this subsection, the prosecuting officer may, upon a showing of probable cause that such material will not be available at trial, obtain a special warrant for the sole purpose of duplicating the material to secure and preserve it as evidence. Application for the special warrant shall be on notice to defendant and include a statement setting out the circumstances which make duplication under subdivision (1) of this subsection impossible, the time and date the materials are to be seized and specify the time and date, not to exceed 24-hours after such seizure, when such material is to be returned. (Added 1973, No. 204 (Adj. Sess.), § 9.)

§ 2811. Procedure

Any party or intervenor shall have the right to trial by jury to determine whether the material is harmful to minors. The verdict of the jury shall be unanimous. At the trial, all parties shall have the right to submit evidence, including expert testimony. (Added 1973, No. 204 (Adj. Sess.), § 10.)

§ 2812. Judgment

(a) If the court or jury, as the case may be, finds the material not to be harmful to minors, the court shall enter said declaration in the judgment and dismiss the suit.

(b) If the court or jury, as the case may be, finds the material to be harmful to minors, the court may in its judgment or in subsequent orders of enforcement thereof enter a permanent injunction against any and all defendants prohibiting them from disseminating, distributing, exhibiting, or displaying the materials declared to be harmful to minors.

(c) A final declaration obtained pursuant to this act may be used to form the basis for an injunction or to establish scienter in a criminal proceeding. (Added 1973, No. 204 (Adj. Sess.), § 11.)

§ 2813. Injunctions

The prosecuting officer may seek a preliminary injunction on notice to defendant and upon a showing of compelling facts which demonstrate that an irreparable harm will be inflicted on the community if the materials are disseminated until such time as a permanent injunction, if warranted, can be obtained. (Added 1973, No. 204 (Adj. Sess.), § 12.)

Chapter 64: Sexual Exploitation Of Children

§ 2821. Definitions

As used in this chapter:

(1) "Child" means any person under 16 years of age.

(2) "Sexual conduct" means any of the following:

(A) any conduct involving contact between the penis and the vulva, the penis and the penis, the penis and the anus, the mouth and the penis, the mouth and the anus, the vulva and the vulva, or the mouth and the vulva;

(B) any intrusion, however slight, by any part of a person's body or any object into the genital or anal opening of another with the intent of arousing, appealing to, or gratifying the lust, passions, or sexual desire of any person;

(C) any intentional touching, not through the clothing, of the genitals, anus, or breasts of another with the intent of arousing, appealing to, or gratifying the lust, passions, or sexual desire of any person;

(D) masturbation;

(E) bestiality; or

(F) sadomasochistic abuse for sexual purposes.

(3) "Performance" means:

(A) an event that is photographed, filmed, or visually recorded; or

(B) a play, dance, or other visual presentation or exhibition before an audience.

(4) "Sexual performance" means any performance or any part of a performance that includes sexual conduct by, with, or on a child.

(5) "Promote" means to procure, issue, manufacture, publish, sell, give, provide, lend, mail, deliver, distribute, disseminate, circulate, present, exhibit, advertise, make available, or offer to do the same, by any means, including electronic transmission, file sharing, or peer-to-peer networks.

(6) "Peer-to-peer network" means a network in which two or more computers or devices share files without requiring a separate server computer or server software. (Added 1983, No. 92; amended 1999, No. 122 (Adj. Sess.), § 1; 1999, No. 124 (Adj. Sess.), § 9; 2019, No. 132 (Adj. Sess.), § 1; 2019, No. 167 (Adj. Sess.), § 30, eff. Oct. 7, 2020.)

§ 2822. Use of a child in a sexual performance

(a) No person shall, with knowledge of the character and content, promote a sexual performance by a child or a performance that contains a lewd exhibition of the genitals, anus, or breasts of a child, or hire, employ, procure, use, cause, or induce a child to engage in such a performance.

(b) In any prosecution arising under this section, the defendant may raise as an affirmative defense that before the child participated in the sexual performance, the defendant, in good faith, had a reasonable and factual basis to conclude that the child had in fact attained 16 years of age; and the defendant did not rely solely upon the oral allegations or representations of the child as to his or her age. (Added 1983, No. 92; amended 1999, No. 122 (Adj. Sess.), § 2; 2019, No. 132 (Adj. Sess.), § 1.)

§ 2823. Consenting to a sexual performance

No person who is the parent, legal guardian, or custodian of a child may, with knowledge of the character and content, consent to the participation of that child in a sexual performance or a performance including a lewd exhibition of the genitals by that child. (Added 1983, No. 92; 2019, No. 132 (Adj. Sess.), § 1.)

§ 2824. Promoting a recording of sexual conduct

(a) No person may, with knowledge of the character and content, promote any photograph, film, or visual recording of sexual conduct by, with, or on a child, or of a lewd exhibition of a child's genitals or anus. This subsection does not apply to paintings, drawings, or to nonvisual or written descriptions of sexual conduct.

(b) In any prosecution arising under this section, the defendant may raise any of the following affirmative defenses:

(1) that the recording was promoted for a bona fide medical, psychological, social work, legislative, judicial, or law enforcement purpose, by or to a physician, psychologist, social worker, legislator, judge, prosecutor, law enforcement officer, or other person having such a bona fide interest in the subject matter;

(2) that the defendant was a bona fide school, museum, or public library, or was a person acting in the course of employment as an employee or official of such an organization or of a retail outlet affiliated with and serving the educational or intended purpose of that school, museum, or library;

(3) that the defendant in good faith had a reasonable basis to conclude that the child in fact had attained 16 years of age when the recording was made. (Added 1983, No. 92; amended 1999, No. 122 (Adj. Sess.), § 3; 2019, No. 132 (Adj. Sess.), § 1.)

§ 2825. Penalties

(a) A person who violates section 2822, 2823, or 2824 of this title shall be imprisoned not more than 10 years or fined not more than $20,000.00, or both.

(b) Upon conviction for a violation of section 2822, 2823, or 2824 of this title of a person who has earlier been convicted under any of those sections, the person shall be imprisoned not less than one year nor more than 15 years or fined not more than $50,000.00, or both.

(c) A person who violates section 2827 of this title by possessing or accessing with intent to view a photograph, film, or visual depiction, including a depiction stored electronically, which constitutes:

(1) a clearly lewd exhibition of a child's genitals or anus, other than a depiction of sexual conduct by a child, shall be imprisoned not more than two years or fined not more than $5,000.00, or both;

(2) sexual conduct by, with, or on a child, shall be imprisoned not more than five years or fined not more than $10,000.00, or both.

(d) A person who violates section 2827 of this title after being convicted of a previous violation of the same section shall be imprisoned not more than 10 years or fined not more than $50,000.00, or both.

(e) A person who violates section 2828 of this title shall be imprisoned not more than five years or fined not more than $10,000.00, or both. (Added 1983, No. 92; amended 1999, No. 122 (Adj. Sess.), § 7; 2019, No. 132 (Adj. Sess.), § 1.)

§ 2826. Evidence of age

The age of a person who participated in sexual conduct or a performance that contains a lewd exhibition of the genitals, anus, or breasts, or who was solicited for either by means designated under section 2828 of this title may be established by any method acceptable under the rules of evidence, including but not limited to the following methods:

(1) inferences drawn by the trier of fact from inspection of a document that depicts sexual conduct;

(2) testimony as to the apparent age of the person by a witness to sexual conduct; or

(3) expert medical testimony based upon the appearance of the person depicted in a recording of sexual conduct. (Added 1983, No. 92; amended 1999, No. 122 (Adj. Sess.), § 4; 2019, No. 132 (Adj. Sess.), § 1.)

§ 2827. Possession of child sexual abuse material

(a) No person shall, with knowledge of the character and content, possess or knowingly access with intent to view any photograph, film, or visual depiction, including any depiction that is stored electronically, of sexual conduct by, with, or on a child or of a clearly lewd exhibition of a child's genitals or anus.

(b) This section shall not apply:

(1) if the depiction was possessed for a bona fide medical, psychological, social work, legislative, judicial, or law enforcement purpose, by a physician, psychologist, social worker, legislator, judge, prosecutor, law enforcement officer, or other person having such a bona fide interest in the subject matter;

(2) if the person was a bona fide school, museum, or public library, or was a person acting in the course of employment as an employee or official of such an organization or of a retail outlet affiliated with and serving the educational or intended purpose of that school, museum, or library; or

(3) to paintings, drawings, or nonvisual or written descriptions of sexual conduct.

(c) In any prosecution arising under this section, the defendant may raise any of the following affirmative defenses, which shall be proven by a preponderance of the evidence:

(1) that the defendant in good faith had a reasonable basis to conclude that the child in fact had attained 16 years of age when the depiction was made;

(2) that the defendant in good faith took reasonable steps, whether successful or not, to destroy or eliminate the depiction. (Added 1999, No. 122 (Adj. Sess.), § 5; amended 2019, No. 132 (Adj. Sess.), § 1.)

§ 2828. Luring a child

(a) No person shall knowingly solicit, lure, or entice, or to attempt to solicit, lure, or entice, a child under 16 years of age or another person believed by the person to be a child under 16 years of age, to engage in a sexual act as defined in section 3251 of this title or engage in lewd and lascivious conduct as defined in section 2602 of this title.

(b) This section applies to solicitation, luring, or enticement by any means, including in person, through written or telephonic correspondence or electronic communication.

(c) This section shall not apply if the person is less than 19 years of age, the child is at least 15 years of age, and the conduct is consensual. (Added 1999, No. 122 (Adj. Sess.), § 6; amended 2005, No. 192 (Adj. Sess.), § 9; 2019, No. 132 (Adj. Sess.), § 1.)

Chapter 65: Perjury

§ 2901. Punishment for perjury

A person who, being lawfully required to depose the truth in a proceeding in a court of justice or in a contested case before a State agency pursuant to 3 V.S.A. chapter 25, commits perjury shall be imprisoned not more than 15 years or fined not more than $10,000.00, or both. (Amended 1971, No. 199 (Adj. Sess.), § 15; 1981, No. 223 (Adj. Sess.), § 23; 1983, No. 244 (Adj. Sess.), § 1; 2005, No. 148 (Adj. Sess.), § 4a; 2019, No. 77, § 13, eff. June 19, 2019.)

§ 2901a. Perjury by inconsistent statements

A person is also guilty of perjury and may be sentenced under section 2901 of this title if in one or more proceedings before or ancillary to a court or grand jury or in a contested case before a State agency pursuant to 3 V.S.A. chapter 25;

(1) he or she knowingly makes two or more statements under oath or affirmation which are material in the proceedings;

(2) the statements are inconsistent to the degree that the person necessarily believed one of them to be false; and

(3) both statements were made within the period of the statute of limitations. (Added 1983, No. 244 (Adj. Sess.), § 2; amended 2005, No. 148 (Adj. Sess.), § 4b.)

§ 2902. Subornation of perjury

A person who is guilty of subornation of perjury by procuring another person to commit the crime of perjury shall be punished as provided in section 2901 of this title.

§ 2903. Attempt to suborn

A person who corruptly endeavors to incite or procure a person to commit the crime of perjury, though no perjury is committed, shall be imprisoned not more than five years or fined not more than $500.00, or both. (Amended 1971, No. 199 (Adj. Sess.), § 15; 1981, No. 223 (Adj. Sess.), § 23.)

§ 2904. False swearing; false declaration

(a) A person of whom an oath is required by law, who willfully swears falsely in regard to any matter or thing respecting which such oath is required, shall be guilty of perjury and punished as provided in section 2901 of this title.

(b) A person who declares, certifies, or verifies in a signed writing that a statement is true and is made under the pains and penalties of perjury, and who willfully makes a false statement in the declaration, certification, or verification, shall be guilty of perjury and punished as provided in section 2901 of this title. (Amended 2019, No. 77, § 5, eff. June 19, 2019.)

§ 2905. In proof of loss to fire insurance company

A person who knowingly swears to any false statement made in a proof of loss to a fire insurance company authorized to do business in this State, with intent to defraud, shall be guilty of perjury and punished as provided in section 2901 of this title.

§ 2906. Information and indictment for perjury

It shall be sufficient in an information or indictment for perjury or subornation of perjury to set forth the substance of the offense charged, by what court or State agency and by whom the oath was administered, and that such court, State agency, or person had competent authority to administer the same, without setting forth, other than aforesaid, the record or other proceedings, or the commission or authority of such court, State agency, or person before whom the perjury was committed. (Amended 2005, No. 148 (Adj. Sess.), § 4c.)

§ 2907. Repealed. 2005, No. 148 (Adj. Sess.), § 4e.

Chapter 69: Railroads

§§ 3101-3104. Repealed. 2007, No. 164 (Adj. Sess.), § 47.

§§ 3105-3109. [Reserved.].

§ 3110. Railroad vandalism

(a) Purpose. The purpose of this section is to prevent acts of vandalism to railroad property that affect the health, safety, and welfare of the traveling public, the neighboring community, and railroad employees; to protect railroad property and freight in transportation by railroad; and otherwise to enhance the safety of transportation by railroad.

(b) Definitions. For purposes of this section:

(1) "Bodily injury" shall have the same meaning as in subdivision 1021(1) of this title.

(2) "Railroad" means any form of nonhighway ground transportation that runs on rails or electromagnetic guideways, including:

(A) commuter or other short-haul railroad passenger service in a metropolitan or suburban area; and

(B) high-speed ground transportation systems that connect metropolitan areas, but does not include rapid transit operations in an urban area that are not connected to the general railroad system of transportation.

(3) "Railroad carrier" means a person providing railroad transportation.

(4) "Railroad property" means all property owned, leased, or operated by a railroad carrier, including a right-of-way, track, bridge, yard, shop, station, tunnel, viaduct, trestle, depot, warehouse, terminal, railroad signal system, train control system, centralized dispatching system, or any other structure, appurtenance, or equipment owned, leased, or used in the operation of any railroad carrier, including a train, locomotive, engine, rail car, work equipment, rolling stock, or safety device. "Railroad property" does not include administrative buildings, administrative offices, or administrative office equipment.

(5) "Right-of-way" means the track or roadbed owned, leased, or operated by a railroad carrier that is located on either side of its tracks and that is readily recognizable to a reasonable person as being railroad property or is reasonably identified as such by fencing or appropriate signs.

(6) "Serious bodily injury" shall have the same meaning as in subdivision 1021(2) of this title.

(c) Vandalism of railroad property. No person shall, with reckless disregard for railroad property or the safety of another, commit an act that causes damage to railroad property.

(d) Penalty for vandalism of railroad property.

(1) A person who violates subsection (c) of this section shall be fined not more than $500.00 or imprisoned for not more than six months, or both, if the violation results in property damage of $900.00 or less.

(2) A person who violates subsection (c) of this section shall be fined not more than $1,000.00 or imprisoned for not more than one year, or both, if the violation results in bodily injury to another person or property damage of greater than $900.00.

(3) A person who violates subsection (c) of this section shall be fined not more than $20,000.00 or imprisoned for not more than 15 years, or both, if the violation results in death or serious bodily injury to another person.

(e) Aggravated railroad vandalism. A person who intentionally causes damage to railroad property that results in death or serious bodily injury to another person shall be guilty of aggravated railroad vandalism.

(f) Penalty for aggravated railroad vandalism. A person who violates subsection (e) of this section shall be fined not more than $25,000.00 or imprisoned for not more than 15 years, or both.

(g) If serious bodily injury or death results to more than one person other than the defendant as a result of a violation of this section, the defendant may be convicted of a separate violation of this section for each decedent or person injured. (Added 2007, No. 164 (Adj. Sess.), § 46.)

Chapter 70: Female Genital Mutilation Or Cutting Prohibited

§ 3151. Female genital mutilation or cutting prohibited

(a) Definitions. As used in this section:

(1) "Health care professional" means an individual, partnership, corporation, facility, or institution licensed or certified or authorized by law to provide professional health care services.

(2) "Midwife" means a midwife licensed pursuant to 26 V.S.A. chapter 85.

(b) Female genital mutilation or cutting prohibited. Except as provided in subsection (c) of this section, no person shall:

(1) Knowingly circumcise, excise, or infibulate the whole or any part of the labia majora or labia minora or clitoris of another person who has not attained 18 years of age.

(2) Knowingly incise, prick, scrape, or cauterize any part of the labia majora or labia minora or clitoris of another person who has not attained 18 years of age.

(c) Exceptions. A medical procedure is not a violation of this section if it is:

(1) necessary to the health of the person on whom it is performed and is performed by a health care professional; or

(2) performed on a person in labor or who has just given birth and is performed for medical purposes connected with that labor or birth by a health care professional, midwife, or person in training to become a health care professional or midwife.

(d) Defense. It is not a defense to a charge under this section that the person on whom the procedure is performed, or any other person, believes that the procedure is required as a matter of custom or ritual or that the person on whom the procedure is performed, or that person's parent or guardian, consented to the procedure.

(e) Transportation prohibited. A person shall not knowingly transport a person into or out of this State for the purpose of conduct that would be a violation of this section.

(f) Penalty. A person who violates subdivision (b)(2) of this section shall be imprisoned not more than two years or fined not more than $500.00, or both. A person who violates subdivision (b)(1) or subsection (e) of this section shall be imprisoned not more than 10 years or fined not more than $20,000.00, or both. (Added 2019, No. 87 (Adj. Sess.), § 2, eff. Feb. 27, 2020.)

Chapter 71: Rape

§§ 3201, 3202. Repealed. 1977, No. 51, § 2.

Chapter 72: Sexual Assault

Subchapter 1: Crimes; Trial

§ 3251. Definitions

As used in this chapter:

(1) A "sexual act" means conduct between persons consisting of contact between the penis and the vulva, the penis and the anus, the mouth and the penis, the mouth and the vulva, or any intrusion, however slight, by any part of a person's body or any object into the genital or anal opening of another.

(2) "Sexual conduct" means any conduct or behavior relating to sexual activities of the complaining witness, including but not limited to prior experience of sexual acts, use of contraceptives, living arrangement, and mode of living.

(3) "Consent" means words or actions by a person indicating a voluntary agreement to engage in a sexual act.

(4) "Serious bodily injury" shall have the same meaning as in subdivision 1021(2) of this title.

(5) "Bodily injury" means physical pain, illness, or any impairment of physical condition.

(6) "Actor" means a person charged with sexual assault or aggravated sexual assault.

(7) "Deadly force" means physical force which a person uses with the intent of causing, or which the person knows or should have known would create a substantial risk of causing, death or serious bodily injury.

(8) "Deadly weapon" means:

(A) any firearm; or

(B) any weapon, device, instrument, material, or substance, whether animate or inanimate, which in the manner it is used or is intended to be used, is known to be capable of producing death or serious bodily injury.

(9) "Law enforcement officer" means a person certified as a law enforcement officer under the provisions of 20 V.S.A. chapter 151. (Added 1977, No. 51, § 1; amended 1985, No. 83, § 1; 1989, No. 293 (Adj. Sess.), § 4; 2005, No. 192 (Adj. Sess.), § 10; 2019, No. 8, § 1, eff. April 23, 2019.)

§ 3252. Sexual assault

(a) No person shall engage in a sexual act with another person and compel the other person to participate in a sexual act:

(1) without the consent of the other person; or

(2) by threatening or coercing the other person; or

(3) by placing the other person in fear that any person will suffer imminent bodily injury.

(b) No person shall engage in a sexual act with another person and impair substantially the ability of the other person to appraise or control conduct by administering or employing drugs or intoxicants without the knowledge or against the will of the other person.

(c) No person shall engage in a sexual act with a child who is under the age of 16, except:

(1) where the persons are married to each other and the sexual act is consensual; or

(2) where the person is less than 19 years old, the child is at least 15 years old, and the sexual act is consensual.

(d) No person shall engage in a sexual act with a child who is under the age of 18 and is entrusted to the actor's care by authority of law or is the actor's child, grandchild, foster child, adopted child, or stepchild.

(e) No person shall engage in a sexual act with a child under the age of 16 if:

(1) the victim is entrusted to the actor's care by authority of law or is the actor's child, grandchild, foster child, adopted child, or stepchild; or

(2) the actor is at least 18 years of age, resides in the victim's household, and serves in a parental role with respect to the victim.

(f)(1) A person who violates subsection (a), (b), (d), or (e) of this section shall be imprisoned not less than three years and for a maximum term of life, and, in addition, may be fined not more than $25,000.00.

(2) A person who violates subsection (c) of this section shall be imprisoned for not more than 20 years, and, in addition, may be fined not more than $10,000.00.

(g) A person convicted of violating subsection (a), (b), (d), or (e) of this section shall be sentenced under section 3271 of this title. (Added 1977, No. 51, § 1; amended 1985, No. 83, § 2; 1989, No. 293 (Adj. Sess.), § 5; 2005, No. 192 (Adj. Sess.), § 10.)

§ 3253. Aggravated sexual assault

(a) A person commits the crime of aggravated sexual assault if the person commits sexual assault under any one of the following circumstances:

(1) At the time of the sexual assault, the actor causes serious bodily injury to the victim or to another.

(2) The actor is joined or assisted by one or more persons in physically restraining, assaulting, or sexually assaulting the victim.

(3) The actor commits the sexual act under circumstances which constitute the crime of kidnapping.

(4) The actor has previously been convicted in this State of sexual assault under subsection 3252(a) or (b) of this title or aggravated sexual assault or has been convicted in any jurisdiction in the United States or territories of an offense which would constitute sexual assault under subsection 3252(a) or (b) of this title or aggravated sexual assault if committed in this State.

(5) At the time of the sexual assault, the actor is armed with a deadly weapon and uses or threatens to use the deadly weapon on the victim or on another.

(6) At the time of the sexual assault, the actor threatens to cause imminent serious bodily injury to the victim or to another and the victim reasonably believes that the actor has the present ability to carry out the threat.

(7) At the time of the sexual assault, the actor applies deadly force to the victim.

(8) The victim is under the age of 13 and the actor is at least 18 years of age.

(9) The victim is subjected by the actor to repeated nonconsensual sexual acts as part of the same occurrence or the victim is subjected to repeated nonconsensual sexual acts as part of the actor's common scheme and plan.

(b) A person who commits the crime of aggravated sexual assault shall be imprisoned not less than ten years and a maximum term of life, and, in addition, may be fined not more than $50,000.00.

(c)(1) Except as provided in subdivision (2) of this subsection, a sentence ordered pursuant to subsection (b) of this section shall include at least a ten-year term of imprisonment. The ten-year term of imprisonment required by this subdivision shall be served and may not be suspended, deferred, or served as a supervised sentence. The defendant shall not be eligible for probation, parole, furlough, or any other type of early release until the expiration of the five-year or ten-year term of imprisonment.

(2) The court may depart downwardly from the ten-year term of imprisonment required by subsection (b) of this section and impose a lesser term of incarceration if the court makes written findings on the record that the downward departure will serve the interests of justice and public safety, provided that in no event may the court impose a term of incarceration of less than five years.

(d) A person convicted of violating this section shall be sentenced under section 3271 of this title. (Added 1977, No. 51, § 1; amended 1989, No. 293 (Adj. Sess.), § 6; 2005, No. 79, § 10; 2005, No. 192 (Adj. Sess.), § 10.)

§ 3253a. Aggravated sexual assault of a child

(a) A person commits the crime of aggravated sexual assault of a child if the actor is at least 18 years of age and commits sexual assault against a child under the age of 16 in violation of section 3252 of this title and at least one of the following circumstances exists:

(1) At the time of the sexual assault, the actor causes serious bodily injury to the victim or to another.

(2) The actor is joined or assisted by one or more persons in physically restraining, assaulting, or sexually assaulting the victim.

(3) The actor commits the sexual act under circumstances which constitute the crime of kidnapping.

(4) The actor has previously been convicted in this State of sexual assault under subsection 3252(a) or (b) of this title, aggravated sexual assault under section 3253 of this title, or aggravated sexual assault of a child under this section, or has been convicted in any jurisdiction in the United States or territories of an offense which would constitute sexual assault under subsection 3252(a) or (b) of this title, aggravated sexual assault under section 3253 of this title, or aggravated sexual assault of a child under this section if committed in this State.

(5) At the time of the sexual assault, the actor is armed with a deadly weapon and uses or threatens to use the deadly weapon on the victim or on another.

(6) At the time of the sexual assault, the actor threatens to cause imminent serious bodily injury to the victim or to another, and the victim reasonably believes that the actor has the present ability to carry out the threat.

(7) At the time of the sexual assault, the actor applies deadly force to the victim.

(8) The victim is subjected by the actor to repeated nonconsensual sexual acts as part of the same occurrence or the victim is subjected to repeated nonconsensual sexual acts as part of the actor's common scheme and plan.

(b) A person who commits the crime of aggravated sexual assault of a child shall be imprisoned for not less than 25 years with a maximum term of life, and, in addition, may be fined not more than $50,000.00. The 25-year term of imprisonment required by this subsection shall be served and may not be suspended, deferred, or served as a supervised sentence. The defendant shall not be eligible for probation, parole, furlough, or any other type of early release until the expiration of the 25-year term of imprisonment. (Added 2009, No. 1, § 30, eff. March 4, 2009.)

§ 3254. Trial procedure; consent

In a prosecution for a crime defined in this chapter or section 2601 of this title:

(1) lack of consent may be shown without proof of resistance;

(2) a person shall be deemed to have acted without the consent of the other person where the actor:

(A) knows that the other person is mentally incapable of understanding the nature of the sexual act or lewd and lascivious conduct; or

(B) knows that the other person is not physically capable of resisting, or declining consent to, the sexual act or lewd and lascivious conduct; or

(C) knows that the other person is unaware that a sexual act or lewd and lascivious conduct is being committed; or

(D) knows that the other person is mentally incapable of resisting, or declining consent to, the sexual act or lewd and lascivious conduct, due to a mental condition or a psychiatric or developmental disability as defined in 14 V.S.A. § 3061. (Added 1977, No. 51, § 1; amended 1993, No. 100, § 13; 2013, No. 96 (Adj. Sess.), § 57.)

§ 3255. Evidence

(a) In a prosecution for a crime defined in this chapter and in sections 2601 and 2602 of this title, for human trafficking or aggravated human trafficking under chapter 60 of this title, or for abuse of a vulnerable adult under chapter 28 of this title or 33 V.S.A. chapter 69:

(1) Neither opinion evidence of nor evidence of the reputation of the complaining witness' sexual conduct shall be admitted.

(2) Evidence shall be required as it is for all other criminal offenses, and additional corroborative evidence set forth by case law regarding sexual assault shall no longer be required.

(3) Evidence of prior sexual conduct of the complaining witness shall not be admitted; provided, however, where it bears on the credibility of the complaining witness or it is material to a fact at issue and its probative value outweighs its private character, the court may admit:

(A) evidence of the complaining witness' past sexual conduct with the defendant;

(B) evidence of specific instances of the complaining witness' sexual conduct showing the source of origin of semen, pregnancy, or disease; and

(C) evidence of specific instances of the complaining witness' past false allegations of violations of this chapter.

(b) In a prosecution for a crime defined in this chapter and in a prosecution pursuant to sections 2601 and 2602 of this title, for human trafficking or aggravated human trafficking under chapter 60 of this title, or for abuse or exploitation of a vulnerable adult under 33 V.S.A. § 6913(b), if a defendant proposes to offer evidence described in subdivision (a)(3) of this section, the defendant shall prior to the introduction of such evidence file written notice of intent to introduce that evidence, and the court shall order an in camera hearing to determine its admissibility. All objections to materiality, credibility, and probative value shall be stated on the record by the prosecutor at the in camera hearing, and the court shall rule on the objections forthwith, and prior to the taking of any other evidence.

(c) In a prosecution for a crime defined in this chapter and in sections 2601 and 2602 of this title or for human trafficking or aggravated human trafficking under chapter 60 of this title, if the defendant takes the deposition of the complaining witness, questions concerning the evidence described in subdivisions (a)(1) and (3) of this section shall not be permitted. (Added 1977, No. 51, § 1; amended 1993, No. 100, § 14; 1995, No. 170 (Adj. Sess.), § 23, eff. Sept. 1, 1996; 2011, No. 55, § 8; 2017, No. 113 (Adj. Sess.), § 50.)

§ 3256. Testing for infectious diseases

(a) The victim of an offense involving a sexual act may obtain an order from the Criminal or Family Division of the Superior Court in which the offender was convicted of the offense, or was adjudicated delinquent, requiring that the offender be tested for the presence of the etiologic agent for acquired immune deficiency syndrome (AIDS) and other sexually-transmitted diseases, including gonorrhea, herpes, chlamydia, and syphilis. If requested by the victim, the State's Attorney shall petition the court on behalf of the victim for an order under this section. For the purposes of this section, "offender" includes a juvenile adjudicated a delinquent.

(b) For purposes of this section, "sexual act" means a criminal offense:

(1) where the underlying conduct of the offender constitutes a sexual act as defined in section 3251 of this title; and

(2) that creates a risk of transmission of the etiologic agent for AIDS to the victim as determined by the federal Centers for Disease Control and Prevention.

(c) If the court determines that the offender was convicted or adjudicated of a crime involving a sexual act with the victim, the court shall order the test to be administered by the Department of Health in accordance with applicable law. If appropriate under the circumstances, the court may include in its order a requirement for follow-up testing of the offender. An order for follow-up testing shall be terminated if the offender's conviction is overturned. A sample taken pursuant to this section shall be used solely for purposes of this section. All costs of testing the offender shall, if not otherwise funded, be paid by the Department of Public Safety.

(d) The results of the offender's test shall be disclosed only to the offender and the victim.

(e) If an offender who is subject to an order pursuant to subsection (c) of this section refuses to comply with the order, the victim, or State's Attorney on behalf of the victim, may seek a civil contempt order pursuant to 12 V.S.A. chapter 5.

(f) After arraignment, a defendant who is charged with an offense involving a sexual act may offer to be tested for the presence of the etiologic agent for acquired immune deficiency syndrome (AIDS) and other

sexually transmitted diseases, including gonorrhea, herpes, chlamydia, and syphilis. Such testing shall follow the same procedures set forth for testing an offender who is subject to an order pursuant to subsection (c) of this section. The defendant's offer to be tested after arraignment shall not be used as evidence at the defendant's trial. If the defendant is subsequently convicted of an offense involving a sexual act, the court may consider the offender's offer for testing as a mitigating factor.

(g) Upon request of the victim at any time after the commission of a crime involving a sexual act under subsection (b) of this section, the State shall provide any of the following services to the victim:

(1) counseling regarding human immunodeficiency virus (HIV);

(2) testing, which shall remain confidential unless otherwise provided by law, for HIV and other sexually transmitted diseases, including gonorrhea, herpes, chlamydia, and syphilis;

(3) counseling by a medically trained professional on the accuracy of the testing, and the risk of transmitting HIV and other sexually transmitted diseases to the victim as a result of the crime involving a sexual act; and

(4) prophylaxis treatment, crisis counseling, and support services.

(h) A victim who so requests shall receive monthly follow-up HIV testing for six months after the initial test.

(i) The State shall provide funding for HIV or AIDS, or both, and sexual assault cross-training between sexual assault programs and HIV and AIDS service organizations.

(j) The record of the court proceedings and test results pursuant to this section shall be sealed.

(k) The Court Administrator's Office shall develop and distribute forms to implement this section in connection with a criminal conviction or adjudication of delinquency.

(l) The Center for Crime Victim Services shall be the primary coordinating agent for the services to be provided in subsections (g), (h), and (i) of this section. (Added 2001, No. 49, § 12, eff. June 12, 2001; amended 2009, No. 154 (Adj. Sess.), § 100; 2015, No. 97 (Adj. Sess.), § 74.)

§ 3257. Sexual exploitation of an inmate

(a) No correctional employee, contractor, or other person providing services to offenders on behalf of the Department of Corrections or pursuant to a court order or in accordance with a condition of parole, probation, supervised community sentence, or furlough shall engage in a sexual act with a person who the employee, contractor, or other person providing services knows:

(1) is confined to a correctional facility; or

(2) is being supervised by the Department of Corrections while on parole, probation, supervised community sentence, or furlough, where the employee, contractor, or other service provider is currently engaged in a direct supervisory relationship with the person being supervised. For purposes of this subdivision, a person is engaged in a direct supervisory relationship with a supervisee if the supervisee is assigned to the caseload of that person.

(b) A person who violates subsection (a) of this section shall be imprisoned for not more than five years or fined not more than $10,000.00, or both. (Added 2005, No. 177 (Adj. Sess.), § 1.)

§ 3258. Sexual exploitation of a minor

(a) No person shall engage in a sexual act with a minor if:

(1) the actor is at least 48 months older than the minor; and

(2) the actor is in a position of power, authority, or supervision over the minor by virtue of the actor's undertaking the responsibility, professionally or voluntarily, to provide for the health or welfare of minors, or guidance, leadership, instruction, or organized recreational activities for minors.

(b) A person who violates subsection (a) of this section shall be imprisoned for not more than one year or fined not more than $2,000.00, or both.

(c) A person who violates subsection (a) of this section and who abuses his or her position of power, authority, or supervision over the minor in order to engage in a sexual act shall be imprisoned for not more than five years or fined not more than $10,000.00, or both. (Added 2009, No. 1, § 13.)

§ 3259. Sexual exploitation of a person in the custody of a law enforcement officer

(a) No law enforcement officer shall engage in a sexual act with a person whom the officer is detaining, arresting, or otherwise holding in custody or who the officer knows is being detained, arrested, or otherwise held in custody by another law enforcement officer.

(b) A person who violates subsection (a) of this section shall be imprisoned for not more than five years or fined not more than $10,000.00, or both. (Added 2019, No. 8, § 2, eff. April 23, 2019.)

Subchapter 2: Sentencing, Treatment, And Supervision

§ 3271. Indeterminate life sentence

(a) A person who commits one of the following offenses shall be sentenced under this section:

(1) Lewd and lascivious conduct with a child, second or subsequent offense, in violation of subdivision 2602(b)(2) of this title.

(2) Sexual assault in violation of subsection 3252(a), (b), (d), or (e) of this title.

(3) Aggravated sexual assault in violation of section 3253 of this title.

(4) Violation of sex offender registry requirements by noncompliant high-risk sex offenders, in violation of subsection 5411d(g) of this title.

(b) If a person is sentenced under this section, the person's maximum sentence shall be imprisonment for life.

(c) If a person sentenced under this section receives a sentence that is wholly or partially suspended, sex offender conditions and treatment shall be a condition of the person's probation agreement.

(d) If a person sentenced under this section receives a sentence for an unsuspended term of incarceration, the person shall not be released until the person successfully completes all sex offender treatment and programming required by the Department of Corrections, unless the Department determines that the person poses a sufficiently low risk of reoffense to protect the community or that a program can be implemented which adequately supervises the person and addresses any risk the person may pose to the community. (Added 2005, No. 192 (Adj. Sess.), § 10; amended 2007, No. 77, § 11.)

§ 3272. Community reentry; prerelease planning

(a) Consistent with 28 V.S.A. § 721, the Department of Corrections shall jointly establish with the community of planned residence a community reentry support team for all offenders designated as high risk under section 5411b of this title. The Department, the reentry support team, and the offender shall jointly begin developing a release plan for each offender subject to this subsection beginning at least 12 months prior to the offender's release. The Department shall designate a person to oversee the creation of prerelease plans developed under this section and to review completed plans.

(b) A release plan developed under this section shall be individually tailored for each offender, shall describe in detail the community reentry programming planned for the offender, and shall include provisions addressing:

(1) the appropriate residence for the offender;

(2) postrelease treatment;

(3) the community support and accountability network available to the offender; and

(4) potential employment for the offender, including job and skills training.

(c) A release plan developed under this section shall include a plan for victim safety developed jointly by the Department and any known victim desiring to participate. A plan developed pursuant to this subsection shall include victim wraparound services when practicable and desired by the victim.

(d) Notwithstanding the provisions of 3 V.S.A. chapter 25, the Department shall develop an internal directive to implement the provisions of this section.

(e) This section shall not be construed to affect in any way the Department's duty to develop and implement plans for offenders to return to the community under 28 V.S.A. § 1(b). (Added 2005, No. 192 (Adj. Sess.), § 14.)

§§ 3273-3280. [Reserved for future use.].

§ 3281. Sexual assault survivors' rights

(a) Short title. This section may be cited as the "Bill of Rights for Sexual Assault Survivors."

(b) Definition. As used in this section, "sexual assault survivor" means a person who is a victim of an alleged sexual offense.

(c) Survivors' rights. When a sexual assault survivor makes a verbal or written report to a law enforcement officer, emergency department, sexual assault nurse examiner, or victim's advocate of an alleged sexual offense, the recipient of the report shall provide written notification to the survivor that he or she has the following rights:

(1) The right to receive a medical forensic examination and any related toxicology testing at no cost to the survivor in accordance with 32 V.S.A. § 1407, irrespective of whether the survivor reports to or cooperates with law enforcement. If the survivor opts to have a medical forensic examination, he or she shall have the following additional rights:

(A) the right to have the medical forensic examination kit or its probative contents delivered to a forensics laboratory within 72 hours of collection;

(B) the right to have the sexual assault evidence collection kit or its probative contents preserved without charge for the duration of the maximum applicable statute of limitations;

(C) the right to be informed in writing of all policies governing the collection, storage, preservation, and disposal of a sexual assault evidence collection kit;

(D) the right to be informed of a DNA profile match on a kit reported to law enforcement or on a confidential kit, on a toxicology report, or on a medical record documenting a medical forensic examination, if the disclosure would not impede or compromise an ongoing investigation; and

(E) upon written request from the survivor, the right to:

(i) receive written notification from the appropriate official with custody not later than 60 days before the date of the kit's intended destruction or disposal; and

(ii) be granted further preservation of the kit or its probative contents.

(2) The right to consult with a sexual assault advocate.

(3) The right to information concerning the availability of protective orders and policies related to the enforcement of protective orders.

(4) The right to information about the availability of, and eligibility for, victim compensation and restitution.

(5) The right to information about confidentiality.

(d) Notification protocols. The Vermont Network Against Domestic and Sexual Violence and the Sexual Assault Nurse Examiner Program, in consultation with other parties referred to in this section, shall develop protocols and written materials to assist all responsible entities in providing notification to victims. (Added 2017, No. 44, § 4.)

Chapter 73: Sabbath Breaking

§§ 3301-3308. Repealed. 1975, No. 207 (Adj. Sess.), § 2, eff. March 27, 1976.

Chapter 74: A Common Day Of Rest

§§ 3351-3353. Repealed. 1983, No. 80, eff. April 29, 1983.

§ 3354. Repealed. 1981, No. 107, § 7, eff. May 14, 1981.

§§ 3354a-3358. Repealed. 1983, No. 80, eff. April 29, 1983.

Chapter 75: Treason And Other Offenses Against The Government

Subchapter 1: Treason And Related Offenses

§ 3401. Definition and punishment of treason

A person owing allegiance to this State, who levies war or conspires to levy war against the same, or adheres to the enemies thereof, giving them aid and comfort, within the State or elsewhere, shall be guilty of treason against this State and shall suffer the punishment of death.

§ 3402. Place of trial; testimony

Such person may be tried in any county in the State, but shall not be convicted except upon testimony equivalent to two witnesses to the same overt act of treason of which he or she stands indicted, or upon confession in open court.

§ 3403. Misprision of treason

A person owing allegiance to this State, knowing such treason to have been committed, or knowing of the intent of a person to commit such treason, who does not, within 14 days from the time of having such knowledge, give information thereof to the Governor of the State, to one of the Justices of the Supreme Court, a Superior judge, or a justice of the peace, shall be guilty of misprision of treason and shall be imprisoned not more than 10 years nor less than five years or fined not more than $2,000.00, or both. (Amended 1965, No. 194, § 10, operative February 1, 1967; 1971, No. 199 (Adj. Sess.), § 15; 2019, No. 77, § 15, eff. June 19, 2019.)

§ 3404. Powers of arrest; proceedings

A district judge, sheriff, deputy sheriff, constable, or police officer having notice or knowledge, or who suspects that a person has committed treason or an offense mentioned in sections 3481-3485 of this title, shall arrest such person without warrant and take him or her before a Justice of the Supreme Court or a Superior judge, who shall have authority to commit such person to jail, or may bind him or her over with sufficient sureties by way of recognizance, for his appearance before the Superior Court of the county in which the offense was committed, to answer to such information or indictment as may be brought against him or her. Section 7173 of this title shall apply to such a Justice of the Supreme Court and to such a Superior judge. (Amended 1965, No. 194, § 10, operative February 1, 1967; 1973, No. 193 (Adj. Sess.), § 3, eff. April 9, 1974;1973, No. 249 (Adj. Sess.), § 47.)

§ 3405. Promotion of anarchy

A person who by speech or directly or indirectly by exhibition, distribution, or promulgation of any written or printed document or paper or pictorial representation, shall advocate, advise, counsel, or incite unlawful assault upon, or the killing of a public official, or the unlawful destruction of property, or the overthrow by force or violence of the government of the State, or who, at any meeting or in the presence of more than three persons in any place or in any manner, shall advise, advocate, or counsel the violation of or unlawful refusal to obey a law of the State respecting the preservation of the peace and the protection of life or property shall be imprisoned not more than three years or fined not more than $1,000.00, or both.

Subchapter 2: Sabotage Prevention Act

§ 3431. Definitions

As used in this subchapter:

(1) "Highway" includes any private or public street, way, or other place used for travel to or from property.

(2) "Road commissioner" means any individual, board, or other body having authority under then existing law to discontinue the use of the highway that it is desired to restrict or close to public use and

travel. The power to discontinue highways or the use thereof vested in any town may, for the purpose of this subchapter, be exercised by the selectboard thereof.

(3) "Public utility" includes any pipeline, gas, electric, heat, water, oil, sewer, telephone, telegraph, radio, railway, railroad, airplane, transportation, communication, or other system, by whomsoever owned or operated, for public use.

§ 3432. Interference with defense or war effort

A person who intentionally destroys, impairs, injures, interferes, or tampers with real or personal property, with reasonable grounds to believe that such act will hinder, delay, or interfere with the preparation of the United States or of any of the states for defense or for war, or with the prosecution of war by the United States, shall be imprisoned not less than one year nor more than 10 years or fined not more than $10,000.00, or both.

§ 3433. Defective materials

A person who intentionally makes or causes to be made or omits to note on inspection any defect in any article or thing with reasonable grounds to believe that such article or thing is intended to be used in connection with the preparation of the United States or any of the states for defense or for war, or for the prosecution of war by the United States, or that such article or thing is one of a number of similar articles or things, some of which are so to be used, intending thereby to hinder, delay, or interfere with the preparation of the United States or of any of the states for defense or for war, or with the prosecution of war by the United States, shall be imprisoned not less than one year nor more than 10 years or fined not more than $10,000.00, or both.

§ 3434. Attempts

A person who attempts to commit any of the crimes defined by this subchapter shall be liable to one-half the punishment prescribed for the completed crime. In addition to the acts that constitute an attempt to commit a crime under the law of this State, the solicitation or incitement of another to commit any of the crimes defined by this subchapter not followed by the commission of the crime, the collection or assemblage of any materials with the intent that the same are to be used then or at a later time in the commission of such crime, or the entry, with or without permission, into a building, enclosure, or other premises of another with the intent to commit any such crime therein or thereon shall constitute an attempt to commit such crime.

§ 3435. Conspiracy

If two or more persons conspire to commit any crime defined by this subchapter, each of such persons shall be guilty of conspiracy and subject to the same punishment as if he or she had committed the crime that he or she conspired to commit, whether or not any act be done in furtherance of the conspiracy. The fact that any of his or her fellow conspirators has been acquitted, has not been arrested or convicted, is not amenable to justice, or has been pardoned or otherwise discharged before or after conviction shall not constitute any defense or ground of suspension of judgment, sentence, or punishment on behalf of any person prosecuted under this section.

§ 3436. Self incrimination of witnesses; immunity from prosecution

No person shall be excused from attending and testifying, or producing any books, papers, or other documents before any court, magistrate, referee, or grand jury upon any investigation, proceeding, or trial, for or relating to or concerned with a violation of any section of this subchapter or attempt to commit such violation, upon the ground or for the reason that the testimony or evidence, documentary or otherwise, required of him or her by the State may tend to convict him or her of a crime or to subject him or her to a penalty or forfeiture; but no person shall be prosecuted or subjected to any penalty or forfeiture for or on account of any transaction, matter or thing concerning which he or she may so testify or produce evidence, documentary or otherwise, and no testimony so given or produced shall be received against him or her, upon any criminal investigation, proceeding or trial, except upon a prosecution for perjury or contempt of court based upon the giving or producing of such testimony.

§ 3437. Posting premises

An individual, partnership, association, corporation, municipal corporation, or state or any political subdivision thereof engaged in, or preparing to engage in the following enterprises, the property of which is enclosed by a fence, wall, building, or water frontage or any combination of the same, may post around such property at each gate, entrance, or dock and for every one hundred feet of water front a sign reading "No entry without permission":

(1) The manufacture, transportation, or storage of any product to be used in the preparation of the United States or of any of the states for defense or for war or in the prosecution of war by the United States.

(2) The manufacture, transportation, distribution, or storage of gas, oil, coal, electricity, or water.

(3) The operation of any public utility.

§ 3438. Trespass on posted premises

A person who, without permission from such owner, shall willfully enter upon premises so posted as provided in section 3437 of this title shall be imprisoned not more than 10 days or fined not more than $50.00, or both.

§ 3439. Arrest

Any peace officer or any person employed as watchman, guard, or in a supervisory capacity on premises posted as provided in section 3437 of this title may stop any person found on any premises to which entry without permission is forbidden by section 3437 and may detain him or her for the purpose of requiring of him or her his or her name, address, and business in such place. If such peace officer or employee has reason to believe from the answers of the person so interrogated that such person has no right to be in such place, he or she shall forthwith arrest such person without a warrant on the charge of violating the provisions of section 3437.

§ 3440. Closing highways

An individual, partnership, association, corporation, municipal corporation or state or any political subdivision thereof engaged in or preparing to engage in the manufacture, transportation, or storage of any product to be used in the preparation of the United States or any of the states for defense or for war or in the prosecution of war by the United States, or in the manufacture, transportation, distribution, or storage of gas, oil, coal, electricity, or water, or any of such natural or artificial persons operating any public utility, who has property so used that he or she or it believes will be endangered if public use and travel is not restricted or prohibited on one or more highways or parts thereof upon which such property abuts, may petition the road commissioners of any city, town, or county to close

one or more of such highways or parts thereof to public use and travel or to restrict by order the use
and travel upon one or more of such highways or parts thereof.

§ 3441. Notice and hearing

Upon receipt of such petition, the road commissioners shall set a day for hearing and give notice thereof
by publication in a newspaper having general circulation in the city, town, or county in which such
property is located, such notice to be at least seven days prior to the date set for hearing. If, after
hearing, the road commissioners determine that the public safety and the safety of the property of the
petitioner so require, they shall by suitable order close to public use and travel or reasonably restrict the
use of and travel upon one or more of such highways or parts thereof. However, the road
commissioners may issue written permits to travel over the highway so closed or restricted to
responsible and reputable persons for such term, under such conditions and in such form as such
commissioners may prescribe. Appropriate notices in letters at least three inches high shall be posted
conspicuously at each end of any highway so closed or restricted by such order. The road commissioners
may at any time revoke or modify any order so made.

§ 3442. Penalties

A person who violates any order made under sections 3440 and 3441 of this title shall be imprisoned not
more than 10 days or fined not more than $50.00, or both.

§ 3443. Effect on labor organizations

Nothing in this subchapter shall be construed to impair, curtail, or destroy the rights of employees and
their representatives to self-organization, to form, join, or assist labor organizations, to bargain
collectively through representatives of their own choosing, and to engage in concerted activities, for the
purpose of collective bargaining or other mutual aid or protection.

§ 3444. Suspension of other laws

All acts and parts of acts inconsistent with this subchapter are hereby suspended in their application to
any proceedings under this subchapter. If conduct prohibited by this subchapter is also made unlawful
by other law, the offender may be convicted for the violation of this subchapter or of such other law.

§ 3445. When subchapter in force

This subchapter shall be in force whenever the United States is at war. However, any violation of this
subchapter, committed while the chapter is in force, may be prosecuted and punished thereafter,
whether or not this subchapter is in force at the time of such prosecution and punishment.

Subchapter 3: Other Offenses

§ 3481. Repealed. 2017, No. 16, § 1.

§ 3482. Furnishing information to enemy

(a) A person shall not furnish, nor attempt to furnish, to a government at war with or threatening war on
the United States, or to a citizen of such government or to a person whom he or she has reason to
believe will furnish or attempt to furnish to such government or citizen, information relative to:

(1) the location, construction, or condition of a military camp, fort, armory, arsenal, or building in which munitions of war are being manufactured or are stored;

(2) the proposed location of such camp, fort, armory, arsenal, or building;

(3) the location or condition or proposed location of a bridge, road, car, boat, canal, dockyard, telephone or telegraph line or equipment, wireless station or equipment, railway or railway equipment, property of a corporation subject to the supervision of the Public Utility Commission;

(4) the topography of the State or a part thereof;

(5) the number, character, condition, or location of the National Guard or the land or naval forces of the United States in this State.

(b) A person who violates a subdivision of subsection (a) of this section shall be imprisoned not more than 10 years. (Amended 1959, No. 329 (Adj. Sess.), § 39; 1971, No. 199 (Adj. Sess.), § 15.)

§ 3483. Injuries to certain property; penalty

(a) While the United States is at war or threatened with war, a person shall not:

(1) injure or attempt or conspire, or have in his or her possession any tool, explosive, or means with intent to use the same or for some one else to use, to injure a bridge, road, car, boat, canal, dockyard, telephone or telegraph line or equipment, wireless station or equipment, railway or highway equipment, road or railway making equipment, property, or a corporation subject to the supervision of the Public Utility Commission, property designed for use by the State or a municipality or railway, telephone, or telegraph company, property of a person, copartnership, or corporation engaged in or about to engage in making munitions of war or property to become the property of the State, or a building belonging to the State or a municipality or to a railway, telephone, or telegraph company or to a corporation subject to the supervision of the Public Utility Commission; or

(2) pollute or place any poisonous substance in any water liable to be used by a person or domestic animal.

(b) A person who violates a subdivision of subsection (a) of this section shall be imprisoned not more than 20 years. (Amended 1959, No. 329 (Adj. Sess.), § 39; 1971, No. 199 (Adj. Sess.), § 15.)

§ 3484. Concerted action by three or more

If three or more persons, acting in concert, with force and violence, attempt to kill, maim, or wound a person, or to rob a person, corporation, or community of money or other property, or to burn, blow up, or otherwise destroy a bank building, store, factory, dwelling house, or other building or depository of property, or a railway car or engine, or a steamboat, vessel, or other watercraft, finished or unfinished, for use in navigable waters, or property of a corporation subject to the supervision of the Public Utility Commission, each person so offending shall suffer the penalty of death. The provisions of this section shall be in force only while the United States is at war or threatened with war. (Amended 1959, No. 329 (Adj. Sess.), § 39, eff. March 1, 1961.)

§ 3485. Penalty when offense is treason

A person who commits an offense punishable under one of sections 3482-3485 of this title, and such offense amounts to treason, shall be punished for treason in lieu of the penalty prescribed in such section. (Amended 2019, No. 77, § 16, eff. June 19, 2019.)

Chapter 76: Weapons Of Mass Destruction

§ 3501. Definitions

(a) As used in this chapter:

(1) "Chemical warfare agents" means:

(A) Any weaponized toxic or poisonous chemical, including the following agents or any analog of the following agents:

(i) Nerve agents, including Tabun (GA), Sarin (GB), Soman (GD), GF, and VX.

(ii) Choking agents, including Phosgene (CG) and Diphosgene (DP).

(iii) Blood agents, including Hydrogen Cyanide (AC), Cyanogen Chloride (CK), and Arsine (SA).

(iv) Blister agents, including mustards (H, HD (sulfur mustard), HN-1, HN-2, HN-3 (nitrogen mustard)), arsenicals, such as Lewisite (L), urticants, such as CX, and incapacitating agents, such as BZ.

(B) A dangerous chemical or hazardous material generally utilized in an industrial or commercial process when a person knowingly and intentionally utilizes the material with the intent to cause harm, and the use places persons at risk of serious bodily injury or death, or endangers the environment.

(2) "Health care provider" means a person, partnership, corporation, facility, or institution, licensed, certified, or authorized, by law, to provide professional health care service in this State to an individual during that individual's medical care, treatment, or confinement.

(3) "Hoax weapon" means any substance, compound, or other item intended to convey the physical appearance or chemical properties of a weapon of mass destruction or asserted to contain a weapon of mass destruction, which is not a weapon of mass destruction or does not contain a weapon of mass destruction.

(4) "Law enforcement agency" means:

(A) A federal law enforcement agency, including the Bureau of Alcohol, Tobacco and Firearms, the Federal Bureau of Investigation, Military Police or Military Criminal Investigative Division, U.S. Marshals Service, Secret Service, Federal Emergency Management Agency, or the Department of Defense Threat Reduction Agency.

(B) One of the following Vermont law enforcement agencies:

(i) The Department of Public Safety.

(ii) A municipal police department.

(iii) A sheriff's department.

(iv) The Attorney General's office.

(v) A State's Attorney's office.

(vi) The Capitol Police Department.

(5) "Nuclear or radiological agents" means any improvised nuclear device (IND), which is any explosive device designed to cause a nuclear yield, any radiological dispersal device (RDD), which is any explosive device utilized to spread radioactive material, or a simple radiological dispersal device (SRDD), which is any container designed to release radiological material as a weapon without an explosion.

(6) "Vector" means a living organism or a molecule, including a recombinant molecule, or a biological product that may be engineered as a result of biotechnology, that is capable of carrying a biological agent or toxin to a host.

(7) "Weapon of mass destruction" means a chemical warfare agent, weaponized biological or biologic warfare agent, nuclear agent, or radiological agent.

(8) "Weaponization" means the deliberate processing, preparation, packaging, or synthesis of any substance or agent for use as a weapon or munition. "Weaponized agents" means those agents or substances that have been prepared for dissemination through any explosive, thermal, pneumatic, mechanical, or other means.

(9) "Weaponized biological or biologic warfare agents" means:

(A) weaponized pathogens, including bacteria, viruses, rickettsia, yeasts, or fungi;

(B) genetically engineered pathogens;

(C) weaponized toxins;

(D) weaponized vectors; and

(E) weaponized endogenous biological regulators (EBRs).

(b) The lawful use of chemicals for legitimate mineral extraction, industrial, agricultural, or commercial purposes is not proscribed by this chapter. (Added 2001, No. 137 (Adj. Sess.), § 3.)

§ 3502. Possession and use of weapons of mass destruction

(a) A person who knowingly and without lawful authority possesses, develops, manufactures, produces, transfers, acquires, or stockpiles any weapon of mass destruction shall be imprisoned not more than 20 years or fined not more than $100,000.00, or both.

(b) A person who uses or directly employs against other persons a weapon of mass destruction in a form that may cause disabling illness or injury in human beings shall be imprisoned not less than 20 years nor more than life and fined not more than $250,000.00.

(c) A person who uses a weapon of mass destruction in a form that may cause widespread damage to or disruption of water or food supplies shall be imprisoned not less than five years nor more than 30 years and fined not more than $250,000.00.

(d) A person who uses a weapon of mass destruction against livestock or crops with the intent to cause widespread and substantial damage to livestock or crops shall be imprisoned not more than 30 years and fined not more than $250,000.00.

(e) A person who uses a weapon of mass destruction in a form that may cause widespread and significant damage to public or private property shall be imprisoned not more than 30 years and fined not more than $250,000.00.

(f) A person who uses recombinant technology or any other biological advance to create new pathogens or more virulent forms of existing pathogens for the purpose of creating a weapon of mass destruction shall be imprisoned not more than 20 years or fined not more than $250,000.00, or both.

(g) A person who knowingly and intentionally places a hoax weapon in any public place, building, house, residence, facility of public transport, vehicular conveyance, train, ship, boat, aircraft, dam or reservoir for storing water, shall be imprisoned not more than five years or fined not more than $10,000.00, or both.

(h) No university, research institution, private company, individual, or hospital engaged in scientific or public health research and, as required, registered with the Centers for Disease Control and Prevention (CDC) pursuant to part 113 (commencing with Section 113.1) of subchapter E of chapter 1 of Title 9 or pursuant to Part 72 (commencing with Section 72.1) of Subchapter E of Chapter 1 of Title 42 of the Code of Federal Regulations, or any successor provisions, shall be subject to this section.

(i) Nothing in this section shall be construed to limit or restrict prosecution under any other applicable laws. (Added 2001, No. 137 (Adj. Sess.), § 3.)

§ 3503. Threats

(a) No person shall communicate a threat to use a weapon of mass destruction, knowing that the threat is likely to cause:

(1) evacuation of a building, place of assembly, or facility of public transport; or

(2) a person to fear serious bodily injury.

(b) A person who violates this section shall:

(1) For a first offense, be imprisoned for not more than two years or fined not more than $5,000.00, or both.

(2) For a second or subsequent offense, be imprisoned for not more than five years or fined not more than $10,000.00, or both.

(c) It shall not be a defense to a prosecution under this section that the defendant did not have the capability or means of committing the specified offense or that the threat was not made to a person who was a subject thereof. The foregoing shall not impair a defendant's right to assert a defense based upon insanity or diminished capacity.

(d) Nothing in this section shall be construed to limit or restrict prosecution under any other applicable laws. (Added 2001, No. 137 (Adj. Sess.), § 3.)

§ 3504. Reporting illnesses, diseases, injuries, and deaths associated with weapons of mass destruction

(a)(1) Illness, disease, injury, or death. A health care provider shall report all cases of persons who exhibit any illness, disease, injury, or death identified by the Department of Health as likely to be caused by a weapon of mass destruction, which may include illnesses, diseases, injuries, or deaths that:

(A) can result from bioterrorism, epidemic, or pandemic disease, or novel and highly fatal infectious agents or biological toxins, and might pose a risk of a significant number of human fatalities or incidents of permanent or long-term disability; or

(B) may be caused by the biological agents listed in 42 C.F.R. Part 72, Appendix A.

(2) This section does not authorize, nor shall it be interpreted to authorize, unreasonable searches and seizures by public health care employees; nor does this section authorize performance of diagnostic tests or procedures for the specific purpose of incriminating patients, unless the patient consents to such specific tests or procedures after notice of his or her constitutional rights and knowing waiver of them.

(3) Health care providers who make good faith reports to the Department of Health under this section shall be immune from prosecution, suit, administrative or regulatory sanctions for defamation, breach of confidentiality or privacy, or any other cause of action based on such reports or errors contained in such reports.

(b) Pharmacists. A pharmacist shall report any unusual or increased prescription requests, unusual types of prescriptions, or unusual trends in pharmacy visits that may result from bioterrorist acts, epidemic or pandemic disease, or novel and highly fatal infectious agents or biological toxins, and might pose a substantial risk of a significant number of human fatalities or incidents of permanent or long-term disability. Prescription-related events that require a report include, but are not limited to:

(1) an unusual increase in the number of prescriptions to treat fever, respiratory, or gastrointestinal complaints;

(2) an unusual increase in the number of prescriptions for antibiotics;

(3) an unusual increase in the number of requests for information on over-the-counter pharmaceuticals to treat fever, respiratory, or gastrointestinal complaints; and

(4) any prescription that treats a disease that is relatively uncommon and may be the result of bioterrorism.

(c)(1) Manner of reporting. A report made pursuant to subsection (a) or (b) of this section shall be made in writing within 24 hours to the Commissioner of Health or designee.

(2) The report shall include as much of the following information as is available:

(A) The patient's name, date of birth, sex, race, and current address (including city and county).

(B) The name and address of the health care provider, and of the reporting individual, if different.

(C) Any other information as determined by the Commissioner of Health.

(3) The Department of Health shall establish a form, which may be filed electronically, for use in filing the reports required by this subsection.

(d)(1) Animal diseases. Every veterinarian, livestock owner, veterinary diagnostic laboratory director, or other person having the care of animals, shall report animals having or suspected of having any disease that can result from bioterrorism, epidemic or pandemic disease, or novel and highly fatal infectious agents or biological toxins, and might pose a risk of a significant number of human and animal fatalities or incidents of permanent or long-term disability.

(2) A report made pursuant to this subsection shall be made, in writing, within 24 hours to the Commissioner of Health or designee, and shall include as much of the following information as is available: the location or suspected location of the animal, the name and address of any known owner, and the name and address of the reporting individual.

(e) Laboratories. For purposes of this section only, the term "health care provider" shall also include out-of-state medical laboratories that have agreed to the reporting requirements of this State. Results must be reported by the laboratory that performs the test, but an in-state laboratory that sends specimens to an out-of-state laboratory is also responsible for reporting results.

(f) Enforcement. The Department of Health may enforce the provisions of this section in accordance with 18 V.S.A. chapters 3 and 11.

(g) Disclosure. Information collected pursuant to this section and in support of investigations and studies undertaken by the Commissioner in response to reports made pursuant to this section shall be privileged and confidential. This subsection shall not apply to the disclosure of information to a law enforcement agency for a legitimate law enforcement purpose.

(h) Rulemaking. The Commissioner of Health shall, after consultation with the Commissioner of Public Safety, adopt rules to implement this section. The rules adopted pursuant to this subsection shall include methods to ensure timely communication from the Department of Health to the Department of Public Safety. (Added 2001, No. 137 (Adj. Sess.), § 3.)

Chapter 77: Trees And Plants

§ 3601. Definitions

As used in this chapter:

(1) "Diameter breast height" or "DBH" means the diameter of a standing tree at four and one-half feet from the ground.

(2) "Harvest" means the cutting, felling, or removal of timber.

(3) "Harvest unit" means the area of land from which timber will be harvested or the area of land on which timber stand improvement will occur.

(4) "Harvester" means a person, firm, company, corporation, or other legal entity that harvests timber.

(5) "Landowner" means the person, firm, company, corporation, or other legal entity that owns or controls the land or owns or controls the right to harvest timber on the land.

(6) "Landowner's agent" means a person, firm, company, corporation, or other legal entity representing the landowner in a timber sale, timber harvest, or land management.

(7) "Stump diameter" means the diameter of a tree stump remaining after cutting, felling, or destruction.

(8) "Forest products" means logs, pulpwood, veneer, bolt wood, wood chips, stud wood, poles, pilings, biomass, fuel wood, or bark.

(9) "Timber" means:

(A) trees of every size, nature, kind, and description; and

(B) sprouts from which trees may grow, seedlings, saplings, bushes, or shrubs that have been planted or cultivated by a person who owns or controls the property where they are located. (Added 2009, No. 147 (Adj. Sess.), § 4; amended 2015, No. 106 (Adj. Sess.), § 1.)

§ 3602. Valuation of trees or timber

Any person who is entitled to damages pursuant to section 3606 of this title or who is entitled to restitution for a violation of section 3606a of this title may provide an assessment of the value, based upon the kind, condition, location, and use of the timber cut down, destroyed, removed, injured, damaged, or carried away or, in the alternative, may assess the value of the timber as follows:

(1) if a tree is no more than six inches in stump diameter or DBH, $50.00;

(2) if a tree is more than six inches and not more than ten inches in stump diameter or DBH, $100.00;

(3) if a tree is more than 10 inches and not more than 14 inches in stump diameter or DBH, $300.00;

(4) if a tree is more than 14 inches and not more than 18 inches in stump diameter or DBH, $750.00;

(5) if a tree is more than 18 inches and not more than 22 inches in stump diameter or DBH, $1,500.00;

(6) if a tree is greater than 22 inches in stump diameter or DBH, $2,000.00;

(7) for a bush or shrub, $50.00. (Added 2009, No. 147 (Adj. Sess.), § 4; amended 2015, No. 106 (Adj. Sess.), § 1.)

§ 3603. Marking harvest units

As a best management practice, a landowner who authorizes timber harvesting or who in fact harvests timber should clearly and accurately mark the harvest unit with visible means. (Added 2009, No. 147 (Adj. Sess.), § 4; amended 2015, No. 106 (Adj. Sess.), § 1.)

§ 3604. Exemptions

The cutting, felling, or destruction of a tree or the harvest of timber by the following shall not be subject to a civil action under section 3606 of this title or a criminal penalty under section 3606a of this title:

(1) The Agency of Transportation, or its representatives, conducting vegetation management.

(2) A municipality conducting brush removal subject to the requirements of 19 V.S.A. § 904.

(3) A utility conducting vegetation management within the boundaries of the utility's established right-of-way.

(4) [Repealed.]

(5) A railroad conducting vegetation management.

(6) A licensed surveyor establishing boundaries between abutting parcels under 27 V.S.A. § 4. (Added 2009, No. 147 (Adj. Sess.), § 4; amended 2015, No. 106 (Adj. Sess.), § 1.)

§ 3605. Repealed. 1971, No. 222 (Adj. Sess.), § 7, eff. April 5, 1972.

§ 3606. Trespass; civil action

(a) In addition to any other civil liability or criminal penalty allowed by law, if a person cuts down, fells, destroys, removes, injures, damages, or carries away any timber placed or growing for any use or purpose whatsoever, or forest products standing, lying, or growing belonging to another person, without permission from the owner of the timber or forest product, or cuts out, alters, or defaces the mark of a log or other valuable forest product, the party injured may recover of such person, in an action on this statute, treble damages for the value of the timber or forest product, and any damage caused to the land or improvements thereon as a result of such action. The injured party or landowner may rely on an assessment of damages based on the kind, condition, location, and use of the timber or forest product by the injured party or landowner, or alternatively, may elect to rely on the values established under section 3602 of this title.

(b) If the defendant in an action brought pursuant to subsection (a) of this section establishes by a preponderance of the evidence that he or she had good reason to believe that the timber or forest products belonged to him or her, or that he or she had a legal right to perform the acts complained of, the plaintiff shall recover single damages only, with costs.

(c) As used in this section, "damages" shall include any damage caused to the land or improvements thereon as a result of a person cutting, felling, destroying, removing, injuring, damaging, or carrying away timber or forest products without the permission of the owner of the property on which the timber stands. (Amended 1959, No. 61, eff. March 26, 1959; amended 2009, No. 147 (Adj. Sess.), § 5; 2015, No. 106 (Adj. Sess.), § 1.)

§ 3606a. Trespass; criminal penalty

(a) No person shall knowingly or recklessly:

(1) cut down, fell, destroy, remove, injure, damage, or carry away any timber or forest product placed or growing for any use or purpose whatsoever, or timber or forest product lying or growing belonging to another person, without permission from the owner of the timber or forest product; or

(2) deface the mark of a log, forest product, or other valuable timber in a river or other place.

(b) Any person who violates subsection (a) of this section shall:

(1) for a first offense, be imprisoned not more than one year or fined not more than $20,000.00, or both; or

(2) for a second or subsequent offense, be imprisoned not more than two years or fined not more than $50,000.00, or both. (Added 2015, No. 106 (Adj. Sess.), § 1.)

§§ 3607, 3608. Repealed. 1971, No. 222 (Adj. Sess.), § 7, eff. April 5, 1972.

§ 3609. Transportation of trees; evidence

A person found transporting upon a public highway one or more pine, spruce, hemlock, cedar, or other evergreen trees, under such condition or circumstances as to reasonably justify any police officer or a person from whom trees of such type have been stolen, or his or her employees, to believe that such trees have been stolen or taken without the consent of the owner, such police officer, person, or his or her employees, or any of them, may stop the person transporting such trees and interrogate such person as to where and from whom he or she obtained such trees and ask such person to produce a bill of sale or a writing showing his or her rightful possession of such trees. If the person interrogated fails to produce a bill of sale or writing showing his or her rightful possession of such trees or refuses to answer such interrogations, or if his or her answers to such interrogations are false, it shall be prima facie evidence that such person has stolen such trees and upon conviction for such an offense he or she shall be imprisoned for not more than six months or fined not more than $300.00, or both. (Amended 1959, No. 199.)

§§ 3610-3612. Repealed. 1971, No. 222 (Adj. Sess.), § 7, eff. April 5, 1972.

§§ 3613, 3614. Repealed. 1971, No. 159 (Adj. Sess.), § 4, eff. March 9, 1972.

Chapter 79: Protection Of Endangered Species

§§ 3651-3653. Repealed. 1981, No. 188 (Adj. Sess.), § 5, eff. date, see note set out below.

Chapter 81: Trespass And Malicious Injuries To Property

Subchapter 1: Injuries To Buildings And Their Appurtenances

§ 3701. Unlawful mischief

(a) A person who, with intent to damage property, and having no right to do so or any reasonable ground to believe that he or she has such a right, does any damage to any property which is valued in an amount exceeding $1,000.00 shall be imprisoned for not more than five years or fined not more than $5,000.00, or both.

(b) A person who, with intent to damage property, and having no right to do so or any reasonable ground to believe that he or she has such a right, does any damage to any property which is valued in an amount exceeding $250.00 shall be imprisoned for not more than one year or fined not more than $1,000.00, or both.

(c) A person who, having no right to do so or any reasonable ground to believe that he or she has such a right, intentionally does any damage to property of any value not exceeding $250.00 shall be imprisoned for not more than six months or fined not more than $500.00, or both.

(d) A person who, with intent to damage property, and having no right to do so or any reasonable ground to believe that he or she has such a right, does any damage to any property by means of an explosive shall be imprisoned for not more than five years or fined not more than $5,000.00, or both.

(e) For the purposes of this section "property" means real or personal property.

(f) A person who suffers damages as a result of a violation of this section may recover those damages together with reasonable attorney's fees in a civil action under this section. (Amended 1971, No. 222 (Adj. Sess.), § 6, eff. April 5, 1972.)

§§ 3702-3704. Repealed. 1971, No. 222 (Adj. Sess.), § 7, eff. April 5, 1972.

§ 3705. Unlawful trespass

(a)(1) A person shall be imprisoned for not more than three months or fined not more than $500.00, or both, if, without legal authority or the consent of the person in lawful possession, he or she enters or remains on any land or in any place as to which notice against trespass is given by:

(A) actual communication by the person in lawful possession or his or her agent or by a law enforcement officer acting on behalf of such person or his or her agent;

(B) signs or placards so designed and situated as to give reasonable notice; or

(C) in the case of abandoned property:

(i) signs or placards, posted by the owner, the owner's agent, or a law enforcement officer, and so designed and situated as to give reasonable notice; or

(ii) actual communication by a law enforcement officer.

(2) As used in this subsection, "abandoned property" means:

(A) real property on which there is a vacant structure that for the previous 60 days has been continuously unoccupied by a person with the legal right to occupy it and with respect to which the municipality has by first-class mail to the owner's last known address provided the owner with notice and an opportunity to be heard; and

(i) property taxes have been delinquent for six months or more; or

(ii) one or more utility services have been disconnected; or

(B) a railroad car that for the previous 60 days has been unmoved and unoccupied by a person with the legal right to occupy it.

(b) Prosecutions for offenses under subsection (a) of this section shall be commenced within 60 days following the commission of the offense and not thereafter.

(c) A person who enters a building other than a residence, whose access is normally locked, whether or not the access is actually locked, or a residence in violation of an order of any court of competent jurisdiction in this State shall be imprisoned for not more than one year or fined not more than $500.00, or both.

(d) A person who enters a dwelling house, whether or not a person is actually present, knowing that he or she is not licensed or privileged to do so shall be imprisoned for not more than three years or fined not more than $2,000.00, or both.

(e) A law enforcement officer shall not be prosecuted under subsection (a) of this section if he or she is authorized to serve civil or criminal process, including citations, summons, subpoenas, warrants, and other court orders, and the scope of his or her entrance onto the land or place of another is no more than necessary to effectuate the service of process. (Added 1969, No. 156 (Adj. Sess.); amended 1971, No. 229 (Adj. Sess.), § 1; 1973, No. 109, § 7; 1979, No. 153 (Adj. Sess.), § 2; 1981, No. 223 (Adj. Sess.), §§ 17, 23; 2013, No. 49, § 3; 2013, No. 75, § 21.)

Subchapter 2: Injuries To Other Property

§§ 3721-3728. Repealed. 1971, No. 222 (Adj. Sess.), § 7, eff. April 5, 1972.

§ 3729. Fire protection apparatus

A person who without lawful authority tampers or interferes with a main, hydrant, gate, or other fire protection apparatus of a municipal water system or with the fire protection apparatus of a private water system used for municipal purposes shall be fined not more than $1,000.00 or imprisoned not more than 10 years, or both. (Amended 1971, No. 199 (Adj. Sess.), § 15.)

§§ 3730, 3731. Repealed. 1971, No. 222 (Adj. Sess.), § 7, eff. April 5, 1972.

§ 3732. Unauthorized removal of books from library

A person who removes from a free public library, or a free town, village, or traveling library, a book, paper, magazine, document, or other reading matter, or an art book, picture, print, plate, or other art work, kept in such library for public use or circulation, without the consent of the librarian or other person in charge of such library, shall be fined not more than $50.00 for each offense, half to the use of the library from which the same was so removed, and the other half to the use of the treasury liable for the costs of prosecution.

§ 3733. Mills, dams or bridges

A person who willfully and maliciously injures, removes, or opens a dam, reservoir, gate, or flume or injures or removes the wheels, mill gear, or machinery of a water mill, or injures, removes, or destroys a public or toll bridge, shall be imprisoned not more than five years or fined not more than $500.00, or both. (Amended 1971, No. 199 (Adj. Sess.), § 15; 1981, No. 223 (Adj. Sess.), § 23.)

§§ 3734-3737. Repealed. 1971, No. 222 (Adj. Sess.), § 7, eff. April 5, 1972.

§ 3738. Obstruction and use of private roads and lands by motor vehicle

A person who, by use of a motor vehicle as defined in 23 V.S.A. § 4:

(1) obstructs a private driveway, barway, or gateway; or

(2) travels over a private road that is so marked, or travels over other private lands; or

(3) enters on private lands for the purpose of camping; without the permission of the owner or occupant shall be fined not more than $500.00. (Added 1967, No. 173; amended 1971, No. 95, § 1, eff. April 22, 1971.)

§ 3739. Operation of vehicles on state owned land

(a) A person who operates a motor vehicle, as defined in 23 V.S.A. § 4, on any land that is owned or held by the State:

(1) except in places or on trails specifically designated and marked by the Secretary of Natural Resources; or

(2) contrary to any rule governing the use of the place or trail shall be fined not more than $500.00. For the purposes of this section "land owned or held by the State" does not include a highway as defined in 23 V.S.A. § 4.

(b) The Secretary of Natural Resources may by rule designate a place or trail for use by motor vehicles when it finds that natural, fish and wildlife, and other recreational activities or aesthetic values will not be substantially adversely affected. The Secretary may by rule specify under which weather and trail conditions or at which times or hours of the day designated trails or places may not be used. (Added 1971, No. 95, § 2, eff. April 22, 1971; amended 1987, No. 76, § 18.)

§ 3740. Damage to State land

A person who operates a motor vehicle, as defined in 23 V.S.A. § 4, on any land, that is owned or held by the State, in such a manner as to purposely and maliciously cause injury, damage, erosion or waste to the land shall be fined not more than $500.00. For the purposes of this section "land" does not include a highway as defined in 23 V.S.A. § 4. (Added 1971, No. 95, § 3, eff. April 22, 1971.)

Subchapter 3: Dead Bodies, Cemeteries, And Monuments

§ 3761. Unauthorized removal of human remains

A person who, not being authorized by law, intentionally excavates, disinters, removes, or carries away a human body, or the remains thereof, interred or entombed in this State or intentionally excavates, disinters, removes, or carries away an object interred or entombed with a human body in this State, or knowingly aids in such excavation, disinterment, removal, or carrying away, or is accessory thereto, shall be imprisoned not more than 15 years or fined not more than $10,000.00, or both. (Amended 1989, No. 142 (Adj. Sess.), § 1.)

§ 3762. Search for concealed bodies

Upon the complaint and oath of a person made to him or her in writing that the remains of a dead person have been disinterred and removed and that the complainant has reason to believe that the remains of such dead person are secreted in a dwelling house or other building, a district judge shall issue a warrant, directed to any sheriff or constable, commanding him or her to make search in such place for such dead person. The officer serving such process shall not be liable for executing such warrant, whether the body of such dead person is found or not. (Amended 1965, No. 194, § 10, operative February 1, 1967; 1973, No. 249 (Adj. Sess.), § 48, eff. April 9, 1974.)

§ 3763. Exception

Section 3762 of this title shall not prevent a surgeon or physician from having in his or her possession a dead human subject for anatomical investigation and instruction of students, if such subject was obtained without violating the law of the State.

§ 3764. Cemeteries and monuments- Grave markers and historical tablets

A person shall not intentionally and without right or authority excavate, steal, remove, injure, or destroy, or procure or cause to be excavated, stolen, removed, injured, or destroyed, a gravestone or monument erected to the memory of a deceased person, or erected and intended for such use, or a grave, tomb, or burial site, or portion thereof, in which the body or remains of a deceased person is interred, or that is intended for the interment of a deceased person, or a monument, tablet, or marker erected for the commemoration of some historical event or place by a historical or patriotic association or society on land on which such association or society has a right to erect the same. (Amended 1989, No. 142 (Adj. Sess.), § 2.)

§ 3765. Repealed. 2001, No. 99 (Adj. Sess.), § 3.

§ 3766. Grave markers and ornaments

(a) A person shall not steal, or cause to be stolen, or intentionally and without lawful authority remove, break down, injure, or destroy, or cause to be removed, broken down, injured, or destroyed, an ornament, token, flag holder, or emblem used to decorate, mark, or distinguish the grave or tomb of a deceased person.

(b) A person shall not buy, sell, or barter, or cause to be bought, sold, or bartered, an ornament, token, flag holder, or emblem that has been used to decorate, mark, or distinguish the grave or tomb of a deceased person. In a prosecution under this subsection, it shall be an affirmative defense, to be proven by a preponderance of the evidence, that the person did not gain possession of the ornament, token, flag holder, or emblem by unlawful means.

(c) A person shall not steal or cause to be stolen, or intentionally and without lawful authority remove, break down, injure, or destroy, or cause to be removed, broken down, injured, or destroyed, flowers, trees, or any other plant matter used to decorate, mark, or distinguish any cemetery property, including the grave or tomb of a deceased person. (Amended 1989, No. 142 (Adj. Sess.), § 4; 2001, No. 99 (Adj. Sess.), § 1, eff. May 8, 2002.)

§ 3767. Penalties

(a) A person who violates a provision of sections 3764-3766 of this title shall, except as provided in subsection (b) of this section, be imprisoned not more than five years or fined not more than $5,000.00, or both.

(b) A person who violates subsection 3766(c) of this title shall be imprisoned not more than one year or fined not more than $500.00, or both. (Amended 1971, No. 199 (Adj. Sess.), § 15; 1981, No. 223 (Adj. Sess.), § 23; 1989, No. 142 (Adj. Sess.), § 5; 2001, No. 99 (Adj. Sess.), § 2, eff. May 8, 2002.)

§ 3768. Repealed. 1973, No. 249 (Adj. Sess.), § 111, eff. April 9, 1974.

§ 3769. Civil action

A person who violates a provision of sections 3764-3766 of this title, shall be further liable in a civil action on this statute, in which the plaintiff may recover damages and reasonable attorney's fees. Such action may be brought in the name of the owner of the property so injured, or in the name of the town in which such burial ground is situated, or in the name of the commissioners, or in the name of the association or corporation that holds lawful possession of such burial ground at the time such damage is committed, or, if the property injured is a gravestone or monument erected to the memory of a deceased person or a grave, tomb, or burial site in which the body or remains of a deceased person is interred, in the name of the surviving heirs or descendants of such deceased person, jointly, or in the name of one or more of them for the benefit of all, or in the name of the historical or patriotic association or society erecting such monument, tablet, or marker. (Amended 1989, No. 142 (Adj. Sess.), § 6.)

§ 3770. Use of damages recovered

Such damages, when recovered by a town, association, society, corporation, or by commissioners, shall be expended under the direction of the party recovering the same for the benefit of the property injured.

§ 3771. Disturbing a funeral service

(a) As used in this section:

(1) "Funeral service" means the ceremonies, rituals, and memorial services held at a church, mortuary, cemetery, or home in connection with the burial or cremation of a dead person.

(2) "Picketing" means a protest, demonstration, or other similar activity directed at a funeral service.

(b) No person shall disturb or attempt to disturb a funeral service by engaging in picketing within 100 feet of the service within one hour prior to and two hours following the publicly announced time of the commencement of the service.

(c) A person who violates this section shall be imprisoned not more than 30 days or fined not more than $500.00, or both. (Added 2005, No. 167 (Adj. Sess.), § 19, eff. May 20, 2006.)

Subchapter 4: Public Utilities

§ 3781. Tapping gas pipes with intent to defraud

A person who taps gas pipes with intent to take gas therefrom, or who connects pipes with such gas pipes so that gas may be used without passing through the meters for measurement, or who knowingly burns gas without measurement by gas meters, without the consent of the owner, shall be imprisoned not more than one year or fined not more than $100.00, or both. The owner of the gas may recover of the person so unlawfully tapping or connecting such pipes or using gas, the actual damages, with costs, in a civil action on this statute.

§ 3782. Tapping electric lines; injuries to electric plants

A person who willfully commits or causes to be committed an act with intent to injure a machine, apparatus, or structure appertaining to the works of a person, firm, association, or corporation engaged in manufacturing, selling, or distributing electrical energy in this State, or whereby such works may be stopped, obstructed, or injured, or who taps an electrical line of a person, firm, association, or corporation so that electricity can be taken therefrom, or knowingly uses electricity taken from such line without the consent of such person, firm, association, or corporation, shall be imprisoned not more than two years or fined not more than $300.00, or both. Such person shall also be liable to such person, firm, association, or corporation or to anyone injured for actual damages, with full costs, in a civil action on this statute.

§ 3783. Repealed. 1973, No. 249 (Adj. Sess.), § 111, eff. April 9, 1974.

§ 3784. Interfering with meters

A person, other than an authorized agent or employee acting for the owner, manufacturer, or operator thereof, who maliciously opens, closes, breaks into, or in any manner adjusts or interferes with a meter, or other regulating or measuring device or appliance attached to or connected with wires, pipe lines, mains, service pipes, or house pipes owned or used by a manufacturer or furnisher of electricity, gas, or water shall be imprisoned not more than three months or fined not more than $100.00, or both.

§ 3785. Injuring lights in streets and public buildings

A person who willfully and maliciously breaks the glass about a street lamp or gaslight, or a lamp or gaslight in the grounds about a public building, or, without authority, lights such a lamp or gaslight or extinguishes the same when lighted, or in any manner interferes therewith, or injures any part of the fixtures supporting such lamp or gaslight, or defaces the same by painting or posting notices thereon, or fastens a horse or animal thereto, shall be imprisoned not more than three months or fined not more than $50.00, or both. (Amended 1981, No. 228 (Adj. Sess.), § 23.)

§ 3786. Tapping cable television systems; damage to equipment

A person who willfully or maliciously damages, or causes to be damaged, any wire, cable, conduit, apparatus, or equipment of a company operating a cable television system, as defined in 30 V.S.A. § 501, or who commits any act with intent to cause damage to any wire, cable, conduit, apparatus, or equipment of a company operating such a system, or who taps, tampers with, or connects any wire or device to the equipment of the cable television company that would degrade the service rendered without authorization of the company may be fined not more than $100.00 and shall be liable in a civil action for three times the actual amount of damages sustained thereby. (Added 1971, No. 202 (Adj. Sess.), § 1, eff. May 1, 1972.)

Subchapter 5: Emergencies On Party Telephone Lines

§ 3801. Definitions

As used in this section:

(1) "Party line" means a subscribers' line telephone circuit, consisting of two or more main telephone stations connected therewith, each station with a distinctive ring or telephone number.

(2) "Emergency" means a situation in which property or human life is in jeopardy and the prompt summoning of aid is essential.

§ 3802. Refusal to surrender line in an emergency

A person shall not willfully refuse to surrender the use of a party line to another person for the purpose of permitting such other person to report a fire or summon police, medical or other aid in case of emergency.

§ 3803. Declaring emergency falsely

A person shall not request the use of a party line on pretext that an emergency exists, knowing that an emergency does not exist.

§ 3804. Notice in telephone directories

Every telephone directory hereafter distributed to the members of the general public shall contain a copy of this subchapter, printed in type which is no smaller than eight-point type and is headed by the word "warning" in larger and bold-faced type. The provisions of this section do not apply to directories published solely for business purposes, commonly known as classified directories.

§ 3805. Penalties

A person who violates this subchapter shall be fined not more than $300.00 or imprisoned for not more than one month, or both.

Subchapter 6: Miscellaneous Provisions

§ 3831. Cutting ice and not fencing hole

A person who takes ice from water over which people are accustomed to pass and does not place around the opening thereby made in the ice suitable guards to prevent a person, team, or vehicle from falling into such hole or opening shall be fined not more than $50.00.

§ 3832. Repealed. 1979, No. 152 (Adj. Sess.).

§ 3833. Unlawful taking of tangible personal property; penalty

A person who, without the consent of the owner, takes and carries away or causes to be taken and carried away any tangible personal property with the intent of depriving the owner temporarily of the lawful possession of his or her property shall be fined not more than $100.00. This section shall not be construed to limit or restrict prosecutions for larceny or theft. (Added 1977, No. 227 (Adj. Sess.), § 2, eff. April 17, 1978.)

§ 3834. Removal of surveying monuments

A person who knowingly removes or alters monuments marking the boundary of lands or knowingly defaces, alters, or removes marks upon any tree, post, or stake that is a monument designating a point, course, or line in the boundary of a parcel of land shall be fined $100.00 and shall be civilly liable for the replacement cost and any consequential damages. However, land surveyors in their professional practice may perpetuate such monumentation by adding additional marks, or by remonumenting nonsubstantial monuments or by the placing of new monuments to preserve monuments to be destroyed or made inaccessible. (Added 1985, No. 116 (Adj. Sess.), § 1.)

Chapter 83: Vagrants

§§ 3901, 3902. Repealed. 2017, No. 105 (Adj. Sess.), § 2.

§ 3903. Repealed. 1973, No. 249 (Adj. Sess.), § 111, eff. April 9, 1974.

§§ 3904-3906. Repealed. 2017, No. 105 (Adj. Sess.), § 2.

Chapter 85: Weapons

Subchapter 1: Generally

§ 4001. Slung shot, blackjack, brass knuckles- Use or possession

A person who uses a slung shot, blackjack, brass knuckles or similar weapon against another person, or attempts so to do, or who possesses a slung shot, blackjack, brass knuckles, or similar weapon, with intent so to use it, shall be imprisoned not more than five years or fined not more than $1,000.00, or both. The provisions of this section do not apply to a law enforcement officer as to the possession and use of a blackjack, billy club, or night stick.

§ 4002. Manufacture, sale, etc.

A person within the State who manufactures or causes to be manufactured, or sells or gives away or parts with, or offers so to do, or keeps for sale or gift, a slung shot, blackjack, brass knuckles, or similar weapon, shall be imprisoned not more than two years or fined not more than $500.00, or both. This section shall not apply to the manufacture of a blackjack, billy club, or nightstick for a law enforcement officer or the sale or gift thereto. (Amended 1981, No. 223 (Adj. Sess.), § 23.)

§ 4003. Carrying dangerous weapons

A person who carries a dangerous or deadly weapon with the intent to injure another shall be imprisoned for not more than two years or fined not more than $2,000.00, or both. It shall be a felony punishable by not more than 10 years of imprisonment or a fine of $25,000.00, or both, if the person intends to injure multiple persons. (Amended 2017, No. 135 (Adj. Sess.), § 1, eff. May 21, 2018.)

§ 4004. Possession of dangerous or deadly weapon in a school bus or school building or on school property

(a) No person shall knowingly possess a firearm or a dangerous or deadly weapon while within a school building or on a school bus. A person who violates this section shall, for the first offense, be imprisoned for not more than one year or fined not more than $1,000.00, or both, and for a second or subsequent offense shall be imprisoned for not more than three years or fined not more than $5,000.00, or both.

(b) No person shall knowingly possess a firearm or a dangerous or deadly weapon on any school property with the intent to injure another person. A person who violates this section shall, for the first offense, be imprisoned for not more than three years or fined not more than $1,000.00, or both, and for a second or subsequent offense shall be imprisoned for not more than five years or fined not more than $5,000.00, or both.

(c) This section shall not apply to:

(1) A law enforcement officer while engaged in law enforcement duties.

(2) Possession and use of firearms or dangerous or deadly weapons if the board of school directors, or the superintendent or principal if delegated authority to do so by the board, authorizes possession or use for specific occasions or for instructional or other specific purposes.

(d) As used in this section:

(1) "School property" means any property owned by a school, including motor vehicles.

(2) "Owned by the school" means owned, leased, controlled, or subcontracted by the school.

(3) "Dangerous or deadly weapon" shall have the same meaning as in section 4016 of this title.

(4) "Firearm" shall have the same meaning as in section 4016 of this title.

(5) "Law enforcement officer" shall have the same meaning as in section 4016 of this title.

(e) The provisions of this section shall not limit or restrict any prosecution for any other offense, including simple assault or aggravated assault. (Amended 1989, No. 143 (Adj. Sess.), § 1; 1999, No. 113 (Adj. Sess.), § 11; 2017, No. 135 (Adj. Sess.), § 3, eff. May 21, 2018.)

§ 4005. While committing a crime

Except as otherwise provided in 18 V.S.A. § 4253, a person who carries a dangerous or deadly weapon, openly or concealed, while committing a felony shall be imprisoned not more than five years or fined not more than $500.00, or both. (Amended 1967, No. 296 (Adj. Sess.), § 1, eff. March 20, 1968; 2011, No. 121 (Adj. Sess.), § 4, eff. May 9, 2012.)

§ 4006. Record of firearm sales

All pawnbrokers and retail merchants dealing in firearms shall keep a record book in which they shall record the sale by them of all revolvers and pistols, and the purchase by them of all secondhand revolvers and pistols. Such record shall include the date of the transaction, the marks of identification of the firearm, including the manufacturer's name, the caliber, model, and manufacturer's number of the firearm, the name, address, birthplace, occupation, age, height, weight, and color of eyes and hair of the purchaser or seller. Such purchaser or seller shall sign his or her name to the record and the pawnbroker or merchant shall preserve such record book for six years after the date of last entry and shall permit all enforcement officers to inspect the same at all reasonable times. A person, partnership or corporation who violates a provision of this section shall be fined not more than $100.00.

§ 4007. Furnishing firearms to children

A person, firm, or corporation, other than a parent or guardian, who sells or furnishes to a minor under the age of 16 years a firearm or other dangerous weapon or ammunition for firearms shall be fined not more than $50.00 nor less than $10.00. This section shall not apply to an instructor or teacher who furnishes firearms to pupils for instruction and drill.

§ 4008. Possession of firearms by children

A child under the age of 16 years shall not, without the consent of his or her parents or guardian, have in his or her possession or control a pistol or revolver constructed or designed for the use of gunpowder or other explosive substance with leaden ball or shot. A child who violates a provision of this section shall be deemed a delinquent child under the provisions of 33 V.S.A. chapter 52.

§ 4009. Negligent use of gun

A person who carelessly or negligently wounds another person by gunshot shall be imprisoned not more than five years or fined not more than $1,000.00, or both. (Amended 1971, No. 199 (Adj. Sess.), § 15.)

§ 4010. Gun suppressors

(a) As used in this section:

(1) "Gun suppressor" means any device for silencing, muffling, or diminishing the report of a portable firearm, including any combination of parts, designed or redesigned, and intended for use in assembling or fabricating a gun suppressor, and any part intended only for use in such assembly or fabrication.

(2) "Sport shooting range" shall have the same meaning as used in 10 V.S.A. § 5227(a).

(b) A person shall not manufacture, make, or import a gun suppressor, except for:

(1) a licensed manufacturer, as defined in 18 U.S.C. § 921, who is registered as a manufacturer pursuant to 26 U.S.C. § 5802;

(2) a licensed importer, as defined in 18 U.S.C. § 921, who is registered as an importer pursuant to 26 U.S.C. § 5802; or

(3) a person who makes a gun suppressor in compliance with the requirements of 26 U.S.C. § 5822.

(c) A person shall not use a gun suppressor in the State, except for use by:

(1) a Level III certified law enforcement officer or Department of Fish and Wildlife employee in connection with his or her duties and responsibilities and in accordance with the policies and procedures of that officer's or employee's agency or department;

(2) the Vermont National Guard in connection with its duties and responsibilities;

(3) a licensed manufacturer or a licensed importer, as defined in 18 U.S.C. § 921, who is also registered as a manufacturer or an importer pursuant to 26 U.S.C. § 5802, who in the ordinary course of his or her business as a manufacturer or as an importer tests the operation of the gun suppressor; or

(4) a person lawfully using a sport shooting range.

(d)(1) A person who violates subsection (b) of this section shall be fined not less than $500.00 for each offense.

(2) A person who violates subsection (c) of this section shall be fined $50.00 for each offense. (Amended 2009, No. 154 (Adj. Sess.), § 238f, eff. June 3, 2010; 2013, No. 141 (Adj. Sess.), § 17, eff. July 1, 2015; 2015, No. 61, § 15, eff. July 2, 2015.)

§ 4011. Aiming gun at another

Any person who shall intentionally point or aim any gun, pistol, or other firearm at or towards another, except in self-defense or in the lawful discharge of official duty, shall be punished by fine not exceeding $50.00. Any person who shall discharge any such firearm so intentionally aimed or pointed shall be punished by imprisonment for not more than one year or fined not more than $100.00, or both.

§ 4012. Reporting treatment of firearm wounds

(a) Every physician attending or treating a case of bullet wound, gunshot wound, powder burn, or any other injury arising from or caused by the discharge of a gun, pistol, or other firearm, or whenever such case is treated in a hospital, sanitarium, or other institution, the manager, superintendent, or other person in charge shall report such case at once to local law enforcement officials or the State police. The provisions of this section shall not apply to such wounds, burns, or injuries received by a member of the armed forces of the United States or State of Vermont while engaged in the actual performance of duty.

(b) A person violating the provisions of this section shall be fined not more than $100.00.

§ 4013. Zip guns; switchblade knives

A person who possesses, sells, or offers for sale a weapon commonly known as a "zip" gun, or a weapon commonly known as a switchblade knife, the blade of which is three inches or more in length, shall be imprisoned not more than 90 days or fined not more than $100.00, or both. (Added 1959, No. 151, eff. May 5, 1959; amended 1981, No. 223 (Adj. Sess.), § 23.)

§ 4014. Purchase of firearms in other states

Residents of the State of Vermont may purchase rifles and shotguns in another state, provided that such residents conform to the applicable provisions of the Gun Control Act of 1968, and regulations thereunder, as administered by the U.S. Bureau of Alcohol, Tobacco, Firearms and Explosives, and provided further that such residents conform to the provisions of law applicable to such purchase in the State of Vermont and in the state in which the purchase is made. (Added 1969, No. 108, § 1, eff. April 19, 1969; amended 2009, No. 54, § 86, eff. June 1, 2009.)

§ 4015. Purchase of firearms by nonresidents

Residents of a state other than the State of Vermont may purchase rifles and shotguns in the State of Vermont, provided that such residents conform to the applicable provisions of the Gun Control Act of 1968, and regulations thereunder, as administered by the U.S. Bureau of Alcohol, Tobacco, Firearms and Explosives, and provided further that such residents conform to the provisions of law applicable to such purchase in the State of Vermont and in the state in which such persons reside. (Added 1969, No. 108, § 2, eff. April 19, 1969; amended 2009, No. 54, § 87, eff. June 1, 2009.)

§ 4016. Weapons in court

(a) As used in this section:

(1) "Courthouse" means a building or any portion of a building designated by the Supreme Court of Vermont as a courthouse.

(2) "Dangerous or deadly weapon" means any firearm, or other weapon, device, instrument, material, or substance, whether animate or inanimate, that in the manner it is used or is intended to be used is known to be capable of producing death or serious bodily injury.

(3) "Firearm" means any weapon, whether loaded or unloaded, that will expel a projectile by the action of an explosive and includes any weapon commonly referred to as a pistol, revolver, rifle, gun, machine gun, or shotgun.

(4) "Law enforcement officer" means a person certified by the Vermont Criminal Justice Council as having satisfactorily completed the approved training programs required to meet the minimum training standards applicable to that person pursuant to 20 V.S.A. § 2358.

(5) "Secured building" means a building with controlled points of public access, metal screening devices at each point of public access, and locked compartments, accessible only to security personnel, for storage of checked firearms.

(b) A person who, while within a courthouse and without authorization from the court,

(1) carries or has in his or her possession a firearm; or

(2) knowingly carries or has in his or her possession a dangerous or deadly weapon, other than a firearm, shall be imprisoned not more than one year or fined not more than $500.00, or both.

(c) Notice of the provisions of subsection (b) of this section shall be posted conspicuously at each public entrance to each courthouse.

(d) No dangerous or deadly weapon shall be allowed in a courthouse that has been certified by the Court Administrator to be a secured building. (Added 1993, No. 45, § 1, eff. June 2, 1993.)

§ 4017. Persons prohibited from possessing firearms; conviction of violent crime

(a) A person shall not possess a firearm if the person has been convicted of a violent crime.

(b) A person who violates this section shall be imprisoned not more than two years or fined not more than $1,000.00, or both.

(c) This section shall not apply to a person who is exempt from federal firearms restrictions under 18 U.S.C. § 925(c).

(d) As used in this section:

(1)(A) "Firearm" means:

(i) any weapon (including a starter gun) that will or is designed to or may readily be converted to expel a projectile by the action of an explosive;

(ii) the frame or receiver of any such weapon; or

(iii) any firearm muffler or firearm silencer.

(B) "Firearm" shall not include an antique firearm.

(2) "Antique firearm" means:

(A) Any firearm (including any firearm with a matchlock, flintlock, percussion cap, or similar type of ignition system) manufactured in or before 1898.

(B) Any replica of any firearm described in subdivision (A) of this subdivision (2) if the replica:

(i) is not designed or redesigned for using rimfire or conventional centerfire fixed ammunition; or

(ii) uses rimfire or conventional centerfire fixed ammunition that is no longer manufactured in the United States and that is not readily available in the ordinary channels of commercial trade.

(C) Any muzzle loading rifle, muzzle loading shotgun, or muzzle loading pistol that is designed to use black powder or a black powder substitute and that cannot use fixed ammunition. As used in this subdivision (C), "antique firearm" shall not include a weapon that incorporates a firearm frame or receiver, a firearm that is converted into a muzzle loading weapon, or any muzzle loading weapon that can be readily converted to fire fixed ammunition by replacing the barrel, bolt, breechblock, or any combination thereof.

(3) "Violent crime" means:

(A)(i) A listed crime as defined in subdivision 5301(7) of this title other than:

(I) lewd or lascivious conduct as defined in section 2601 of this title;

(II) recklessly endangering another person as defined in section 1025 of this title;

(III) operating a vehicle under the influence of alcohol or other substance with either death or serious bodily injury resulting as defined in 23 V.S.A. § 1210(f) and (g);

(IV) careless or negligent operation resulting in serious bodily injury or death as defined in 23 V.S.A. § 1091(b);

(V) leaving the scene of an accident resulting in serious bodily injury or death as defined in 23 V.S.A. § 1128(b) or (c); or

(VI) a misdemeanor violation of chapter 28 of this title, relating to abuse, neglect, and exploitation of vulnerable adults; or

(ii) a comparable offense and sentence in another jurisdiction if the offense prohibits the person from possessing a firearm under 18 U.S.C. § 922(g)(1) or 18 U.S.C. § 921(a)(20).

(B) An offense involving sexual exploitation of children in violation of chapter 64 of this title, or a comparable offense and sentence in another jurisdiction if the offense prohibits the person from possessing a firearm under 18 U.S.C. § 922(g)(1) or 18 U.S.C. § 921(a)(20).

(C) A violation of 18 V.S.A. § 4231(b)(2), (b)(3), or (c)(selling, dispensing, or trafficking cocaine); 4232(b)(2) or (b)(3)(selling or dispensing LSD); 4233(b)(2), (b)(3), or (c)(selling, dispensing, or trafficking heroin); 4234(b)(2) or (b)(3)(selling or dispensing depressants, stimulants, and narcotics); 4234a(b)(2), (b)(3), or (c)(selling, dispensing, or trafficking methamphetamine); 4235(c)(2) or (c)(3)(selling or dispensing hallucinogenic drugs); 4235a(b)(2) or (b)(3)(selling or dispensing Ecstasy), or a comparable offense and sentence in another jurisdiction if the offense prohibits the person from possessing a firearm under 18 U.S.C. § 922(g)(1) or 18 U.S.C. § 921(a)(20).

(D) A conviction of possession with intent to distribute a controlled substance other than cannabis in another jurisdiction if the offense prohibits the person from possessing a firearm under 18 U.S.C. § 922(g)(1) or 18 U.S.C. § 921(a)(20). (Added 2015, No. 14, § 1; amended 2017, No. 83, § 161(3).)

§ 4018. Drones

(a) No person shall equip a drone with a dangerous or deadly weapon or fire a projectile from a drone. A person who violates this section shall be imprisoned not more than one year or fined not more than $1,000.00, or both.

(b) As used in this section:

(1) "Drone" shall have the same meaning as in 20 V.S.A. § 4621.

(2) "Dangerous or deadly weapon" shall have the same meaning as in section 4016 of this title. (Added 2015, No. 169 (Adj. Sess.), § 3, eff. Oct. 1, 2016.)

§ 4019. Firearms transfers; background checks

(a) As used in this section:

(1) "Firearm" shall have the same meaning as in subsection 4017(d) of this title.

(2) "Immediate family member" means a spouse, parent, stepparent, child, stepchild, sibling, stepsibling, grandparent, step-grandparent, grandchild, step-grandchild, great-grandparent, step-great-grandparent, great-grandchild, and step-great-grandchild.

(3) "Law enforcement officer" shall have the same meaning as in subdivision 4016(a)(4) of this title.

(4) "Licensed dealer" means a person issued a license as a dealer in firearms pursuant to 18 U.S.C. § 923(a).

(5) "Proposed transferee" means an unlicensed person to whom a proposed transferor intends to transfer a firearm.

(6) "Proposed transferor" means an unlicensed person who intends to transfer a firearm to another unlicensed person.

(7) "Transfer" means to transfer ownership of a firearm by means of sale, trade, or gift.

(8) "Unlicensed person" means a person who has not been issued a license as a dealer, importer, or manufacturer in firearms pursuant to 18 U.S.C. § 923(a).

(b)(1) Except as provided in subsection (e) of this section, an unlicensed person shall not transfer a firearm to another unlicensed person unless:

(A) the proposed transferor and the proposed transferee physically appear together with the firearm before a licensed dealer and request that the licensed dealer facilitate the transfer; and

(B) the licensed dealer agrees to facilitate the transfer.

(2) A person shall not, in connection with the transfer or attempted transfer of a firearm pursuant to this section, knowingly make a false statement or exhibit a false identification intended to deceive a licensed dealer with respect to any fact material to the transfer.

(c)(1) A licensed dealer who agrees to facilitate a firearm transfer pursuant to this section shall comply with all requirements of State and federal law and shall, unless otherwise expressly provided in this section, conduct the transfer in the same manner as the licensed dealer would if selling the firearm from his or her own inventory, but shall not be considered a vendor.

(2) A licensed dealer shall return the firearm to the proposed transferor and decline to continue facilitating the transfer if the licensed dealer determines that the proposed transferee is prohibited by federal or State law from purchasing or possessing the firearm.

(3) A licensed dealer may charge a reasonable fee to facilitate the transfer of a firearm between a proposed transferor and a proposed transferee pursuant to this section.

(d)(1) An unlicensed person who transfers a firearm to another unlicensed person in violation of subdivision (b)(1) of this section shall be imprisoned not more than one year or fined not more than $500.00, or both.

(2) A person who violates subdivision (b)(2) of this section shall be imprisoned not more than one year or fined not more than $500.00, or both.

(e) This section shall not apply to:

(1) the transfer of a firearm by or to a law enforcement agency;

(2) the transfer of a firearm by or to a law enforcement officer or member of the U.S. Armed Forces acting within the course of his or her official duties;

(3) the transfer of a firearm from one immediate family member to another immediate family member; or

(4) a person who transfers the firearm to another person in order to prevent imminent harm to any person, provided that this subdivision shall only apply while the risk of imminent harm exists.

(f) A licensed dealer who facilitates a firearm transfer pursuant to this section shall be immune from any civil or criminal liability for any actions taken or omissions made when facilitating the transfer in reliance on the provisions of this section. This subsection shall not apply to reckless or intentional misconduct by a licensed dealer. (Added 2017, No. 94 (Adj. Sess.), § 6, eff. April 11, 2018.)

§ 4020. Sale of firearms to persons under 21 years of age prohibited

(a) A person shall not sell a firearm to a person under 21 years of age. A person who violates this subsection shall be imprisoned for not more than one year or fined not more than $1,000.00, or both.

(b) This section shall not apply to:

(1) a law enforcement officer;

(2) an active or veteran member of the Vermont National Guard, of the National Guard of another state, or of the U.S. Armed Forces;

(3) a person who provides the seller with a certificate of satisfactory completion of a Vermont hunter safety course or an equivalent hunter safety course that is approved by the Commissioner; or

(4) a person who provides the seller with a certificate of satisfactory completion of a hunter safety course in another state or a province of Canada that is approved by the Commissioner.

(c) As used in this section:

(1) "Firearm" shall have the same meaning as in subsection 4017(d) of this title.

(2) "Law enforcement officer" shall have the same meaning as in subsection 4016(a) of this title.

(3) "Commissioner" means the Commissioner of Fish and Wildlife. (Added 2017, No. 94 (Adj. Sess.), § 7, eff. April 11, 2018.)

§ 4021. Large capacity ammunition feeding devices

(a) A person shall not manufacture, possess, transfer, offer for sale, purchase, or receive or import into this State a large capacity ammunition feeding device. As used in this subsection, "import" shall not include the transportation back into this State of a large capacity ammunition feeding device by the same person who transported the device out of State if the person possessed the device on or before the effective date of this section.

(b) A person who violates this section shall be imprisoned for not more than one year or fined not more than $500.00, or both.

(c)(1) The prohibition on possession of large capacity ammunition feeding devices established by subsection (a) of this section shall not apply to a large capacity ammunition feeding device lawfully possessed on or before the effective date of this section.

(2) The prohibition on possession, transfer, sale, and purchase of large capacity ammunition feeding devices established by subsection (a) of this section shall not apply to a large capacity ammunition feeding device lawfully possessed by a licensed dealer as defined in subdivision 4019(a)(4) of this title prior to April 11, 2018 and transferred by the dealer on or before October 1, 2018.

(d)(1) This section shall not apply to any large capacity ammunition feeding device:

(A) manufactured for, transferred to, or possessed by the United States or a department or agency of the United States, or by any state or by a department, agency, or political subdivision of a state;

(B) transferred to or possessed by a federal law enforcement officer or a law enforcement officer certified as a law enforcement officer by the Vermont Criminal Justice Council pursuant to 20 V.S.A. § 2358, for legitimate law enforcement purposes, whether the officer is on or off duty;

(C) transferred to a licensee under Title I of the Atomic Energy Act of 1954 for purposes of establishing and maintaining an on-site physical protection system and security organization required by federal law, or possessed by an employee or contractor of such a licensee on-site for these purposes, or off-site for purposes of licensee-authorized training or transportation of nuclear materials;

(D) possessed by an individual who is retired from service with a law enforcement agency after having been transferred to the individual by the agency upon his or her retirement, provided that the individual is not otherwise prohibited from receiving ammunition;

(E) manufactured, imported, transferred, or possessed by a manufacturer or importer licensed under 18 U.S.C. chapter 44:

(i) for the purposes of testing or experimentation authorized by the U.S. Attorney General, or for product development;

(ii) for repair and return to the person from whom it was received; or

(iii) for transfer in foreign or domestic commerce for delivery and possession outside the State of Vermont; or

(F) [Repealed.]

(2) This section shall not apply to a licensed dealer as defined in subdivision 4019(a)(4) of this title for the sole purpose of transferring or selling a large capacity ammunition feeding device to a person to whom this section does not apply under subdivision (1) of this subsection (d).

(e)(1) As used in this section, "large capacity ammunition feeding device" means a magazine, belt, drum, feed strip, or similar device that has a capacity of, or that can be readily restored or converted to accept:

(A) more than 10 rounds of ammunition for a long gun; or

(B) more than 15 rounds of ammunition for a hand gun.

(2) The term "large capacity ammunition feeding device" shall not include:

(A) an attached tubular device designed to accept, and capable of operating only with, .22 caliber rimfire ammunition;

(B) a large capacity ammunition feeding device that is manufactured or sold solely for use by a lever action or bolt action long gun or by an antique firearm as defined in subdivisions 4017(d)(2)(A) and (B) of this title; or

(C) a large capacity ammunition feeding device that is manufactured or sold solely for use with a firearm that is determined to be a curio or relic by the Bureau of Alcohol, Tobacco, Firearms and Explosives. As used in this subdivision, "curio or relic" means a firearm that is of special interest to collectors by reason of some quality other than its association with firearms intended for sporting use or as offensive or defensive weapons. (Added 2017, No. 94 (Adj. Sess.), § 8, eff. April 11, 2018; amended 2017, No. 94 (Adj. Sess.), § 11, eff. July 1, 2019.)

§ 4022. Bump-fire stocks; possession prohibited

(a) As used in this section, "bump-fire stock" means a butt stock designed to be attached to a semiautomatic firearm and intended to increase the rate of fire achievable with the firearm to that of a fully automatic firearm by using the energy from the recoil of the firearm to generate a reciprocating action that facilitates the repeated activation of the trigger.

(b) A person shall not possess a bump-fire stock. A person who violates this subsection shall be imprisoned not more than one year or fined not more than $1,000.00, or both.

(c) The Department of Public Safety shall develop, promote, and execute a collection process that permits persons to voluntarily and anonymously relinquish bump-fire stocks prior to the effective date of this section. (Added 2017, No. 94 (Adj. Sess.), § 9, eff. Oct. 1, 2018.)

Subchapter 2: Extreme Risk Protection Orders

§ 4051. Definitions

As used in this subchapter:

(1) "Court" means the Family Division of the Superior Court.

(2) "Dangerous weapon" means an explosive or a firearm.

(3) "Explosive" means dynamite, or any explosive compound of which nitroglycerin forms a part, or fulminate in bulk or dry condition, or blasting caps, or detonating fuses, or blasting powder or any other similar explosive. The term does not include a firearm or ammunition therefor or any components of ammunition for a firearm, including primers, smokeless powder, or black gunpowder.

(4) "Federally licensed firearms dealer" means a licensed importer, licensed manufacturer, or licensed dealer required to conduct national instant criminal background checks under 18 U.S.C. § 922(t).

(5) "Firearm" shall have the same meaning as in subsection 4017(d) of this title.

(6) "Law enforcement agency" means the Vermont State Police, a municipal police department, or a sheriff's department. (Added 2017, No. 97 (Adj. Sess.), § 1, eff. April 11, 2018.)

§ 4052. Jurisdiction and venue

(a) The Family Division of the Superior Court shall have jurisdiction over proceedings under this subchapter.

(b) Emergency orders under section 4054 of this title may be issued by a judge of the Criminal, Civil, or Family Division of the Superior Court.

(c) Proceedings under this chapter shall be commenced in the county where the law enforcement agency is located, the county where the respondent resides, or the county where the events giving rise to the petition occur. (Added 2017, No. 97 (Adj. Sess.), § 1, eff. April 11, 2018.)

§ 4053. Petition for extreme risk protection order

(a) A State's Attorney or the Office of the Attorney General may file a petition requesting that the court issue an extreme risk protection order prohibiting a person from purchasing, possessing, or receiving a dangerous weapon or having a dangerous weapon within the person's custody or control. The petitioner shall submit an affidavit in support of the petition.

(b) Except as provided in section 4054 of this title, the court shall grant relief only after notice to the respondent and a hearing. The petitioner shall have the burden of proof by clear and convincing evidence.

(c)(1) A petition filed pursuant to this section shall allege that the respondent poses an extreme risk of causing harm to himself or herself or another person by purchasing, possessing, or receiving a dangerous weapon or by having a dangerous weapon within the respondent's custody or control.

(2)(A) An extreme risk of harm to others may be shown by establishing that:

(i) the respondent has inflicted or attempted to inflict bodily harm on another; or

(ii) by his or her threats or actions the respondent has placed others in reasonable fear of physical harm to themselves; or

(iii) by his or her actions or inactions the respondent has presented a danger to persons in his or her care.

(B) An extreme risk of harm to himself or herself may be shown by establishing that the respondent has threatened or attempted suicide or serious bodily harm.

(3) The affidavit in support of the petition shall state:

(A) the specific facts supporting the allegations in the petition;

(B) any dangerous weapons the petitioner believes to be in the respondent's possession, custody, or control; and

(C) whether the petitioner knows of an existing order with respect to the respondent under 15 V.S.A. chapter 21 (abuse prevention orders) or 12 V.S.A. chapter 178 (orders against stalking or sexual assault).

(d) The court shall hold a hearing within 14 days after a petition is filed under this section. Notice of the hearing shall be served pursuant to section 4056 of this title concurrently with the petition and any ex parte order issued under section 4054 of this title.

(e)(1) The court shall grant the petition and issue an extreme risk protection order if it finds by clear and convincing evidence that the respondent poses an extreme risk of causing harm to himself or herself or another person by purchasing, possessing, or receiving a dangerous weapon or by having a dangerous weapon within the respondent's custody or control.

(2) An order issued under this subsection shall prohibit a person from purchasing, possessing, or receiving a dangerous weapon or having a dangerous weapon within the person's custody or control for a period of up to six months. The order shall be signed by the judge and include the following provisions:

(A) A statement of the grounds for issuance of the order.

(B) The name and address of the court where any filings should be made, the names of the parties, the date of the petition, the date and time of the order, and the date and time the order expires.

(C) A description of how to appeal the order.

(D) A description of the requirements for relinquishment of dangerous weapons under section 4059 of this title.

(E) A description of how to request termination of the order under section 4055 of this title. The court shall include with the order a form for a motion to terminate the order.

(F) A statement directing the law enforcement agency, approved federally licensed firearms dealer, or other person in possession of the firearm to release it to the owner upon expiration of the order.

(G) A statement in substantially the following form:

"To the subject of this protection order: This order shall be in effect until the date and time stated above. If you have not done so already, you are required to surrender all dangerous weapons in your custody, control, or possession to [insert name of law enforcement agency], a federally licensed firearms dealer, or a person approved by the court. While this order is in effect, you are not allowed to purchase, possess, or receive a dangerous weapon; attempt to purchase, possess, or receive a dangerous weapon; or have a dangerous weapon in your custody or control. You have the right to request one hearing to terminate this order during the period that this order is in effect, starting from the date of this order. You may seek the advice of an attorney regarding any matter connected with this order."

(f) If the court denies a petition filed under this section, the court shall state the particular reasons for the denial in its decision.

(g) No filing fee shall be required for a petition filed under this section.

(h) Form petitions and form orders shall be provided by the Court Administrator and shall be maintained by the clerks of the courts.

(i) When findings are required under this section, the court shall make either written findings of fact or oral findings of fact on the record.

(j) Every final order issued under this section shall bear the following language: "VIOLATION OF THIS ORDER IS A CRIME SUBJECT TO A TERM OF IMPRISONMENT OR A FINE, OR BOTH, AS PROVIDED BY 13 V.S.A. § 4058, AND MAY ALSO BE PROSECUTED AS CRIMINAL CONTEMPT PUNISHABLE BY FINE OR IMPRISONMENT, OR BOTH."

(k) Affidavit forms required pursuant to this section shall bear the following language: "MAKING A FALSE STATEMENT IN THIS AFFIDAVIT IS A CRIME SUBJECT TO A TERM OF IMPRISONMENT OR A FINE, OR BOTH, AS PROVIDED BY 13 V.S.A. § 4058." (Added 2017, No. 97 (Adj. Sess.), § 1, eff. April 11, 2018.)

§ 4054. Emergency relief; temporary ex parte order

(a)(1) A State's Attorney or the Office of the Attorney General may file a motion requesting that the court issue an extreme risk protection order ex parte, without notice to the respondent. A law enforcement officer may notify the court that an ex parte extreme risk protection order is being requested pursuant to this section, but the court shall not issue the order until after the motion is submitted.

(2) The petitioner shall submit an affidavit in support of the motion alleging that the respondent poses an imminent and extreme risk of causing harm to himself or herself or another person by purchasing, possessing, or receiving a dangerous weapon or by having a dangerous weapon within the respondent's custody or control. The affidavit shall state:

(A) the specific facts supporting the allegations in the motion, including the imminent danger posed by the respondent; and

(B) any dangerous weapons the petitioner believes to be in the respondent's possession, custody, or control.

(b)(1) The court shall grant the motion and issue a temporary ex parte extreme risk protection order if it finds by a preponderance of the evidence that at the time the order is requested the respondent poses an imminent and extreme risk of causing harm to himself or herself or another person by purchasing, possessing, or receiving a dangerous weapon or by having a dangerous weapon within the respondent's custody or control. The petitioner shall cause a copy of the order to be served on the respondent pursuant to section 4056 of this title, and the court shall deliver a copy to the holding station.

(2)(A) An extreme risk of harm to others may be shown by establishing that:

(i) the respondent has inflicted or attempted to inflict bodily harm on another; or

(ii) by his or her threats or actions the respondent has placed others in reasonable fear of physical harm to themselves; or

(iii) by his or her actions or inactions the respondent has presented a danger to persons in his or her care.

(B) An extreme risk of harm to himself or herself may be shown by establishing that the respondent has threatened or attempted suicide or serious bodily harm.

(c)(1) Unless the petition is voluntarily dismissed pursuant to subdivision (2) of this subsection, the court shall hold a hearing within 14 days after the issuance of a temporary ex parte extreme risk protection order to determine if a final extreme risk protection order should be issued. If not voluntarily dismissed, the temporary ex parte extreme risk protection order shall expire when the court grants or denies a motion for an extreme risk protection order under section 4053 of this title.

(2) The prosecutor may voluntarily dismiss a motion filed under this section at any time prior to the hearing if the prosecutor determines that the respondent no longer poses an extreme risk of causing harm to himself or herself or another person by purchasing, possessing, or receiving a dangerous weapon or by having a dangerous weapon within the respondent's custody or control. If the prosecutor voluntarily dismisses the motion pursuant to this subdivision, the court shall vacate the temporary ex parte extreme risk protection order and direct the person in possession of the dangerous weapon to return it to the respondent consistent with section 4059 of this title.

(d)(1) An order issued under this section shall prohibit a person from purchasing, possessing, or receiving a dangerous weapon or having a dangerous weapon within the person's custody or control for a period of up to 14 days. The order shall be in writing and signed by the judge and shall include the following provisions:

(A) A statement of the grounds for issuance of the order.

(B) The name and address of the court where any filings should be made, the names of the parties, the date of the petition, the date and time of the order, and the date and time the order expires.

(C) The date and time of the hearing when the respondent may appear to contest the order before the court. This opportunity to contest shall be scheduled as soon as reasonably possible, which in no event shall be more than 14 days after the date of issuance of the order.

(D) A description of the requirements for relinquishment of dangerous weapons under section 4059 of this title.

(E) A statement in substantially the following form:

"To the subject of this protection order: This order shall be in effect until the date and time stated above. If you have not done so already, you are required to surrender all dangerous weapons in your custody, control, or possession to [insert name of law enforcement agency], a federally licensed firearms dealer, or a person approved by the court. While this order is in effect, you are not allowed to purchase, possess, or receive a dangerous weapon; attempt to purchase, possess, or receive a dangerous weapon; or have a dangerous weapon in your custody or control. A hearing will be held on the date and time noted above to determine if a final extreme risk prevention order should be issued. Failure, to appear at that hearing may result in a court making an order against you that is valid for up to six months. You may seek the advice of an attorney regarding any matter connected with this order."

(2)(A) The court may issue an ex parte extreme risk protection order by telephone or by reliable electronic means pursuant to this subdivision if requested by the petitioner.

(B) Upon receipt of a request for electronic issuance of an ex parte extreme risk protection order, the judicial officer shall inform the petitioner that a signed or unsigned motion and affidavit may be submitted electronically. The affidavit shall be sworn to or affirmed by administration of the oath over the telephone to the petitioner by the judicial officer. The administration of the oath need not be made part of the affidavit or recorded, but the judicial officer shall note on the affidavit that the oath was administered.

(C) The judicial officer shall decide whether to grant or deny the motion and issue the order solely on the basis of the contents of the motion and the affidavit or affidavits provided. If the motion is granted, the judicial officer shall immediately sign the original order, enter on its face the exact date and time it is issued, and transmit a copy to the petitioner by reliable electronic means. The petitioner shall cause a copy of the order to be served on the respondent pursuant to section 4056 of this title.

(D) On or before the next business day after the order is issued:

(i) the petitioner shall file the original motion and affidavit with the court; and

(ii) the judicial officer shall file the signed order, the motion, and the affidavit with the clerk. The clerk shall enter the documents on the docket immediately after filing.

(e) Form motions and form orders shall be provided by the Court Administrator and shall be maintained by the clerks of the courts.

(f) Every order issued under this section shall bear the following language: "VIOLATION OF THIS ORDER IS A CRIME SUBJECT TO A TERM OF IMPRISONMENT OR A FINE, OR BOTH, AS PROVIDED BY 13 V.S.A. §

4058, AND MAY ALSO BE PROSECUTED AS CRIMINAL CONTEMPT PUNISHABLE BY FINE OR IMPRISONMENT, OR BOTH."

(g) Affidavit forms required pursuant to this section shall bear the following language: "MAKING A FALSE STATEMENT IN THIS AFFIDAVIT IS A CRIME SUBJECT TO A TERM OF IMPRISONMENT OR A FINE, OR BOTH, AS PROVIDED BY 13 V.S.A. § 4058."

(h) If the court denies a petition filed under this section, the court shall state the particular reasons for the denial in its decision. (Added 2017, No. 97 (Adj. Sess.), § 1, eff. April 11, 2018.)

§ 4055. Termination and renewal motions

(a)(1) The respondent may file a motion to terminate an extreme risk protection order issued under section 4053 of this title or an order renewed under subsection (b) of this section. A motion to terminate shall not be filed more than once during the effective period of the order. The State shall have the burden of proof by clear and convincing evidence.

(2) The court shall grant the motion and terminate the extreme risk protection order unless it finds by clear and convincing evidence that the respondent continues to pose an extreme risk of causing harm to himself or herself or another person by purchasing, possessing, or receiving a dangerous weapon or by having a dangerous weapon within the respondent's custody or control.

(b)(1) A State's Attorney or the Office of the Attorney General may file a motion requesting that the court renew an extreme risk protection order issued under this section or section 4053 of this title for an additional period of up to six months. The motion shall be accompanied by an affidavit and shall be filed not more than 30 days and not less than 14 days before the expiration date of the order. The motion and affidavit shall comply with the requirements of subsection 4053(c) of this title, and the moving party shall have the burden of proof by clear and convincing evidence.

(2) The court shall grant the motion and renew the extreme risk protection order for an additional period of up to six months if it finds by clear and convincing evidence that the respondent continues to pose an extreme risk of causing harm to himself or herself or another person by purchasing, possessing, or receiving a dangerous weapon or by having a dangerous weapon within the respondent's custody or control. The order shall comply with the requirements of subdivision 4053(e)(2) and subsections 4053(j) and (k) of this title.

(c) The court shall hold a hearing within 14 days after a motion to terminate or a motion to renew is filed under this section. Notice of the hearing shall be served pursuant to section 4056 of this title concurrently with the motion.

(d) If the court denies a motion filed under this section, the court shall state the particular reasons for the denial in its decision.

(e) Form termination and form renewal motions shall be provided by the Court Administrator and shall be maintained by the clerks of the courts.

(f) When findings are required under this section, the court shall make either written findings of fact or oral findings of fact on the record. (Added 2017, No. 97 (Adj. Sess.), § 1, eff. April 11, 2018.)

§ 4056. Service

(a) A petition, ex parte temporary order, or final order issued under this subchapter shall be served in accordance with the Vermont Rules of Civil Procedure and may be served by any law enforcement officer. A court that issues an order under this chapter during court hours shall promptly transmit the order electronically or by other means to a law enforcement agency for service, and shall deliver a copy to the holding station.

(b) A respondent who attends a hearing held under section 4053, 4054, or 4055 of this title at which a temporary or final order under this subchapter is issued and who receives notice from the court on the record that the order has been issued shall be deemed to have been served. A respondent notified by the court on the record shall be required to adhere immediately to the provisions of the order. However, even when the court has previously notified the respondent of the order, the court shall transmit the order for additional service by a law enforcement agency.

(c) Extreme risk protection orders shall be served by the law enforcement agency at the earliest possible time and shall take precedence over other summonses and orders. Orders shall be served in a manner calculated to ensure the safety of the parties. Methods of service that include advance notification to the respondent shall not be used. The person making service shall file a return of service with the court stating the date, time, and place at which the order was delivered personally to the respondent.

(d) If service of a notice of hearing issued under section 4053 or 4055 of this title cannot be made before the scheduled hearing, the court shall continue the hearing and extend the terms of the order upon request of the petitioner for such additional time as it deems necessary to achieve service on the respondent. (Added 2017, No. 97 (Adj. Sess.), § 1, eff. April 11, 2018.)

§ 4057. Procedure

(a) Except as otherwise specified, proceedings commenced under this subchapter shall be in accordance with the Vermont Rules for Family Proceedings and shall be in addition to any other available civil or criminal remedies.

(b) The Court Administrator shall establish procedures to ensure access to relief after regular court hours or on weekends and holidays. The Court Administrator is authorized to contract with public or private agencies to assist petitioners to seek relief and to gain access to Superior Courts. Law enforcement agencies shall assist in carrying out the intent of this section.

(c) The Court Administrator shall ensure that the Superior Court has procedures in place so that the contents of orders and pendency of other proceedings can be known to all courts for cases in which an extreme risk protection order proceeding is related to a criminal proceeding. (Added 2017, No. 97 (Adj. Sess.), § 1, eff. April 11, 2018.)

§ 4058. Enforcement; criminal penalties

(a) Law enforcement officers are authorized to enforce orders issued under this chapter. Enforcement may include collecting and disposing of dangerous weapons pursuant to section 4059 of this title and making an arrest in accordance with the provisions of Rule 3 of the Vermont Rules of Criminal Procedure.

(b)(1) A person who intentionally commits an act prohibited by a court or fails to perform an act ordered by a court, in violation of an extreme risk protection order issued pursuant to section 4053, 4054, or 4055 of this title, after the person has been served with notice of the contents of the order as provided for in this subchapter, shall be imprisoned not more than one year or fined not more than $1,000.00, or both.

(2) A person who files a petition for an extreme risk protection order under this subchapter, or who submits an affidavit accompanying the petition, knowing that information in the petition or the affidavit is false, or that the petition or affidavit is submitted with the intent to harass the respondent, shall be imprisoned for not more than one year or fined not more than $1,000.00, or both.

(c) In addition to the provisions of subsections (a) and (b) of this section, violation of an order issued under this subchapter may be prosecuted as criminal contempt under Rule 42 of Vermont Rules of Criminal Procedure. The prosecution for criminal contempt may be initiated by the State's Attorney in the county in which the violation occurred. The maximum penalty that may be imposed under this subsection shall be a fine of $1,000.00 or imprisonment for six months, or both. A sentence of imprisonment upon conviction for criminal contempt may be stayed, in the discretion of the court, pending the expiration of the time allowed for filing notice of appeal or pending appeal if any appeal is taken. (Added 2017, No. 97 (Adj. Sess.), § 1, eff. April 11, 2018.)

§ 4059. Relinquishment, storage, and return of dangerous weapons

(a) A person who is required to relinquish a dangerous weapon other than a firearm in the person's possession, custody, or control by an extreme risk protection order issued under section 4053, 4054, or 4055 of this title shall upon service of the order immediately relinquish the dangerous weapon to a cooperating law enforcement agency. The law enforcement agency shall transfer the weapon to the Bureau of Alcohol, Tobacco, Firearms and Explosives for proper disposition.

(b)(1) A person who is required to relinquish a firearm in the person's possession, custody, or control by an extreme risk protection order issued under section 4053, 4054, or 4055 of this title shall, unless the court orders an alternative relinquishment pursuant to subdivision (2) of this subsection, upon service of the order immediately relinquish the firearm to a cooperating law enforcement agency or an approved federally licensed firearms dealer.

(2)(A) The court may order that the person relinquish a firearm to a person other than a cooperating law enforcement agency or an approved federally licensed firearms dealer unless the court finds that relinquishment to the other person will not adequately protect the safety of any person.

(B) A person to whom a firearm is relinquished pursuant to subdivision (A) of this subdivision (2) shall execute an affidavit on a form approved by the Court Administrator stating that the person:

(i) acknowledges receipt of the firearm;

(ii) assumes responsibility for storage of the firearm until further order of the court and specifies the manner in which he or she will provide secure storage;

(iii) is not prohibited from owning or possessing firearms under State or federal law; and

(iv) understands the obligations and requirements of the court order, including the potential for the person to be subject to civil contempt proceedings pursuant to subdivision (C) of this subdivision (2) if the person permits the firearm to be possessed, accessed, or used by the person who relinquished the item or by any other person not authorized by law to do so.

(C) A person to whom a firearm is relinquished pursuant to subdivision (A) of this subdivision (2) shall be subject to civil contempt proceedings under 12 V.S.A. chapter 5 if the person permits the firearm to be possessed, accessed, or used by the person who relinquished the item or by any other person not authorized by law to do so. In the event that the person required to relinquish the firearm or any other person not authorized by law to possess the relinquished item obtains access to, possession of, or use of a relinquished item, all relinquished items shall be immediately transferred to the possession of a law enforcement agency or approved federally licensed firearms dealer pursuant to subdivision (b)(1) of this section.

(c) A law enforcement agency or an approved federally licensed firearms dealer that takes possession of a firearm pursuant to subdivision (b)(1) of this section shall photograph, catalogue, and store the item in accordance with standards and guidelines established by the Department of Public Safety pursuant to 20 V.S.A. § 2307(i)(3).

(d) Nothing in this section shall be construed to prohibit the lawful sale of firearms or other items.

(e) An extreme risk protection order issued pursuant to section 4053 of this title or renewed pursuant to section 4055 of this title shall direct the law enforcement agency, approved federally licensed firearms dealer, or other person in possession of a firearm under subsection (b) of this section to release it to the owner upon expiration of the order.

(f)(1) A law enforcement agency, an approved federally licensed firearms dealer, or any other person who takes possession of a firearm for storage purposes pursuant to this section shall not release it to the owner without a court order unless the firearm is to be sold pursuant to subdivision (2)(A) of this subsection. If a court orders the release of a firearm stored under this section, the law enforcement agency or firearms dealer in possession of the firearm shall make it available to the owner within three business days after receipt of the order and in a manner consistent with federal law.

(2)(A)(i) If the owner fails to retrieve the firearm within 90 days after the court order releasing it, the firearm may be sold for fair market value. Title to the firearm shall pass to the law enforcement agency or firearms dealer for the purpose of transferring ownership, except that the Vermont State Police shall follow the procedure described in 20 V.S.A. § 2305.

(ii) The law enforcement agency or firearms dealer shall make a reasonable effort to notify the owner of the sale before it occurs. In no event shall the sale occur until after the court issues a final extreme risk protection order pursuant to section 4053 of this title.

(iii) As used in this subdivision (2)(A), "reasonable effort" shall mean notice shall be served as provided for by Rule 4 of the Vermont Rules of Civil Procedure.

(B) Proceeds from the sale of a firearm pursuant to subdivision (A) of this subdivision (2) shall be apportioned as follows:

(i) associated costs, including the costs of sale and of locating and serving the owner, shall be paid to the law enforcement agency or firearms dealer that incurred the cost; and

(ii) any proceeds remaining after payment is made to the law enforcement agency or firearms dealer pursuant to subdivision (i) of this subdivision (2)(B) shall be paid to the original owner.

(g) A law enforcement agency shall be immune from civil or criminal liability for any damage or deterioration of a firearm stored or transported pursuant to this section. This subsection shall not apply if the damage or deterioration occurred as a result of recklessness, gross negligence, or intentional misconduct by the law enforcement agency.

(h) This section shall be implemented consistent with the standards and guidelines established by the Department of Public Safety under 20 V.S.A. § 2307(i).

(i) Notwithstanding any other provision of this chapter:

(1) A dangerous weapon shall not be returned to the respondent if the respondent's possession of the weapon would be prohibited by state or federal law.

(2) A dangerous weapon shall not be taken into possession pursuant to this section if it is being or may be used as evidence in a pending criminal matter. (Added 2017, No. 97 (Adj. Sess.), § 1, eff. April 11, 2018.)

§ 4060. Appeals

An extreme risk protection order issued by the court under section 4053 or 4055 of this title shall be treated as a final order for the purposes of appeal. Appeal may be taken by either party to the Supreme Court under the Vermont Rules of Appellate Procedure, and the appeal shall be determined forthwith. (Added 2017, No. 97 (Adj. Sess.), § 1, eff. April 11, 2018.)

§ 4061. Effect on other laws

This chapter shall not be construed to prevent a court from prohibiting a person from possessing firearms under any other provision of law. (Added 2017, No. 97 (Adj. Sess.), § 1, eff. April 11, 2018.)

Chapter 87: Computer Crimes

§ 4101. Definitions

As used in this chapter:

(1) "Access" means to instruct, communicate with, store data in, enter data in, retrieve data from, or otherwise make use of any resources of a computer, computer system, or computer network.

(2) "Computer" means an electronic device which performs logical, arithmetic, and memory functions by the manipulations of electronic, photonic or magnetic impulses, and includes all input, output, processing, storage, software, or communications facilities which are connected or related to such a device in a system or network, including devices available to the public for limited or designated use or other devices used to access or connect to such a system or network.

(3) "Computer network" means the interconnection of remote user terminals with a computer through communications lines, or a complex consisting of two or more interconnected computers.

(4) "Computer program" means a series of instructions or statements or related data that, in actual or modified form, is capable of causing a computer or a computer system to perform specified functions in a form acceptable to a computer, that permits the functioning of a computer system in a manner designed to provide appropriate products from such computer system.

(5) "Computer software" means a set of computer programs, procedures, and associated documentation concerned with the operation of a computer system.

(6) "Computer system" means a set of connected computer equipment, devices and software.

(7) "Data" means any representation of information, knowledge, facts, concepts, or instructions that are being prepared or have been prepared and are intended to be entered, processed, or stored, are being entered, processed, or stored, or have been entered, processed, or stored in a computer, computer system, or computer network.

(8) "Property" includes electronically produced data, and computer software and programs in either machine or human readable form, and any other tangible or intangible item of value.

(9) "Services" includes computer time, data processing, and storage functions. (Added 1999, No. 35, § 1.)

§ 4102. Unauthorized access

A person who knowingly and intentionally and without lawful authority, accesses any computer, computer system, computer network, computer software, computer program, or data contained in such computer, computer system, computer program, or computer network shall be imprisoned not more than six months or fined not more than $500.00, or both. (Added 1999, No. 35, § 1.)

§ 4103. Access to computer for fraudulent purposes

(a) A person shall not intentionally and without lawful authority access or cause to be accessed any computer, computer system, or computer network for any of the following purposes:

(1) executing any scheme or artifice to defraud;

(2) obtaining money, property, or services by means of false or fraudulent pretenses, representations, or promises; or

(3) in connection with any scheme or artifice to defraud, damaging, destroying, altering, deleting, copying, retrieving, interfering with or denial of access to, or removing any program or data contained therein.

(b) Penalties. A person convicted of the crime of access to computer for fraudulent purposes shall be:

(1) if the value of the matter involved does not exceed $500.00, imprisoned not more than one year or fined not more than $500.00, or both;

(2) if the value of the matter involved does not exceed $500.00, for a second or subsequent offense, imprisoned not more than two years or fined not more than $1,000.00, or both; or

(3) if the value of the matter involved exceeds $500.00, imprisoned not more than 10 years or fined not more than $10,000.00, or both. (Added 1999, No. 35, § 1.)

§ 4104. Alteration, damage, or interference

(a) A person shall not intentionally and without lawful authority, alter, damage, or interfere with the operation of any computer, computer system, computer network, computer software, computer program, or data contained in such computer, computer system, computer program, or computer network.

(b) Penalties. A person convicted of violating this section shall be:

(1) if the damage or loss does not exceed $500.00 for a first offense, imprisoned not more than one year or fined not more than $5,000.00, or both;

(2) if the damage or loss does not exceed $500.00 for a second or subsequent offense, imprisoned not more than two years or fined not more than $10,000.00, or both; or

(3) if the damage or loss exceeds $500.00, imprisoned not more than 10 years or fined not more than $25,000.00, or both. (Added 1999, No. 35, § 1; amended 2013, No. 199 (Adj. Sess.), § 15.)

§ 4105. Theft or destruction

(a)(1) A person shall not intentionally and without claim of right deprive the owner of possession, take, transfer, copy, conceal, or retain possession of, or intentionally and without lawful authority, destroy any computer system, computer network, computer software, computer program, or data contained in such computer, computer system, computer program, or computer network.

(2) Copying a commercially available computer program or computer software is not a crime under this section, provided that the computer program and computer software has a retail value of $500.00 or less and is not copied for resale.

(b) Penalties. A person convicted of violating this section shall be:

(1) if the damage or loss does not exceed $500.00 for a first offense, imprisoned not more than one year or fined not more than $5,000.00, or both;

(2) if the damage or loss does not exceed $500.00 for a second or subsequent offense, imprisoned not more than two years or fined not more than $10,000.00, or both; or

(3) if the damage or loss exceeds $500.00, imprisoned not more than 10 years or fined not more than $25,000.00, or both. (Added 1999, No. 35, § 1; amended 2013, No. 199 (Adj. Sess.), § 15.)

§ 4106. Civil liability

A person damaged as a result of a violation of this chapter may bring a civil action against the violator for damages, costs, and fees, including reasonable attorney's fees, and such other relief as the court deems appropriate. (Added 1999, No. 35, § 1; amended 2013, No. 199 (Adj. Sess.), § 15.)

§ 4107. Venue

For the purposes of venue under this chapter, any violation of this chapter shall be considered to have been committed in the State of Vermont if the State of Vermont is the state from which or to which any use of a computer or computer network was made, whether by wires, electromagnetic waves, microwaves, or any other means of communication. (Added 1999, No. 35, § 1.)

Chapter 151: Limitation Of Prosecutions And Actions

§ 4501. Limitation of prosecutions for certain crimes

(a) Prosecutions for aggravated sexual assault, aggravated sexual assault of a child, sexual assault, sexual exploitation of a minor as defined in subsection 3258(c) of this title, human trafficking, aggravated human trafficking, murder, manslaughter, arson causing death, and kidnapping may be commenced at any time after the commission of the offense.

(b) Prosecutions for lewd and lascivious conduct, sexual abuse of a vulnerable adult under subsection 1379(a) of this title, grand larceny, robbery, burglary, embezzlement, forgery, bribery offenses, false claims, fraud under 33 V.S.A. § 141(d), and felony tax offenses shall be commenced within six years after the commission of the offense, and not after.

(c) Prosecutions for any of the following offenses shall be commenced within 40 years after the commission of the offense, and not after:

(1) lewd and lascivious conduct alleged to have been committed against a child under 18 years of age;

(2) maiming;

(3) lewd or lascivious conduct with a child;

(4) sexual exploitation of children under chapter 64 of this title; and

(5) sexual abuse of a vulnerable adult under subsection 1379(b) of this title.

(d) Prosecutions for arson and first degree aggravated domestic assault shall be commenced within 11 years after the commission of the offense, and not after.

(e) Prosecutions for other felonies and for misdemeanors shall be commenced within three years after the commission of the offense, and not after. (Amended 1981, No. 52, § 1; 1981, No. 223 (Adj. Sess.), § 11; 1985, No. 82, § 4; 1987, No. 48, § 7; 1989, No. 292 (Adj. Sess.), § 1; 1993, No. 163 (Adj. Sess.), § 1; 1995, No. 27, § 1; 2009, No. 58, § 15; 2011, No. 6, § 1, 2011, No. 55, § 4; 2013, No. 62, § 1, eff. June 3, 2013; 2013, No. 170 (Adj. Sess.), § 7, eff. Sept. 1, 2014; 2017, No. 44, § 5; 2019, No. 39, § 1, eff. May 30, 2019.)

§ 4502. Repealed. 1981, No. 223 (Adj. Sess.), § 24.

§ 4503. Proceedings begun after time limitation

(a) If a prosecution for a felony or misdemeanor, other than arson and murder, is commenced after the time limited by section 4501 or 4502 of this title, such proceedings shall be void.

(b) If a defendant knowingly and voluntarily waives the statute of limitations in writing and with the consent of the prosecution, the court shall have jurisdiction over the offense and the proceedings shall be valid. (Amended 2009, No. 99 (Adj. Sess.), § 1.)

§ 4504. Limitation on actions for penalty- Accruing to prosecutor

Actions upon a statute for a penalty or forfeiture given in whole or in part to a person who prosecutes for the same, shall be commenced within one year after the commission of the offense, and not after.

§ 4505. Penalty accruing to State, county, or town

Actions founded upon a statute for a penalty or forfeiture given in whole or in part to the State, county, or town shall be commenced within two years after the commission of the offense, and not after, unless otherwise provided.

§ 4506. Penalty accruing to party aggrieved

Actions upon a statute for a penalty or forfeiture given in whole or in part to the party aggrieved shall be commenced within four years after the commission of the offense, and not after.

§ 4507. Prosecutions limited by other statutes

Sections 4501-4506 of this title shall not apply to an action, complaint, information, or indictment limited by a statute to be commenced within a shorter or longer time than is prescribed in such sections.

§ 4508. When prosecution deemed commenced

For the purpose of determining whether a period of limitation prescribed by law has run, a prosecution for a felony or misdemeanor shall be deemed commenced upon the occurrence of the earliest of the following events:

(1) the arrest of the defendant without warrant;

(2) the issuance to him or her by a law enforcement or prosecuting officer of a citation to appear; or

(3) the presentation of an information or indictment to a judicial officer for the purpose of obtaining a summons or arrest warrant. (Amended 1973, No. 118, § 6, eff. Oct. 1, 1973.)

§§ 4509, 4510. Repealed. 1973, No. 118, § 25, eff. Oct. 1, 1973.

§ 4511. Actions against moneyed corporations for penalty

The provisions of this chapter shall not apply to actions against moneyed corporations or against the directors or stockholders thereof, to recover a penalty or forfeiture imposed or to enforce a liability created by the act of incorporation or other law. Such actions shall be brought by the aggrieved party within six years after the discovery of the facts upon which the penalty or forfeiture attached or by which the liability was created.

Chapter 153: Place Of Trial

Subchapter 1: Venue

§ 4601. General rule

When not otherwise provided, criminal causes shall be tried in the Criminal Division of the Superior Court in the unit where an offense within the jurisdiction of such court is committed. (Amended 1973, No. 118, § 7, eff. Oct. 1, 1973; 1973, No. 193 (Adj. Sess.), § 3, eff. April 9, 1974; 2009, No. 154 (Adj. Sess.), § 101.)

§ 4602. When act in one county or unit causes death in another

A person feloniously wounding or poisoning a person in one unit of the Criminal Division of the Superior Court, whose death results therefrom in another unit, may be tried in the Criminal Division of the Superior Court in either unit, if the offense is within the jurisdiction of such court. (Amended 1973, No.

118, § 8, eff. Oct. 1, 1973; 1973, No. 193 (Adj. Sess.), § 3, eff. April 1, 1974; 2009, No. 154 (Adj. Sess.), § 101a.)

§ 4603. Offense on boundary

If an offense is committed on the boundary of two or more units of the Superior Court, or within 100 rods of such boundary, such offense may be alleged in the information or indictment to have been committed and may be prosecuted in the Criminal Division of the Superior Court in any of such counties or in the Criminal Division of the Superior Court in any of such units, if the offense is within the jurisdiction of such court. (Amended 1973, No. 118, § 9, eff. Oct. 1, 1973; 1973, No. 193 (Adj. Sess.), § 3, eff. April 9, 1974; 2009, No. 154 (Adj. Sess.), § 101b.)

§ 4604. Repealed. 1969, No. 22, § 8.

§ 4605. Repealed. 1973, No. 249 (Adj. Sess.), § 111, eff. April 9, 1974.

Subchapter 2: Change Of Venue

§ 4631. Authority

The Supreme Court may by rule provide for change of venue in criminal prosecutions upon motion, for the prevention of prejudice to the defendant or for the convenience of parties and witnesses and in the interests of justice. The court to which a prosecution is transferred shall thereby have jurisdiction of the cause, and the same proceedings shall be had therein as though the venue had not been changed. (Amended 1969, No. 22, § 1; 1973, No. 118, § 10, eff. Oct. 1, 1973; 1973, No. 193 (Adj. Sess.), § 3, eff. April 9, 1974; 2009, No. 154 (Adj. Sess.), § 102.)

§§ 4632-4634. Repealed. 1973, No. 118, § 25, eff. Oct. 1, 1973.

§ 4635. Order for removal of defendant

When a motion for change of venue has been granted and the defendant is in custody, the judge granting the motion shall issue an order in writing to the officer having the defendant in custody, commanding him or her to deliver the defendant to the keeper of the jail serving the unit in which the further proceedings are ordered to be had. (Amended 1969, No. 22, § 4; 1973, No. 118, § 11, eff. Oct. 1, 1973; 2009, No. 154 (Adj. Sess.), § 103.)

§ 4636. Service and return

The officer having the defendant in custody shall forthwith remove and deliver him or her as directed in the order, leave a copy of the same with his or her return indorsed thereon with the keeper of the jail to which the defendant is committed and return the original order with his or her return indorsed thereon to the clerk of the court in which the defendant was informed against or indicted. (Amended 1969, No. 22, § 5; 1973, No. 118, § 12, eff. Oct. 1, 1973.)

§ 4637. Repealed. 1973, No. 118, § 25, eff. Oct. 1, 1973.

§ 4638. Which State's Attorney to prosecute

The State's Attorney of the county in which the respondent is informed or complained against or indicted shall appear in behalf of the State in the court to which the case is removed, and in proceedings relating thereto he or she shall have the same powers and be subject to the same duties and liabilities as though the trial were had in the county for which he or she is the attorney. (Amended 1969, No. 22, § 7; 2009, No. 154 (Adj. Sess.), § 104.)

Chapter 155: Search Warrants

§ 4701. Issuance of search warrants for code violations

A district judge may issue a warrant to any law enforcement officer or official inspector for searching in the daytime a dwelling house or other premises for violations of local codes or ordinances. (Amended 1969, No. 210 (Adj. Sess.), § 1, eff. March 4, 1970; 1973, No. 118, § 13, eff. Oct. 1, 1973; 1973, No. 249 (Adj. Sess.), § 49, eff. April 9, 1974.)

§ 4702. Affidavit

A search warrant shall not be granted pursuant to section 4701 of this title except upon the oath of a law enforcement officer or official inspector that he or she has reason to suspect and does suspect that the premises are in violation of a local code or ordinance. (Amended 1969, No. 210 (Adj. Sess.), § 2, eff. March 24, 1970; 1973, No. 118, § 14, eff. Oct. 1, 1973.)

§ 4703. Payment of fees

When the State's Attorney of a county in which a search is to be made applies for a search warrant or certifies in writing on the warrant that the search ought to be made, the fees for such warrant and the service thereof shall be paid by the State. (Amended 1973, No. 118, § 15, eff. Oct. 1, 1973; 2017, No. 93 (Adj. Sess.), § 13.)

Chapter 157: Insanity As A Defense

§ 4801. Test of insanity in criminal cases

(a) The test when used as a defense in criminal cases shall be as follows:

(1) A person is not responsible for criminal conduct if at the time of such conduct as a result of mental disease or defect he or she lacks adequate capacity either to appreciate the criminality of his or her conduct or to conform his or her conduct to the requirements of law.

(2) The terms "mental disease or defect" do not include an abnormality manifested only by repeated criminal or otherwise anti-social conduct. The terms "mental disease or defect" shall include congenital and traumatic mental conditions as well as disease.

(b) The defendant shall have the burden of proof in establishing insanity as an affirmative defense by a preponderance of the evidence. (Amended 1983, No. 75.)

§ 4802. M'Naghten test abolished

The M'Naghten test of insanity in criminal cases is hereby abolished.

§§ 4803-4813. Repealed. 1969, No. 20, § 14.

§ 4814. Order for examination

(a) Any court before which a criminal prosecution is pending may order the Department of Mental Health to have the defendant examined by a psychiatrist at any time before, during, or after trial, and before final judgment in any of the following cases:

(1) when the defendant enters a plea of not guilty, or when such a plea is entered in the defendant's behalf, and then gives notice of the defendant's intention to rely upon the defense of insanity at the time of the alleged crime, or to introduce expert testimony relating to a mental disease, defect, or other condition bearing upon the issue of whether he or she had the mental state required for the offense charged;

(2) when the defendant, the State, or an attorney, guardian, or other person acting on behalf of the defendant, raises before such court the issue of whether the defendant is mentally competent to stand trial for the alleged offense;

(3) when the court believes that there is doubt as to the defendant's sanity at the time of the alleged offense; or

(4) when the court believes that there is doubt as to the defendant's mental competency to be tried for the alleged offense.

(b) Such order may be issued by the court on its own motion, or on motion of the State, the defendant, or an attorney, guardian, or other person acting on behalf of the defendant. (Added 1969, No. 20, § 1; amended 1973, No. 118, § 16, eff. Oct. 1, 1973; 1991, No. 231 (Adj. Sess.), § 6; 1995, No. 174 (Adj. Sess.), § 3; 2005, No. 174 (Adj. Sess.), § 19; 2007, No. 15, § 22.)

§ 4815. Place of examination; temporary commitment

(a) It is the purpose of this section to provide a mechanism by which a defendant is examined in the least restrictive environment deemed sufficient to complete the examination and prevent unnecessary pre-trial detention and substantial threat of physical violence to any person, including a defendant.

(b) The order for examination may provide for an examination at any jail or correctional center, or at the State Hospital, or at its successor in interest, or at such other place as the court shall determine, after hearing a recommendation by the Commissioner of Mental Health.

(c) A motion for examination shall be made as soon as practicable after a party or the court has good faith reason to believe that there are grounds for an examination. An attorney making such a motion shall be subject to the potential sanctions of Rule 11 of the Vermont Rules of Civil Procedure.

(d) Upon the making of a motion for examination, the court shall order a mental health screening to be completed by a designated mental health professional while the defendant is still at the court.

(e) If the screening cannot be commenced and completed at the courthouse within two hours from the time of the defendant's appearance before the court, the court may forgo consideration of the screener's recommendations.

(f) The court and parties shall review the recommendation of the designated mental health professional and consider the facts and circumstances surrounding the charge and observations of the defendant in court. If the court finds sufficient facts to order an examination, it may be ordered to be completed in the least restrictive environment deemed sufficient to complete the examination, consistent with subsection (a) of this section.

(g)(1) Inpatient examination at the Vermont State Hospital, or its successor in interest, or a designated hospital. The court shall not order an inpatient examination unless the designated mental health professional determines that the defendant is a person in need of treatment as defined in 18 V.S.A. § 7101(17).

(2) Before ordering the inpatient examination, the court shall determine what terms, if any, shall govern the defendant's release from custody under sections 7553-7554 of this title.

(3) An order for inpatient examination shall provide for placement of the defendant in the custody and care of the Commissioner of Mental Health.

(A) If a Vermont State Hospital psychiatrist, or a psychiatrist of its successor in interest, or a designated hospital psychiatrist determines that the defendant is not in need of inpatient hospitalization prior to admission, the Commissioner shall release the defendant pursuant to the terms governing the defendant's release from the Commissioner's custody as ordered by the court. The Commissioner of Mental Health shall ensure that all individuals who are determined not to be in need of inpatient hospitalization receive appropriate referrals for outpatient mental health services.

(B) If a Vermont State Hospital psychiatrist, or a psychiatrist of its successor in interest, or designated hospital psychiatrist determines that the defendant is in need of inpatient hospitalization:

(i) The Commissioner shall obtain an appropriate inpatient placement for the defendant at the Vermont State Hospital psychiatrist, or a psychiatrist of its successor in interest, or a designated hospital and, based on the defendant's clinical needs, may transfer the defendant between hospitals at any time while the order is in effect. A transfer to a designated hospital outside the no refusal system is subject to acceptance of the patient for admission by that hospital.

(ii) The defendant shall be returned to court for further appearance on the following business day if the defendant is no longer in need of inpatient hospitalization, unless the terms established by the court pursuant to subdivision (2) of this section permit the defendant to be released from custody.

(C) The defendant shall be returned to court for further appearance within two business days after the Commissioner notifies the court that the examination has been completed, unless the terms established by the court pursuant to subdivision (2) of this section permit the defendant to be released from custody.

(4) If the defendant is to be released pursuant to subdivision (3)(A), (3)(B)(ii), or (3)(C) of this subsection and is not in the custody of the Commissioner of Corrections, the defendant shall be returned to the defendant's residence or such other appropriate place within the State of Vermont by the Department of Mental Health at the expense of the court.

(5) If it appears that an inpatient examination cannot reasonably be completed within 30 days, the court issuing the original order, on request of the Commissioner and upon good cause shown may order placement at the hospital extended for additional periods of 15 days in order to complete the

examination, and the defendant on the expiration of the period provided for in such order shall be returned in accordance with this subsection.

(6) For the purposes of this subsection, "in need of inpatient hospitalization" means an individual has been determined under clinical standards of care to require inpatient treatment.

(h) Except upon good cause shown, defendants charged with misdemeanor offenses who are not in the custody of the Commissioner of Corrections shall be examined on an outpatient basis for mental competency. Examinations occurring in the community shall be conducted at a location within 60 miles of the defendant's residence or at another location agreed to by the defendant.

(i) As used in this section:

(1) "No refusal system" means a system of hospitals and intensive residential recovery facilities under contract with the Department of Mental Health that provides high intensity services, in which the facilities shall admit any individual for care if the individual meets the eligibility criteria established by the Commissioner in contract.

(2) "Successor in interest" shall mean the mental health hospital owned and operated by the State that provides acute inpatient care and replaces the Vermont State Hospital. (Added 1969, No. 20, § 2; amended 1987, No. 248 (Adj. Sess.), § 2; 1989, No. 187 (Adj. Sess.), § 5; 1991, No. 231 (Adj. Sess.), § 7; 1995, No. 134 (Adj. Sess.), § 1; 1995, No. 174 (Adj. Sess.), § 3; 2005, No. 71, §§ 113a, 113b; 2005, No. 174 (Adj. Sess.), § 20; 2005, No. 215 (Adj. Sess.), § 124; 2007, No. 15, § 22; 2009, No. 119 (Adj. Sess.), § 12; 2011, No. 79 (Adj. Sess.), § 15, eff. April 12, 2012.)

§ 4816. Scope of examination; report; evidence

(a) Examinations provided for in section 4815 of this title shall have reference to:

(1) mental competency of the person examined to stand trial for the alleged offense; and

(2) sanity of the person examined at the time of the alleged offense.

(b) A competency evaluation for an individual thought to have a developmental disability shall include a current evaluation by a psychologist skilled in assessing individuals with developmental disabilities.

(c) As soon as practicable after the examination has been completed, the examining psychiatrist or psychologist, if applicable, shall prepare a report containing findings in regard to each of the matters listed in subsection (a) of this section. The report shall be transmitted to the court issuing the order for examination, and copies of the report sent to the State's Attorney, and to the respondent's attorney if the respondent is represented by counsel.

(d) No statement made in the course of the examination by the person examined, whether or not he or she has consented to the examination, shall be admitted as evidence in any criminal proceeding for the purpose of proving the commission of a criminal offense or for the purpose of impeaching testimony of the person examined.

(e) The relevant portion of a psychiatrist's report shall be admitted into evidence as an exhibit on the issue of the person's mental competency to stand trial and the opinion shall be conclusive on the issue if agreed to by the parties and if found by the court to be relevant and probative on the issue.

(f) Introduction of a report under subsection (d) of this section shall not preclude either party or the court from calling the psychiatrist who wrote the report as a witness or from calling witnesses or introducing other relevant evidence. Any witness called by either party on the issue of the defendant's competency shall be at the State's expense, or, if called by the court, at the court's expense. (Added 1969, No. 20, § 3; amended 1995, No. 134 (Adj. Sess.), § 2; 2009, No. 146 (Adj. Sess.), § C25a; 2009, No. 156 (Adj. Sess.), § F.6.)

§ 4817. Competency to stand trial; determination

(a) A person shall not be tried for a criminal offense if he or she is incompetent to stand trial.

(b) If a person indicted, complained, or informed against for an alleged criminal offense, an attorney or guardian acting in his or her behalf, or the State, at any time before final judgment, raises before the court before which such person is tried or is to be tried, the issue of whether such person is incompetent to stand trial, or if the court has reason to believe that such person may not be competent to stand trial, a hearing shall be held before such court at which evidence shall be received and a finding made regarding his or her competency to stand trial. However, in cases where the court has reason to believe that such person may be incompetent to stand trial due to a mental disease or mental defect, such hearing shall not be held until an examination has been made and a report submitted by an examining psychiatrist in accordance with sections 4814-4816 of this title.

(c) A person who has been found incompetent to stand trial for an alleged offense may be tried for that offense if, upon subsequent hearing, such person is found by the court having jurisdiction of his or her trial for the offense to have become competent to stand trial. (Added 1969, No. 20, § 4.)

§ 4818. Failure to indict by reason of insanity

When a grand jury before which an indictment is heard returns the indictment as not found by reason of insanity of the person so charged at the time of the alleged offense, the grand jury shall so certify to the court. (Added 1969, No. 20, § 5.)

§ 4819. Acquittal by reason of insanity

When a person tried on information, complaint, or indictment is acquitted by a jury by reason of insanity at the time of the alleged offense, the jury shall state in its verdict of not guilty that the same is given for such cause. (Added 1969, No. 20, § 6.)

§ 4820. Hearing regarding commitment

When a person charged on information, complaint, or indictment with a criminal offense:

(1) Is reported by the examining psychiatrist following examination pursuant to sections 4814-4816 of this title to have been insane at the time of the alleged offense.

(2) Is found upon hearing pursuant to section 4817 of this title to be incompetent to stand trial due to a mental disease or mental defect.

(3) Is not indicted upon hearing by grand jury by reason of insanity at the time of the alleged offense, duly certified to the court.

(4) Upon trial by court or jury is acquitted by reason of insanity at the time of the alleged offense; the court before which such person is tried or is to be tried for such offense, shall hold a hearing for the

purpose of determining whether such person should be committed to the custody of the Commissioner of Mental Health. Such person may be confined in jail or some other suitable place by order of the court pending hearing for a period not exceeding 15 days. (Added 1969, No. 20, § 7; amended 1987, No. 248 (Adj. Sess.), § 3; 1989, No. 187 (Adj. Sess.), § 5; 1995, No. 174 (Adj. Sess.), § 3; 2005, No. 174 (Adj. Sess.), § 21; 2007, No. 15, § 22.)

§ 4821. Notice of hearing; procedures

The person who is the subject of the proceedings, his or her attorney, the legal guardian, if any, the Commissioner of Mental Health or the Commissioner of Disabilities, Aging, and Independent Living, and the State's Attorney or other prosecuting officer representing the State in the case shall be given notice of the time and place of a hearing under 4820 of this title. Procedures for hearings for persons with a mental illness shall be as provided in 18 V.S.A. chapter 181. Procedures for hearings for persons with an intellectual disability shall be as provided in 18 V.S.A. chapter 206, subchapter 3. (Added 1969, No. 20, § 8; amended 1987, No. 248 (Adj. Sess.), § 4; 1989, No. 187 (Adj. Sess.), § 5; 1995, No. 174 (Adj. Sess.), § 3; 2005, No. 174 (Adj. Sess.), § 22; 2007, No. 15, § 22; 2013, No. 96 (Adj. Sess.), § 58.)

§ 4822. Findings and order; persons with a mental illness

(a) If the court finds that the person is a person in need of treatment or a patient in need of further treatment as defined in 18 V.S.A. § 7101, the court shall issue an order of commitment directed to the Commissioner of Mental Health that shall admit the person to the care and custody of the Department of Mental Health for an indeterminate period. In any case involving personal injury or threat of personal injury, the committing court may issue an order requiring a court hearing before a person committed under this section may be discharged from custody.

(b) An order of commitment issued pursuant to this section shall have the same force and effect as an order issued under 18 V.S.A. §§ 7611-7622, and a person committed under this order shall have the same status and the same rights, including the right to receive care and treatment, to be examined and discharged, and to apply for and obtain judicial review of his or her case, as a person ordered committed under 18 V.S.A. §§ 7611-7622.

(c) Notwithstanding the provisions of subsection (b) of this section, at least 10 days prior to the proposed discharge of any person committed under this section, the Commissioner of Mental Health shall give notice of the discharge to the committing court and State's Attorney of the county where the prosecution originated. In all cases requiring a hearing prior to discharge of a person found incompetent to stand trial under section 4817 of this title, the hearing shall be conducted by the committing court issuing the order under that section. In all other cases, when the committing court orders a hearing under subsection (a) of this section or when, in the discretion of the Commissioner of Mental Health, a hearing should be held prior to the discharge, the hearing shall be held in the Family Division of the Superior Court to determine if the committed person is no longer a person in need of treatment or a patient in need of further treatment as set forth in subsection (a) of this section. Notice of the hearing shall be given to the Commissioner, the State's Attorney of the county where the prosecution originated, the committed person, and the person's attorney. Prior to the hearing, the State's Attorney may enter an appearance in the proceedings and may request examination of the patient by an independent psychiatrist, who may testify at the hearing.

(d) The court may continue the hearing provided in subsection (c) of this section for a period of 15 additional days upon a showing of good cause.

(e) If the court determines that commitment shall no longer be necessary, it shall issue an order discharging the patient from the custody of the Department of Mental Health.

(f) The court shall issue its findings and order not later than 15 days from the date of hearing. (Added 1969, No. 20, § 9; amended 1977, No. 95, § 1, eff. May 5, 1977; 1977, No. 252 (Adj. Sess.), § 38; 1987, No. 248 (Adj. Sess.), § 5; 1989, No. 187 (Adj. Sess.), § 5; 1995, No. 174 (Adj. Sess.), § 3; 2009, No. 154, § 238; 2011, No. 79 (Adj. Sess.), § 15a, eff. April 2, 2012; 2013, No. 96 (Adj. Sess.), § 58; 2013, No. 131 (Adj. Sess.), § 107.)

§ 4823. Findings and order; persons with an intellectual disability

(a) If the court finds that such person is a person in need of custody, care, and habilitation as defined in 18 V.S.A. § 8839, the court shall issue an order of commitment directed to the Commissioner of Disabilities, Aging, and Independent Living for care and habilitation of such person for an indefinite or limited period in a designated program.

(b) Such order of commitment shall have the same force and effect as an order issued under 18 V.S.A. § 8843 and persons committed under such an order shall have the same status, and the same rights, including the right to receive care and habilitation, to be examined and discharged, and to apply for and obtain judicial review of their cases, as persons ordered committed under 18 V.S.A. § 8843.

(c) Section 4822 of this title shall apply to persons proposed for discharge under this section; however, judicial proceedings shall be conducted in the Criminal Division of the Superior Court in which the person then resides, unless the person resides out of State in which case the proceedings shall be conducted in the original committing court. (Added 1987, No. 248 (Adj. Sess.), § 6; amended 1989, No. 187 (Adj. Sess.), § 5; 1995, No. 174 (Adj. Sess.), § 3; 2005, No. 174 (Adj. Sess.), § 23; 2009, No. 154, § 238; 2013, No. 96 (Adj. Sess.), § 58.)

§ 4824. Reporting; National Instant Criminal Background Check System

(a) If the court finds that a person is a person in need of treatment pursuant to section 4822 of this title, the Court Administrator shall within 48 hours report the name of the person subject to the order to the National Instant Criminal Background Check System, established by Section 103 of the Brady Handgun Violence Prevention Act of 1993. The report shall include only information sufficient to identify the person, the reason for the report, and a statement that the report is made in accordance with 18 U.S.C. § 922(g)(4).

(b) A report required by this section shall be submitted notwithstanding 18 V.S.A. § 7103 or any other provision of law.

(c) A report required by this section is confidential and exempt from public inspection and copying under the Public Records Act except as provided in subsection (d) of this section. The report shall not be used for any purpose other than for submission to the National Instant Criminal Background Check System pursuant to this section, where it may be used for any purpose permitted by federal law, including in connection with the issuance of a firearm-related permit or license.

(d) A copy of the report required by this section shall be provided to the person who is the subject of the report. The report shall include written notice to the person who is the subject of the report that the person is not permitted to possess a firearm. (Added 2015, No. 14, § 4, eff. Oct. 1, 2015.)

§ 4825. Persons prohibited by federal law from possessing firearms due to mental illness; petition for relief from disability

(a)(1) A person who is prohibited from possessing firearms by 18 U.S.C. § 922(g)(4) may petition the Family Division of the Superior Court for an order that the person be relieved from the firearms disability imposed by that section. When the petition is filed, the petitioner shall provide notice and a copy of the petition to the State's Attorney or the Attorney General, who shall be the respondent in the matter. The petition shall be filed in the county where the offense or the adjudication occurred.

(2)(A) The court shall grant a petition filed under this section without hearing if neither the State's Attorney nor the Attorney General files an objection within six months after receiving notice of the petition. If the court grants the petition pursuant to this subdivision, the court shall make findings and issue an order in accordance with this section.

(B) The court shall grant the petition filed under this section without hearing if the petitioner and the respondent stipulate to the granting of the petition. The respondent shall file the stipulation with the court, and the court shall make findings and issue an order in accordance with this section.

(b) In determining a petition filed under this section, unless the petition is granted pursuant to subdivision (a)(2) of this subsection, the court shall consider:

(1) the circumstances regarding the firearms disabilities imposed on the person by 18 U.S.C. § 922(g)(4);

(2) the petitioner's record, including his or her mental health and criminal history records; and

(3) the petitioner's reputation, as demonstrated by character witness statements, testimony, or other character evidence.

(c)(1) The court shall grant a petition filed under this section if it finds that the petitioner has demonstrated by a preponderance of the evidence that the person is no longer a person in need of treatment as defined in 18 V.S.A. § 7101(17).

(2) As the terms are used in this subsection, a finding that the person is no longer a person in need of treatment shall also mean that granting the relief will not be contrary to the public interest.

(d) If a petition filed under this section is granted, the court shall enter an order declaring that the basis under which the person was prohibited from possessing firearms by 18 U.S.C. § 922(g)(4) no longer applies. The court shall inform the Federal Bureau of Investigation, the U.S. Attorney General, and the National Instant Criminal Background Check System of its decision.

(e) If the court denies the petition, the petitioner may appeal the denial to the Vermont Supreme Court. The appeal shall be on the record, and the Supreme Court may review the record de novo.

(f) If the court denies a petition filed under this section, no further petition shall be filed by the person until at least one year after the order of the trial court, or of the Supreme Court if an appeal is taken, becomes final.

(g) At the time a petition is filed pursuant to this section, the respondent shall give notice of the petition to a victim of the offense, if any, who is known to the respondent. The victim shall have the right to offer the respondent a statement prior to any stipulation or to offer the court a statement. The disposition of the petition shall not be unnecessarily delayed pending receipt of a victim's statement. The respondent's inability to locate a victim after a reasonable effort has been made shall not be a bar to granting a petition.

(h) As used in this section, "reasonable effort" means attempting to contact the victim by first-class mail at the victim's last known address and by telephone at the victim's last known telephone number. (Added 2015, No. 14, § 7, eff. Oct. 1, 2015.)

Chapter 159: Extradition And Fresh Pursuit

Subchapter 1: Generally

§§ 4901, 4902. Repealed. 1973, No. 118, § 25, eff. Oct. 1, 1973.

§ 4903. Transporting prisoner through State

Whenever an offender is apprehended in a neighboring state, and it may be necessary to transport him or her through this State to the place where the offense was committed, a Superior Court judge, upon application and proof that lawful process has issued against the offender, shall issue a warrant under his or her hand and seal, directed to a sheriff or his or her deputy, or to a person by name who shall be sworn to the faithful performance of his or her duty, authorizing such conveyance. (Amended 1965, No. 194, § 10, operative February 1, 1967; 1973, No. 193 (Adj. Sess.), § 3, eff. April 9, 1974; 2009, No. 154 (Adj. Sess.), § 105.)

§ 4904. Duty of officer

Such person or officer shall cause the offender to be conveyed to the line of this State nearest to the state where the offense was committed, there to be delivered to some proper officer ready to receive him or her. All persons to whom the warrant may be directed are required to obey such order, upon payment or tender of the lawful fees therefor.

§ 4905. By officers of New York state

The authorities of the state of New York shall have the same power and authority to detain and transport through this State persons convicted of offenses and sentenced to be confined in a penitentiary in the state of New York, which they have to detain and transport them in such state.

§ 4906. By officers of New Hampshire

The authorities of the state of New Hampshire shall have the same power and authority to detain and transport through this State prisoners arrested in New Hampshire and held for trial or commitment by a court of record in New Hampshire, which they have to detain and transport them in that state.

§ 4907. Service of criminal process returnable in Massachusetts

(a) Jurisdiction to serve criminal process returnable to a court in the commonwealth of Massachusetts is hereby given to officers who, by the laws of such commonwealth, may serve such process, over a building situated partly in such commonwealth and partly in this State.

(b) Subsection (a) of this section shall take effect when the commonwealth of Massachusetts has given like jurisdiction to similar officers in this State to serve criminal process returnable to a court in Vermont.

§ 4908. Powers of officers from another state

A sheriff, deputy sheriff, constable, or other officer or justice of a neighboring state, with his or her assistants, in the execution of any lawful process issuing from and returnable to a court in such state, may pass through this State and convey such persons or things as he or she may have in his or her custody by virtue of such process, in as full and ample a manner as an officer of this State might do.

§ 4909. Impeding officers of other states

If a person assaults or obstructs an officer or his or her assistants passing through this State in the execution of any warrant or like process, he or she shall be liable to the same punishment as for assaulting or obstructing an officer of this State.

§ 4910. Receiving person from officer of another state

A sheriff shall receive a person charged with crime, delivered to him or her by an officer of another state having a warrant from proper authority for delivering the person, and shall take him or her forthwith before a district judge for examination. (Amended 1965, No. 194, § 10, operative February 1, 1967; 1973, No. 249 (Adj. Sess.), § 50, eff. April 9, 1974.)

Subchapter 2: Uniform Criminal Extradition Act

§ 4941. Definitions

The word "Governor," as used in this subchapter, shall include any person performing the functions of Governor by authority of the law of this State. The words "executive authority" shall include the Governor, and any person performing the functions of governor in a state other than this state. The word "state" referring to a state other than this State shall mean any other state or territory organized or unorganized of the United States of America.

§ 4942. Duty of Governor

Subject to the qualifications of this subchapter, and the provisions of the constitution of the United States controlling, and acts of Congress in pursuance thereof, it is the duty of the Governor of this State to have arrested and delivered up to the executive authority of any other state of the United States any person charged in that state with treason, felony, or other crime, who has fled from justice and is found in this State.

§ 4943. Form of demand

(a) A demand for the extradition of a person charged with crime in another state shall not be recognized by the Governor unless in writing alleging, except in cases arising under section 4946 of this title, that the accused was present in the demanding state at the time of the commission of the alleged crime, and that thereafter he or she fled from the state, and accompanied by a copy of an indictment found or by an information supported by affidavit in the state having jurisdiction of the crime, or by a copy of an affidavit made before a magistrate therein, together with a copy of any warrant that was issued thereon or by a copy of a judgment of conviction or of a sentence imposed in execution thereof, together with a statement by the executive authority of the demanding state that the person claimed has escaped from confinement or has broken the terms of his or her bail, probation, or parole. The indictment, information, or affidavit made before the magistrate must substantially charge the person demanded with having committed a crime under the law of that state; and the copy of the indictment, information, affidavit, judgment of conviction, or sentence must be authenticated by the executive authority making the demand.

(b) A warrant of extradition shall not be issued unless the documents presented by the executive authority making the demand show that:

(1) Except in cases arising under section 4946 of this title, the accused was present in the demanding state at the time of the commission of the alleged crime, and thereafter fled from that state;

(2) The accused is now in this State; and

(3) He or she is lawfully charged by indictment found or by information filed by a prosecuting officer and supported by affidavit to the facts, or by affidavit made before a magistrate in that state, with having committed a crime under the laws of that state or that he or she has been convicted of a crime in that state and has escaped from confinement or broken the terms of his or her bail, probation, or parole.

§ 4944. Investigation
When a demand shall be made upon the Governor by the executive authority of another state for the surrender of a person so charged with crime, the Governor may call upon the Attorney General or any prosecuting officer in this State to investigate or assist in investigating the demand, and to report to him or her the situation and circumstances of the person so demanded, and whether he or she ought to be surrendered.

§ 4945. Extradition of persons imprisoned or awaiting trial in another state or who have left the demanding state under compulsion
(a) When it is desired to have returned to this State a person charged in this State with a crime, and such person is imprisoned or is held under criminal proceedings then pending against him or her in another state, the Governor of this State may agree with the executive authority of such other state for the extradition of such person before the conclusion of such proceedings or his or her term of sentence in such other state, upon condition that such person be returned to such other state at the expense of this State as soon as the prosecution in this State is terminated.

(b) The Governor of this State may also surrender on demand of the executive authority of any other state any person in this State who is charged in the manner provided in section 4963 of this title, with having violated the laws of the state whose executive authority is making the demand, even though such person left the demanding state involuntarily.

§ 4946. Extradition of person not in demanding state at time crime committed
The Governor of this State may also surrender, on demand of the executive authority of any other state, any person in this State who is charged in such other state in the manner provided in section 4943 of this title with committing an act in this State, or in a third state, intentionally resulting in a crime in the state whose executive authority makes the demand; and the provisions of this subchapter not otherwise inconsistent shall apply to such cases, notwithstanding that the accused was not in that state at the time of the commission of the crime, and has not fled therefrom.

§ 4947. Governor to issue warrant

If the Governor shall decide that the demand should be complied with, he or she shall issue a warrant of arrest, that shall be sealed with the State Seal, and be directed to any sheriff, constable, or other person whom he or she may think fit to entrust with the execution thereof. Such warrant must substantially recite the facts necessary to the validity of its issue.

§ 4948. Manner and place of executing warrant

Such warrant shall authorize the officer or other person to whom directed to arrest the accused at any place where he or she may be found within the State and to command the aid of all sheriffs and other peace officers in the execution of such warrant, and to deliver the accused, subject to the provisions of this subchapter, to the duly authorized agent of the demanding state.

§ 4949. Authority of arresting officer

Such officer or other person empowered to make the arrest shall have the same authority in arresting the accused to command assistance therein, as sheriffs and other officers have by law in the execution of any criminal process directed to them, with the like penalties against those who refuse their assistance.

§ 4950. Rights of accused person; application for writ of habeas corpus

A person arrested upon such warrant shall not be delivered over to the agent whom the executive authority demanding him or her shall have appointed to receive him or her unless he or she shall first be taken forthwith before a judge of a court of record in this State, who shall inform him or her of the demand made for his or her surrender and of the crime with which he or she is charged, and that he or she has the right to demand and procure legal counsel. If the prisoner or his or her counsel shall state that he or she or they desire to test the legality of the arrest, the judge of such court of record shall fix a reasonable time to be allowed him or her within which to apply for a writ of habeas corpus. When such writ is applied for, notice thereof, and of the time and place of hearing thereon, shall be given to the State's Attorney of the county in which the arrest is made and in which the accused is in custody, and to the agent of the demanding state.

§ 4951. Penalty for noncompliance

An officer who shall deliver a person in his or her custody under the Governor's warrant to the agent for extradition of the demanding state in disobedience of section 4950 of this title shall be imprisoned not more than six months or fined not more than $1,000.00, or both.

§ 4952. Confinement in jail when necessary

(a) The officer or person executing the Governor's warrant of arrest, or the agent of the demanding state to whom the prisoner may have been delivered, may, when necessary, confine the prisoner in the jail of any county or city through which he or she or she may pass; and the keeper of such jail shall receive and safely keep the prisoner until the person having charge of him or her is ready to proceed on his or her route, such person being chargeable with the expense of keeping.

(b) The officer or agent of a demanding state to whom a prisoner may have been delivered following extradition proceedings in another state, or to whom a prisoner may have been delivered after waiving extradition in such other state, and who is passing through this State with such a prisoner for the purpose of immediately returning such prisoner to the demanding state may, when necessary, confine the prisoner in the jail of any county or city through which he or she may pass; and the keeper of such jail shall receive and safely keep the prisoner until the officer or agent having charge of him or her is ready to proceed on his or her route, such officer or agent, however, being chargeable with the expense of keeping. However, such officer or agent shall produce and show to the keeper of such jail satisfactory written evidence of the fact that he or she is actually transporting such prisoner to the demanding state after a requisition by the executive authority of such demanding state. Such prisoner shall not be entitled to demand a new requisition while in this State.

§ 4953. Arrest prior to requisition

Whenever any person within this State shall be charged on the oath of any credible person before any judge or magistrate of this State with the commission of any crime in any other state, and, except in cases arising under section 4946 of this title, with having fled from justice, or with having been convicted of a crime in that state and having escaped from confinement, or having broken the terms of his or her bail, probation, or parole, or whenever complaint shall have been before a Superior Court judge within this State, setting forth on the affidavit of a credible person in another state that a crime has been committed in such other state and that the accused has been charged in that state with the commission of a crime, and, except in cases arising under section 4946, has fled from justice, or with having been convicted of a crime in that state and having escaped from confinement, or having broken the terms of his or her bail, probation, or parole and is believed to have been found in this State, such judge shall issue a warrant to any sheriff or constable directing him or her to apprehend the person charged, wherever he or she may be found in this State, and bring him or her before the same or any other Superior Court judge who may be available in or convenient of access to the place where the arrest may be made, to answer the charge or complaint and affidavit; and a certified copy of the sworn charge or complaint and affidavit upon which the warrant is issued shall be attached to the warrant. (Amended 1965, No. 194, § 10, operative February 1, 1967; 1973, No. 193 (Adj. Sess.), § 3, eff. April 9, 1974; 2009, No. 154 (Adj. Sess.), § 106.)

§ 4954. Arrest without a warrant

The arrest of a person may be lawfully made by an officer or a private citizen without a warrant upon reasonable information that the accused stands charged in the courts of another state with a crime punishable by death or imprisonment for a term exceeding one year. When so arrested, the accused shall be taken before a Superior Court judge as soon as may be, and complaint shall be made against him or her under oath, setting forth the ground for the arrest as in section 4953 of this title; and thereafter his or her answer shall be heard as if he or she had been arrested on a warrant. (Amended 1965, No. 194, § 10, operative February 1, 1967; 1973, No. 193 (Adj. Sess.), § 3, eff. April 9, 1974; 2009, No. 154 (Adj. Sess.), § 107.)

§ 4955. Commitment to await extradition; bail

If upon examination it appears that the person held is the person charged with having committed the crime alleged and that the person probably committed the crime, and, except in cases arising under section 4946 of this title, that the person has fled from justice, the judge or magistrate shall commit the person to jail by a warrant, reciting the accusation, for such a time, not exceeding 30 days, to be specified in the warrant as will enable the arrest of the accused to be made under a warrant of the Governor on a requisition of the executive authority of the state having jurisdiction of the offense, unless the accused give bail as provided in section 4956 of this title, or until the person shall be legally discharged. On request of the state, the hearing may be continued for up to three working days, only for the purpose of determining whether the person probably committed the crime. Findings under this section may be based upon hearsay evidence or upon copies of affidavits, whether certified or not, made outside this State. It shall be sufficient for a finding that a person probably committed the crime that there is a current grand jury indictment from another state. (Amended 1989, No. 289 (Adj. Sess.).)

§ 4956. Bail when ordered

Unless the offense with which the prisoner is charged is shown to be an offense punishable by death or life imprisonment under the laws of the state in which it was committed, the judge or magistrate shall admit the person arrested to bail by bond or undertaking, with sufficient sureties, and in such sum as he or she deems proper, for his or her appearance before him at a time specified in such bond or undertaking, and for his or her surrender, to be arrested upon the warrant of the governor of this state.

§ 4957. Extending time of commitment

If the accused is not arrested under warrant of the Governor by the expiration of the time specified in the warrant, bond or undertaking, such judge may discharge him or her or may recommit him or her for a further period not to exceed 60 days, or may again take bail for his or her appearance and surrender as provided in section 4956 of this title, but within a period not to exceed 60 days after the date of such new bond.

§ 4958. Forfeiture of bail

If the prisoner is admitted to bail, and fails to appear and surrender himself or herself according to the condition of his or her bond, the court, by proper order, shall declare the bond forfeited and order his or her immediate arrest without warrant if he or she be within this State. Recovery may be had thereon in the name of the State as in the case of other bonds or undertakings given by the accused in criminal proceedings within this State.

§ 4959. Persons under prosecution in this State at time of requisition

If a criminal prosecution has been instituted against such person under the laws of this state and is still pending, the governor in his or her discretion either may surrender him or her on the demand of the executive authority of another state, or may hold him or her until he or she has been tried and discharged, or convicted and punished in this State.

§ 4960. Guilt or innocence of accused not in issue

The guilt or innocence of the accused as to the crime of which he or she is charged may not be inquired into by the Governor or in any proceeding after the demand for extradition accompanied by a charge of crime in legal form as provided in this chapter shall have been presented to the Governor, except as it may be involved in identifying the person held as the person charged with the crime.

§ 4961. Governor may recall or reissue warrant

The Governor may recall his or her warrant of arrest, or may issue another warrant when he or she deems proper.

§ 4962. Fugitives from this State; duty of governors

Whenever the Governor of this State shall demand a person charged with crime or with escaping from confinement or breaking the terms of his or her bail, probation or parole in this State from the chief executive of any other state, or from the chief judge or another judge of the United States district court for the District of Columbia authorized to receive such demand under laws of the United States, he or she shall issue a warrant under the seal of this State, to some agent, commanding his or her to receive the person so charged if delivered to his or her and convey his or her to the sheriff of the county in this State in which the offense was committed.

§ 4963. Manner of applying for requisition

(a) When the return to this State of a person charged with a crime in this State is required, the State's Attorney of the county in which the offense is committed, or the Attorney General shall present to the Governor his or her written application for a requisition for the return of the person so charged, in which application shall be stated the name of the person so charged, the crime charged against him or her, and the approximate time, place and circumstances of its commission, the state in which he or she is believed to be, including the location of the accused therein at the time the application is made, and certifying that in the opinion of the State's Attorney or the Attorney General the ends of justice require the arrest and return of the accused to this state for trial, and that the proceeding is not instituted to enforce a private claim.

(b) When the return to this State is required of a person who has been convicted of a crime in this State and has escaped from confinement or broken the terms of his or her bail, probation, or parole, the Attorney General or the State's Attorney of the county in which the offense was committed, the State probation officer or the warden of the institution or sheriff of the county, from which escape was made, shall present to the Governor a written application for a requisition for the return of such person, in which application shall be stated the name of the person, the crime of which he or she was convicted, the circumstances of his or her escape from confinement or of the breach of the terms of his or her bail, probation or parole, the state in which he or she is believed to be, including the location of the person therein at the time application is made.

(c) The application shall be verified by affidavit, shall be executed in duplicate and shall be accompanied by two certified copies of the indictment returned, or information and affidavit filed, or of the complaint, stating the offense with which the accused is charged or of the judgment of conviction or of the sentence. The State's Attorney, the Attorney General, the State probation officer, warden, or sheriff may also attach such further affidavits and other documents in duplicate as he or she shall deem proper to be submitted with such application. One copy of the application with the action of the Governor indicated by endorsement thereon, and one of the certified copies of the indictment or complaint or information and affidavit, or of the judgment of conviction or of the sentence shall be filed in the office of the Governor to remain of record in that office. The other copies of all papers shall be forwarded with the Governor's requisition.

§ 4964. Immunity from civil process

A person brought into this State on, or after waiver of, extradition based on a criminal charge shall not be subject to service of personal process in civil actions arising out of the same facts as the criminal proceeding to answer that he or she is returned, until he or she has been convicted in the criminal proceeding, or if acquitted, until he or she has had ample opportunity to return to the state from which he or she was extradited.

§ 4965. No immunity from other criminal prosecutions

After a person has been brought back to this State upon, or after waiver of, extradition proceedings, he or she may be tried in this State for other crimes that he or she may be charged with having committed in this State, as well as that specified in the requisition for his or her extradition.

§ 4966. Payment of expenses

In proceedings under the preceding sections of this subchapter, the complainant shall pay the actual costs and charges and for the support in jail of a person committed thereunder at the rate of $4.00 a week and shall advance the money therefor from time to time or give to the jailer satisfactory security therefor. When complainant neglects for 24 hours to advance such money or give such security after he or she has been required by the jailer so to do, the jailer may discharge the person so committed and shall forthwith notify the authority issuing the warrant.

§ 4967. Written waiver of extradition proceedings

(a) Any person arrested in this State charged with having committed any crime in another state or alleged to have escaped from confinement, or broken the terms of his or her bail, probation, or parole may waive the issuance and service of the warrant provided for in sections 4947 and 4948 of this title and all other procedure incidental to extradition proceedings, by executing or subscribing in the presence of a judge of any court of record within this State a writing that states that he or she consents to return to the demanding state; provided however, before such waiver shall be executed or subscribed by such person it shall be the duty of such judge to inform such person of his or her rights to the issuance and service of a warrant of extradition and to obtain a writ of habeas corpus as provided for in section 4950 of this title.

(b) If and when such consent has been duly executed, it shall forthwith be forwarded to the office of the Governor of this State and filed therein. The judge shall direct the officer having such person in custody to deliver forthwith such person to the duly accredited agent or agents of the demanding state, and shall deliver or cause to be delivered to such agent or agents a copy of such consent; provided however, that nothing in this section shall be deemed to limit the rights of the accused person to return voluntarily and without formality to the demanding state, nor shall this waiver procedure be deemed to be an exclusive procedure or to limit the powers, rights or duties of the officers of the demanding state or of this State.

§ 4968. Nonwaiver by this State

Nothing contained in this subchapter shall be deemed to constitute a waiver by this state of its right, power or privilege to try such demanded person for crime committed within this State, or of its right, power or privilege to regain custody of such person by extradition proceedings or otherwise for the purpose of trial, sentence or punishment for any crime committed within this State, nor shall any proceedings had under this subchapter that result in, or fail to result in, extradition be deemed a waiver by this State of any of its rights, privileges or jurisdiction in any way whatsoever.

§ 4969. Uniform interpretation

This subchapter shall be so interpreted and construed as to effectuate its general purpose to make uniform the law of those states that enact it.

Subchapter 3: Uniform Act On Fresh Pursuit

§ 5041. Definition

The term "fresh pursuit" as used in this subchapter shall include fresh pursuit as defined by the common law, and also the pursuit of a person who has committed a felony or who is reasonably suspected of having committed a felony or who is reasonably suspected of operating a motor vehicle while under the influence of alcohol. It shall also include the pursuit of a person suspected of having committed a supposed felony, though no felony has actually been committed, if there is reasonable ground for believing that a felony has been committed. Fresh pursuit as used herein shall not necessarily imply instant pursuit, but pursuit without unreasonable delay. (Amended 1985, No. 228 (Adj. Sess.), § 1; 2017, No. 83, § 161(3).)

§ 5042. Powers of law enforcement officers

Any member of a duly organized state, county, or municipal law enforcement unit of another state of the United States who enters this State in fresh pursuit, and continues within this State in such fresh pursuit, of a person in order to arrest him or her on the ground that he or she is believed to have committed a felony or operated a motor vehicle while under the influence of alcohol in such other state, shall have the same authority to arrest and hold in custody such person as a sheriff of this State has to arrest and hold in custody a person on the ground that he or she is believed to have committed a felony or operated a motor vehicle while under the influence of alcohol in this State. (Amended 1985, No. 228 (Adj. Sess.), § 2; 2017, No. 83, § 161(3).)

§ 5043. Hearing, commitment, discharge

If an arrest is made in this State by an officer of another state in accordance with the provisions of section 5042 of this title, he or she shall without unnecessary delay take the person arrested before a Superior judge of the unit in which the arrest was made, who shall conduct a hearing for the purpose of determining the lawfulness of the arrest. If the judge determines that the arrest was lawful, he or she shall commit the person arrested to await for a reasonable time the issuance of an extradition warrant by the Governor of this State or admit such person to bail pending the issuance of such warrant. If the judge determines that the arrest was unlawful, he or she shall discharge the person arrested. (Amended 1965, No. 194, § 10, operative February 1, 1967; 1973, No. 193 (Adj. Sess.), § 3, eff. April 9, 1974; 2009, No. 154 (Adj. Sess.), § 108.)

§ 5044. Construction and separability

Section 5042 of this title shall not be construed so as to make unlawful any arrest in this State that would otherwise be lawful. For the purpose of this subchapter the word "state" shall include the District of Columbia. If any part of this subchapter is for any reason declared void, it is declared to be the intent of this subchapter that such invalidity shall not affect the validity of the remaining portions of this subchapter.

§ 5045. Short title; interpretation

This subchapter may be cited as the Uniform Act on Fresh Pursuit and shall be so interpreted and construed as to effectuate its general purpose to make uniform the law of the states that enact it.

Chapter 161: Inquests As To Criminal Matters

Subchapter 1: Inquests As To Death

§§ 5101-5103. Repealed. 1973, No. 249 (Adj. Sess.), § 111, eff. April 9, 1974.

Subchapter 2: Inquests As To Criminal Matters

§ 5131. Application for inquest

Upon the written application of the State's Attorney, a judge of the Superior Court may institute and conduct an inquest upon any criminal matter under investigation by the State's Attorney. (Amended 1965, No. 194, § 10, operative February 1, 1967; 1973, No. 193 (Adj. Sess.), § 3, eff. April 9, 1974; 2009, No. 154 (Adj. Sess.), § 109.)

§ 5132. Procedure

A judge may issue necessary process to bring witnesses before him or her to give evidence in any matter there under investigation. The witnesses shall be sworn and paid the same fees as witnesses in the Criminal Division of the Superior Court. A judge so conducting an inquest shall not be disqualified from trying the cause that was the subject of inquiry at such inquest. (Amended 1973, No. 249 (Adj. Sess.), § 51, eff. April 9, 1974; 2009, No. 154, § 238.)

§ 5133. Stenographer

Upon the approval of the judge and at the expense of the State, a stenographer shall take and transcribe the testimony of the witnesses for the use of the State's Attorney. The order approving such appointment of the stenographer shall be in writing.

§ 5134. Oath of secrecy

Before entering upon his or her duties, such stenographer shall be sworn to keep secret all matters and things coming before the judge at such inquest. Such oath shall be in writing, and the stenographer shall not disclose testimony so taken by him or her except to the Attorney General, State's Attorney, and the judge holding the inquest. The minutes of testimony so taken shall be the property of the State and the same or copy thereof shall not go out of the possession of such Attorney General, State's Attorney, or their successors except to an attorney appointed by the Supreme Court or Superior Court to act in the place of or assist a State's Attorney. However, nothing in this section shall prevent the stenographer from disclosing such evidence on an order of the Supreme or Superior Court, or a prosecuting attorney from disclosing such evidence to a defendant in such manner as the Supreme Court may by rule provide. (Amended 1973, No. 118, § 17, eff. Oct. 1, 1973; 1973, No. 193 (Adj. Sess.), § 3, eff. April 9, 1974.)

§ 5135. Penalty

A stenographer approved under section 5133 of this title, who violates a provision of section 5134 of this title, shall be imprisoned not more than one year or fined not more than $1,000.00 nor less than $100.00, or both.

§ 5136. Accounts; forms

After the close of such inquest such judge shall forward his or her account forthwith to the Commissioner of Finance and Management, who shall audit the same and issue his or her warrant therefor in favor of such judge. The Commissioner shall prepare and furnish to the proper officers the necessary forms for carrying into effect the provisions of this section. (Added 1959, No. 329 (Adj. Sess.), § 8; 1971, No. 92, § 1.)

§ 5137. State's Attorney to attend

The authority instituting an inquest under this subchapter shall at once notify the State's Attorney of the hearing, and he or she shall attend the hearing and conduct the examination of witnesses.

Subchapter 3: Investigations Ordered By Superior Judge Or Attorney General

§ 5161. Investigation of crime by experts

To prevent a failure of Justice, a Superior Judge or the Attorney General may order an examination to be made by an expert or experts, either within or without the State, in the investigation of a crime supposed to have been committed within the State. Such order shall be made only on the petition of the State's Attorney for the county in which the crime is supposed to have been committed, setting forth the facts because of which the order is applied for, and verified by affidavit, and shall name the expert or experts by whom the examination is to be made, and limit the expense of the examination. Such expense shall be paid in the manner provided for the payment of witness fees in State causes in the Superior Court.

§ 5162. Autopsy

Upon the petition of the State's Attorney, a Superior Judge or the Attorney General may order an autopsy or exhumation and autopsy to be performed by the chief medical examiner or under his or her direction in the preparation of a State cause for trial in any court, or in the interest of public health, welfare, or safety or in the furtherance of the administration of the law. Upon completion of the autopsy, the chief medical examiner shall submit a report to the State's Attorney and shall complete and sign a certificate of death. (Amended 1969, No. 265 (Adj. Sess.), § 1; 1971, No. 33, § 1.)

Chapter 163: Public Defenders

Subchapter 1: General Provisions

§ 5201. Definitions

In this chapter, the term:

(1) "Detain" means to have in custody or otherwise deprive of freedom of action.

(2) "Expenses," when used with reference to representation under this chapter, includes the expenses of investigation, other preparation, and trial.

(3) "Needy person" means a person who at the time his or her need is determined is financially unable, without undue hardship, to provide for the full payment of an attorney and all other necessary expenses of representation or who is otherwise unable to employ an attorney.

(4) "Serious crime" includes:

(A) a felony;

(B) a misdemeanor the maximum penalty for which is a fine of more than $1,000.00 or any period of imprisonment unless the judge, at the arraignment but before the entry of a plea, determines and states on the record that he or she will not sentence the defendant to a fine of more than $1,000.00 or a period of imprisonment if the defendant is convicted of the misdemeanor; and

(C) an act that, but for the age of the person involved, would be a serious crime.

(5) "Serious crime" does not include the following misdemeanor offenses unless the judge at arraignment but before the entry of a plea determines and states on the record that a sentence of imprisonment or a fine over $1,000.00 may be imposed on conviction:

(A) [Repealed.]

(B) Big game violations (10 V.S.A. § 4518)

(C) Simple assault by mutual consent (13 V.S.A. § 1023(b))

(D) Bad checks (13 V.S.A. § 2022)

(E) Petit larceny (13 V.S.A. § 2502)

(F) Theft of services under $500.00 (13 V.S.A. § 2582)

(G) Retail theft under $900.00 (13 V.S.A. § 2577)

(H) Unlawful mischief (13 V.S.A. § 3701(c))

(I) Unlawful trespass (13 V.S.A. § 3705(a))

(J) Disorderly conduct (13 V.S.A. § 1026)

(K) Possession of cannabis- first offense (18 V.S.A. § 4230(a)(1))

(L) Violation of municipal ordinances (Added 1971, No. 161 (Adj. Sess.), § 6, eff. date, see note; amended 1973, No. 118, § 18, eff. Oct. 1, 1973; 1975, No. 254 (Adj. Sess.), § 25; 1995, No. 21, § 2; 2007, No. 108 (Adj. Sess.), § 2; 2015, No. 147 (Adj. Sess.), § 8, eff. May 31, 2016.)

§ 5202. Construction with other laws

The protections provided by this chapter do not exclude any protection or sanction that the law otherwise provides. (Added 1971, No. 161 (Adj. Sess.), § 6, eff. date, see note.)

§ 5203. Federal courts

This chapter applies only to representation in or with respect to the courts of this State. It does not prohibit the Defender General, the Deputy Defender General, or public defenders from representing a needy person in a federal court of the United States, if:

(1) the matter arises out of or is related to an action pending or recently pending in a court of criminal jurisdiction of the State;

(2) representation is under a plan of the U.S. District Court as required by the Criminal Justice Act of 1964 (18 U.S.C. § 3006A); or

(3) representation is in or with respect to a matter arising out of or relating to immigration status. (Added 1971, No. 161 (Adj. Sess.), § 6, eff. date, see note; amended 1987, No. 183 (Adj. Sess.), § 22; 2017, No. 177 (Adj. Sess.), § 2.)

§ 5204. Court rules

The Supreme Court shall make such rules as shall further the intent and purposes of this chapter. Those rules shall be controlling in all courts of this State. (Added 1971, No. 161 (Adj. Sess.), § 6, eff. date, see note.)

§ 5205. Court assigned attorneys

(a) The Supreme Court shall prescribe reasonable rates of compensation for the services of attorneys, assigned under sections 5272 or 5274 of this title, who have not entered into a contract with the Defender General to provide assigned counsel services.

(b) The Defender General shall enter into contract with a member of the bar to serve as assigned counsel coordinator, who shall determine those expenses, necessary to representation, for which assigned counsel shall be reimbursed. The Defender General may not supervise the duties of the assigned counsel coordinator, but the assigned counsel coordinator shall consult with the Defender General concerning the assigned counsel budget.

(c) The Defender General may enter into contracts, as provided by section 5253 of this title, with attorneys to provide assigned counsel services. Payment and expenses of assigned counsel, and of the assigned counsel coordinator, shall be made from funds appropriated to the Office of the Defender General for the compensation of assigned counsel. (Added 1971, No. 161 (Adj. Sess.), § 6, eff. date, see note; amended 1981, No. 146 (Adj. Sess.), § 1, eff. April 8, 1982.)

§ 5206. Appointment of counsel by court; use of uncounseled convictions

(a) Prior to any decision regarding the appointment of counsel under the provisions of subdivisions 5201(4)(B) and (5) of this title, the judge shall inquire of the prosecutor whether a term of imprisonment or a fine over $1,000.00 will be sought.

(b) At the request of the prosecutor or on the judge's own motion, at any time prior to the commencement of trial and if there is a change of circumstances or new information, the judge may vacate the commitment to not sentence the defendant to a fine of not more than $1,000.00 or to a period of incarceration upon conviction. If the judge vacates the commitment, the judge shall inform the defendant of the right to apply for the appointment of counsel at State expense.

(c) A prior uncounseled criminal conviction of a crime listed in subdivisions (A) through (L) of subdivision (5) of section 5201 of this title in which counsel was denied and the defendant was otherwise entitled to appointed counsel under this subchapter, shall not be used to subject that defendant to the enhanced statutory penalty for a subsequent conviction for the same offense.

(d) Notwithstanding subdivision 5201(4)(B) of this title, a needy person who is charged with an offense which provides for a felony penalty for the next subsequent conviction for the same offense shall be entitled to counsel under this chapter. (Added 1995, No. 21, § 3.)

Subchapter 2: Notice And Nature Of Rights

§ 5231. Right to representation, services, and facilities

(a) A needy person who is being detained by a law enforcement officer without charge or judicial process, or who is charged with having committed or is being detained under a conviction of a serious crime, is entitled:

(1) To be represented by an attorney to the same extent as a person having his or her own counsel; and

(2) To be provided with the necessary services and facilities of representation. Any such necessary services and facilities of representation that exceed $1,500.00 per item must receive prior approval from the court after a hearing involving the parties. The court may conduct the hearing outside the presence of the State, but only to the extent necessary to preserve privileged or confidential information. This obligation and requirement to obtain prior court approval shall also be imposed in like manner upon the Attorney General or a State's Attorney prosecuting a violation of the law.

(b) The attorney, services and facilities, and court costs shall be provided at public expense to the extent that the person, at the time the court determines need, is unable to provide for the person's payment without undue hardship. (Added 1971, No. 161 (Adj. Sess.), § 6, eff. date, see note; amended 1995, No. 178 (Adj. Sess.), § 63; 2009, No. 33, § 34.)

§ 5232. Particular proceedings

Counsel shall be assigned under section 5231 of this title to represent needy persons in any of the following:

(1) extradition proceedings;

(2) habeas corpus and other proceedings wherein the person is confined in a penal or mental institution in this state and seeks release therefrom; or

(3) proceedings arising out of a petition brought in a juvenile court when the court deems the interests of justice require representation of either the child or his or her parents or guardian or both, including any subsequent proceedings arising from an order therein. (Added 1971, No. 161 (Adj. Sess.), § 6, eff. date, see note.)

§ 5233. Extent of services

(a) A needy person who is entitled to be represented by an attorney under section 5231 of this title is entitled:

(1) to be counseled and defended at all stages of the matter beginning with the earliest time when a person providing the person's own counsel would be entitled to be represented by an attorney and including revocation of probation or parole;

(2) to be represented in any appeal; and

(3) to be represented in any other postconviction proceeding which may have more than a minimal effect on the length or conditions of detention where the attorney considers:

(A) the claims, defenses, and other legal contentions to be warranted by existing law or by a nonfrivolous argument for the extension, modification, or reversal of existing law or the establishment of new law; and

(B) the allegations and other factual contentions to have evidentiary support, or likely to have evidentiary support after a reasonable opportunity for further investigation and discovery.

(b) A needy person's right to a benefit under this section is not affected by having provided a similar benefit at the person's own expense, or by having waived it, at an earlier stage. (Added 1971, No. 161 (Adj. Sess.), § 6, eff. date, see note; amended 2003, No. 157 (Adj. Sess.), § 10, eff. June 8, 2004; 2015, No. 137 (Adj. Sess.), § 6, eff. May 25, 2016.)

§ 5234. Notice of rights; representation provided

(a) If a person who is being detained by a law enforcement officer without charge or judicial process, or who is charged with having committed or is being detained under a conviction of a serious crime, is not represented by an attorney under conditions in which a person having his or her own counsel would be entitled to be so represented, the law enforcement officer, magistrate, or court concerned shall:

(1) Clearly inform him or her of the right of a person to be represented by an attorney and of a needy person to be represented at public expense; and

(2) If the person detained or charged does not have an attorney and does not knowingly, voluntarily and intelligently waive his or her right to have an attorney when detained or charged, notify the appropriate public defender that he or she is not so represented. This shall be done upon commencement of detention, formal charge, or post-conviction proceeding, as the case may be. As used in this subsection, the term "commencement of detention" includes the taking into custody of a probationer or parolee.

(b) Upon commencement of any later judicial proceeding relating to the same matter, the presiding officer shall clearly inform the person so detained or charged of the right of a needy person to be represented by an attorney at public expense.

(c) Information given to a person by a law enforcement officer under this section is effective only if it is communicated to a person in a manner meeting standards under the constitution of the United States relating to admissibility in evidence against him or her of statements of a detained person.

(d) Information meeting the standards of subsection (c) of this section and given to a person by a law enforcement officer under this section gives rise to a rebuttable presumption that the information was effectively communicated if:

(1) It is in writing or otherwise recorded;

(2) The recipient records his or her acknowledgment of receipt and time of receipt of the information; and

(3) The material so recorded under subdivisions (1) and (2) of this subsection is filed with the court next concerned. (Added 1971, No. 161 (Adj. Sess.), § 6, eff. date, see note; amended 1973, No. 109, § 8, eff. 30 days from April 25, 1973.)

§ 5235. Notice to public defender

If a law enforcement officer, magistrate, or court determines that a person is entitled to be represented by an attorney at public expense, the officer, magistrate, or court, as the case may be, shall promptly notify the appropriate public defender. (Added 1971, No. 161 (Adj. Sess.), § 6, eff. date, see note.)

§ 5236. Determination of financial need

(a) The determination whether a person covered by sections 5231-5234 of this title is a needy person shall be deferred until his or her first appearance in court or in a suit for payment or reimbursement under section 5255 of this title, whichever occurs earlier. Thereafter, the court shall determine, with respect to each proceeding, whether the person is a needy person. As used in this section, an appeal is a separate proceeding. The determination of need, for purposes of an appeal, shall be based on a separate application submitted on or after the date of the order appealed from, except that an appeal from a proceeding under 33 V.S.A. chapter 51, 52, or 53 is not a separate proceeding and does not require a separate application.

(b) In determining whether a person is a needy person and the extent of his or her ability to pay, the court may consider such factors as income, property owned, outstanding obligations, and the number and ages of dependents as specified in rules of the Supreme Court adopted pursuant to section 5204 of this title. Release on bail does not necessarily disqualify a person from being a needy person. In each case, the person, subject to the penalties for perjury, shall certify in writing or by other record such information relating to ability to pay as the Supreme Court prescribes.

(c) A determination of whether a person is a needy person under this section shall be made by the clerk of the court, or any other judicial officer of the court. After review of the initial determination by the presiding judge of the trial court the applicant, the State, or the Office of the Defender General may appeal the determination to a single Justice of the Supreme Court of this State, in accordance with the rules of the Supreme Court.

(d) In determining whether a person is a needy person under this section and the extent of the person's ability to pay, the clerk of court or the judicial officer who is making that determination may require the applicant to provide proof of income at a time to be determined by the clerk or judicial officer.

(e)(1) The Commissioner of Taxes or the Commissioner's designee, when requested by the clerk of court or the judicial officer, shall furnish the requester with a nonspecific report of the adjusted gross income as shown on the Vermont tax return of the applicant or, in the case of a joint return, the applicant and the applicant's spouse as it relates to the federal poverty income guidelines in effect as of December 31 of the year for which the tax information is requested. Such report shall only identify whether the income of the applicant (or the applicant and the applicant's spouse in the case of a joint return) is at or below the federal poverty income guidelines applicable to family size or is within the following percentages of those guidelines:

101-124%

125-150%

151-175%

176-200%, or

over 200%

(2) Information furnished to the requester shall be made available to the applicant and the court.

(f) Any financial information furnished or disclosed under subsections (d) and (e) of this section shall be confidential and available for review only by the clerk or judicial officer or the person submitting the financial information. In the event of an appeal, any identifying information shall be confidential and not made part of the public record.

(g) A person who knowingly violates subsection (f) of this section shall be fined not more than $500.00, and shall be liable in a civil action for any damages resulting from improper disclosure. (Added 1971, No. 161 (Adj. Sess.), § 6, eff. date, see note; amended 1987, No. 266 (Adj. Sess.); 1991, No. 231 (Adj. Sess.), § 1; 1993, No. 60, § 57; 1995, No. 178 (Adj. Sess.), § 62; 1997, No. 45, §§ 1, 2, eff. June 19, 1997; 1997, No. 139 (Adj. Sess.), § 3; 1997, No. 156 (Adj. Sess.), § 25, eff. April 29, 1998; 2013, No. 131 (Adj. Sess.), § 108.)

§ 5237. Waiver

A person who has been appropriately informed under section 5234 of this title may waive in writing, or by other record, any right provided by this chapter, if the court, at the time of or after waiver, finds of record that he has acted with full awareness of his rights and of the consequences of a waiver and if the waiver is otherwise according to law. The court shall consider such factors as the person's age, education, and familiarity with the English language, and the complexity of the crime involved. (Added 1971, No. 161 (Adj. Sess.), § 6, eff. date, see note.)

§ 5238. Co-payment and reimbursement orders

(a) On or before June 1 of each year, the Defender General shall calculate an average direct cost per case of representation extended in the preceding calendar year by category of case. The categories of cases for which calculations are made shall be: felonies; misdemeanors; postconviction and miscellaneous criminal-related proceedings, including violations of probation, extraditions, and habeas corpus; juvenile proceedings, not including juvenile delinquency proceedings; and appeals. The calculations shall be based on all representation supported by the budget of the Defender General whether provided by public defenders, contractors or assigned counsel. The administrative costs of running the Office of Defender General shall not be included in the calculation.

(b) The court shall require any person assigned counsel pursuant to section 5236 of this title to pay for all or part of the cost of representation based upon his or her ability to pay. Unless the person and cohabiting family members are found to be financially unable to pay, in all cases the court shall order a minimum payment of $50.00. This assignment fee shall be paid within 60 days of assignment of counsel. If the court finds that the income of the person and cohabiting family members for the past year equaled or exceeded 125 percent of the federal poverty level applicable to their family size, the balance to be paid by the person found eligible, when added to the minimum assignment fee, shall be equal to the amount calculated according to the following chart:

Income as a percentage of federal poverty level applicable to family size	Defendant's percentage of average direct cost per case for category of case
125-150%	25%
151-175	50
176-200	75
over 200	100

(c) The amount to be paid under subsection (b) of this section shall be divided by the court between a co-payment and reimbursement amount. A separate payment amount shall be calculated for each proceeding. If a defendant is charged with more than one related offense, the court may impose one payment amount calculated based on the category of case for the offense with the highest possible punishment.

(d) To the extent that the court finds that the eligible person has income or assets available to enable payment of an immediate co-payment, it shall order such a co-payment to cover in whole or in part the amount of the costs of representation to be borne by the eligible person. The co-payment shall be paid to the clerk of the court. Any portion of the co-payment not paid to the clerk may be included in a reimbursement order.

(e) The remainder of the amount to be paid by the person found eligible shall be ordered to be paid in a reimbursement order. Unless the court extends the time because the eligible person is incarcerated or good cause is shown, the reimbursement amount shall become due 60 days from the date of the order.

(f) A person who may be or has been ordered to pay all or part of the cost of representation by co-payment or reimbursement order may at any time petition the court making the order for remission of all of the amount or any part thereof. If it appears to the satisfaction of the court that payment of the amount due will impose manifest hardships on the defendant or the defendant's immediate family or that the circumstances of case disposition and the interests of justice so require, the court may remit all or part of the amount due or modify the method of payment.

(g) A juvenile shall not be ordered to pay any part of the cost of representation.

(h) A copayment or reimbursement order under this section shall be made by the clerk of the court or any other judicial officer of the court. The applicant, the State, or the Office of the Defender General may appeal the order to a single Justice of the Supreme Court of this State, in accordance with the rules of the Supreme Court. (Added 1991, No. 231 (Adj. Sess.), § 2; amended 1993, No. 60, § 57a; 1995, No. 77 (Adj. Sess.), § 9, eff. Mar. 21, 1996; 2011, No. 128 (Adj. Sess.), § 38; 2015, No. 133 (Adj. Sess.), § 2, eff. May 25, 2016.)

§ 5239. Public Defender Special Fund

(a) The Public Defender Special Fund is hereby created. All co-payments, reimbursements, and assignment fees paid by persons receiving representation under this chapter, as well as all amounts recovered pursuant to section 5255 of this title and 23 V.S.A. § 1210(j), shall be deposited in the Fund.

(b) The Special Fund created by subsection (a) of this section shall be organized and managed as follows:

(1) The Fund shall be managed on the State Central Accounting System under the control of the Commissioner of Finance and Management with the actual monies held under the authority and responsibility of the State Treasurer.

(2) [Repealed.]

(3) All interest earned by the Fund shall be credited to the General Fund.

(4) All monies to be expended from the Fund shall be appropriated annually by the General Assembly, or allocated pursuant to the authority granted by the General Assembly to the Commissioner of Finance and Management with regard to excess receipts.

(5) Expenditures from the Fund shall not exceed available revenues, except that the Commissioner of Finance and Management may anticipate receipts to the Fund and issue warrants based thereon, and in so doing may establish limits on expenditures in anticipation of receipts.

(6) All cash balances in the Fund at the end of the fiscal year shall be carried forward and remain in the Fund unspent until authorized by the General Assembly.

(7) All monies remaining in the Fund when it is terminated shall revert to the General Fund.

(8) Any negative cash balance in the Fund at the end of a fiscal year shall be carried forward and applied against the Fund's receipts for the next fiscal year. (Added 1991, No. 231 (Adj. Sess.), § 3, eff. May 28, 1992; amended 1993, No. 60, § 58, eff. May 28, 1993; 1993, No. 210 (Adj. Sess.), § 55, eff. June 17, 1994; 1995, No. 77 (Adj. Sess.), § 10, eff. Mar. 21, 1996; 2009, No. 67 (Adj. Sess.), § 85, eff. Feb. 25, 2010; 2011, No. 56, § 8, eff. May 31, 2011.)

§ 5240. Collection of reimbursements

(a) If persons receiving representation under this chapter fail to make reimbursement on the date specified in the court order, the Court Administrator shall refer the uncollected reimbursement orders to the Commissioner of Taxes, and the Commissioner is authorized to proceed to collection in the name of the State.

(b) The Commissioner is authorized to use setoff debt collection, as provided in 32 V.S.A. §§ 5931-5940, for collecting reimbursements.

(c) The Commissioner of Taxes is authorized to contract with private collection agencies for the sole purpose of collection of reimbursements imposed by judicial order, and such order shall be deemed reasonable notice of the debt. The Commissioner may agree to pay a collection agency a fixed rate or a percentage of the amount actually collected and remitted to the State. Notwithstanding 32 V.S.A. § 502, the Commissioner may charge against such collections any cost of such collections.

(d) If a person provided representation under this chapter is convicted of a crime in the matter for which representation was provided, the sentence shall include an order to pay any reimbursements ordered and unpaid. The order shall be enforced as a condition of probation, supervised community sentence, or parole if the convicted person is sentenced to probation, supervised community sentence, or imprisonment and later placed on parole.

(e) The amount specified to be paid by a reimbursement order shall be considered a fine, forfeiture, or penalty for purposes of section 7171 of this title and may be collected as provided in that section. (Added 1991, No. 231 (Adj. Sess.), § 4, eff. May 28, 1992; amended 2011, No. 128 (Adj. Sess.), § 39.)

§ 5241. Ineffective assistance claim

(a) No action shall be brought for professional negligence against a criminal defense attorney under contract with or providing ad hoc legal services for the Office of the Defender General unless the plaintiff has first successfully prevailed in a claim for postconviction relief based upon ineffective assistance of counsel in the same or a substantially related matter. Failure to prevail in a claim for postconviction relief based upon ineffective assistance of counsel under contract with or providing ad hoc legal services for the Office of the Defender General shall bar any claim against the attorney based upon the attorney's representation in the same or a substantially related matter.

(b) In the performance of duties pursuant to a contract with or providing ad hoc legal services to the Office of the Defender General, an attorney shall have the benefit of immunity to the same extent as an attorney employed by the Defender General. (Added 2011, No. 100 (Adj. Sess.), § 1; amended 2015, No. 58, § E.203, eff. June 11, 2015; 2017, No. 177 (Adj. Sess.), § 3.)

Subchapter 3: Office Of Defender General

§ 5251. Creation of office

The Office of Defender General is established. The Office shall consist of the Defender General who shall be the head of the Office, a Deputy Defender General, if one is appointed in accordance with subsection 5253(e) of this title, and such public defenders and deputy public defenders selected by the Defender General and within the limits of funds and staffing authorized by the General Assembly. (Added 1971, No. 161 (Adj. Sess.), § 6, eff. date, see note; amended 1973, No. 266 (Adj. Sess.), § 2; 1981, No. 146 (Adj. Sess.), § 2, eff. April 8, 1982; 1987, No. 183 (Adj. Sess.), § 23.)

§ 5252. Appointment; compensation

(a) The Defender General shall be appointed by the Governor subject to the advice and consent of the Senate.

(b) There shall be included in the qualifications for appointment that the Defender General shall be an attorney-at-law who has been engaged in the practice of law or as a judge in the State of Vermont for a period of at least five out of the 10 years preceding his or her appointment. Further, he or she shall be an attorney or judge who has spent a substantial part of his or her last five years in the practice of criminal law or presiding over the adjudication of criminal cases.

(c) The Defender General shall be appointed for a term of four years and until his or her successor is appointed and qualified.

(d) [Repealed.] (Added 1971, No. 161 (Adj. Sess.), § 6, eff. date, see note; amended 1973, No. 266 (Adj. Sess.), § 3; 1975, No. 227 (Adj. Sess.), § 5, eff. April 7, 1976; 1977, No. 109, § 33(g).)

§ 5253. Powers and duties

(a) The Defender General has the primary responsibility for providing needy persons with legal services under this chapter. He or she shall have also the duty of providing legal services to those persons in the custody of the Commissioner of Corrections. He or she may provide these services personally, through public defenders employed under subsection 5254(a) of this title, or through attorneys-at-law as provided by subsection (b) of this section. No other official or agency of the State may supervise the Defender General or assign him or her duties in addition to those prescribed by this chapter. He or she may not practice law other than in the performance of his or her duties under this chapter or engage in any other occupation, except as provided in section 5203 of this title.

(b) When necessary or appropriate, the Defender General may contract for the services of investigators or additional attorneys-at-law to provide services to needy persons covered by this chapter or to carry out any other function of the Office of Defender General provided that:

(1) the services performed shall meet the professional standards that this chapter prescribes for services performed by the Office of the Defender General;

(2) the services are subject to the supervision and control of the Defender General, except as otherwise provided in section 5205 involving contracts providing for representation in cases involving conflict of interest; and

(3) the services contracted under this subsection shall be approved by the Secretary of Administration.

(c) The Defender General shall supervise the training of all public defenders, and for this purpose he or she may establish a training course.

(d) The Defender General shall consult and cooperate with interested professional groups with respect to the causes of crime, the development of effective means for discouraging crime, the rehabilitation of convicted criminals, the administration of criminal justice, and the administration of the Office of the Defender General.

(e) The Defender General may appoint a Deputy Defender General with the approval of the Governor, remove the Deputy at his or her pleasure, and shall be responsible for the Deputy's acts. The Deputy shall perform such duties as the Defender General shall direct, and in the absence or disability of the Defender General perform the duties of the Defender General. In case a vacancy occurs in the Office of the Defender General, the Deputy shall assume and discharge the duties of such office until the vacancy is filled. (Added 1971, No. 161 (Adj. Sess.), § 6, eff. date, see note; amended 1973, No. 77, § 42; 1973, No. 266 (Adj. Sess.), § 4; 1981, No. 146 (Adj. Sess.), § 3, eff. April 8, 1982; 1987, No. 183 (Adj. Sess.), § 24.)

§ 5254. Personnel designation and expenditures

(a) The Defender General, Deputy Defender General, public defenders, and deputy public defenders shall be exempt from the classified State service.

(b) Clerical and office staff in the Office of the Defender General and in all local offices shall be hired by the Defender General. Clerical and office staff shall be State employees paid by the State, and shall receive those benefits and compensation available to classified State employees who are similarly situated, unless otherwise covered by the provisions of a collective bargaining agreement setting forth the terms and conditions of employment, negotiated pursuant to the provisions of 3 V.S.A. chapter 27. Clerical and office staff employed by the Office of the Defender General shall not be part of the classified service as set forth in 3 V.S.A. chapter 13.

(c) The Deputy Defender General shall be entitled to compensation at an annual rate that does not exceed an amount $500.00 less than the salary of the Defender General. The public defenders and deputy public defenders shall be entitled to compensation at annual rates not to exceed an amount $1,000.00 less than the salary of the Defender General.

(d) The Defender General is responsible for assuming expenses for his or her office and all local offices. The entirety of expenditures shall not exceed those set in the annual budget of the Office of the Defender General and such expenditures shall be subject to the provisions of 32 V.S.A. § 702. (Added 1971, No. 161 (Adj. Sess.), § 6, eff. date, see note; amended 1973, No. 77, § 41; 1973, No. 266 (Adj. Sess.), § 5; 1977, No. 109, § 14; 1983, No. 88, § 15; 1987, No. 183 (Adj. Sess.), § 25; 1997, No. 92 (Adj. Sess.), §§ 6a, 8; 2015, No. 58, § E.203.1.)

§ 5255. Recovery from defendant

(a) The Defender General or Commissioner of Taxes, on behalf of the State, may recover reimbursement from each person who has received legal assistance or other benefit under this chapter:

(1) To which the person was not entitled;

(2) With respect to which the person was not a needy person when the person received it; or

(3) With respect to which the person has failed to make the certification required by section 5236(b) of this title;

and for which the person refuses to reimburse. Suit must be brought within six years after the date on which the aid was received.

(b) The Defender General or the Commissioner of Taxes, on behalf of the State, may recover reimbursement from each person, other than a person covered by subsection (a) of this section, who has received legal assistance under this chapter and who, on the date on which suit is brought, is financially able to reimburse the State for it according to the standards of ability to pay applicable under subdivision 5201(3), section 5231, and subsection 5238(b) of this title, but refuses to do so. Suit must be brought within three years after the date on which the benefit was received. The amount of recovery shall be equal to the average cost per case for representation supported by the budget of the Defender General for the calendar year in which legal assistance was completed as determined by the Defender General, less any reimbursement or co-payment actually paid for representation.

(c) Amounts recovered under this section shall be paid into the Public Defender Special Fund. (Added 1971, No. 161 (Adj. Sess.), § 6, eff. date, see note; 1991, No. 231 (Adj. Sess.), § 5, eff. May 28, 1992.)

§ 5256. Reports

The Defender General shall submit an annual report of his or her activities to the House and Senate Committees on Judiciary showing the number of persons represented under this chapter, the crimes involved, the outcome of each case, and the expenditures totaled by kind made in carrying out the responsibilities imposed by this chapter. (Added 1971, No. 161 (Adj. Sess.), § 6, eff. date, see note; amended 2011, No. 139 (Adj. Sess.), § 13, eff. May 14, 2012.)

§ 5257. Expenses

The Defender General shall be reimbursed for all reasonable expenses, including mileage and other travel expense, lodging, and subsistence, incurred in carrying out his or her responsibilities under this chapter. (Added 1971, No. 161 (Adj. Sess.), § 6, eff. date, see note.)

§ 5258. Audit

(a) In the 1995 audit and thereafter as appropriate, the auditor of accounts shall conduct an audit of the assignment of counsel to needy persons under section 5231 of this title, determination of financial need under section 5236 of this title, co-payment and reimbursement orders under section 5238 of this title and collection of reimbursements under section 5240 of this title.

(b) The audit shall evaluate compliance with statutory and legal requirements and internal controls. If noncompliance is found, the auditor shall recommend that proper corrections be made. The auditor shall recommend uniform practice by the responsible agencies and the courts throughout the State. The auditor shall report his or her findings in accordance with 32 V.S.A. § 163(5).

(c) The 1995 audit required by this section shall be funded in the amount of $5,000.00 from the special fund created under section 5239 of this title. (Added 1995, No. 21, § 5.)

§ 5259. Duty to investigate

(a) The Defender General shall investigate issues related to the health, safety, and welfare of inmates in correctional facilities and shall receive the cooperation of all State agencies in carrying out this duty. Issues that require an investigation by the Defender General shall, at a minimum, include:

(1) the death of an inmate;

(2) a suicide attempt that requires more than 24 hours of emergency hospitalization; and

(3) a critical incident that results in injury to an inmate from an assault, use of force, or accident in a correctional facility that requires more than 24 hours of emergency hospitalization.

(b)(1) When an incident enumerated in subdivisions (a)(1)-(3) of this section occurs, the Department of Corrections shall notify the Defender General as soon as reasonably practicable.

(2) The Commissioner shall report weekly to the Defender General regarding any critical incident that negatively impacts the health, safety, or welfare of an inmate, the conditions of confinement, or the adequacy of care provided to inmates.

(c) In carrying out the duties under this section, the Defender General:

(1) Shall be given reasonable unaccompanied access to the correctional facility and inmates and is authorized to speak with any relevant personnel from the Department of Corrections and other State

agencies subject to the individual's constitutional rights and to legitimate law enforcement concerns regarding preservation of a criminal investigation, if any.

(2) Shall be given broad access to records concerning the incident and any inmates involved in the incident. In response to a request for records from the Defender General, the Commissioner of Corrections shall provide the records promptly and no subpoena or public records request shall be required. Records subject to this section include video or audio recordings.

(d) The Defender General is authorized to protect the confidentiality of sources in the course of an investigation pursuant to this section. Work product generated in the course of representation of a client that contains confidential communication between an inmate and the Defender General shall not be discoverable and records of communications between inmates and the Defender General may be redacted.

(e) Where appropriate, the Defender General shall report to the Department of Corrections and the Joint Committee on Corrections Oversight identifying any concerns and suggested policy changes that arise from an incident that resulted in an investigation. (Added 2013, No. 110 (Adj. Sess.), § 1, eff. April 22, 2014.)

Subchapter 4: Office Of Public Defender

§ 5271. Offices established

The Defender General may establish public defender offices to carry out his or her responsibilities under this chapter. Each public defender office shall be headed by a public defender selected by the Defender General within the limits of funds and staffing authorized by the General Assembly. (Added 1971, No. 161 (Adj. Sess.), § 6, eff. date, see note; amended 1973, No. 266 (Adj. Sess.), § 6; 1981, No. 146 (Adj. Sess.), § 4, eff. April 8, 1982.)

§ 5272. Appointment; co-counsel; compensation

Upon notification under section 5234 of this title or upon request by the person concerned, a public defender shall represent the person with respect to whom the notification is made. If the public defender assigned to the court's jurisdiction is unable to represent the person, the court concerned shall assign an attorney to represent the person. Representation may include co-counsel or associate counsel in appropriate cases. Compensation of the appointed counsel shall be made from funds appropriated to the Office of the Defender General for the compensation of assigned counsel. (Added 1971, No. 161 (Adj. Sess.), § 6, eff. date, see note; amended 1973, No. 77, § 43; 1981, No. 146 (Adj. Sess.), § 5, eff. April 8, 1982.)

§ 5273. Qualifications

(a) The Deputy Defender General and a public defender must be licensed to practice law in this State and otherwise competent to counsel and defend a person charged with crime.

(b) The Deputy Defender General and a public defender may not otherwise engage in the practice of criminal law, except as otherwise provided in section 5203 of this title. This limitation shall not apply to the assigned counsel coordinator or to attorneys providing services under contract pursuant to section 5253 of this title. (Added 1971, No 161 (Adj. Sess.), § 6, eff. date, see note; amended 1981, No. 146 (Adj. Sess.), § 6, eff. April 8, 1982; 1987, No. 183 (Adj. Sess.), § 26.)

§ 5274. Replacement

At any stage, including appeal or other post-conviction proceedings, the Defender General or the court for good cause may assign a replacement attorney. The replacement attorney has the same functions with respect to the needy person as the attorney whom he or she replaces. (Added 1971, No. 161 (Adj. Sess.), § 6, eff. date, see note.)

§ 5275. Additional fees forbidden

A person who represents a needy person under this chapter may not receive any fee for his or her services in addition to that provided under this chapter. (Added 1971, No. 161 (Adj. Sess.), § 6, eff. date, see note.)

§ 5276. Reports

An attorney who is assigned by a court to represent a needy person under section 5272 or 5274 of this title shall report to the Defender General on his or her representation of the needy person, as prescribed by the Defender General. (Added 1971, No. 161 (Adj. Sess.), § 6, eff. date, see note.)

§ 5277. Use of State facilities

An attorney representing a person under this chapter is entitled to use any State technical services and facilities for the development or evaluation of evidence that are available to the prosecutor. (Added 1971, No. 161 (Adj. Sess.), § 6, eff. date, see note.)

Chapter 165: Victims

§ 5301. Definitions

As used in this chapter:

(1) "Disposition" means the sentencing or determination of penalty or punishment to be imposed upon a person convicted of a crime or against whom a finding of sufficient facts for conviction is made.

(2) "Family member" means a spouse, child, sibling, parent, next of kin, domestic partner, or legal guardian of a victim.

(3) "Restitution" means money or services that a court orders a defendant to pay or render to a victim as a part of the disposition.

(4) "Victim" means a person who sustains physical, emotional, or financial injury or death as a direct result of the commission or attempted commission of a crime or act of delinquency and shall also include the family members of a minor, a person who has been found to be incompetent, or a homicide victim.

(5) "Affected person" means any of the following persons who has requested notification in writing from the court or the Department of Corrections:

(A) witnesses;

(B) jurors;

(C) family members who are not covered by subdivision (4) of this section;

(D) any other persons who demonstrate to the court that the release or escape of a defendant will constitute a threat of physical, emotional, or financial injury or death.

(6) "Release" means release from a correctional facility to furlough or to probation or parole supervision, release from a correctional facility upon expiration of sentence or release from a correctional facility on bail after the defendant's initial appearance.

(7) "Listed crime" means any of the following offenses:

(A) stalking as defined in section 1062 of this title;

(B) aggravated stalking as defined in subdivision 1063(a)(3) or (4) of this title;

(C) domestic assault as defined in section 1042 of this title;

(D) first degree aggravated domestic assault as defined in section 1043 of this title;

(E) second degree aggravated domestic assault as defined in section 1044 of this title;

(F) sexual assault as defined in section 3252 of this title or its predecessor as it was defined in section 3201 or 3202 of this title;

(G) aggravated sexual assault as defined in section 3253 of this title;

(H) lewd or lascivious conduct as defined in section 2601 of this title;

(I) lewd or lascivious conduct with a child as defined in section 2602 of this title;

(J) murder as defined in section 2301 of this title;

(K) aggravated murder as defined in section 2311 of this title;

(L) manslaughter as defined in section 2304 of this title;

(M) aggravated assault as defined in section 1024 of this title;

(N) assault and robbery with a dangerous weapon as defined in subsection 608(b) of this title;

(O) arson causing death as defined in section 501 of this title;

(P) assault and robbery causing bodily injury as defined in subsection 608(c) of this title;

(Q) maiming as defined in section 2701 of this title;

(R) kidnapping as defined in section 2405 of this title or its predecessor as it was defined in section 2401 of this title;

(S) unlawful restraint in the second degree as defined in section 2406 of this title;

(T) unlawful restraint in the first degree as defined in section 2407 of this title;

(U) recklessly endangering another person as defined in section 1025 of this title;

(V) violation of abuse prevention order as defined in section 1030 of this title, excluding violation of an abuse prevention order issued pursuant to 15 V.S.A. § 1104 (emergency relief) or 33 V.S.A. § 6936 (emergency relief);

(W) operating vehicle under the influence of alcohol or other substance with either death or serious bodily injury resulting as defined in 23 V.S.A. § 1210(f) and (g);

(X) careless or negligent operation resulting in serious bodily injury or death as defined in 23 V.S.A. § 1091(b);

(Y) leaving the scene of an accident with serious bodily injury or death as defined in 23 V.S.A. § 1128(b) or (c);

(Z) burglary into an occupied dwelling as defined in subsection 1201(c) of this title;

(AA) the attempt to commit any of the offenses listed in this section;

(BB) abuse (section 1376 of this title), abuse by restraint (section 1377 of this title), neglect (section 1378 of this title), sexual abuse (section 1379 of this title), financial exploitation (section 1380 of this title), and exploitation of services (section 1381 of this title);

(CC) aggravated sexual assault of a child in violation of section 3253a of this title;

(DD) human trafficking in violation of section 2652 of this title; and

(EE) aggravated human trafficking in violation of section 2653 of this title. (Added 1985, No. 182 (Adj. Sess.), § 2, eff. Sept. 1, 1986; amended 1989, No. 290 (Adj. Sess.), § 1; 1995, No. 170 (Adj. Sess.), § 5, eff. Sept. 1, 1996; 1999, No. 4, § 1; 2005, No. 79, § 3; 2009, No. 1, § 13a, eff. March 4, 2009; 2009, No. 58, § 3; 2011, No. 55, § 6; 2013, No. 96 (Adj. Sess.), § 59; 2015, No. 133 (Adj. Sess.), § 3, eff. May 25, 2016; 2017, No. 83, § 161(3).)

§ 5302. Reporting to law enforcement agencies

Victims are eligible for the services set forth under this chapter only if the crime has been reported to law enforcement authorities. (Added 1985, No. 182 (Adj. Sess.), § 2, eff. Sept. 1, 1986.)

§ 5303. Legislative purpose

(a) The fundamental objective underlying this chapter is the protection of victims of crime. This chapter seeks to ensure that crime victims are treated with the dignity and respect they deserve while functioning in a system in which they find themselves through no fault of their own. This chapter seeks to accommodate that objective and balance crime victims' needs and rights with criminal defendants' rights.

(b) This chapter also seeks to reduce the financial, emotional, and physical consequences of criminal victimization, to prevent victimization by the law enforcement and criminal justice system, and to assist victims with problems that result from their victimization.

(c) Victims of crime shall be treated with courtesy and sensitivity by the court system and the State's Attorney's office. Those responsible should ensure that the process of criminal prosecution moves smoothly and expeditiously and, after the conclusion of a prosecution, should cooperate in an appropriate manner with victims who seek to enforce their civil rights and remedies, which cooperation may include preserving and producing evidence, documents, and testimony to the victims for use in such efforts. (Added 1985, No. 182 (Adj. Sess.), § 2, eff. Sept. 1, 1986; amended 1995, No. 170 (Adj. Sess.), § 1, eff. Sept. 1, 1996.)

§ 5304. Victims Assistance Program

(a) The Center for Crime Victim Services shall create and maintain a Victims Assistance Program. Except as otherwise provided by law, victim advocates shall provide victims the following services:

(1) Information. Victims shall be informed as to the level of protection available, procedures to be followed in order to receive applicable witness fees, the right to seek restitution as an element of the final disposition of the case, and the right to appear at sentencing in accordance with section 7006 of this title.

(2) Notification. Victims, other than victims of acts of delinquency, shall be notified in a timely manner when a court proceeding involving their case is scheduled to take place and when a court proceeding to which they have been summoned will not take place as scheduled. Victims shall also be notified as to the final disposition of the case, and shall be notified of their right to request notification of a person's release or escape under section 5305 of this title.

(3) Services. Victims shall be entitled to:

(A) receive short-term counseling and support from the victim advocate and referrals for further services;

(B) assistance in obtaining financial assistance and minimizing loss of pay or other benefits resulting from involvement in the criminal justice process;

(C) assistance in documenting and preparing requests for restitution and insurance reimbursement;

(D) assistance in obtaining protection through local law enforcement agencies from harm and threats of harm arising out of their cooperation with the court system;

(E) assistance in the return of property from law enforcement agencies;

(F) assistance and support in dealing with law enforcement agencies; and

(G) transportation as needed to court proceedings.

(b) A victim may decline any service provided by the Victims Assistance Program under this section. (Added 1985, No. 182 (Adj. Sess.), § 2, eff. Sept. 1, 1986; amended 1989, No. 290 (Adj. Sess.), § 2; 1991, No. 263 (Adj. Sess.), § 2; 1995, No. 170 (Adj. Sess.), § 3, eff. Sept. 1, 1996; 2015, No. 97 (Adj. Sess.), § 75.)

§ 5305. Information concerning release from custody

(a) Victims, other than victims of acts of delinquency, and affected persons shall have the right to request notification by the agency having custody of the defendant before the defendant is released, including a release on bail or conditions of release, furlough, or other community program, upon termination or discharge from probation, or whenever the defendant escapes, is recaptured, dies, or receives a pardon or commutation of sentence. Notice shall be given to the victim or affected person as expeditiously as possible at the address or telephone number provided to the agency having custody of the defendant by the person requesting notice. Any address or telephone number so provided shall be kept confidential. The prosecutor's office shall ensure that victims are made aware of their right to notification of an offender's scheduled release date pursuant to this section.

(b) If the defendant is released on conditions at arraignment, the prosecutor's office shall inform the victim of a listed crime of the conditions of release.

(c) If requested by a victim of a listed crime, the Department of Corrections shall:

(1) at least 30 days before a parole board hearing concerning the defendant, inform the victim of the hearing and of the victim's right to testify before the parole board or to submit a written statement for the parole board to consider; and

(2) promptly inform the victim of the decision of the parole board, including providing to the victim any conditions attached to the defendant's release on parole. (Added 1985, No. 182 (Adj. Sess.), § 2; amended 1989, No. 290 (Adj. Sess.), § 3; 1995, No. 170 (Adj. Sess.), § 4, eff. Sept. 1, 1996; 2015, No. 155 (Adj. Sess.), § 1; 2019, No. 148 (Adj. Sess.), § 15, eff. Jan. 1, 2021.)

§ 5306. Victim advocates

In order to carry out the provisions of the Victims Assistance Program, State's Attorneys are authorized to hire victim advocates who shall serve at their pleasure unless otherwise modified by a collective bargaining agreement entered into pursuant to 3 V.S.A. chapter 27. Nothing in this section shall be construed to limit the subjects for bargaining pursuant to 3 V.S.A. § 904. (Added 1985, No. 182 (Adj. Sess.), § 2, eff. Sept. 1, 1986; amended 2017, No. 81, § 10, eff. June 15, 2017.)

§ 5307. Cooperation

State's attorneys, local law enforcement agencies, local social service agencies, and courts shall cooperate to afford victims of crimes the right and services described in this chapter; however, victim advocates shall not delegate to these agencies or to the courts the duties imposed on them under section 5304 of this title. (Added 1985, No. 182 (Adj. Sess.), § 2, eff. Sept. 1, 1986.)

§ 5308. Notice and right to be present at arraignment

If practicable the victim of a listed crime shall be given notice of the defendant's arraignment by the law enforcement agency that issued the citation or made the arrest. The victim of a listed crime shall have the right to be present at the defendant's arraignment. The prosecutor's office shall inform the victim about the issues concerning bail and the prosecutor shall advise the court of the victim's position regarding bail. (Added 1995, No. 170 (Adj. Sess.), § 6, eff. Sept. 1, 1996.)

§ 5309. Presence in courtroom

The victim of a listed crime shall be entitled to be present during all court proceedings subject to the provisions of Rule 615 of the Vermont Rules of Evidence. (Added 1995, No. 170 (Adj. Sess.), § 7, eff. Sept. 1, 1996.)

§ 5310. Nondisclosure of information about victim

A witness testifying in a criminal proceeding, including any discovery proceedings, shall not be compelled to disclose the victim's residential address or place of employment on the record unless the court finds, based upon a preponderance of the evidence, that nondisclosure of the information will prejudice the defendant. (Added 1995, No. 170 (Adj. Sess.), § 8, eff. Sept. 1, 1996.)

§ 5311. Prompt return of property

A law enforcement agency holding property of any individual shall take reasonable care of the property. Upon authorization of the prosecutor, the law enforcement agency holding the property, unless it is contraband or subject to forfeiture, shall promptly notify the individual that the property is no longer needed for evidentiary purposes and may be picked up by the individual. (Added 1995, No. 170 (Adj. Sess.), § 9, eff. Sept. 1, 1996.)

§ 5312. Victim's interest in speedy prosecution

(a) The prosecutor's office shall make every effort to inform a victim of a listed crime of any pending motion that may substantially delay any deposition, change of plea, trial, sentencing hearing, or restitution hearing. The prosecutor shall inform the court of how the victim was notified and the victim's position on the motion, if any. In the event the victim was not notified, the prosecutor shall inform the court why notification did not take place.

(b) If a victim of a listed crime objects to a delay, the court shall consider the victim's objection. (Added 1995, No. 170 (Adj. Sess.), § 9a, eff. Sept. 1, 1996; amended 2007, No. 40, § 2.)

§ 5313. Limitations on employer

An employer may not discharge or discipline a victim of a listed crime or a victim's family member or representative for honoring a subpoena to testify. (Added 1995, No. 170 (Adj. Sess.), § 9b, eff. Sept. 1, 1996.)

§ 5314. Information from law enforcement agency

(a) Information to all victims. After initial contact between a victim and a law enforcement agency responsible for investigating a crime, the agency shall promptly give in writing to the victim:

(1) an explanation of the victim's rights under this chapter and chapter 167 of this title;

(2) information concerning the availability of:

(A) assistance to victims, including medical, housing, counseling, and emergency services;

(B) compensation for victims under chapter 167 of this title, and the name, street address, and telephone number of the Center for Crime Victim Services;

(C) protection for the victim, including protective court orders; and

(D) access by the victim and the defendant to records related to the case which are public under the provisions of 1 V.S.A. chapter 5, subchapter 3 (access to public records).

(b) Information to victims of listed crimes. As soon as practicable, the law enforcement agency shall use reasonable efforts to give to the victim of a listed crime, as relevant, all of the following:

(1) Information as to the accused's identity unless inconsistent with law enforcement purposes.

(2) Information as to whether the accused has been taken into custody.

(3) The file number of the case and the name, office street address, and telephone number of the law enforcement officer currently assigned to investigate the case.

(4) The prosecutor's name, office street address, and telephone number.

(5) An explanation that no individual is under an obligation to respond to questions that may be asked outside a courtroom or deposition.

(6) Information concerning any bail or conditions of release imposed on the defendant by a judicial officer prior to arraignment or an initial court appearance. (Added 1995, No. 170 (Adj. Sess.), § 10, eff. Sept. 1, 1996; amended 2015, No. 97 (Adj. Sess.), § 76; 2015, No. 155 (Adj. Sess.), § 2.)

§ 5315. Information concerning appeal or post-conviction remedies

If the defendant appeals or pursues a post-conviction remedy, the prosecutor's office shall promptly inform the victim of a listed crime of that fact, shall explain the significance of such a proceeding and shall promptly notify the victim of the date, time, and place of any hearing and of the decision. (Added 1995, No. 170 (Adj. Sess.), § 11, eff. Sept. 1, 1996.)

§ 5316. Complete identification by prosecution and defense

Any individual associated with the prosecution or defense of a listed crime, including attorneys, investigators, or experts, who comes in contact with the victim or the victim's family shall properly identify himself or herself and by whom he or she is employed. (Added 1995, No. 170 (Adj. Sess.), § 12, eff. Sept. 1, 1996.)

§ 5317. General requirements for information

(a) The information required to be furnished to victims under this chapter shall be provided upon request of the victim and, unless otherwise specifically provided, may be furnished either orally or in writing.

(b) A person responsible for furnishing information may rely upon the most recent name, address, and telephone number furnished by the victim.

(c) The court, State's Attorneys, public defenders, law enforcement agencies, and the Departments of Corrections and of Public Safety shall develop and implement an automated notification system to deliver the information required to be furnished to victims under this chapter. (Added 1995, No. 170 (Adj. Sess.), § 13, eff. Sept. 1, 1996; amended 2009, No. 154 (Adj. Sess.), § 109a.)

§ 5318. Derivative rights of member of victim's family

(a) If the victim is a minor or is unable to exercise his or her rights under the provisions of this chapter, section 7006 of this title, or 28 V.S.A. § 507, a family member of the victim shall be permitted to do so in place of the victim. If more than one family member of the victim's family attempts to exercise the victim's rights, the court may designate one of them to exercise those rights based on the best interests of the victim. If no family member is able to exercise such rights, a victim's advocate or other representative may, in situations where a victim is authorized by law to address the court or Parole Board, attend and read to the court or Parole Board a written statement prepared by the victim or the victim's family member without the assistance of the prosecutor or a law enforcement officer.

(b) If a victim is a minor or is incapacitated, incompetent, or deceased, a family member of the victim may exercise the rights of the victim under sections 5305, 5308-5317, and 7006 of this title; 28 V.S.A. §§ 205, 252, and 507; and 33 V.S.A. § 5233. (Added 1995, No. 170 (Adj. Sess.), § 14, eff. Sept. 1, 1996; amended 2013, No. 131 (Adj. Sess.), § 109.)

§ 5319. Victim not a party

The rights of victims contained in this chapter do not entitle a victim to be a party in any proceeding, or to any procedural rights that are not specifically provided for in this chapter, including any right to request a delay or rescheduling of any proceeding. (Added 1995, No. 170 (Adj. Sess.), § 15, eff. Sept. 1, 1996.)

§ 5320. Repealed. 2007, No. 185 (Adj. Sess.), § 13, eff. June 5, 2008.

§ 5321. Appearance by victim

(a) The victim of a crime has the following rights in any sentencing proceedings concerning the person convicted of that crime, or in the event a proposed plea agreement filed with the court recommends a deferred sentence, at any change of plea hearing concerning the person charged with committing that crime:

(1) to be given advance notice by the prosecutor's office of the date of the proceedings; and

(2) to appear, personally, to express reasonably his or her views concerning the crime, the person convicted, and the need for restitution.

(b) The change of plea hearing or sentencing shall not be delayed or voided by reason of the failure to give the victim the required notice or the failure of the victim to appear.

(c) In accordance with court rules, at the sentencing or change of plea hearing, the court shall ask if the victim is present and, if so, whether the victim would like to be heard regarding sentencing or the proposed deferral of sentencing. In imposing the sentence or considering whether to defer sentencing, the court shall consider any views offered at the hearing by the victim. If the victim is not present, the court shall ask whether the victim has expressed, either orally or in writing, views regarding sentencing or the proposed deferral of sentencing and shall take those views into consideration in imposing the sentence or considering whether to defer sentencing.

(d) At or before the sentencing hearing, the prosecutor's office shall instruct the victim of a listed crime, in all cases where the court imposes a sentence that includes a period of incarceration, that a sentence of incarceration is to the custody of the Commissioner of Corrections and that the Commissioner of Corrections has the authority to affect the actual time the defendant shall serve in incarceration through good time credit, furlough, work-release, and other early release programs. In addition, the prosecutor's office shall explain the significance of a minimum and maximum sentence to the victim and shall also explain the function of parole and how it may affect the actual amount of time the defendant may be incarcerated.

(e) At or before a change of plea hearing where the plea agreement filed with the court proposes a deferred sentence, the prosecutor's office shall instruct the victim of a listed crime about the significance of a deferred sentence and the potential consequences of a violation of conditions imposed by the court. In addition, the prosecutor's office shall consult with the victim concerning any proposed probation conditions prior to the hearing.

(f) The prosecutor's office shall use all reasonable efforts to keep the victim informed and consult with the victim throughout the plea agreement negotiation process in any case involving a victim of a listed crime. (Added 1999, No. 4, § 3; amended 2015, No. 5, § 2, eff. April 9, 2015; 2015, No. 155 (Adj. Sess.), § 3.)

§ 5322. Confidentiality

When responding to a request for public records, or on any State website or State payment report, the State of Vermont shall not disclose to the public the name or any other identifying information, including the town of residence or the type or purpose of the payment, of an applicant to the Victims Compensation Program, a victim named in a restitution judgment order, or a recipient of the Domestic and Sexual Violence Survivors' Transitional Employment Program. (Added 2011, No. 55, § 12.)

Chapter 167: Crime Victims

Subchapter 1: Compensation To Victims Of Crime

§ 5351. Definitions

As used in this chapter:

(1) "Board" means the Victims Compensation Board established under this chapter.

(2) "Dependent" means the victim's spouse or a person who is legally dependent for support upon a victim.

(3) "Crime" includes delinquent acts and an act of terrorism, as defined in 18 U.S.C. § 2331, committed outside the United States against a resident of this State.

(4) "Injury" means actual bodily harm or pregnancy, or emotional harm resulting from the crime.

(5) "Pecuniary loss" means, in the case of a victim, the amount of medical or medically related expenses, loss of wages, and any other expenses that the Board feels became necessary as a direct result of the crime. Medical or medically related expenses may include, but are not limited to, the costs of individual or family psychological, psychiatric, or mental health counseling and the costs of replacing or repairing eyeglasses, hearing aids, dentures, or any prosthetic devices that were taken, lost, or destroyed during the commission of the crime. In the case of a dependent, "pecuniary loss" means the cost of psychological, psychiatric, or mental health counseling, funeral expenses for the victim, and, upon demonstration of financial hardship, temporary living expenses.

(6) "Unreimbursed pecuniary loss" means a pecuniary loss:

(A) that is not covered by medical, hospitalization, or disability insurance or workers' compensation; and

(B) that has not been ordered by the court to be restored to the victim or dependent by the person who caused the loss; or

(C) that has been ordered by the court to be restored to the victim or dependent but has not been paid by the person who caused the loss.

(7) "Victim" means:

(A) a person who sustains injury or death as a direct result of the commission or attempted commission of a crime; or

(B) an intervenor who is injured or killed in an attempt to assist the person described in subdivision (A) of this subdivision (7) or the police; or

(C) a surviving immediate family member of a homicide victim, including a spouse, domestic partner, parent, sibling, child, grandparent, or other survivor who may suffer severe emotional harm as a result of the victim's death as determined on a case-by-case basis in the discretion of the Board; or

(D) a resident of this State who is injured or killed as the result of a crime committed outside the United States.

(8) "Profits from crimes" means:

(A) any property obtained through or income generated from the commission of a crime in which the defendant was convicted;

(B) any property obtained by or income generated from the sale, conversion, or exchange of proceeds of a crime, including any gain realized by such sale, conversion, or exchange;

(C) any property that the defendant obtained or any income generated as a result of having committed the crime, including any assets obtained through the use of unique knowledge acquired during the commission of or in preparation for the commission of the crime, as well as any property obtained or income generated from the sale, conversion, or exchange of such property and any gain realized by such sale, conversion, or exchange; and

(D) any property defendant obtained or any income generated from the sale of tangible property the value of which is increased by the notoriety gained from the conviction of an offense by the person accused or convicted of the crime. (Added 1989, No. 214 (Adj. Sess.), § 1; amended 1991, No. 107, § 2; 1995, No. 22, § 1; 1997, No. 61, §§ 56a, 56b; 2003, No. 92 (Adj. Sess.), § 3, eff. April 13, 2004; 2007, No. 173 (Adj. Sess.), § 1; 2009, No. 55, § 1, eff. June 1, 2009.)

§ 5352. Victims Compensation Board

(a) The Victims Compensation Board is established for the purpose of awarding compensation to victims of crimes and to their dependents. The Board shall consist of five members appointed by the Governor as follows: one physician licensed to practice in this State, one attorney admitted to practice in this State, one individual who is a crime victim, and two public members. Each member shall serve for a term of three years. A vacancy shall be filled in the same manner as the original appointment for the remainder of the unexpired term.

(b) The Board shall function independently. In order to maximize eligibility for federal reimbursement, the Center for Crime Victim Services shall coordinate the Victims Compensation Program with other programs compensating victims of crime, including offender restitution and counseling costs for victims of child sexual abuse.

(c) The Board shall meet at least monthly to review and determine applications. Members of the Board are entitled to compensation and expenses as provided under 32 V.S.A. § 1010.

(d) The Board shall adopt rules under 3 V.S.A. chapter 25 necessary to carry out the purposes of this chapter, including rules relating to evaluation and determination of awards under this chapter.

(e) The Board may employ such staff as needed to carry out the provisions of this chapter. Staff retained by the Board shall not be considered State employees. (Added 1989, No. 214 (Adj. Sess.), § 1; amended 1991, No. 263 (Adj. Sess.), § 3; 2015, No. 97 (Adj. Sess.), § 77.)

§ 5353. Application for compensation

(a) A victim or a dependent of a victim shall, upon application, be eligible for compensation if:

(1) a law enforcement official has filed a report concluding that a crime was committed which resulted in the injury or death of the victim; and

(2) the crime was committed in this State; or

(3) the victim is a Vermont resident, the state in which the crime occurred does not have an eligible crime Victims Compensation Program and the applicant would have been eligible for compensation under this chapter if the crime had been committed in this State; or

(4) the victim is a Vermont resident who is injured or killed by an act of terrorism outside the United States, to the extent that compensation is not otherwise available under federal law.

(b) Victims of crimes subject to federal jurisdiction, and their dependents, shall be eligible for compensation on the same basis as victims of State crimes.

(c) The application for compensation shall be signed by the applicant and shall contain at least the following information which shall be provided subject to the penalties of perjury:

(1) A description of the date, nature, and circumstances of the crime.

(2) A complete financial statement, including pecuniary losses and the extent to which the applicant has been or may be indemnified for these expenses from any source.

(3) When appropriate, a statement indicating the extent of any disability resulting from the injury.

(4) When reasonably available, copies of all law enforcement reports and reports from all health care providers who treated or examined the victim at the time of or after the crime or who treated or examined the dependent.

(5) The applicant's Social Security number for the purpose of making cash payment to the applicant in accordance with section 5356 of this title.

(d) In any case in which the person entitled to compensation under this chapter is a minor or is mentally incompetent or unable to apply because of his or her physical condition, the application may be made on the person's behalf by a parent, spouse, guardian, or other person authorized to administer the estate.

(e) In any case in which a victim otherwise eligible for compensation under this chapter dies without making an application, the Board may, upon application, award medical or medically related expenses to the victim's estate.

(f) The Board may award funeral expenses to the next of kin of a deceased victim who is not survived by a dependent.

(g) A victim or a dependent of a victim shall be eligible for compensation for pecuniary losses sustained as a result of a crime that occurred after July 1, 1987 if the losses occurred on or after July 1, 1990.

(h) A victim who is under the age of 18 at the time the application for compensation is filed shall be eligible for compensation for pecuniary losses sustained as a result of a crime, no matter when the crime occurred, if the losses occurred on or after July 1, 1990.

(i) A victim shall be eligible for compensation for pecuniary losses sustained as a result of a crime which occurred before July 1, 1987 if at the time of application the case is being investigated or is being prosecuted. (Added 1989, No. 214 (Adj. Sess.), § 1; amended 1991, No. 107, §§ 1, 3, 5; 1997, No. 147 (Adj. Sess.), § 53; 2005, No. 162 (Adj. Sess.), § 2, eff. Jan. 1, 2007; 2007, No. 173 (Adj. Sess.), § 5.)

§ 5354. Review of applications

(a) The Board shall review applications to determine whether compensation should be awarded under this chapter.

(b) If, in the opinion of the Board, a report by an impartial medical expert relating to the applicant's health care history, the applicant's condition after the injury or the cause of the victim's death would be of material assistance, the Board may order such an examination and report, at the Board's expense.

(c) In making its determination, the board shall consider all relevant information presented to the Board. (Added 1989, No. 214 (Adj. Sess.), § 1.)

§ 5355. Approval or rejection of application

(a) After review of the evidence relevant to the application for compensation, the Board shall approve the application if a preponderance of the evidence shows that as a direct result of the crime an injury occurred that resulted in a pecuniary loss to the victim or the dependent.

(b) An application for assistance shall be denied if any of the following apply:

(1) The application was not made within the period of time permitted for commencing prosecution of the crime. The Board may extend the time for filing for good cause shown.

(2) The victim violated a criminal law of this State that caused or contributed to the victim's injuries or death.

(c) If the Board intends to deny an application, the Board shall send the applicant written notice of the decision personally or by certified mail. The notice shall include a statement of the reasons for the action and shall advise the applicant that the applicant may file a petition with the Board for review of its preliminary decision within 30 days of the date on which the notice is mailed. After the hearing, the Board shall affirm or reverse the preliminary denial, explaining the reasons therefor in writing.

(d) The decision of the Board shall be final. (Added 1989, No. 214 (Adj. Sess.), § 1; amended 1991, No. 107, § 4.)

§ 5356. Amount of compensation

(a) If the application is approved, the Board shall authorize cash payments, not to exceed $10,000.00, to or on behalf of the applicant, equal to the unreimbursed pecuniary loss directly resulting from the injury or death of the victim. Applications approved in any fiscal year shall not exceed funds appropriated and authorized in that fiscal year for this purpose.

(b) Funds available to the Board for payments include fees collected and deposited by the court into the Victims Compensation Fund as described in section 7282 of this title and monies from inmate labor contributions from the prison industries enhancement program or from any other source.

(c) The Board may reimburse health care facilities and health care providers as defined in 18 V.S.A. § 9402 at 60 percent of the billed charges for compensation claims for uninsured crime victims who do not qualify for the hospital's patient assistance program, Medicaid, or Medicare. The health care facility or health care provider shall not bill any balance to the uninsured crime victim. (Added 1989, No. 214 (Adj. Sess.), § 1; amended 1995, No. 63, § 53; 2007, No. 173 (Adj. Sess.), § 2; 2015, No. 34, § 2, eff. May 26, 2015.)

§ 5357. Subrogation; lien; disposition of proceeds

The State shall be subrogated to the rights of the victim, assignee, heir, or dependent to whom cash payments are granted to the extent of the cash payments granted, less the amount of any fine imposed by the court on the perpetrator of the crime. The State shall have a lien therefor and may commence an action or intervene in any action to protect and enforce the lien. Such subrogation rights shall be against any person liable for the pecuniary loss. (Added 1989, No. 214 (Adj. Sess.), § 1; amended 2017, No. 107 (Adj. Sess.), § 1, eff. April 19, 2018.)

§ 5358. Duties of law enforcement agency

Every law enforcement agency shall inform victims of crimes and their dependents of the provisions of this chapter and provide application forms to persons who desire to seek compensation. The Board shall provide application forms and other information which local law enforcement agencies may require to comply with this section. (Added 1989, No. 214 (Adj. Sess.), § 1.)

§ 5358a. Application information; confidentiality

(a) All documents reviewed by the Victims Compensation Board for purposes of approving an application for compensation shall be confidential and shall not be disclosed without the consent of the victim except as provided in this section and subsection 7043(c) of this title.

(b) For the purpose of requesting restitution, the amount of assistance provided by the Victims Compensation Board shall be established by copies of bills submitted to the Victims Compensation Board reflecting the amount paid by the Board and stating that the services for which payment was made were for uninsured pecuniary losses.

(c) The following shall be confidential and shall be redacted by the Victims Compensation Board for any purpose including restitution: the victim's residential address, telephone number, and other contact information and the victim's Social Security number. In cases involving stalking, sexual offenses, and domestic violence, the following information shall also be confidential and shall not be disclosed by the Victims Compensation Board for any purpose, including restitution, absent a court order:

(1) the victim's employer's name, telephone number, address, or any other contact information; and

(2) the victim's medical or mental health provider's name, telephone number, address, or any other contact information.

(d) Meetings of the Victims Compensation Board relating to victims compensation or offender restitution shall not be subject to the Vermont Open Meeting Law, 1 V.S.A. chapter 5, subchapter 2. Annually, the Board shall hold an open meeting to present information and data concerning the victims compensation and offender restitution programs, including aggregate information on cases, pecuniary loss, expense reimbursement, restitution orders, profits from crimes, and nonidentifying information on the amounts of compensation awarded to victims. (Added 2011, No. 145 (Adj. Sess.), § 6, eff. May 15, 2012; amended 2019, No. 127 (Adj. Sess.), § 1.)

Subchapter 2: Center For Crime Victim Services

§ 5359. Victims Compensation Special Fund

(a) There is created a fund to be known as the Victims Compensation Fund. This Fund shall be administered by the Victims Compensation Board established by section 5352 of this title. The purpose of this Fund shall be to support the activities and the operating costs of the Victims Compensation Board and the Center for Crime Victim Services.

(b) The Victims Compensation Fund shall consist of:

(1) Fees imposed by the court clerk and designated for deposit into the Fund pursuant to section 7282 of this title.

(2) Restitution as ordered by the court pursuant to section 7043 of this title.

(3) Funds received from inmate labor contribution from the prison industries enhancement program or from any other source.

(4) Appropriations by the General Assembly.

(c) Balances in the Fund at the end of the fiscal year shall be carried forward and remain in the Fund. (Added 2003, No. 57, § 13a, eff. June 4, 2003; amended 2015, No. 97 (Adj. Sess.), § 78.)

§ 5360. Domestic and Sexual Violence Special Fund

A Domestic and Sexual Violence Special Fund is established, to be managed in accordance with 32 V.S.A. chapter 7, subchapter 5 and administered by the Center for Crime Victim Services created in section 5361 of this title. The revenues of the Fund shall consist of that portion of the additional surcharge on penalties and fines imposed by section 7282 of this title deposited in the Domestic and Sexual Violence Special Fund and that portion of the town clerks' fee for issuing and recording civil marriage or civil union licenses in 32 V.S.A. § 1712(1) deposited in the Domestic and Sexual Violence Special Fund. The

Fund may be expended by the Center for Crime Victim Services for budgeted grants to the Vermont Network against Domestic and Sexual Violence and for the Criminal Justice Training Council position dedicated to domestic violence training, pursuant to 20 V.S.A. § 2365(c). (Added 2011, No. 162 (Adj. Sess.), § E.220.1; amended 2015, No. 97 (Adj. Sess.), § 79.)

§ 5361. Center for Crime Victim Services

(a) The Center for Crime Victim Services is created and shall be responsible for the following:

(1) strengthen and coordinate programs serving crime victims;

(2) promote the rights and needs of crime victims statewide;

(3) [Repealed.]

(4) assist in the development and administration of other programs and services for crime victims and witnesses, as needed;

(5) administer the federal Victims of Crime Act funds (VOCA); and

(6) serve as a clearinghouse for information regarding victims of crime.

(b) The Center shall be governed by and attached to the Victims Compensation Board for administrative support.

(c) The Board may employ such staff as necessary to carry out its responsibilities under this chapter and chapter 165 of this title. (Added 1991, No. 263 (Adj. Sess.), § 1; amended 1993, No. 88 § 2; 2003, No. 57, § 2, eff. July 1, 2004; 2015, No. 97 (Adj. Sess.), § 80.)

§ 5362. Restitution Unit

(a) A Restitution Unit is created within the Center for Crime Victim Services for purposes of ensuring that crime victims receive restitution when it is ordered by the court.

(b) The Restitution Unit shall administer the Restitution Fund established under section 5363 of this title.

(c) The Restitution Unit shall have the authority to:

(1) Collect restitution from the offender when it is ordered by the court under section 7043 of this title.

(2) Enforce a restitution obligation as a civil judgment under section 7043 of this title. The Restitution Unit shall enforce restitution orders issued prior to July 1, 2004 pursuant to the law in effect on the date the order is issued.

(3)(A) Share and access information, including information maintained by the National Criminal Information Center, consistent with Vermont and federal law, from the court, the Departments of Corrections, of Motor Vehicles, of Taxes, and of Labor, and law enforcement agencies in order to carry out its collection and enforcement functions. The Restitution Unit, for purposes of establishing and enforcing restitution payment obligations, is designated as a law enforcement agency for the sole purpose of requesting and obtaining access to information needed to identify or locate a person, including access to information maintained by the National Criminal Information Center.

(B) Provide information to the Department of Corrections concerning supervised offenders, including an offender's restitution payment history and balance, address and contact information, employment information, and information concerning the Restitution Unit's collection efforts.

(C) The Restitution Unit is specifically authorized to collect, record, use, and disseminate Social Security numbers as needed for the purpose of collecting restitution and enforcing restitution judgment orders issued by the court, provided that the Social Security number is maintained on a separate form that is confidential and exempt from public inspection and copying under the Public Records Act.

(4) Investigate and verify losses as determined by the Restitution Unit, including losses that may be eligible for advance payment from the Restitution Special Fund, and verify the amount of insurance or other payments paid to or for the benefit of a victim, and reduce the amount collected or to be collected from the offender or disbursed to the victim from the Crime Victims' Restitution Special Fund accordingly. The Restitution Unit, when appropriate, shall submit to the Court a proposed revised restitution order, with copies provided to the victim and the offender. No hearing shall be required.

(5) Adopt such administrative rules as are reasonably necessary to carry out the purposes set forth in this section.

(6)(A) Report offenders' payment histories to credit reporting agencies. The Unit shall not make a report under this subdivision (6) until after it has notified the offender of the proposed report by first class mail or other like means to give actual notice, and provided the offender a period not to exceed 20 days to contest the accuracy of the information with the Unit. The Unit shall immediately notify each credit bureau organization to which information has been furnished of any increases or decreases in the amount of restitution owed by the offender.

(B) Obtain offenders' credit reports from credit reporting agencies. The Unit shall not obtain a report under this subdivision (6) until after it has notified the offender by first class mail or other means likely to give actual notice of its intent to obtain the report.

(7) Enter into a repayment contract with a juvenile or adult accepted into a diversion program and to bring a civil action to enforce the contract when a diversion program has referred an individual pursuant to 3 V.S.A. § 164a.

(8) Contract with one or more sheriff's departments for the purposes of serving process, warrants, demand letters, and mittimuses in restitution cases, and contract with one or more law enforcement agencies or other investigators for the purpose of investigating and locating offenders and enforcing restitution judgment orders.

(9) Collect from an offender subject to a restitution judgment order all fees and direct costs, including reasonable attorney's fees, incurred by the Restitution Unit as a result of enforcing the order and investigating and locating the offender. (Added 2003, No. 57, § 3, eff. June 4, 2003; amended 2003, No. 92 (Adj. Sess.), § 1; 2005, No. 51, § 2; amended 2005, No. 103 (Adj. Sess.), § 3, eff. April 5, 2006; 2005, No. 162 (Adj. Sess.), § 4, eff. Jan. 1, 2007; 2007, No. 40, § 3; 2011, No. 145 (Adj. Sess.), § 3; 2013, No. 126 (Adj. Sess.), § 1.)

§ 5363. Crime Victims' Restitution Special Fund

(a) There is hereby established in the State Treasury a fund to be known as the Crime Victims' Restitution Special Fund, to be administered by the Restitution Unit established by section 5362 of this title, and from which payments may be made to provide restitution to crime victims.

(b)(1) There shall be deposited into the Fund:

(A) all monies collected by the Restitution Unit pursuant to section 7043 and subdivision 5362(c)(7) of this title;

(B) all fees imposed by the clerk of court and designated for deposit into the Fund pursuant to section 7282 of this title;

(C) all monies donated to the Restitution Unit or the Crime Victims' Restitution Special Fund; and

(D) such sums as may be appropriated to the Fund by the General Assembly.

(2) If a person donates funds, or if a restitution recipient has declined to accept payment of restitution, the donated or declined amounts shall be retained in the Crime Victims' Restitution Special Fund.

(3) If a victim who is entitled to receive an advance payment of restitution from the Crime Victims Restitution Special Fund cannot be located, the Restitution Unit shall report the amount to the Treasurer within the time limits provided by 27 V.S.A. § 1247(d), and the Treasurer shall report it as unclaimed property. Notwithstanding any other provision of law, in no event shall the advance payments from the Restitution Special Fund to which the victim is entitled be subject to ultimate deposit in the General or Education Fund.

(c) The Restitution Unit shall make disbursements from the Restitution Special Fund only to pay restitution obligations arising under section 7043 of this title, to support the Restitution Unit, or pursuant to subsection (d) of this section.

(d)(1) The Restitution Unit is authorized to advance up to $5,000.00 to a victim or to a deceased victim's heir or legal representative if the victim:

(A) was first ordered by the court to receive restitution on or after July 1, 2004;

(B) is a natural person or the natural person's legal representative;

(C) has not been reimbursed under subdivision (2) of this subsection; and

(D) is a natural person and has been referred to the Restitution Unit by a diversion program pursuant to 3 V.S.A. § 164a.

(2) The Restitution Unit may make advances of up to $5,000.00 under this subsection to the following persons or entities:

(A) a victim service agency approved by the Restitution Unit if the agency has advanced monies which would have been payable to a victim under subdivision (1) of this subsection;

(B) a victim who is a natural person or the natural person's legal representative in a case where the defendant, before or after an adjudication of guilt, enters into a drug court contract requiring payment of restitution.

(3) An advance under this subsection shall not be made to the government or to any governmental subdivision or agency.

(4) An advance under this subsection shall not be made to a victim who:

(A) fails to provide the Restitution Unit with the documentation necessary to support the victim's claim for restitution;

(B) violated a criminal law of this State that caused or contributed to the victim's material loss; or

(C) has crime-related losses that are eligible for payment from the Victims Compensation Special Fund.

(5) An advance under this subsection shall not be made for the amount of cash loss included in a restitution judgment order.

(6) An advance under this subsection shall not be made for:

(A) jewelry or precious metals; or

(B) luxury items or collectibles identified in rules adopted by the Unit pursuant to subdivision 5362(c)(5) of this title.

(e) If the Restitution Unit collects in excess of $10,000.00 from an offender, the amount in excess of $10,000.00 shall first be paid to that offender's victims until the victims have received the full amount of restitution ordered. Any excess remaining after the victims have received the full amount of restitution ordered shall be divided between the Victims Compensation Fund and the Crime Victims Special Restitution Fund in proportion to the amount which each paid.

(f)(1) In no event shall the amount of restitution advanced to the victims of a single crime spree during a single fiscal year under this title exceed five percent of the balance of the Fund at the end of the prior fiscal year. If this section applies, an advance payment to a victim shall be reduced by the same percentage that the Restitution Unit reduces the total amount advanced to all victims in connection with the crime spree. Unless otherwise ordered by the court, the Restitution Unit shall determine the offenders and crimes encompassed within a crime spree.

(2) A victim whose advance payment is reduced pursuant to this subsection shall be entitled to receive additional advance payments during subsequent fiscal years until the restitution order has been satisfied or the $10,000.00 cap has been reached, whichever occurs first.

(g) All balances in the Fund at the end of any fiscal year shall be carried forward and remain a part of the Fund. Disbursements from the Fund shall be made by the State Treasurer on warrants drawn by the Commissioner of Finance and Management.

(h) Notwithstanding anything in this section or any other provision of law to the contrary, revenue from the surcharge fees deposited into the Crime Victims' Restitution Special Fund shall be used to support the Restitution Unit and restitution for crime victims, and as otherwise authorized by the General Assembly. (Added 2003, No. 57, § 4, eff. June 4, 2003; amended 2003, No. 92 (Adj. Sess.), § 2; 2005, No.

51, § 3; 2007, No. 40, § 4, eff. July 1, 2012; 2011, No. 3, § 84, eff. Feb. 17, 2011; 2011, No. 55, § 13; 2011, No. 145 (Adj. Sess.), § 4; 2013, No. 126 (Adj. Sess.), § 2.)

§ 5364. Subrogation lien

The State shall be subrogated to the rights of the victim, assignee, heir, or dependent to whom restitution payments are made to the extent of the payments made. The State shall have a lien therefor and may commence an action or intervene in any action to protect and enforce such lien. Such subrogation rights shall be against any person liable for the pecuniary loss. (Added 2005, No. 51, § 4.)

§ 5365. Access to financial records

(a) As used in this section:

(1) "Depositor" means an owner of an account in a financial institution and includes "share account holders" of credit unions.

(2) "Financial institution" means a savings and loan association, a trust company, a savings bank, an industrial bank, a banking organization, a commercial bank, or a credit union organized under the laws of this State or authorized to do business in this State.

(3) "Offender" means a person who owes restitution.

(4) "Restitution" means an unsatisfied obligation to pay restitution that was ordered in connection with a criminal case and about which, prior to the issuance of the order, the offender had notice and an opportunity to contest the amount owed.

(5) "Restitution unit" means the State of Vermont restitution unit.

(b) Upon receipt of a duly authorized written request from the restitution unit to identify depository accounts held by an offender, a financial institution shall search its depositor records in order to identify accounts in which the offender has an ownership or beneficial interest.

(c) A financial institution shall notify the restitution unit of all accounts identified in response to a request filed under subsection (b) of this section. The notification shall contain the following information, if available to the financial institution through its search procedure, for each account identified:

(1) The full name, date of birth, and address that the offender provided for himself or herself to the financial institution.

(2) The offender's Social Security number.

(3) The offender's account number.

(4) The amount of deposits contained in the offender's account.

(5) Whether the offender is the sole owner of the account.

(d) The financial institution shall not provide notice in any form to a depositor identified by the restitution unit pursuant to this section. Failure to provide notice to a depositor shall not constitute a violation of the financial institution's duty of good faith to its customers.

(e) A financial institution may charge the restitution unit a fee for services provided under this section, provided that the fee shall not exceed the actual costs incurred by the financial institution.

(f) The information provided to each other by the financial institution and the restitution unit pursuant to this section shall be confidential and shall be used only for the purpose of collecting unpaid restitution. (Added 2007, No. 40, § 5.)

§ 5366. Delay in debt collection by health care provider

(a) When a person files a claim under this chapter, no health care provider that has been given notice of the claim shall conduct any debt collection activities relating to medical or dental treatment received by the person in connection with the claim until an award is made on the claim or until the claim is determined to be noncompensable pursuant to section 5355 of this title. The period during which the health care provider is prohibited from conducting debt collection activities under this section shall be excluded in determining the applicable limitations period for commencing an action to collect the debt.

(b) As used in this section:

(1) "Debt collection activities" means repeatedly calling or writing to the claimant and threatening to turn the matter over to a debt collection agency or to an attorney for collection, enforcement, or filing of other process. The term shall not include routine billing or inquiries about the status of the claim.

(2) "Health care provider" shall have the same meaning as in 18 V.S.A. § 9402. (Added 2007, No. 173 (Adj. Sess.), § 3.)

Subchapter 3: Sex Offender Registration; Law Enforcement Notification

§ 5401. Definitions

As used in this subchapter:

(1) "Address" means the actual location of the sex offender's dwelling, including the street address, if any.

(2) "Department" means the Department of Public Safety.

(3) "Local law enforcement agency" means the municipal police department or statutorily established college or university police department. If the municipality, college, or university has no police department, the law enforcement agency that serves the municipality, college, or university.

(4) "Mental abnormality" means a congenital or acquired condition that affects the emotional or volitional capacity of a person in a manner that predisposes the person to the commission of criminal sexual acts to a degree that makes the person a menace to the health and safety of other persons.

(5) "Minor" means a person under the age of 18 years.

(6) "Personality disorder" means a condition where a person exhibits personality traits that are inflexible and maladaptive and cause either significant functional impairment or subjective distress.

(7) "Predatory" means an act directed at a stranger, or a person with whom a relationship has been established or promoted for the primary purpose of victimization.

(8) "Release" means release from confinement or custody or placement into the community for any reason, including release on bail pending appeal, probation, parole, furlough, work release, early release, alternative sanctions, house arrest, daily interrupt, community placement, or completion of sentence. It shall also mean probation or parole supervision of an out-of-state sex offender under an interstate agreement or compact.

(9) "Registry" means the Sex Offender Registry maintained by the Department of Public Safety.

(10) "Sex offender" means:

(A) A person who is convicted in any jurisdiction of the United States, including a state, territory, commonwealth, the District of Columbia, or military, federal, or tribal court of any of the following offenses:

(i) sexual assault as defined in section 3252 of this title;

(ii) aggravated sexual assault as defined in section 3253 of this title;

(iii)   lewd and lascivious conduct as defined in section 2601 of this title;

(iv) sexual abuse of a vulnerable adult as defined in section 1379 of this title;

(v) second or subsequent conviction for voyeurism as defined in subsection 2605(b) or (c) of this title;

(vi) kidnapping with intent to commit sexual assault as defined in subdivision 2405(a)(1)(D) of this title;

(vii) aggravated sexual assault of a child in violation of section 3253a of this title;

(viii) human trafficking in violation of subdivisions 2652(a)(1)-(4) of this title;

(ix) aggravated human trafficking in violation of subdivision 2653(a)(4) of this title;

(x) a federal conviction in federal court for any of the following offenses:

(I) sex trafficking of children as defined in 18 U.S.C. § 1591;

(II) aggravated sexual abuse as defined in 18 U.S.C. § 2241;

(III) sexual abuse as defined in 18 U.S.C. § 2242;

(IV) sexual abuse of a minor or ward as defined in 18 U.S.C. § 2243;

(V) abusive sexual contact as defined in 18 U.S.C. § 2244;

(VI) offenses resulting in death as defined in 18 U.S.C. § 2245;

(VII) sexual exploitation of children as defined in 18 U.S.C. § 2251;

(VIII) selling or buying of children as defined in 18 U.S.C. § 2251A;

(IX) material involving the sexual exploitation of minors as defined in 18 U.S.C. § 2252;

(X) material containing child pornography as defined in 18 U.S.C. § 2252A;

(XI) production of sexually explicit depictions of a minor for import into the United States as defined in 18 U.S.C. § 2260;

(XII) transportation of a minor for illegal sexual activity as defined in 18 U.S.C. § 2421;

(XIII) coercion and enticement of a minor for illegal sexual activity as defined in 18 U.S.C. § 2422;

(XIV) transportation of minors for illegal sexual activity, travel with the intent to engage in illicit sexual conduct with a minor, and engaging in illicit sexual conduct in foreign places as defined in 18 U.S.C. § 2423;

(XV) transmitting information about a minor to further criminal sexual conduct as defined in 18 U.S.C. § 2425;

(XVI) trafficking in persons as defined in 18 U.S.C. sections 2251-2252(a), 2260, or 2421-2423 if the violation included sexual abuse, aggravated sexual abuse, or the attempt to commit aggravated sexual abuse; and

(xi) an attempt to commit any offense listed in this subdivision (A).

(B) A person who is convicted of any of the following offenses against a victim who is a minor, except that, for purposes of this subdivision, conduct that is criminal only because of the age of the victim shall not be considered an offense for purposes of the Registry if the perpetrator is under the age of 18 and the victim is at least 12 years old:

(i) any offense listed in subdivision (A) of this subdivision (10);

(ii) kidnapping as defined in subdivision 2405(a)(1)(D) of this title;

(iii) lewd and lascivious conduct with a child as defined in section 2602 of this title;

(iv) slave traffic as defined in section 2635 of this title;

(v) sexual exploitation of children as defined in chapter 64 of this title;

(vi) procurement or solicitation as defined in subdivision 2632(a)(6) of this title;

(vii) aggravated sexual assault of a child as defined in section 3253a of this title;

(viii) sex trafficking of children or sex trafficking by force, fraud, or coercion as defined in section 2652 of this title;

(ix) sexual exploitation of a minor as defined in section 3258 of this title;

(x) an attempt to commit any offense listed in this subdivision (B).

(C) A person who takes up residence within this State, other than within a correctional facility, and who has been convicted in any jurisdiction of the United States, including a state, territory, commonwealth, the District of Columbia, or military, federal, or tribal court, for a sex crime the elements of which would constitute a crime under subdivision (A) or (B) of this subdivision (10) if committed in this State.

(D) A person 18 years of age or older who resides in this State, other than in a correctional facility, and who is currently or, prior to taking up residence within this State, was required to register as a sex offender in any jurisdiction of the United States, including a state, territory, commonwealth, the District of Columbia, or military, federal, or tribal court; except that, for purposes of this subdivision, conduct that is criminal only because of the age of the victim shall not be considered an offense for purposes of the registry if the perpetrator is under the age of 18 and the victim is at least 12 years old.

(E) A nonresident sex offender who crosses into Vermont and who is employed, carries on a vocation, or is a student.

(11) "Sexually violent offense" means sexual assault or aggravated sexual assault, as described in sections 3252 and 3253 of this title, or a comparable offense in another jurisdiction of the United States, or any attempt to commit sexual assault, aggravated sexual assault, or a comparable offense in another jurisdiction of the United States.

(12) "Sexually violent predator" means a person who is a sex offender, who has been convicted of a sexually violent offense, as defined in subdivision (11) of this section, and who suffers from a mental abnormality or personality disorder that makes the person likely to engage in predatory sexually violent offenses.

(13) "Employed, carries on a vocation" includes employment that is full-time or part-time for a period of time exceeding 14 days or for an aggregate period of time exceeding 30 days during any calendar year, whether financially compensated, volunteered, or for the purpose of governmental or educational benefit.

(14) "Student" means a person who is enrolled on a full-time or part-time basis in any public or private educational institution in Vermont, including any secondary school, trade or professional institution, or institution of higher learning.

(15)(A) "Conviction" means a judgment of guilt following a verdict or finding of guilt, a plea of guilty, a plea of nolo contendere, an Alford Plea, or a judgment of guilt pursuant to a deferred sentence.

(B) A sex offender whose sentence is deferred shall have no duty to register unless:

(i) the offender violates the terms of the deferred sentence agreement and is sentenced on the conviction, in which case the offender's name shall remain on the Registry for the period of time required by subsection 5407(e) or (f) of this title; or

(ii) the court finds that the interests of justice warrant placing the offender's name on the Registry while the sentence is deferred, in which case the offender's name shall be removed from the Registry upon his or her successful completion of the deferred sentence agreement.

(C) A sex offender treated as a youthful offender pursuant to 33 V.S.A. chapter 52A shall have no duty to register unless the offender's youthful offender status is revoked and he or she is sentenced for the offense in the Criminal Division of Superior Court.

(16) "Risk" means the degree of dangerousness that a sex offender poses to others. "High-risk" means a high degree of dangerousness that a sex offender poses to others. Dangerousness includes the probability of a sexual reoffense. (Added 1995, No. 124 (Adj. Sess.), § 1, eff. Sept. 1, 1996; amended 1997, No. 57, § 7, eff. June 26, 1997; 2001, No. 49, § 2, eff. Sept. 1, 2001; 2003, No. 157 (Adj. Sess.), § 2;

2005, No. 79, § 5; 2005, No. 83, § 3; 2005, No. 192 (Adj. Sess.), § 24, eff. May 26, 2006; 2009, No. 1, § 13b, eff. March 4, 2009; 2009, No. 58, § 6; 2011, No. 31, § 1, eff. May 17, 2011; 2011, No. 55, § 9; 2015, No. 31, § 1; 2017, No. 15, § 1, eff. May 1, 2017; 2017, No. 72, § 1.)

§ 5402. Sex Offender Registry

(a) The Department of Public Safety shall establish and maintain a Sex Offender Registry, that shall consist of the information required to be filed under this subchapter.

(b) All information contained in the Registry may be disclosed for any purpose permitted under the law of this State, including use by:

(1) local, state, and federal law enforcement agencies exclusively for lawful law enforcement activities;

(2) state and federal governmental agencies for the exclusive purpose of conducting confidential background checks;

(3) any employer, including a school district, who is authorized by law to request records and information from the Vermont Criminal Information Center, where such disclosure is necessary to protect the public concerning persons required to register under this subchapter. The identity of a victim of an offense that requires registration shall not be released;

(4) a person identified as a sex offender in the Registry for the purpose of reviewing the accuracy of any record relating to him or her. The identity of a victim of an offense that requires registration shall not be released; and

(5) probate courts for purposes of conducting checks on persons applying for changes of name under 15 V.S.A. § 811.

(c) The Departments of Corrections and of Public Safety shall adopt rules, forms and procedures under 3 V.S.A. chapter 25 to implement the provisions of this subchapter. (Added 1995, No. 124 (Adj. Sess.), § 1, eff. Sept. 1, 1996; amended 1999, No. 152 (Adj. Sess.), § 78a, eff. May 29, 2000; 2001, No. 49, § 3, eff. Sept. 1, 2001; 2009, No. 58, § 13.)

§ 5403. Reporting to Department of Public Safety

(a) Upon conviction and prior to sentencing, the court shall order the sex offender to provide the court with the following information, which the court shall forward to the Department forthwith:

(1) name;

(2) date of birth;

(3) current address;

(4) Social Security number;

(5) current employment; and

(6) name and address of any postsecondary educational institution at which the sex offender is enrolled as a student.

(b) Within 14 days after sentencing, the court shall forward to the Department:

(1) the sex offender's conviction record, including offense, date of conviction, sentence, and any conditions of release or probation; and

(2) an order issued pursuant to section 5405a of this title, on a form developed by the Court Administrator, that the defendant comply with Sex Offender Registry requirements.

(c) The Departments of Corrections and of Public Safety shall jointly develop a process for the Department of Corrections to notify the Department of Public Safety when an offender who is under Department of Corrections supervision is required to be placed on the Sex Offender Registry because of a conviction that occurred in another jurisdiction of the United States, including a state, territory, commonwealth, the District of Columbia, or military, federal, or tribal court. The report shall include the offense of which the defendant was convicted that requires the placement of his or her name on the Registry. (Added 1995, No. 124 (Adj. Sess.), § 1, eff. Sept. 1, 1996; amended 2003, No. 157 (Adj. Sess.), § 3; 2015, No. 31, § 2; 2017, No. 11, § 26.)

§ 5404. Reporting upon release from confinement or supervision

(a) Upon receiving a sex offender from the court on a probationary sentence or supervised community sentence and prior to releasing a sex offender from a correctional facility to serve probation, parole, furlough, or a supervised community sentence, the Department of Corrections shall forward to the Department the following information concerning the sex offender:

(1) an update of the information listed in subsection 5403(a) of this title;

(2) the address upon release and whether the offender will be living with a child under 18 years of age;

(3) the name, address, and telephone number of the probation and parole office in charge of monitoring the sex offender; and

(4) documentation of any treatment or counseling received.

(b) As part of planning for the release of a sex offender from a correctional facility to the community upon completion of the offender's maximum sentence, the Department of Corrections shall notify the offender of his or her obligation to report to the Department to register as a sex offender in compliance with section 5407 of this chapter prior to the offender's scheduled release date. The Department of Corrections shall assist the offender with registration as a sex offender and advise the offender that failure to register with the Department prior to release is a crime subject to section 5409 of this chapter.

(c) The Department of Corrections shall notify the Department of Public Safety within 24 hours of the time a sex offender changes his or her address or place of employment, or enrolls in or separates from any postsecondary educational institution, or begins residing with a child under 18 years of age. In addition, the Department of Corrections shall provide the Department with any updated information requested by the Department.

(d) With respect to a sex offender residing with a child under 18 years of age under circumstances enumerated in subsection (a) or (c) of this section, the Department of Corrections shall communicate with the Department for Children and Families. If placement in a home with a child is being considered by the Department of Corrections, the Department of Corrections shall notify the Department for Children and Families, and the departments shall work together to determine whether such a placement is appropriate. If the Department of Corrections does not have a role in the placement of the offender in the community, but knows the offender will be residing with a person under 18 years of age, the Department of Corrections shall notify the Department for Children and Families at least 24 hours prior to releasing the offender from confinement.

(e) The information required to be provided by subsection (a) of this section shall also be provided by the Department of Corrections to a sex offender's parole or probation officer within three days of the time a sex offender is placed on probation or parole by the court or the Parole Board.

(f) If it has not been previously submitted, upon receipt of the information to be provided to the Department pursuant to subsection (a) of this section, the Department shall immediately transmit the conviction data and fingerprints to the Federal Bureau of Investigation. (Added 1995, No. 124 (Adj. Sess.), § 1, eff. Sept. 1, 1996; amended 2001, No. 49, § 4, eff. Sept. 1, 2001; 2003, No. 157 (Adj. Sess.), § 4; 2009, No. 1, § 14; 2015, No. 1, § 1, eff. Feb. 25, 2015.)

§ 5405. Court determination of sexually violent predators

(a) The General Assembly finds that some sexual offenders should be subject to increased sex offender registry and community notification procedures. It is the intent of the General Assembly that State's Attorneys utilize the provisions in this section to petition the court to designate those offenders who pose a greater risk to the public as sexually violent predators to ensure that those offenders will be required to register as sex offenders for life, and that they will be among those offenders who are included on the State's Internet Sex Offender Registry.

(b) Within 15 days after the conviction of a sex offender, the State may file a petition with the court requesting that the person be designated as a sexually violent predator.

(c) The determination of whether a person is a sexually violent predator shall be made by the court at the time of sentencing.

(d) The court shall order a presentence investigation that shall include a psychosexual evaluation of the offender.

(e) In making a determination of whether the person is a sexually violent predator, the court shall examine the following:

(1) the person's criminal history;

(2) any testimony presented at trial, including expert testimony as to the person's mental state;

(3) the person's history of treatment for a personality disorder or mental abnormality connected with his or her criminal sexual behavior;

(4) any mitigating evidence, including treatment history, evidence of modified behavior, or expert testimony, that the convicted sex offender wishes to provide to the court prior to the determination; and

(5) any other relevant evidence.

(f) The standard of proof when the court makes such a determination shall be clear and convincing evidence that the convicted sex offender suffers from a mental abnormality or personality disorder that makes the person likely to engage in predatory sexually violent offenses.

(g) The court shall determine whether the offender was eligible to be charged as a habitual offender as provided in section 11 of this title or a violent career criminal as provided in section 11a of this title and shall make findings as to such.

(h) After making its determinations, the court shall issue a written decision explaining the reasons for its determinations and provide a copy of the decision to the Department within 14 days.

(i) A person who is determined to be a sexually violent predator shall be subject to sex offender lifetime registration and community notification and inclusion on the Internet Sex Offender Registry as provided in this subchapter. (Added 1995, No. 124 (Adj. Sess.), § 1, eff. Sept. 1, 1996; amended 2001, No. 49, § 5, eff. Sept. 1, 2001; 2005, No. 79, § 8; 2017, No. 11, § 27.)

§ 5405a. Court determination of Sex Offender Registry requirements

(a)(1) The court shall determine at sentencing whether Sex Offender Registry requirements apply to the defendant.

(2) If the State and the defendant do not agree as to the applicability of Sex Offender Registry requirements to the defendant, the State shall file a motion setting forth the Sex Offender Registry requirements applicable to the defendant within 14 days of the entry of a guilty plea. To the extent the defendant opposes the motion, the State and the defendant shall present evidence at the sentencing as to the applicability of Sex Offender Registry requirements to the defendant.

(b) The court shall consider the following when determining under this section whether Sex Offender Registry requirements apply to the defendant:

(1) the report issued pursuant to subsection 5403(c) of this title;

(2) the presentence investigation report regarding the offense for which the defendant is being sentenced;

(3) the court's own judgment of conviction and any evidence that was presented at trial; and

(4) any other evidence admitted at sentencing and deemed relevant by the court to the defendant's Registry status.

(c) The State shall bear the burden of proving by a preponderance of the evidence the applicability of Sex Offender Registry requirements to the defendant under this section.

(d) Within 14 days after the sentencing or the presentation of evidence pursuant to subdivision (a)(2) of this section, the court shall issue an order determining whether Sex Offender Registry requirements apply to the defendant. The order shall include:

(1) the offense of which the defendant was convicted that requires the placement of his or her name on the Sex Offender Registry;

(2) any prior convictions that affect:

(A) the defendant's Sex Offender Registry Status;

(B) the length of time that the defendant is required to register as a sex offender; or

(C) whether information regarding the defendant is required to be electronically posted on the Internet under section 5411a of this title;

(3) the length of time that the defendant is required to register as a sex offender;

(4) whether the defendant is designated as a sexually violent predator under section 5405 of this title;

(5) whether the defendant was immediately released or remanded to the custody of the Department of Corrections; and

(6) whether information regarding the defendant is required to be electronically posted on the Internet under section 5411a of this title. (Added 2015, No. 31, § 3; amended 2017, No. 11, § 28.)

§ 5406. Department of Corrections duty to provide notice

Upon receiving a sex offender from the court on a probationary sentence or any alternative sentence under community supervision by the Department of Corrections, or upon the release of a sex offender from a correctional facility, the Department of Corrections shall do each of the following:

(1) inform the sex offender of the duty to register and keep the registration current as provided in section 5407 of this title;

(2) inform the sex offender that if the sex offender changes residence to another state, the sex offender shall notify the Department of the new address and shall also register with the designated law enforcement agency in the new state not later than three days after establishing residence in the new state, if the new state has a registration requirement;

(3) require the sex offender to read and sign a form stating that the duty of the sex offender to register under this section has been explained and is understood. The registration form shall be sent to the Department without delay; and

(4) inform the sex offender that if he or she crosses into another state for purposes of employment, carrying on a vocation, or being a student, the sex offender must notify the Department of the new address, and shall register with the designated law enforcement agency in the other state, if the other state has a registration requirement. (Added 1995, No. 124 (Adj. Sess.), § 1, eff. Sept. 1, 1996; amended 2001, No. 49, § 6, eff. Sept. 1, 2001.)

§ 5407. Sex offender's responsibility to report

(a) Except as provided in section 5411d of this title, a sex offender shall report to the Department as follows:

(1) if convicted of a registry offense in another state, within 10 days after either establishing residence in this State or crossing into this State for purposes of employment, carrying on a vocation, or being a student, the sex offender shall provide the information listed in subsection 5403(a) of this title;

(2) annually within 10 days after the registrant's birthday, or if a person is determined to be a sexually violent predator, that person shall report to the Department every 90 days;

(3) within three days after any change of address, or if a person is designated as a high-risk sex offender pursuant to section 5411b of this title, that person shall report to the Department within 36 hours, and shall report whether a child under the age of 18 resides at such address;

(4) within three days after the registrant enrolls in or separates from any postsecondary educational institution;

(5) within three days after any change in place of employment;

(6) within three days of any name change;

(7) within three days of a child under 18 years of age moving into the residence of the registrant;

(8) within 24 hours of being released from probation, parole, furlough, or a supervised community sentence; and

(9) prior to the offender's scheduled release date from a correctional facility to the community and if the offender is not subject to probation, furlough, or a community sentence upon release that requires supervision by the Department of Corrections.

(b) If a sex offender changes residence to another state, or crosses into another state for purposes of employment, carrying on a vocation, or being a student, the sex offender shall notify the Department of the new address and shall also register with the designated law enforcement agency in the new state not later than three days after establishing residence in the new state, if the new state has a registration requirement.

(c) Upon a sex offender's change of residence to another state, the Department shall immediately notify the designated law enforcement agency in the new state, if the new state has a registration requirement.

(d) The report required by this section shall include the information required by sections 5403 and 5404 of this chapter.

(e) Except as provided for in subsection (f) of this section, a person required to register as a sex offender under this subchapter shall continue to comply with this section, except during periods of incarceration, until 10 years have elapsed since the person was released from prison or discharged from parole, supervised release, or probation, whichever is later. The 10-year period shall not be affected or reduced in any way by the actual duration of the offender's sentence as imposed by the court, nor shall it be reduced by the sex offender's release on parole or ending of probation or other early release.

(f) A person required to register as a sex offender under this subchapter shall continue to comply with this section for the life of that person, except during periods of incarceration, if that person:

(1) has at least one prior conviction for an offense described in subdivision 5401(10) of this subchapter or a comparable offense in another jurisdiction of the United States;

(2) has been convicted of a sexual assault as defined in section 3252 of this title or aggravated sexual assault as defined in section 3253 of this title, or a comparable offense in another jurisdiction of the United States, including a state, territory, commonwealth, the District of Columbia, or military, federal, or tribal court; however, if a person convicted under section 3252 is not more than six years older than the victim of the assault and if the victim is 14 years of age or older, then the offender shall not be required to register for life if the age of the victim was the basis for the conviction;

(3) has been determined to be a sexually violent predator pursuant to section 5405 of this title; or

(4) has been designated as a noncompliant high-risk sex offender pursuant to section 5411d of this title.

(g) The Department shall adopt forms and procedures for the purpose of verifying the addresses of persons required to register under this subchapter in accordance with the requirements set forth in Section (b)(3) of the Jacob Wetterling Crimes Against Children and Sexually Violent Offender Registration Act. Every 90 days for sexually violent predators and annually for other registrants, the Department shall verify addresses of registrants by sending a nonforwardable address verification form to each registrant at the address last reported by the registrant. The registrant shall be required to sign and return the form to the Department within 10 days of receipt. If the registrant's name appears on the list of address verification forms automatically generated by the Registry, it shall be deemed that the sex offender has received that form.

(h) A registrant who has no permanent address shall report to the Department to notify it as to his or her temporary residence. Temporary residence, for purposes of this section, need not include an actual dwelling or numbered street address, but shall identify a specific location. A registrant shall not be required to check in daily if he or she makes acceptable other arrangements with the Department to keep his or her information current. The Department may enter into an agreement with a local law enforcement agency to perform this function, but shall maintain responsibility for compliance with this subsection.

(i) If the Department is notified by an offender that he or she is living with a child under the age of 18, the Department shall notify the Department for Children and Families within three days. (Added 1995, No. 124 (Adj. Sess.), § 1, eff. Sept. 1, 1996; amended 2001, No. 49, § 7, eff. Sept. 1, 2001; 2003, No. 157 (Adj. Sess.), § 5; 2005, No. 192 (Adj. Sess.), § 25, eff. May 26, 2006; 2007, No. 77, § 7, eff. June 7, 2007; 2009, No. 1, § 15; 2009, No. 58, § 7; 2015, No. 1, § 2, eff. Feb. 25, 2015; 2015, No. 31, § 4.)

§ 5408. Record of addresses; arrest warrant

The Department shall maintain a record of the addresses of all sex offenders. The record shall be updated at least every three months. At any time, if the Department is unable to verify the whereabouts and address of a sex offender subject to this subchapter, it shall immediately notify the local law enforcement agency in writing that the sex offender's whereabouts are unknown. The Department shall also send a copy of the notification to the State's Attorney of the county in which the sex offender's most recent address is located. (Added 1995, No. 124 (Adj. Sess.), § 1, eff. Sept. 1, 1996; amended 2005, No. 192 (Adj. Sess.), § 21, eff. May 26, 2006.)

§ 5409. Penalties

(a) Except as provided in subsection (b) of this section, a sex offender who knowingly fails to comply with any provision of this subchapter shall:

(1) Be imprisoned for not more than two years or fined not more than $1,000.00, or both. A sentence imposed under this subdivision shall run consecutively to any sentence being served by the sex offender at the time of sentencing.

(2) For the second or subsequent offense, be imprisoned not more than three years or fined not more than $5,000.00, or both. A sentence imposed under this subdivision shall run consecutively to any sentence being served by the sex offender at the time of sentencing.

(b) A sex offender who knowingly fails to comply with any provision of this subchapter for a period of more than five consecutive days shall be imprisoned not more than five years or fined not more than $5,000.00, or both. A sentence imposed under this subsection shall run consecutively to any sentence being served by the sex offender at the time of sentencing.

(c) It shall be presumed that every sex offender knows and understands his or her obligations under this subchapter.

(d)(1) An affidavit by the administrator of the Sex Offender Registry that describes the failure to comply with the provisions of this subchapter shall be prima facie evidence of a violation of this subchapter.

(2) Certified records of the sex offender registry shall be admissible into evidence as business records. (Added 1995, No. 124 (Adj. Sess.), § 1, eff. Sept. 1, 1996; amended 2001, No. 49, § 8, eff. Sept. 1, 2001; 2005, No. 192 (Adj. Sess.), § 22, eff. May 26, 2006; 2009, No. 58, § 8.)

§ 5410. Victim notification

If requested by a victim, the Department shall promptly notify the victim of the initial registration of a sex offender and any time the sex offender changes address, where such disclosure is necessary to protect the victim or the public concerning a person required to register under this subchapter. (Added 1995, No. 124 (Adj. Sess.), § 1, eff. Sept. 1, 1996.)

§ 5411. Notification to local law enforcement and local community

(a) Upon receiving a sex offender's registration materials from the Department of Corrections, notification that a nonresident sex offender has crossed into Vermont for the purpose of employment, carrying on a vocation, or being a student, or a sex offender's release or change of address, including changes of address that involve taking up residence in this State, the Department shall immediately notify the local law enforcement agency of the following information, which may be used only for lawful law enforcement activities:

(1) name;

(2) general physical description;

(3) nature of offense;

(4) sentence;

(5) the fact that the Registry has on file additional information, including the sex offender's photograph and fingerprints;

(6) current employment;

(7) name and address of any postsecondary educational institution at which the sex offender is enrolled as a student; and

(8) whether the offender complied with treatment recommended by the Department of Corrections.

(b)(1) Except as provided for in subsections (c) and (e) of this section, the Department, the Department of Corrections, and any authorized local law enforcement agency shall release Registry information concerning persons required to register under State law if the requestor can articulate a concern about the behavior of a specific person regarding the requestor's personal safety or the safety of another, or the requestor has reason to believe that a specific person may be a registered sex offender and can articulate a concern regarding the requestor's personal safety or the safety of another. However, the identity of a victim of an offense shall not be released.

(2) The Department, the Department of Corrections, and any authorized local law enforcement agency shall release the following Registry information if the requestor meets the requirements in subdivision (1) of this subsection:

(A) a general physical description of the offender;

(B) date of birth;

(C) the date and nature of the offense;

(D) whether the offender complied with treatment recommended by the Department of Corrections; and

(E) whether there is an outstanding warrant for the offender's arrest.

(c)(1) Except as provided for in subsection (e) of this section, upon request of a member of the public about a specific person, the Department, the Department of Corrections, and any authorized local law enforcement agency shall release Registry information on sex offenders whose information is required to be posted on the Internet in accordance with section 5411a of this title.

(2) The Department, the Department of Corrections, and any authorized local law enforcement agency shall release the following Registry information to a requestor in accordance with subdivision (1) of this subsection:

(A) the offender's known aliases;

(B) the offender's date of birth;

(C) a general physical description of the offender;

(D) the offender's town of residence;

(E) the date and nature of the offender's conviction;

(F) if the offender is under the supervision of the Department of Corrections, the name and telephone number of the local Department of Corrections office in charge of monitoring the offender;

(G) whether the offender complied with treatment recommended by the Department of Corrections;

(H) whether there is an outstanding warrant for the offender's arrest; and

(I) the reason for which the offender information is accessible under subdivision (1) of this subsection.

(3)(A) The Department, the Department of Corrections, and any authorized local law enforcement agency may, at the discretion of an authorized law enforcement officer, release the current address of an offender listed in subdivision (1) of this subsection if the requestor can articulate a concern regarding the requestor's personal safety or the safety of another, and the requirements of subsection (d) of this section have been satisfied.

(B) For purposes of this subdivision, "authorized law enforcement officer" means a sheriff, a chief of police, the Commissioner of Public Safety, the State's Attorney of Essex County, or a designee. The designee shall be a certified law enforcement officer whose authority is granted or given by the sheriff, chief of police, Commissioner of Public Safety, or State's Attorney of Essex County, either through explicit order or Department policy.

(d) The Department, the Department of Corrections, and any local law enforcement agency authorized to release Registry information shall keep a log of requests for registry information and follow the procedure for verification of the requestor's identity recommended by the Department. Such log shall include the requestor's name, address, telephone number, the name of the person for whom the request was made, the reason for the request, and the date of the request. Information about requestors shall be confidential and shall only be accessible to criminal justice agencies.

(e) After 10 years have elapsed from the completion of the sentence, a person required to register as a sex offender for life pursuant to section 5407 of this title who is not designated as a noncompliant high-risk sex offender pursuant to section 5411d of this title may petition the Criminal Division of the Superior Court for a termination of community notification, including the Internet. The State shall make a reasonable attempt to notify the victim of the proceeding, and consider victim testimony regarding the petition. If the registrant was convicted of a crime that requires lifetime registration, there shall be a rebuttable presumption that the person is a high-risk sex offender. Should the registrant present evidence that he or she is not a high-risk offender, the State shall have the burden of proof to establish by a preponderance of the evidence that the person remains a high risk to reoffend. The court shall consider whether the offender has successfully completed sex offender treatment. The court may require the offender to submit to a psychosexual evaluation. If the court finds that there is a high risk of reoffense, notification shall continue. The Vermont Rules of Civil Procedure shall apply to these proceedings. A lifetime registrant may petition the court to be removed from community notification requirements once every 60 months. The presumption under this section that a lifetime registrant is a high-risk offender shall not automatically subject the offender to increased public access to his or her status as a sex offender and related information under subdivision (c)(1) of this section or section 5411a of this title.

(f) Registry information shall not be released under this section unless it is released pursuant to written protocols governing the manner and circumstances of the release developed by the Department, the Department of Corrections, or an authorized law enforcement agency. The protocols shall include consultation between the department or agency releasing the information and the Department of Corrections' staff member responsible for supervising the offender. (Added 1995, No. 124 (Adj. Sess.), § 1, eff. Sept. 1, 1996; amended 1999, No. 152 (Adj. Sess.), § 78b, eff. May 29, 2000; 2001, No. 49, § 9, eff. Sept. 1, 2001; 2003, No. 157 (Adj. Sess.), § 6; 2005, No. 192 (Adj. Sess.), §§ 23, 26, 31, eff. May 26, 2006; 2007, No. 77, § 8, eff. June 7, 2007; 2009, No. 154, § 238.)

[Section 5411a effective July 1, 2015; see also contingent amendment to section 5411a and proviso .]

§ 5411a. Electronic posting of the Sex Offender Registry

(a) Notwithstanding 20 V.S.A. §§ 2056a-2056e, the Department shall electronically post information on the Internet in accordance with subsection (b) of this section regarding the following sex offenders, upon the offender's release from confinement or, if the offender was not subject to confinement, upon the offender's sentencing:

(1) Sex offenders who have been convicted of:

(A) aggravated sexual assault of a child (13 V.S.A. § 3253a);

(B) aggravated sexual assault (13 V.S.A. § 3253);

(C) sexual assault (13 V.S.A. § 3252);

(D) kidnapping with intent to commit sexual assault (13 V.S.A. § 2405(a)(1)(D));

(E) lewd or lascivious conduct with child (13 V.S.A. § 2602);

(F) a second or subsequent conviction for voyeurism (13 V.S.A. § 2605(b) or (c));

(G) slave traffic if a registrable offense under subdivision 5401(10)(B)(iv) of this title (13 V.S.A. § 2635);

(H) sex trafficking of children or sex trafficking by force, fraud, or coercion (13 V.S.A. § 2635a);

(I) sexual exploitation of a minor (13 V.S.A. § 3258(c));

(J) any offense regarding the sexual exploitation of children (chapter 64 of this title);

(K) sexual abuse of a vulnerable adult (13 V.S.A. § 1379);

(L) human trafficking as defined in subdivisions 2652(a)(1)-(4) of this title;

(M) aggravated human trafficking as defined in subdivision 2653(a)(4) of this title;

(N) a federal conviction in federal court for any of the following offenses:

(i) sex trafficking of children as defined in 18 U.S.C. § 1591;

(ii) aggravated sexual abuse as defined in 18 U.S.C. § 2241;

(iii) sexual abuse as defined in 18 U.S.C. § 2242;

(iv) sexual abuse of a minor or ward as defined in 18 U.S.C. § 2243;

(v) abusive sexual contact as defined in 18 U.S.C. § 2244;

(vi) offenses resulting in death as defined in 18 U.S.C. § 2245;

(vii) sexual exploitation of children as defined in 18 U.S.C. § 2251;

(viii) selling or buying of children as defined in 18 U.S.C. § 2251A;

(ix) material involving the sexual exploitation of minors as defined in 18 U.S.C. § 2252;

(x) material containing child pornography as defined in 18 U.S.C. § 2252A;

(xi) production of sexually explicit depictions of a minor for import into the United States as defined in 18 U.S.C. § 2260;

(xii) transportation of a minor for illegal sexual activity as defined in 18 U.S.C. § 2421;

(xiii) coercion and enticement of a minor for illegal sexual activity as defined in 18 U.S.C. § 2422;

(xiv) transportation of minors for illegal sexual activity, travel with the intent to engage in illicit sexual conduct with a minor, and engaging in illicit sexual conduct in foreign places as defined in 18 U.S.C. § 2423;

(xv) transmitting information about a minor to further criminal sexual conduct as defined in 18 U.S.C. § 2425;

(xvi) trafficking in persons as defined in 18 U.S.C. sections 2251-2252(a), 2260, or 2421-2423 if the violation included sexual abuse, aggravated sexual abuse, or the attempt to commit aggravated sexual abuse;

(O) an attempt to commit any offense listed in this subdivision (a)(1).

(2) Sex offenders who have at least one prior conviction for an offense described in subdivision 5401(10) of this subchapter.

(3) Sex offenders who have failed to comply with sex offender registration requirements and for whose arrest there is an outstanding warrant for such noncompliance. Information on offenders shall remain on the Internet only while the warrant is outstanding.

(4) Sex offenders who have been designated as sexual predators pursuant to section 5405 of this title.

(5)(A) Sex offenders who have not complied with sex offender treatment recommended by the Department of Corrections or who are ineligible for sex offender treatment. The Department of Corrections shall establish rules for the administration of this subdivision and shall specify what circumstances constitute noncompliance with treatment and criteria for ineligibility to participate in treatment. Offenders subject to this provision shall have the right to appeal the Department of Corrections' determination in Superior Court in accordance with Rule 75 of the Vermont Rules of Civil Procedure. This subdivision shall apply prospectively and shall not apply to those sex offenders who did not comply with treatment or were ineligible for treatment prior to March 1, 2005.

(B) The Department of Corrections shall notify the Department if a sex offender who is compliant with sex offender treatment completes his or her sentence but has not completed sex offender treatment. As long as the offender complies with treatment, the offender shall not be considered noncompliant under this subdivision and shall not be placed on the Internet Registry in accordance with this subdivision alone. However, the offender shall submit to the Department proof of continuing treatment compliance every three months. Proof of compliance shall be a form provided by the Department that the offender's treatment provider shall sign, attesting to the offender's continuing compliance with recommended treatment. Failure to submit such proof as required under this subdivision (B) shall result in the offender's placement on the Internet Registry in accordance with subdivision (A) of this subdivision (5).

(6) Sex offenders who have been designated by the Department of Corrections, pursuant to section 5411b of this title, as high-risk.

(7) A person 18 years of age or older who resides in this State, other than in a correctional facility, and who is currently or, prior to taking up residence within this State was required to register as a sex offender in any jurisdiction of the United States, including a state, territory, commonwealth, the District of Columbia, or military, federal, or tribal court; except that, for purposes of this subdivision:

(A) conduct that is criminal only because of the age of the victim shall not be considered an offense for purposes of the Registry if the perpetrator is under the age of 18 and the victim is at least 12 years old; and

(B) information shall be posted electronically only if the offense for which the person was required to register in the other jurisdiction was:

(i) a felony; or

(ii) a misdemeanor punishable by more than six months of imprisonment.

(b) The Department shall electronically post the following information on sex offenders designated in subsection (a) of this section:

(1) the offender's name and any known aliases;

(2) the offender's date of birth;

(3) a general physical description of the offender;

(4) a digital photograph of the offender;

(5) the offender's town of residence;

(6) the date and nature of the offender's conviction;

(7) if the offender is under the supervision of the Department of Corrections, the name and telephone number of the local Department of Corrections office in charge of monitoring the sex offender;

(8) whether the offender complied with treatment recommended by the Department of Corrections;

(9) a statement that there is an outstanding warrant for the offender's arrest, if applicable;

(10) the reason for which the offender information is accessible under this section;

(11) whether the offender has been designated high risk by the Department of Corrections pursuant to section 5411b of this title; and

(12) if the offender has not been subject to a risk assessment, a statement that the offender has not been so assessed and that such a person is presumed to be high risk, provided that the Department of Corrections shall permit a person subject to this subdivision to obtain a risk assessment at the person's own expense.

(c) The Department shall have the authority to take necessary steps to obtain digital photographs of offenders whose information is required to be posted on the Internet and to update photographs as necessary. An offender shall annually report to the Department or a local law enforcement agency for the purpose of being photographed for the Internet.

(d) An offender's street address shall not be posted electronically. The identity of a victim of an offense that requires registration shall not be released.

(e) Information regarding a sex offender shall not be posted electronically if the conduct that is the basis for the offense is criminal only because of the age of the victim and the perpetrator is within 38 months of age of the victim.

(f) Information regarding a sex offender shall not be posted electronically prior to the offender reaching 18 years of age, but such information shall be otherwise available pursuant to section 5411 of this title.

(g) Information on sex offenders shall be posted on the Internet for the duration of time for which they are subject to notification requirements under section 5401 et seq. of this title.

(h) Posting of the information shall include the following language: "This information is made available for the purpose of complying with 13 V.S.A. § 5401 et seq., which requires the Department of Public Safety to establish and maintain a Registry of persons who are required to register as sex offenders and to post electronically information on sex offenders. The Registry is based on the Legislature's decision to facilitate access to publicly available information about persons convicted of sexual offenses. EXCEPT FOR OFFENDERS SPECIFICALLY DESIGNATED ON THIS SITE AS HIGH-RISK, THE DEPARTMENT OF PUBLIC SAFETY HAS NOT CONSIDERED OR ASSESSED THE SPECIFIC RISK OF REOFFENSE WITH REGARD TO ANY INDIVIDUAL PRIOR TO HIS OR HER INCLUSION WITHIN THIS REGISTRY AND HAS MADE NO DETERMINATION THAT ANY INDIVIDUAL INCLUDED IN THE REGISTRY IS CURRENTLY DANGEROUS. THE MAIN PURPOSE OF PROVIDING THIS DATA ON THE INTERNET IS TO MAKE INFORMATION MORE EASILY AVAILABLE AND ACCESSIBLE, NOT TO WARN ABOUT ANY SPECIFIC INDIVIDUAL. IF YOU HAVE QUESTIONS OR CONCERNS ABOUT A PERSON WHO IS NOT LISTED ON THIS SITE OR YOU HAVE QUESTIONS ABOUT SEX OFFENDER INFORMATION LISTED ON THIS SITE, PLEASE CONTACT THE DEPARTMENT OF PUBLIC SAFETY OR YOUR LOCAL LAW ENFORCEMENT AGENCY. PLEASE BE AWARE THAT MANY NONOFFENDERS SHARE A NAME WITH A REGISTERED SEX OFFENDER. Any person who uses information in this Registry to injure, harass, or commit a criminal offense against any person included in the Registry or any other person is subject to criminal prosecution."

(i) The Department shall post electronically general information about the Sex Offender Registry and how the public may access Registry information. Electronically posted information regarding sex offenders listed in subsection (a) of this section shall be organized and available to search by the sex offender's name and the sex offender's county, city, or town of residence.

(j) The Department shall adopt rules for the administration of this section and shall expedite the process for the adoption of such rules. The Department shall not implement this section prior to the adoption of such rules.

(k) If a sex offender's information is required to be posted electronically pursuant to subdivision (a)(2) of this section, the Department shall list the offender's convictions for any crime listed in subdivision 5401(10) of this title, regardless of the date of the conviction or whether the offender was required to register as a sex offender based upon that conviction.

(l) A sex offender's street address shall not be posted electronically if the offender has a developmental disability, receives funding from the Department of Disabilities, Aging, and Independent Living (DAIL) for 24-hour supervision and treatment, and resides in a residence that is equipped with alarms. However, this information shall be otherwise available pursuant to this section. An agency designated pursuant to 18 V.S.A. § 8907 to provide mental health and developmental disability services (DA), or a specialized service agency (SSA) operating under an agreement entered into pursuant to 18 V.S.A. § 8912 that is providing supervision for the offender shall immediately notify the administrator of the Sex Offender Registry and local law enforcement if the individual's level of supervision is decreased from 24 hours or if the offender leaves his or her residence without authorization, and thereafter this subsection shall cease to apply to that offender. If after notice and hearing, the Commissioner of DAIL finds that the DA or SSA has failed to notify the administrator of the Sex Offender Registry and local law enforcement of a decrease from 24-hour supervision or absence without authorization by the offender within 24 hours of the change in status, the Commissioner may impose an administrative penalty of not more than $1,000.00 for each day of the violation. A DA or SSA shall have the right to a de novo appeal of a decision under this subsection pursuant to Rule 75 of the Vermont Rules of Civil Procedure.

(m) Information regarding a sex offender whose sentence is deferred shall not be posted electronically unless the offender violates the terms of the deferred sentence agreement and is sentenced on the conviction. (Added 2003, No. 157 (Adj. Sess.), § 7, eff. Oct. 1, 2004; amended 2005, No. 83, § 13; 2005, No. 192 (Adj. Sess.), § 29, eff. May 26, 2006; 2007, No. 77, § 9, eff. June 7, 2007; 2009, No. 58, §§ 9, 14; 2009, No. 66 (Adj. Sess.), §§ 2, 3; 2009, No. 157 (Adj. Sess.), § 3; 2011, No. 31, § 2, eff. May 17, 2011; 2011, No. 55, § 10; 2013, No. 181 (Adj. Sess.), § 2, eff. June 10, 2014; 2015, No. 133 (Adj. Sess.), § 4, eff. May 25, 2016; 2017, No. 15, § 2, eff. May 1, 2017.)

[Contingent amendment to section 5411a; see also section 5411a set out above and proviso .]

§ 5411a. Electronic posting of the Sex Offender Registry

(a) Notwithstanding 20 V.S.A. §§ 2056a-2056e, the Department shall electronically post information on the Internet in accordance with subsection (b) of this section regarding the following sex offenders, upon the offender's release from confinement or, if the offender was not subject to confinement, upon the offender's sentencing:

(1) Sex offenders who have been convicted of:

(A) aggravated sexual assault of a child (13 V.S.A. § 3253a);

(B) aggravated sexual assault (13 V.S.A. § 3253);

(C) sexual assault (13 V.S.A. § 3252);

(D) kidnapping with intent to commit sexual assault (13 V.S.A. § 2405(a)(1)(D));

(E) lewd or lascivious conduct with child (13 V.S.A. § 2602);

(F) a second or subsequent conviction for voyeurism (13 V.S.A. § 2605(b) or (c));

(G) slave traffic if a registrable offense under subdivision 5401(10)(B)(iv) of this title (13 V.S.A. § 2635);

(H) sex trafficking of children or sex trafficking by force, fraud, or coercion (13 V.S.A. § 2635a);

(I) sexual exploitation of a minor (13 V.S.A. § 3258(c));

(J) any offense regarding the sexual exploitation of children (chapter 64 of this title);

(K) sexual abuse of a vulnerable adult (13 V.S.A. § 1379);

(L) human trafficking as defined in subdivisions 2652(a)(1)-(4) of this title;

(M) aggravated human trafficking as defined in subdivision 2653(a)(4) of this title;

(N) a federal conviction in federal court for any of the following offenses:

(i) sex trafficking of children as defined in 18 U.S.C. § 1591;

(ii) aggravated sexual abuse as defined in 18 U.S.C. § 2241;

(iii) sexual abuse as defined in 18 U.S.C. § 2242;

(iv) sexual abuse of a minor or ward as defined in 18 U.S.C. § 2243;

(v) abusive sexual contact as defined in 18 U.S.C. § 2244;

(vi) offenses resulting in death as defined in 18 U.S.C. § 2245;

(vii) sexual exploitation of children as defined in 18 U.S.C. § 2251;

(viii) selling or buying of children as defined in 18 U.S.C. § 2251A;

(ix) material involving the sexual exploitation of minors as defined in 18 U.S.C. § 2252;

(x) material containing child pornography as defined in 18 U.S.C. § 2252A;

(xi) production of sexually explicit depictions of a minor for import into the United States as defined in 18 U.S.C. § 2260;

(xii) transportation of a minor for illegal sexual activity as defined in 18 U.S.C. § 2421;

(xiii) coercion and enticement of a minor for illegal sexual activity as defined in 18 U.S.C. § 2422;

(xiv) transportation of minors for illegal sexual activity, travel with the intent to engage in illicit sexual conduct with a minor, and engaging in illicit sexual conduct in foreign places as defined in 18 U.S.C. § 2423;

(xv) transmitting information about a minor to further criminal sexual conduct as defined in 18 U.S.C. § 2425;

(xvi) trafficking in persons as defined in 18 U.S.C. sections 2251-2252(a), 2260, or 2421-2423 if the violation included sexual abuse, aggravated sexual abuse, or the attempt to commit aggravated sexual abuse;

(O) an attempt to commit any offense listed in this subdivision (a)(1).

(2) Sex offenders who have at least one prior conviction for an offense described in subdivision 5401(10) of this subchapter.

(3) Sex offenders who have failed to comply with sex offender registration requirements and for whose arrest there is an outstanding warrant for such noncompliance. Information on offenders shall remain on the Internet only while the warrant is outstanding.

(4) Sex offenders who have been designated as sexual predators pursuant to section 5405 of this title.

(5)(A) Sex offenders who have not complied with sex offender treatment recommended by the Department of Corrections or who are ineligible for sex offender treatment. The Department of Corrections shall establish rules for the administration of this subdivision and shall specify what circumstances constitute noncompliance with treatment and criteria for ineligibility to participate in treatment. Offenders subject to this provision shall have the right to appeal the Department of Corrections' determination in Superior Court in accordance with Rule 75 of the Vermont Rules of Civil Procedure. This subdivision shall apply prospectively and shall not apply to those sex offenders who did not comply with treatment or were ineligible for treatment prior to March 1, 2005.

(B) The Department of Corrections shall notify the Department if a sex offender who is compliant with sex offender treatment completes his or her sentence but has not completed sex offender treatment. As long as the offender complies with treatment, the offender shall not be considered noncompliant under this subdivision and shall not be placed on the Internet Registry in accordance with this subdivision alone. However, the offender shall submit to the Department proof of continuing treatment compliance every three months. Proof of compliance shall be a form provided by the Department that the offender's treatment provider shall sign, attesting to the offender's continuing compliance with recommended treatment. Failure to submit such proof as required under this subdivision (B) shall result in the offender's placement on the Internet Registry in accordance with subdivision (A) of this subdivision (5).

(6) Sex offenders who have been designated by the Department of Corrections, pursuant to section 5411b of this title, as high-risk.

(7) A person 18 years of age or older who resides in this State, other than in a correctional facility, and who is currently or, prior to taking up residence within this State was required to register as a sex offender in any jurisdiction of the United States, including a state, territory, commonwealth, the District of Columbia, or military, federal, or tribal court; except that, for purposes of this subdivision:

(A) conduct that is criminal only because of the age of the victim shall not be considered an offense for purposes of the Registry if the perpetrator is under the age of 18 and the victim is at least 12 years old; and

(B) information shall be posted electronically only if the offense for which the person was required to register in the other jurisdiction was:

(i) a felony; or

(ii) a misdemeanor punishable by more than six months of imprisonment.

(b) The Department shall electronically post the following information on sex offenders designated in subsection (a) of this section:

(1) the offender's name and any known aliases;

(2) the offender's date of birth;

(3) a general physical description of the offender;

(4) a digital photograph of the offender;

(5) the offender's town of residence;

(6) the offender's address or, if the offender does not have a fixed address, other information about where the offender habitually lives, if:

(A) the Department determines that all the information to be electronically posted about the offender is correct; and

(B)(i) the offender has been designated as high-risk by the Department of Corrections pursuant to section 5411b of this title;

(ii) the offender has not complied with sex offender treatment;

(iii) there is an outstanding warrant for the offender's arrest;

(iv) the offender is subject to the Registry for a conviction of a sex offense against a child under 13 years of age; or

(v) the offender's name has been electronically posted for an offense committed in another jurisdiction which required the person's address to be electronically posted in that jurisdiction;

(7) the date and nature of the offender's conviction;

(8) if the offender is under the supervision of the Department of Corrections, the name and telephone number of the local Department of Corrections office in charge of monitoring the sex offender;

(9) whether the offender complied with treatment recommended by the Department of Corrections;

(10) a statement that there is an outstanding warrant for the offender's arrest, if applicable; and

(11) the reason for which the offender information is accessible under this section.

(12) whether the offender has been designated high risk by the Department of Corrections pursuant to section 5411b of this title; and

(13) if the offender has not been subject to a risk assessment, a statement that the offender has not been so assessed and that such a person is presumed to be high risk, provided that the Department of Corrections shall permit a person subject to this subdivision to obtain a risk assessment at the person's own expense.

(c) The Department shall have the authority to take necessary steps to obtain digital photographs of offenders whose information is required to be posted on the Internet and to update photographs as necessary. An offender shall annually report to the Department or a local law enforcement agency for the purpose of being photographed for the Internet.

(d) The identity of a victim of an offense that requires registration shall not be released.

(e) Information regarding a sex offender shall not be posted electronically if the conduct that is the basis for the offense is criminal only because of the age of the victim and the perpetrator is within 38 months of age of the victim.

(f) Information regarding a sex offender shall not be posted electronically prior to the offender reaching 18 years of age, but such information shall be otherwise available pursuant to section 5411 of this title.

(g) Information on sex offenders shall be posted on the Internet for the duration of time for which they are subject to notification requirements under section 5401 et seq. of this title.

(h) Posting of the information shall include the following language: "This information is made available for the purpose of complying with 13 V.S.A. § 5401 et seq., which requires the Department of Public Safety to establish and maintain a Registry of persons who are required to register as sex offenders and to post electronically information on sex offenders. The Registry is based on the Legislature's decision to facilitate access to publicly available information about persons convicted of sexual offenses. EXCEPT FOR OFFENDERS SPECIFICALLY DESIGNATED ON THIS SITE AS HIGH-RISK, THE DEPARTMENT OF PUBLIC SAFETY HAS NOT CONSIDERED OR ASSESSED THE SPECIFIC RISK OF REOFFENSE WITH REGARD TO ANY INDIVIDUAL PRIOR TO HIS OR HER INCLUSION WITHIN THIS REGISTRY AND HAS MADE NO DETERMINATION THAT ANY INDIVIDUAL INCLUDED IN THE REGISTRY IS CURRENTLY DANGEROUS. THE MAIN PURPOSE OF PROVIDING THIS DATA ON THE INTERNET IS TO MAKE INFORMATION MORE EASILY AVAILABLE AND ACCESSIBLE, NOT TO WARN ABOUT ANY SPECIFIC INDIVIDUAL. IF YOU HAVE QUESTIONS OR CONCERNS ABOUT A PERSON WHO IS NOT LISTED ON THIS SITE OR YOU HAVE QUESTIONS ABOUT SEX OFFENDER INFORMATION LISTED ON THIS SITE, PLEASE CONTACT THE DEPARTMENT OF PUBLIC SAFETY OR YOUR LOCAL LAW ENFORCEMENT AGENCY. PLEASE BE AWARE THAT MANY NONOFFENDERS SHARE A NAME WITH A REGISTERED SEX OFFENDER. Any person who uses information in this Registry to injure, harass, or commit a criminal offense against any person included in the Registry or any other person is subject to criminal prosecution."

(i) The Department shall post electronically general information about the Sex Offender Registry and how the public may access Registry information. Electronically posted information regarding sex offenders listed in subsection (a) of this section shall be organized and available to search by the sex offender's name and the sex offender's county, city, or town of residence.

(j) The Department shall adopt rules for the administration of this section and shall expedite the process for the adoption of such rules. The Department shall not implement this section prior to the adoption of such rules.

(k) If a sex offender's information is required to be posted electronically pursuant to subdivision (a)(2) of this section, the Department shall list the offender's convictions for any crime listed in subdivision 5401(10) of this title, regardless of the date of the conviction or whether the offender was required to register as a sex offender based upon that conviction.

(l) A sex offender's street address shall not be posted electronically if the offender has a developmental disability, receives funding from the Department of Disabilities, Aging, and Independent Living (DAIL) for 24-hour supervision and treatment, and resides in a residence that is equipped with alarms. However, this information shall be otherwise available pursuant to this section. An agency designated pursuant to

18 V.S.A. § 8907 to provide mental health and developmental disability services (DA), or a specialized service agency (SSA) operating under an agreement entered into pursuant to 18 V.S.A. § 8912 that is providing supervision for the offender shall immediately notify the administrator of the Sex Offender Registry and local law enforcement if the individual's level of supervision is decreased from 24 hours or if the offender leaves his or her residence without authorization, and thereafter this subsection shall cease to apply to that offender. If after notice and hearing, the Commissioner of DAIL finds that the DA or SSA has failed to notify the administrator of the Sex Offender Registry and local law enforcement of a decrease from 24-hour supervision or absence without authorization by the offender within 24 hours of the change in status, the Commissioner may impose an administrative penalty of not more than $1,000.00 for each day of the violation. A DA or SSA shall have the right to a de novo appeal of a decision under this subsection pursuant to Rule 75 of the Vermont Rules of Civil Procedure.

(m) Information regarding a sex offender whose sentence is deferred shall not be posted electronically unless the offender violates the terms of the deferred sentence agreement and is sentenced on the conviction. (Added 2003, No. 157 (Adj. Sess.), § 7, eff. Oct. 1, 2004; amended 2005, No. 83, § 13; 2005, No. 192 (Adj. Sess.), § 29, eff. May 26, 2006; 2007, No. 77, § 9, eff. June 7, 2007; 2009, No. 58, §§ 9, 14; 2009, No. 66 (Adj. Sess.), §§ 2, 3; 2009, No. 157 (Adj. Sess.), § 3; 2011, No. 31, § 2, eff. May 17, 2011; 2011, No. 55, § 10; 2013, No. 181 (Adj. Sess.), § 2, eff. June 10, 2014; 2015, No. 31, § 8; 2015, No. 133 (Adj. Sess.), § 4, eff. May 25, 2016; 2017, No. 15, § 2, eff. May 1, 2017.)

§ 5411b. Designation of high-risk sex offender

(a) The Department of Corrections shall evaluate a sex offender for the purpose of determining whether the offender is "high-risk" as defined in section 5401 of this title. The designation of high-risk under this section is for the purpose of identifying an offender as one who should be subject to increased public access to his or her status as a sex offender and related information, including Internet access.

(b) After notice and an opportunity to be heard, a sex offender who is designated as high risk shall have the right to appeal de novo to the Superior Court in accordance with Rule 75 of the Vermont Rules of Civil Procedure.

(c) The Department of Corrections shall adopt rules for the administration of this section. The Department of Corrections shall not implement this section prior to the adoption of such rules.

(d) The Department of Corrections shall identify those sex offenders under the supervision of the Department as of the date of passage of June 28, 2005 who are high risk and shall designate them as such no later than September 1, 2009. (Added 2003, No. 157 (Adj. Sess.), § 8, eff. March 1, 2005; amended 2005, No. 83, § 16; 2009, No. 58, § 10.)

§ 5411c. Active community notification by the Department of Public Safety, the Department of Corrections, and local law enforcement

(a) Notwithstanding other provisions to the contrary, the Department, the Department of Corrections, and any authorized local law enforcement agency are authorized to notify members of the public at their discretion about any sex offender whose information is required to be posted on the Internet in accordance with section 5411a of this title.

(b) The Department, the Department of Corrections, and any authorized local law enforcement agency are authorized to notify members of the public at their discretion about a sex offender whose information is not required to be posted on the Internet in accordance with section 5411a of this title only under circumstances that constitute a compelling risk to public safety and only after consultation with the Vermont Crime Information Center and the Department of Corrections.

(c) Registry information shall not be released under this section unless it is released pursuant to written protocols governing the manner and circumstances of the release developed by the Department, the Department of Corrections, or an authorized law enforcement agency. The protocols shall include consultation between the department or agency releasing the information and the department of corrections' staff member responsible for supervising the offender.

(d) Active community notification regarding registered sex offenders who may pose a danger to members of the community is an important public safety tool that the General Assembly intends for authorized agencies to use at their discretion in accordance with this subchapter. (Added 2005, No. 192 (Adj. Sess.), § 27, eff. May 26, 2006.)

§ 5411d. Designation of noncompliant high-risk sex offender

(a) Prior to releasing a person from total confinement, the Department of Corrections shall designate the person as a noncompliant high-risk sex offender if the person meets all of the following criteria:

(1) is incarcerated on or after June 7, 2007 for lewd and lascivious conduct with a child as defined in section 2602 of this title, sexual assault as defined in section 3252 of this title, aggravated sexual assault as defined in section 3253 of this title, or any attempt to commit a crime listed herein, or a comparable offense in another jurisdiction of the United States;

(2) is not subject to indeterminate life sentences under section 3271 of this title;

(3) is designated as a high risk sex offender pursuant to section 5411b of this title; and

(4) is noncompliant with sex offender treatment as defined by Department of Corrections' directives.

(b) Noncompliant high-risk sex offenders shall report to the Department as follows:

(1) In person, within 15 days from the date of release from Department of Corrections' supervision, and within every 30 days thereafter.

(2) Prior to any change of address. However, if the change of address is unanticipated, the offender shall report within one day of the change of address.

(3) Prior to enrollment in or separation from any postsecondary educational institution. However, if the change in school status is unanticipated, the offender shall report within one day of the change.

(4) Within one day of any change in a place of employment.

(c) In addition to the Registry information required in section 5403 of this title, a noncompliant high-risk sex offender shall provide the Department with the make, model, color, registration, and license plate number of any vehicle the person operates prior to operation. An offender found in operation of a vehicle not on the list provided to the Department shall be considered to be in violation of this subsection.

(d) The Department shall arrange for the noncompliant high-risk sex offender to have his or her digital photograph updated annually for purposes of the electronic Registry as provided in section 5411a of this title. An offender who is requested by the Department to report to the Department or a local law enforcement agency for the purpose of being photographed for the Internet Registry shall comply with the request within 30 days.

(e) The Department shall conduct periodic unannounced Registry compliance checks on noncompliant high-risk sex offenders to verify the accuracy of Registry information. The Department may enter into an agreement with a local law enforcement agency to perform duties under this subsection and under subdivision (b)(1) of this section, but shall maintain responsibility for compliance with this subsection.

(f)(1) A noncompliant high-risk sex offender may petition the Criminal Division of the Superior Court to be relieved from the heightened Registry requirements in this section once every five years from the date of designation. The offender shall have the burden of proving by a preponderance of the evidence that he or she:

(A) no longer qualifies as a high-risk offender as defined in section 5401 of this title and rules adopted by the Department of Corrections in accordance with section 5411b of this title; and

(B) has complied with and completed sex offender treatment as provided by Department of Corrections' directives.

(2) The Vermont Rules of Civil Procedure shall apply to these proceedings.

(3) If the court finds that the offender is not high risk and has successfully completed treatment, the court shall order that the offender is no longer considered a noncompliant high risk offender and is subsequently relieved from the heightened registry requirements of this section; however, the offender shall still continue to comply with Sex Offender Registry and other requirements as provided elsewhere in this subchapter.

(g)(1) A noncompliant high-risk sex offender who knowingly fails to comply with any of the Registry requirements under this section shall be imprisoned for not less than five years and a maximum term of life and, in addition, may be fined not more than $50,000.00. A sentence may be suspended in whole or in part, or the person may be eligible for parole or release on conditional reentry or furlough, provided the person is subject to intensive supervision by the Department of Corrections.

(2) In a criminal proceeding for violating any of the Registry requirements under this section, a defendant shall be prohibited from challenging his or her status as a noncompliant high-risk sex offender.

(h) A noncompliant high-risk sex offender convicted of violating this section shall be sentenced under section 3271 of this title. (Added 2007, No. 77, § 10, eff. June 7, 2007; amended 2009, No. 154, § 238.)

§ 5412. Immunity

The Department, the Department of Corrections, any authorized local law enforcement agency, and their employees shall be immune from liability in carrying out the provisions under this subchapter except in instances of gross negligence or willful misconduct, provided that the agencies complied with the rules adopted pursuant to this subchapter. (Added 1995, No. 124 (Adj. Sess.), § 1, eff. Sept. 1, 1996;

amended 2003, No. 157 (Adj. Sess.), § 9; 2005, No. 83, § 14; 2005, No. 192 (Adj. Sess.), § 28, eff. May 26, 2006.)

§ 5413. Expungement of records

A person whose conviction of a sex offense is reversed and dismissed shall not be required to register for that conviction under the provisions of this subchapter and any information about that conviction contained in the Registry shall be removed and destroyed. If any information about that conviction was provided to any person or agency under subsection 5402(b) of this subchapter, that person or agency shall be notified that the conviction was reversed and shall be required to remove and destroy the information. If the person whose conviction is reversed and dismissed has more than one entry in the Registry, only the entry related to the dismissed case shall be removed and destroyed. (Added 1995, No. 124 (Adj. Sess.), § 1, eff. Sept. 1, 1996.)

§ 5414. Participation in national sex offender registration

The Department shall participate in the National Sex Offender Registry Program managed by the Federal Bureau of Investigation in accordance with guidelines issued by the U.S. Attorney General, including transmission of current address information and other information on registrants to the extent provided by the guidelines. (Added 2001, No. 49, § 11, eff. Sept. 1, 2001.)

§ 5415. Enforcement; special investigation units

(a) Special investigation units, created pursuant to 24 V.S.A. § 1940, shall be responsible for the investigation of violations of this chapter's Registry requirements and are authorized to conduct in-person Registry compliance checks in a time, place, and manner it deems appropriate in furtherance of the purposes of this chapter. This section shall not be construed to prohibit local law enforcement from enforcing the provisions of this chapter.

(b) On or before November 1, 2019, and annually thereafter, local law enforcement agencies shall report to the Vermont Crime Information Center about any in-person Registry compliance checks that the agency has conducted during the preceding 12 months. The report shall include the total number of in-person compliance checks conducted during the 12-month period, the number of offenders who were in compliance, the number of offenders who were out of compliance, and the reasons for being out of compliance.

(c) The Department of Public Safety shall report to the Senate and House Committees on Judiciary on or before December 15, 2009, and annually thereafter, regarding its efforts under this section. (Added 2009, No. 1, § 16, eff. March 4, 2009; 2019, No. 77, § 17, eff. June 19, 2019.)

§ 5416. Persons subject to erroneous Sex Offender Registry requirements; petition to correct

(a) A person may petition the court for an order declaring that the person has been inadvertently subject to erroneous Sex Offender Registry requirements and directing the Department of Public Safety to correct the error. The petitioner shall provide notice of the petition to the State's Attorney or the Attorney General, who shall be the respondent in the matter.

(b) A petition filed under this section shall include:

(1) the court's order issued under subdivision 5403(b)(2) of this title to comply with Sex Offender Registry requirements, if available; and

(2) the factual basis for the petitioner's allegation that he or she was subject to an erroneous Sex Offender Registry requirement.

(c) The court shall grant a petition filed under this section if it finds that the petitioner has demonstrated by a preponderance of the evidence that he or she was by court order subject to an erroneous Sex Offender Registry requirement. As used in this subsection, "erroneous Sex Offender Registry requirement" includes the person's name being erroneously placed on the Sex Offender Registry or the Internet Sex Offender Registry, or the person being erroneously subject to lifetime registration under subsection 5407(f) of this title.

(d) If a petition filed under this section is granted, the court shall enter an order declaring that the person had been inadvertently subject to erroneous Sex Offender Registry requirements. The court shall provide the order to the Department of Public Safety and direct the Department to take any action necessary to correct the error, including, if appropriate, removing the person's name from the Sex Offender Registry and the Internet Sex Offender Registry.

(e)(1) If the court denies a petition filed under this section, no further petition shall be filed by the person with respect to the alleged error.

(2) This subsection shall not apply if the petition is based on:

(A) newly discovered evidence;

(B) an expungement order issued under chapter 230 of this title;

(C) a successful petition under chapter 182 of this title (innocence protection); or

(D) a successful petition for postconviction relief. (Added 2015, No. 31, § 5.)

Subchapter 4: Profits From Crime

§ 5421. Notice of profits from a crime

(a) Every person, firm, corporation, partnership, association, or other legal entity that knowingly contracts for, pays, or agrees to pay any profits from a crime, as defined in subdivision 5351(8) of this title, to a person charged with or convicted of that crime shall give written notice to the Attorney General of the payment or obligation to pay as soon as is practicable after discovering that the payment is or will be a profit from a crime.

(b) The Attorney General, upon receipt of notice of a contract, agreement to pay, or payment of profits of the crime shall send written notice of the existence of such profits to all known victims of the crime at their last known addresses. (Added 2009, No. 55, § 2, eff. June 1, 2009.)

§ 5422. Actions to recover profits from a crime

(a) Notwithstanding any other provision of law, including any statute of limitations, any crime victim shall have the right to bring a civil action in a court of competent jurisdiction to recover money damages from a person convicted of that crime, or the legal representative of that convicted person, within three years of the discovery of any profits from the crime. Any damages awarded in such action shall be recoverable only up to the value of the profits of the crime. This section shall not limit the right of a victim to proceed or recover under another cause of action.

(b) The Attorney General may, within three years of the discovery of any profits from the crime, bring a civil action on behalf of the State to enforce the subrogation rights described in section 5357 of this title.

(c) If the full value of any profits from the crime has not yet been claimed by either the victim of the crime or the victim's representative, the Attorney General, or both, within three years of the discovery of such profits, then the State may bring a civil action in a court of competent jurisdiction to recover the costs incurred by providing the defendant with counsel, if any, and other costs reasonably incurred or to be incurred in the incarceration of the defendant.

(d) Upon the filing of an action pursuant to subsection (a) of this section, the victim shall deliver a copy of the summons and complaint to the Attorney General. Upon receipt of a copy of the summons and complaint, the Attorney General shall send written notice of the alleged existence of profits from the crime to all other known victims at their last known addresses.

(e) To avoid the wasting of assets identified in the complaint as newly discovered profits of the crime, the Attorney General, acting on behalf of the plaintiff and all other victims, shall have the right to apply for all remedies that are also otherwise available to the victim. (Added 2009, No. 55, § 2, eff. June 1, 2009.)

Subchapter 5: Sexual Assault Nurse Examiners

§ 5431. Definition; certification

(a) As used in this subchapter, "SANE" means a sexual assault nurse examiner.

(b) A person licensed under 26 V.S.A. chapter 28 (nursing) may obtain a specialized certification from the SANE Program as a sexual assault nurse examiner if he or she demonstrates compliance with the requirements for specialized certification as established by the SANE Board. (Added 2015, No. 38, § 12, eff. May 28, 2015; amended 2017, No. 68, § 1.)

§ 5432. SANE Board

(a) The SANE Board is created for the purpose of advising the Sexual Assault Nurse Examiners Program.

(b) The SANE Board shall be composed of the following members:

(1) the Executive Director of the Vermont State Nurses Association or designee;

(2) the President of the Vermont Association of Hospitals and Health Systems;

(3) the Director of the Vermont Forensic Laboratory or designee;

(4) the Director of the Vermont Network Against Domestic and Sexual Violence or designee;

(5) an attorney with experience prosecuting sexual assault crimes, appointed by the Attorney General;

(6) the Executive Director of the Vermont Center for Crime Victim Services or designee;

(7) a law enforcement officer assigned to one of Vermont's special units of investigation, appointed by the Commissioner of Public Safety;

(8) a law enforcement officer employed by a municipal police department, appointed by the Executive Director of the Vermont Criminal Justice Council;

(9) three sexual assault nurse examiners, appointed by the Attorney General;

(10) a health care provider as defined in 18 V.S.A. § 9402 whose practice includes the care of victims of sexual assault, appointed by the Commissioner of Health;

(11) a pediatrician whose practice includes the care of victims of sexual assault, appointed by the Vermont Chapter of the American Academy of Pediatrics;

(12) the Coordinator of the Vermont Victim Assistance Program or designee;

(13) the President of the Vermont Alliance of Child Advocacy Centers or designee;

(14) the Chair of the Vermont State Board of Nursing or designee;

(15) the Commissioner for Children and Families or designee; and

(16) the Commissioner of Health or designee.

(c) The SANE Board shall advise the SANE Program on the following:

(1) statewide program priorities;

(2) training and educational requirements;

(3) a standardized sexual assault protocol and kit to be used by all physicians and hospitals in this State when providing forensic examinations of victims of alleged sexual offenses; and

(4) statewide policy development related to sexual assault nurse examiner programs. (Added 2015, No. 38, § 12, eff. May 28, 2015; amended 2017, No. 68, § 1.)

§ 5433. SANE Program Clinical Coordinator

A clinical coordinator position shall be funded by either the Vermont Center for Crime Victim Services or through other identified State funding options for the purpose of staffing the SANE Program. The position shall be contracted through the Vermont Network Against Domestic and Sexual Violence. The Clinical Coordinator shall consult with the SANE Board in performing the following duties:

(1) overseeing the recruitment and retention of SANEs in the State of Vermont;

(2) administering a statewide educational program, including:

(A) the initial SANE certification training;

(B) ongoing training to ensure currency of practice for SANEs; and

(C) advanced training programs as needed;

(3) providing consultation, technical assistance, and training to SANEs and acute care hospitals regarding the standards of care for sexual assault patients;

(4) providing training and outreach to criminal justice and community-based agencies as needed;

(5) coordinating and managing a system for ensuring best practices; and

(6) granting certifications, pursuant to section 5431 of this title, to candidates who demonstrate compliance with the requirements for specialized certification as established by the SANE Board. (Added 2015, No. 38, § 12, eff. May 28, 2015; amended 2017, No. 68, § 1.)

§ 5434. Repealed. 2017, No. 68, § 1.

§ 5435. Access to a sexual assault nurse examiner

(a) On or before September 1, 2017, the Vermont Association of Hospitals and Health Systems (VAHHS) and the Vermont SANE Program shall enter into a memorandum of understanding (MOU) to ensure improved access to sexual assault nurse examiners (SANE) for victims of sexual assault in underserved regions. Improved access may include all acute care hospitals to provide patients with care from a paid employee who is also a certified sexual assault nurse examiner or access to a shared regional staffing pool that includes certified sexual assault nurse examiners.

(b) The Vermont SANE Program shall develop and offer an annual training regarding standards of care and forensic evidence collection to emergency department appropriate health care providers at acute care hospitals in Vermont. Personnel who are certified sexual assault nurse examiners shall not be subject to this subsection.

(c) On or before January 1, 2018, the SANE Program shall report to the General Assembly on training participation rates pursuant to subsection (b) of this section. (Added 2017, No. 68, § 1.)

Chapter 169: Vermont Sentencing Commission

 [Section 5451 repealed on July 1, 2021.]

§ 5451. Creation of Commission

(a) The Vermont Sentencing Commission is established for the purpose of overseeing criminal sentencing practices in the State, reducing geographical disparities in sentencing, and making recommendations regarding criminal sentencing to the General Assembly.

(b) The Commission shall consist of the following members:

(1) the Chief Justice of the Vermont Supreme Court or designee;

(2) the Chief Superior Judge or designee, provided that the designee is a sitting or retired Vermont judge;

(3) a District or Superior Court Judge with substantial criminal law experience appointed by the administrative judge;

(4) the Chair of the Senate Committee on Judiciary;

(5) the Chair of the House Committee on Judiciary;

(6) the Attorney General or designee;

(7) the Defender General or designee;

(8) the Executive Director of the Department of State's Attorneys and Sheriffs or designee;

(9) the Appellate Defender;

(10) a State's Attorney appointed by the Executive Director of the Department of State's Attorneys and Sheriffs;

(11) a staff public defender with experience in juvenile defense matters appointed by the Defender General;

(12) an attorney with substantial criminal law experience appointed by the Vermont Bar Association;

(13) the Commissioner of Corrections or designee;

(14) the Commissioner of Public Safety or designee;

(15) the Executive Director of the Vermont Center for Crime Victim Services or designee;

(16) the Executive Director of the Vermont Crime Research Group; and

(17) one member of the public appointed by the Governor.

(c) The Chief Justice shall appoint a chair and vice chair of the Commission. Legislative members of the Commission shall serve only while in office. A substitute shall be appointed for a legislator who no longer serves in such capacity. All other members of the Commission shall serve on the Committee for renewable two-year terms for as long as the member continues to hold the position that made the member eligible for appointment to or membership on the Committee. Vacancies shall be appointed in the same manner as original appointments.

(d) The Commission shall meet at least quarterly and at any additional times at the call of the Chair. The Commission shall take minutes of its meetings and may hold public hearings. Ten members of the Commission shall constitute a quorum.

(e) The Commission shall have the assistance and cooperation of the Judiciary, the Department of Public Safety, the Department of Corrections, the Department for Children and Families, the Department of State's Attorneys and Sheriffs, the Office of Defender General, the Vermont Center for Crime Victim Services, and all other State and local agencies and departments.

(f) Legislative members of the Commission shall be entitled to per diem compensation and reimbursement for expenses in accordance with 2 V.S.A. § 406. Members of the Commission who are not otherwise compensated by their employer shall be entitled to per diem compensation and reimbursement for expenses in the same manner as board members are compensated under 32 V.S.A. § 1010. (Added 2005, No. 192 (Adj. Sess.), § 16, eff. May 26, 2006; amended 2017, No. 142 (Adj. Sess.), § 1, eff. May 21, 2018.)

[Section 5452 repealed on July 1, 2021.]

§ 5452. Duties

(a) In addition to the general responsibilities set forth in section 5451 of this title, the Commission shall:

(1) report on historical and existing sentencing practices in Vermont, including the frequency and duration of incarcerative and nonincarcerative sentences for particular offenses;

(2) report on geographical sentencing disparities which result in a defendant's sentence for an offense varying substantially on the basis of the county in which it is committed;

(3) propose a system of statewide discretionary sentencing ranges that take into account historical and existing sentencing practices and establish rational and consistent statewide sentencing standards;

(4) review alternatives to the traditional prosecutorial model and make recommendations for alternative sentencing methods to the General Assembly;

(5) review practices involving probation, parole, early or conditional release, preapproved furlough, supervised community sentence, graduated sanctions, and the awarding of sentencing credits, and make recommendations concerning such practices to the Department of Corrections and the General Assembly;

(6) review developments in criminal law, including statutory modifications and judicial decisions, and make recommendations to the General Assembly when the Commission determines that legislative changes are advisable;

(7) review proposed legislation and make recommendations concerning the proposals to the General Assembly; and

(8) consider any other issue the Commission finds relevant to criminal sentencing and the criminal justice system.

(b) [Repealed.]

(c) It shall be a priority for the Sentencing Commission to develop responses to the significant impacts that increased opioid addiction has had on the criminal justice system. The Commission shall consider:

(1) whether and under what circumstances offenses committed as a result of opioid addiction should be classified as civil rather than criminal offenses;

(2) whether the possession or sale of specific, lesser amounts of opioids and other regulated drugs should be classified as civil rather than criminal offenses;

(3) how to maximize treatment for offenders as a response to offenses committed as a result of opioid addiction. (Added 2005, No. 192 (Adj. Sess.), § 16, eff. May 26, 2006; amended 2011, No. 139 (Adj. Sess.), § 51(d), eff. May 14, 2012; 2017, No. 142 (Adj. Sess.), § 2, eff. May 21, 2018.)

Chapter 181: Arrest, Complaint, And Binding Over

Subchapter 1: Arrest And Complaint

§ 5501. Repealed. 1973, No. 118, § 25, eff. Oct. 1, 1973.

§ 5502. Copy of process for accused

When an officer does not within six hours deliver a true copy of the warrant or process by which he or she detains a person in a criminal proceeding, to a person who demands such copy and tenders the fees therefor, he or she shall forfeit to such person $200.00.

§ 5503. Recognizance by complainant

A warrant to apprehend a person charged with a criminal offense shall not be granted by a district judge except on information or complaint of an informing or complaining officer, until such magistrate has taken security to his or her satisfaction, by way of recognizance to the person so charged, that the prosecutor will answer the damages if he or she does not prosecute his or her information to effect, and a minute of such recognizance shall be made as in civil causes. (Amended 1965, No. 194, § 10, operative February 1, 1967; 1973, No. 249 (Adj. Sess.), § 52, eff. April 9, 1974.)

§ 5504. Repealed. 2017, No. 93 (Adj. Sess.), § 14.

§§ 5505-5510. Repealed. 1973, No. 118, § 25, eff. Oct. 1, 1973.

§ 5511. Notification of unemancipated minor's parent or guardian

(a) A law enforcement officer who arrests an unemancipated minor shall take reasonable steps to notify, as soon as reasonably practicable, a parent or guardian of the minor:

(1) that the minor has been arrested;

(2) the location where the minor is being held if still in law enforcement custody; and

(3) the nature of the criminal charge against the minor.

(b) If the minor is cited to appear in court, a copy of the citation shall promptly be mailed to the last known address of a parent or guardian of the minor. (Added 1997, No. 153 (Adj. Sess.), § 2.)

Subchapter 2: Binding Over To County And District Courts

§§ 5551-5553. Repealed. 1971, No. 258 (Adj. Sess.), § 19.

Chapter 182: Innocence Protection

Subchapter 1: Postconviction Dna Testing

§ 5561. Petition for postconviction DNA testing

(a) A person convicted of a qualifying crime may at any time file a petition requesting forensic DNA testing of any evidence that may contain biological evidence that was obtained during the investigation or prosecution of the crime. The petition shall:

(1) specifically identify the crime for which the petitioner asserts that he or she is innocent and the evidence which the petitioner seeks to have subjected to DNA testing;

(2) contain the petitioner's certification, under oath, that the petitioner did not commit the crime for which he or she was convicted;

(3) contain the petitioner's certification, under oath, that the petition is true and accurate; and

(4) allege facts showing that DNA testing may be material to the petitioner's claim of innocence.

(b) As used in this section:

(1) "Biological evidence" means:

(A) a sexual assault forensic examination kit; or

(B) semen, blood, saliva, hair, skin tissue, or other identified biological material.

(2) "Person convicted of a qualifying crime" means a person convicted of:

(A) one of the following crimes as defined in this title:

(1) arson causing death, § 501;

(2) assault and robbery with a dangerous weapon, § 608(b);

(3) assault and robbery causing bodily injury, § 608(c);

(4) aggravated assault, § 1024;

(5) murder, § 2301;

(6) manslaughter, § 2304;

(7) aggravated murder, § 2311;

(8) kidnapping, § 2405;

(9) unlawful restraint, §§ 2406 and 2407;

(10) maiming, § 2701;

(11) sexual assault, § 3252;

(12) aggravated sexual assault, § 3253;

(13) burglary into an occupied dwelling, § 1201(c); or

(14) lewd and lascivious conduct with a child, § 2602.

(B) any felony not listed in subdivision (b)(1) of this section, if the petition is filed within 30 months after the conviction becomes final, the person presents specific facts demonstrating that DNA evidence will provide substantial evidence of the person's innocence, and the court finds that the interests of justice would be served by permitting the petition.

(c)(1) The petition shall be filed in the Superior Court of the county where the conviction was imposed, and shall not be heard by a judge who presided over the trial, sentencing, or any motion hearing related to evidence to be admitted at the trial.

(2)(A) Unless subdivision (B) of this subdivision (2) applies, the petitioner shall provide copies of the petition to the Attorney General and to the State's Attorney in the district where the conviction was obtained.

(B) If the petitioner is not represented by counsel, the court shall provide copies of the petition to the Attorney General and to the State's Attorney in the district where the conviction was obtained.

(3) Within 30 days after it receives the petition, the State shall agree to perform the requested DNA testing in a timely manner or file a response to the petition. The petitioner may file a reply to the State's response only within 30 days after the response is filed.

(4) The court shall schedule a hearing on the petition within 90 days after the State's response is filed unless the State notifies the court that it has agreed to provide the testing in a timely manner or the court dismisses the petition pursuant to subsection (d) of this section.

(5) Time limits under this subsection may be extended for good cause shown or by consent of the parties.

(d) The court shall dismiss the petition without a hearing if it determines that:

(1) the petition, response, reply if any, files, and records conclusively establish that the petitioner is entitled to no relief; or

(2) the petition was not made to demonstrate innocence or the appropriateness of a lesser sentence and will unreasonably delay the execution of sentence or administration of justice.

(e) No person shall file a petition requesting forensic DNA testing pursuant to this chapter if the person's conviction resulted from a plea agreement until after July 1, 2008. (Added 2007, No. 60, § 1.)

§ 5562. Assignment of counsel

The court may appoint counsel if the petitioner is unable financially to employ counsel and may order that all necessary costs and expenses incident to the matter, including court costs, stenographic services, printing, and reasonable compensation for legal services, be paid by the State from the appropriation to the Defender General. On appeal, the Supreme Court may make a similar order. (Added 2007, No. 60, § 1.)

§ 5563. Victim notification

(a) If the address of a victim of the crime that the petitioner claims to be innocent of in the petition is known, the State's Attorney or Attorney General shall give written notice of a petition under this section to the victim upon the victim's request. If the victim's current address is not known, the State's Attorney or the Attorney General shall consult with the Department of Corrections Victim Services Division to verify the victim's last known address. The notice shall be by any reasonable means to the victim's last known address and shall indicate whether the petitioner is represented by public or private counsel. Upon the victim's request, the State's Attorney or Attorney General shall give the victim notice of the time and place of any hearing on the petition and shall inform the victim of the disposition of the petition and the outcome of any hearing. If DNA testing is ordered, the State's Attorney or the Attorney General shall inform the victim whether the test results require further court hearings, the time and place of any hearings, and the outcome of the hearings.

(b) The rights of victims contained in this section do not entitle a victim to be a party in any proceeding, or to any procedural rights that are not specifically provided for in this section, including any right to request a delay or rescheduling of any proceeding. (Added 2007, No. 60, § 1.)

§ 5564. Discovery

(a) Upon motion by the petitioner or the State, and after providing the nonmovant with reasonable opportunity to respond to the motion, the court may permit reasonable discovery and the right to depose witnesses. The court in its discretion may delay ruling on any discovery motions until after it has determined whether to dismiss the petition pursuant to subsection 5561(d) of this section.

(b) A discovery order issued pursuant to this section may include the following:

(1) The court may order the State to locate and provide the petitioner with any documents, notes, logs, or reports relating to items of physical evidence collected in connection with the case or to help the petitioner locate items of biological evidence that the State contends have been lost or destroyed. The court may further order the State to take reasonable measures to locate biological evidence that may be in its custody or to help the petitioner locate evidence that may be in the custody of a public or private hospital, public or private laboratory, or other facility.

(2) If evidence has previously been subjected to DNA testing, the court may order production of laboratory reports prepared in connection with the testing and may order production of the underlying data and the laboratory notes.

(3) If any DNA or other biological evidence testing was previously conducted by either the prosecution or the defense without knowledge of the other party, the court may order that the previous testing be disclosed.

(4) If the court orders DNA testing under this subchapter, the court shall order the production of any laboratory reports prepared in connection with the testing and may order production of the underlying data, bench notes, or other laboratory notes. (Added 2007, No. 60, § 1.)

§ 5565. [Reserved.]

§ 5566. Order; necessary findings; confidentiality

(a) The court shall grant the petition and order DNA testing if it makes all of the following findings:

(1) A reasonable probability exists that the petitioner would not have been convicted or would have received a lesser sentence for the crime that the petitioner claims to be innocent of in the petition if the results of the requested DNA testing had been available to the trier of fact at the time of the original prosecution.

(2) One or more of the items of evidence that the petitioner seeks to have tested is still in existence.

(3) The evidence to be tested was obtained in connection with the offense that is the basis of the challenged conviction and:

(A) was not previously subjected to DNA testing; or

(B) although previously subjected to DNA testing, can be subjected to additional DNA testing that provides a reasonable likelihood of significantly more probative results.

(4)(A)(i) The chain of custody of the evidence to be tested establishes that the evidence has not been tampered with, replaced, or altered in any material respect; or

(ii) if the chain of custody does not establish the integrity of the evidence, the testing itself has the potential to establish the integrity of the evidence.

(B) For purposes of this subchapter, evidence that has been in the custody of a law enforcement agency, a governmental body, or a public or private hospital shall be presumed to satisfy the chain-of-custody requirement of this subdivision.

(b) The court may designate in its order:

(1) the type of DNA analysis to be used;

(2) the testing procedures to be followed;

(3) the preservation of some portion of the sample for replicating the testing;

(4) additional DNA testing, if the results of the initial testing are inconclusive or otherwise merit additional scientific analysis.

(c) DNA profile information from biological samples taken from any person pursuant to a petition under this subchapter shall be confidential except for use and dissemination consistent with this chapter and 20 V.S.A. chapter 113, and shall be exempt from any law requiring disclosure of information to the public. (Added 2007, No. 60, § 1.)

§ 5567. Appeals

An order entered on the petition may be appealed to the Vermont Supreme Court pursuant to the Rules of Appellate Procedure. (Added 2007, No. 60, § 1.)

§ 5568. Choice of laboratory; payment

(a) If the court orders DNA testing under this subchapter, the testing shall be conducted at a facility mutually agreed upon by the petitioner and the State and approved by the court. If the parties are unable to agree, the court shall designate the testing facility and provide the parties with a reasonable opportunity to be heard on the issue.

(b) The court shall impose reasonable conditions on the testing to protect the parties' interests in the integrity of the evidence and the testing process.

(c)(1) The State shall bear the costs of testing performed at the state crime laboratory.

(2) Except as provided in subdivision (3) of this subsection, the court may require the petitioner or the State, or both, to pay for testing performed at a private laboratory.

(3) If the State Crime Laboratory does not have the ability or resources to conduct the type of DNA testing to be performed, the State shall bear the costs of testing at a private laboratory that does have such capabilities or resources. (Added 2007, No. 60, § 1.)

§ 5569. Procedure after test results obtained

(a) The results of any postconviction DNA testing conducted pursuant to this subchapter shall be disclosed to the State's Attorney, the Attorney General, the Department of Corrections if the petitioner is under the Department's custody or supervision, the petitioner, and the court.

(b) If the results of forensic DNA testing ordered under this subchapter support the facts alleged in the petition, the court shall schedule a hearing as soon as practicable after the results are received to determine the appropriate relief to be granted. The petitioner and the State shall be permitted to submit motions and be heard at the hearing.

(c) At or subsequent to the hearing, the court may issue an order including the following:

(1) setting aside or vacating the petitioner's judgment of conviction;

(2) granting the petitioner a new trial;

(3) granting the petitioner a new sentencing hearing;

(4) discharging the petitioner from custody;

(5) specifying the disposition of any evidence that remains after the completion of the testing;

(6) granting the petitioner additional discovery on matters related to DNA test results or the conviction or sentence under attack, including documents pertaining to the original criminal investigation and the identities of other suspects; or

(7) providing such other relief as the court deems appropriate.

(d) If, as a result of DNA evidence, the person's conviction for an offense is reversed or vacated, the information or indictment is dismissed, the person is acquitted after a second or subsequent trial, or the person is pardoned:

(1) The court shall order the removal and destruction of the person's name and any information about that conviction from the Sex Offender Registry established under section 5402 of this title, the Child Abuse Registry established under 33 V.S.A. § 4916, the Vulnerable Adult Registry established under 33 V.S.A. § 6911, and any other registry on which the person's name appears solely because of his or her conviction of that offense. If the person has more than one entry on a registry, only the entry related to the offense for which, as a result of DNA evidence, the person's conviction was reversed or vacated, the information or indictment was dismissed, the person was acquitted after a second or subsequent trial, or the person received a pardon shall be removed and destroyed.

(2) It shall not be a violation of Vermont law for the person to respond, when asked, that he or she has never previously been convicted of a crime, and that his or her innocence of the crime charged has been established. This subdivision shall not apply if the person has been convicted of a crime other than the

one for which, as a result of DNA evidence, the person's conviction was reversed, the information or indictment was dismissed, the person was acquitted after a second or subsequent trial, or the person was pardoned.

(e) An order issued under this section may be appealed to the Vermont Supreme Court pursuant to the Rules of Appellate Procedure. (Added 2007, No. 60, § 1.)

§ 5570. Successive petitions

(a) The court shall not be required to entertain a second or successive petition for similar relief on behalf of the same petitioner unless it appears the petition will be assisted by the availability of more advanced DNA technology.

(b) The court may entertain a second or successive petition if it determines that doing so would serve the interests of justice. (Added 2007, No. 60, § 1.)

Subchapter 2: Compensation For Wrongful Convictions

§ 5572. Right of action; procedure

(a) A person convicted and imprisoned for a crime of which the person was exonerated pursuant to this chapter shall have a cause of action for damages against the State.

(b) An action brought under this subchapter shall be filed in Washington County Superior Court. Notice of the action shall be served upon the Attorney General.

(c) The Vermont Rules of Civil Procedure shall apply to actions brought under this subchapter, and the plaintiff shall have a right to trial by jury. The Vermont Rules of Appellate Procedure shall apply to appeals from orders and judgments issued under this subchapter.

(d) The Attorney General may consider, adjust, determine, and settle any claim for damages brought against the State of Vermont under this subchapter. (Added 2007, No. 60, § 1; amended 2015, No. 133 (Adj. Sess.), § 5, eff. May 25, 2016.)

§ 5573. Complaint

(a) A complaint filed under this subchapter shall be supported by facts and shall allege that:

(1) the complainant has been convicted of a felony crime, been sentenced to a term of imprisonment, and served at least six months of the sentence in a correctional facility; and

(2) the complainant was exonerated through the complainant's conviction being reversed or vacated, the information or indictment being dismissed, the complainant being acquitted after a second or subsequent trial, or the granting of a pardon.

(b) The court may dismiss the complaint, upon its own motion or upon motion of the State, if it determines that the complaint does not state a claim for which relief may be granted. (Added 2007, No. 60, § 1; amended 2013, No. 126 (Adj. Sess.), § 4.)

§ 5574. Burden of proof; judgment; damages

(a) A claimant shall be entitled to judgment in an action under this subchapter if the claimant establishes each of the following by clear and convincing evidence:

(1) The complainant was convicted of a felony crime, was sentenced to a term of imprisonment, and served at least six months of the sentence in a correctional facility.

(2)(A) the complainant's conviction was reversed or vacated, the complainant's information or indictment was dismissed, or the complainant was acquitted after a second or subsequent trial; or

(B) the complainant was pardoned for the crime for which he or she was sentenced.

(3) The complainant is actually innocent of the felony or felonies that are the basis for the claim. As used in this chapter, a person is "actually innocent" of a felony or felonies if he or she did not engage in any illegal conduct alleged in the charging documents for which he or she was charged, convicted, and imprisoned.

(4) The complainant did not fabricate evidence or commit or suborn perjury during any proceedings related to the crime with which he or she was charged.

(b) A claimant awarded judgment in an action under this subchapter shall be entitled to damages in an amount to be determined by the trier of fact for each year the claimant was incarcerated, provided that the amount of damages shall not be less than $30,000.00 nor greater than $60,000.00 for each year the claimant was incarcerated, adjusted proportionally for partial years served. The damage award may also include:

(1) economic damages, including lost wages and costs incurred by the claimant for his or her criminal defense and for efforts to prove his or her innocence;

(2) up to 10 years of eligibility for State-funded health coverage equivalent to Medicaid services;

(3) compensation for any reasonable reintegrative services and mental and physical health care costs incurred by the claimant for the time period between his or her release from mistaken incarceration and the date of the award;

(4) reasonable attorney's fees and costs for the action brought under this subchapter.

(c) Damages awarded under this section:

(1) shall not be subject to any State taxes, except for the portion of the judgment awarded as attorney's fees; and

(2) shall not be offset by any services awarded to the claimant pursuant to this section or by any expenses incurred by the State or any political subdivision of the State, including expenses incurred to secure or maintain the claimant's custody or to feed, clothe, or provide medical services for the claimant.

(d) The claimant's acceptance of a damages award, compromise, or settlement as a result of a claim under this subchapter shall be in writing and, except when procured by fraud, shall be final and conclusive on the claimant, and constitute a complete release by the claimant of any claim against the State and a complete bar to any action by the claimant against the State with respect to the same subject matter.

(e) A claimant shall be entitled to compensation under this subchapter only for the years in which he or she would not otherwise have been incarcerated for another sentence. (Added 2007, No. 60, § 1;

amended 2013, No. 79, § 16, eff. Jan. 1, 2014; 2013, No. 126 (Adj. Sess.), § 5; 2015, No. 5, § 3, eff. April 9, 2015.)

§ 5575. Payment

(a) Any award made or compromise or settlement against the State of Vermont agreed upon by the Attorney General in response to an action brought under this subchapter shall be paid by the State Treasurer out of the treasury, and the Emergency Board shall reimburse the State Treasurer therefor from time to time.

(b) If the State elects to self-insure for liability as defined in 12 V.S.A. § 5601, any award, compromise, or settlement against the State of Vermont agreed to by the Attorney General shall be paid by the Treasurer from the liability self-insurance fund.

(c) To the extent that an award, settlement, or compromise is covered by a policy of liability insurance, payment will be governed by the terms of the policy. (Added 2007, No. 60, § 1.)

§ 5576. Limitations

(a) Except as provided in subsection (b) of this section, an action for compensation under this subchapter shall be commenced within three years after the person is exonerated pursuant to subchapter 1 of this chapter through the person's conviction being reversed or vacated, the information or indictment being dismissed, the person being acquitted after a second or subsequent trial, or through the granting of a pardon.

(b)(1) If the State challenges the exoneration of a person entitled to bring an action under this subchapter, the limitations period shall not commence until the challenge is finally resolved.

(2) If a person entitled to bring an action under this subchapter is not provided the notice required by section 5577 of this title, the person shall have an additional year within which to bring the action. (Added 2007, No. 60, § 1.)

§ 5577. Notice of right of action

(a) A copy of this subchapter shall be provided to a person by a court:

(1) exonerating a person pursuant to subchapter 1 of this chapter through vacating or reversing the person's conviction, dismissing the information or indictment, entering judgment on an acquittal after a second or subsequent trial; or

(2) receiving notice of a pardon.

(b) A person receiving a copy of this subchapter pursuant to subsection (a) of this section shall be required to acknowledge its receipt in writing on a form established by the Court Administrator. The acknowledgement shall be entered on the docket by the court and shall be admissible in an action filed under this subchapter. (Added 2007, No. 60, § 1.)

§ 5578. Applicability; retroactivity

Notwithstanding 1 V.S.A. § 214(b), this subchapter and any amendments thereto shall apply to any exoneration that occurs on or after July 1, 2007. (Added 2015, No. 133 (Adj. Sess.), § 6, eff. May 25, 2016.)

Subchapter 3: Law Enforcement Practices

§ 5581. Eyewitness identification policy

(a) On or before January 1, 2015, every State, county, and municipal law enforcement agency and every constable who exercises law enforcement authority pursuant to 24 V.S.A. § 1936a and who is trained in compliance with 20 V.S.A. § 2358 shall adopt an eyewitness identification policy.

(b) The written policy shall contain, at a minimum, the following essential elements as identified by the Law Enforcement Advisory Board:

(1) Protocols guiding the use of a show-up identification procedure.

(2) The photo or live lineup shall be conducted by a blind administrator who does not know the suspect's identity. For law enforcement agencies with limited staff, this can be accomplished through a procedure in which photographs are placed in folders, randomly numbered and shuffled, and then presented to an eyewitness such that the administrator cannot see or track which photograph is being presented to the witness until after the procedure is completed.

(3) Instructions to the eyewitness, including that the perpetrator may or may not be among the persons in the identification procedure.

(4) In a photo or live lineup, fillers shall possess the following characteristics:

(A) All fillers selected shall resemble the eyewitness's description of the perpetrator in significant features such as face, weight, build, or skin tone, including any unique or unusual features such as a scar or tattoo.

(B) At least five fillers shall be included in a photo lineup, in addition to the suspect.

(C) At least four fillers shall be included in a live lineup, in addition to the suspect.

(5) If the eyewitness makes an identification, the administrator shall seek and document a clear statement from the eyewitness, at the time of the identification and in the eyewitness's own words, as to the eyewitness's confidence level that the person identified in a given identification procedure is the perpetrator.

(c) The model policy issued by the Law Enforcement Advisory Board shall encourage ongoing law enforcement training in eyewitness identification procedures for State, county, and municipal law enforcement agencies and constables who exercise law enforcement authority pursuant to 24 V.S.A. § 1936a and are trained in compliance with 20 V.S.A. § 2358.

(d) If a law enforcement agency does not adopt a policy by January 1, 2015 in accordance with this section, the model policy issued by the Law Enforcement Advisory Board shall become the policy of that law enforcement agency or constable. (Added 2013, No. 193 (Adj. Sess.), § 1, eff. June 17, 2014.)

Subchapter 4: Custodial Interrogation

§ 5585. Electronic recording of a custodial interrogation

(a) As used in this section:

(1) "Custodial interrogation" means any interrogation:

(A) involving questioning by a law enforcement officer that is reasonably likely to elicit an incriminating response from the subject; and

(B) in which a reasonable person in the subject's position would consider himself or herself to be in custody, starting from the moment a person should have been advised of his or her Miranda rights and ending when the questioning has concluded.

(2) "Electronic recording" or "electronically recorded" means an audio and visual recording that is an authentic, accurate, unaltered record of a custodial interrogation, or if law enforcement does not have the current capacity to create a visual recording, an audio recording of the interrogation.

(3) "Place of detention" means a building or a police station that is a place of operation for the State police, a municipal police department, county sheriff department, or other law enforcement agency that is owned or operated by a law enforcement agency at which persons are or may be questioned in connection with criminal offenses or detained temporarily in connection with criminal charges pending a potential arrest or citation.

(4) "Statement" means an oral, written, sign language, or nonverbal communication.

(b)(1) A custodial interrogation that occurs in a place of detention concerning the investigation of a felony violation of chapter 53 (homicide) or 72 (sexual assault) of this title shall be electronically recorded in its entirety.

(2) In consideration of best practices, law enforcement shall strive to record simultaneously both the interrogator and the person being interrogated.

(c)(1) The following are exceptions to the recording requirement in subsection (b) of this section:

(A) exigent circumstances;

(B) a person's refusal to be electronically recorded;

(C) interrogations conducted by other jurisdictions;

(D) a reasonable belief that the person being interrogated did not commit a felony violation of chapter 53 (homicide) or 72 (sexual assault) of this title and, therefore, an electronic recording of the interrogation was not required;

(E) the safety of a person or protection of his or her identity; and

(F) equipment malfunction.

(2) If law enforcement does not make an electronic recording of a custodial interrogation as required by this section, the prosecution shall prove by a preponderance of the evidence that one of the exceptions identified in subdivision (1) of this subsection applies. If the prosecution does not meet the burden of proof, the evidence is still admissible, but the court shall provide cautionary instructions to the jury regarding the failure to record the interrogation. (Added 2013, No. 193 (Adj. Sess.), § 4, eff. Oct. 1, 2015.)

Chapter 183: Indictment And Information; Grand Jury

Subchapter 1: Grand Jury

§§ 5601-5605. Repealed. 1973, No. 118, § 25, eff. Oct. 1, 1973.

§ 5606. Penalties

A court reporter or other person taking, recording, or transcribing testimony given before a grand jury who reveals any matter or thing coming before the grand jury, except as the Supreme Court may authorize by rule, shall be imprisoned not more than one year or fined not more than $1,000.00 nor less than $100.00, or both. (Amended 1973, No. 118, § 19, eff. Oct. 1, 1973.)

Subchapter 2: Indictment And Information

§§ 5651-5654. Repealed. 1973, No. 118, § 25, eff. Oct. 1, 1973.

Subchapter 3: Respondent's Application To Require Filing Of Information

§ 5701. Repealed. 1973, No. 118, § 25, eff. Oct. 1, 1973.

§§ 5702-5705. Repealed. 1959, No. 142, § 10, eff. Feb. 1, 1960.

§§ 5706, 5707. Repealed. 1973, No. 118, § 25, eff. Oct. 1, 1973.

Chapter 185: Proceedings Before Justices Of The Peace And Appeals Therefrom

§§ 5901-5905. Repealed. 1973, No. 249 (Adj. Sess.), § 111, eff. April 9, 1974.

§ 5906. Repealed. 1959, No. 142, § 10, eff. Feb. 1, 1960.

§§ 5907-5913. Repealed. 1973, No. 249 (Adj. Sess.), § 111, eff. April 9, 1974.

Chapter 201: Pleadings And Proof; Trial

Subchapter 1: Trial Generally

§ 6501. Rights of accused

On the trial of an information or indictment, the party accused may defend himself or herself, be heard by counsel, produce witnesses and proofs in his or her favor, and shall be confronted with the witnesses produced against him or her.

§ 6502. Presumption of innocence

The presumption of innocence in criminal causes shall attend the accused until the jury renders a verdict of guilty, and the court shall charge the jury accordingly. This presumption of innocence is a proper subject of comment in argument.

§ 6503. Repealed. 1971, No. 161 (Adj. Sess.), § 9, eff. date, see note set out below.

§ 6504. Employment of counsel on behalf of State

In the examination of a person charged with a crime exceeding the jurisdiction of a Criminal Division of the Superior Court to try and determine, commenced upon the complaint of a complaining officer not entitled to draw a salary, and in the trial of person before such court upon the complaint of such an officer, charging him or her with a crime within the jurisdiction of such court to try and determine, where the fine is payable to the State, such officer may employ counsel at the expense of the State, when the State's Attorney is disqualified or unable seasonably to attend at such examination or trial. (Amended 1965, No. 194, § 10, operative February 1, 1967; 1973, No. 249 (Adj. Sess.), § 53, eff. April 9, 1974; 2009, No. 154, § 238.)

§ 6505. Payment

The Commissioner of Finance and Management shall allow counsel so employed a reasonable compensation for his or her services and expenses and shall issue his or her warrant for the amount allowed. Compensation shall not be allowed where it appears to the Commissioner that the prosecution was superfluous and instituted to enhance costs, nor in the trial of a person upon a complaint for intoxication or for any other offense against the title relating to alcoholic beverages, except where the respondent pleads not guilty. (Amended 1959, No. 329 (Adj. Sess.), § 8; 2017, No. 83, § 146.)

§§ 6506, 6507. Repealed. 1973, No. 118, § 25, eff. Oct. 1, 1973.

Subchapter 2: Pleadings And Proof

§§ 6551-6554. Repealed. 1973, No. 118, § 25, Oct. 1, 1973.

§ 6555. Nolle prosequi when proof shows greater offense than charged

If, upon the trial of a person charged with an offense, the facts given in evidence amount in law to a greater offense than the one charged, such person shall not by reason thereof be acquitted, but the court, in its discretion, may allow a nolle prosequi to be entered in order that he or she may be prosecuted for the greater offense.

§ 6556. Former acquittal a bar

A person shall not be held to answer on a second complaint, information, or indictment for an offense of which he or she was acquitted by a jury upon the merits on a former trial. Such acquittal may be pleaded in bar of a subsequent prosecution for the same offense, notwithstanding defects in the form or substance of the complaint, information, or indictment on which he or she was acquitted.

§ 6557. Exceptions

When a person is acquitted by reason of a variance between the complaint, information, or indictment and the proof, or upon an exception to the form or substance of the complaint, information, or indictment, he or she may be arraigned again on a new complaint, information, or indictment and may be tried and convicted for the same offense notwithstanding such former acquittal.

§ 6558. Allegation and proof of ownership

In the prosecution of an offense committed upon, or in relation to, or in any way affecting real estate, or an offense committed in stealing, embezzling, injuring, or fraudulently receiving or concealing money or other personal estate, it shall be sufficient and not deemed a variance if it is proved on trial that, at the time when the offense was committed, the actual or constructive possession, or the general or special property in whole or in part of such real or personal estate was in the person alleged in the complaint, information, or indictment to be the owner thereof.

§ 6559. Allegation and proof of intent to defraud

When an intent to defraud is required to constitute a criminal offense, it shall be sufficient to allege in the complaint, information, or indictment an intent to defraud, without naming the person or body corporate intended to be defrauded. On trial it shall be sufficient and shall not be deemed a variance if there appears to have been an intent to defraud the United States, a state, county, town, city, district, a body corporate, a public officer in his or her official capacity, a partnership or members thereof, or a person.

§ 6560. Truth as defense in prosecution for libel or defamation

If a person is prosecuted by information or indictment for uttering and publishing a libel or for defaming the civil authority of the State, under a plea of not guilty, he or she may give evidence as to the truth of the words contained in such supposed libel, as set forth in the information or indictment. If he or she proves their truth to the satisfaction of the jury, it shall find the respondent not guilty in its verdict.

§§ 6561-6564. Repealed. 1973, No. 118, § 25, eff. Oct. 1, 1973.

§ 6565. Pleas

(a) In prosecutions for felonies, the State's Attorney shall place on record in open court the content of the plea agreement, including the offenses charged and the disposition of those charges.

(b) No plea agreement shall be binding upon the court nor shall it limit the court in the judgment and sentence to be imposed. A defendant may not withdraw a plea of guilty or nolo contendere except as provided in Rule 32(d) of the Vermont Rules of Criminal Procedure.

(c)(1) Prior to accepting a plea of guilty or a plea of nolo contendere from a defendant in a criminal proceeding pursuant to Rule 11 of the Vermont Rules of Criminal Procedure, the court shall address the defendant personally in open court, informing the defendant and determining that the defendant understands that, if he or she is not a citizen of the United States, admitting to facts sufficient to warrant a finding of guilt or pleading guilty or nolo contendere to a crime may have the consequences of deportation or denial of U.S. citizenship.

(2) If the court fails to advise the defendant in accordance with this subsection, and he or she later at any time shows that the plea and conviction may have or has had a negative consequence regarding his or her immigration status, the court, upon the defendant's motion, shall vacate the judgment and permit the defendant to withdraw the plea or admission and enter a plea of not guilty.

(d) Each State's Attorney shall submit an annual report to the Office of the Executive Director of the State's Attorneys, in such form as the Executive Director may require, providing information as to the use of plea agreements. (Added 1981, No. 223 (Adj. Sess.), § 21; amended 1983, No. 229 (Adj. Sess.), § 2; 2005, No. 121 (Adj. Sess.), § 1, eff. Sept. 1, 2006; 2017, No. 14, § 1.)

Chapter 203: Evidence

Subchapter 1: Generally

§ 6601. Respondent as witness

In the trial of complaints, informations, indictments and other proceedings against persons charged with crimes or offenses, the person so charged shall, at his or her own request and not otherwise, be deemed a competent witness. The credit to be given to his or her testimony shall be left solely to the jury, under the instructions of the court but the failure of such person to testify shall not be a matter of comment to the jury by either the court or the prosecutor and shall not be considered by the jury as evidence against him or her.

§ 6602. Repealed. 1973, No. 118, § 25, eff. Oct. 1, 1973.

§ 6603. Failure to obey summons to testify

A person legally summoned to attend a court in this State to testify in a criminal cause, who willfully or wrongfully refuses to attend and testify, shall be fined not less than $10.00 nor more than $100.00 or imprisoned not more than six months, or both.

§ 6604. Counseling or aiding in nonattendance of witness

A person who knowingly and wrongfully counsels, aids, or assists a person so summoned to testify, to absent himself or herself from attendance before such court, shall be fined not more than $50.00 nor less than $10.00.

§ 6605. Recognizance by witness; commitment

In a proceeding before a court or magistrate for the investigation or prosecution of a criminal offense, the court or magistrate may order any witness appearing before such court or magistrate to enter into a sufficient recognizance with surety for his or her appearance before any court or magistrate where his or her attendance in such investigation or prosecution is necessary. If the witness refuses to enter into such recognizance with surety, he or she may be committed to jail in the county where his or her attendance as a witness is required, on a warrant of the court or magistrate making the order, and there detained until such time as his or her attendance to testify is required.

§ 6606. Separate examination of witnesses

On the trial of a person for a criminal offense or on the examination of a person charged therewith before a Criminal Division of the Superior Court, on the request of the prosecuting attorney or the party accused, the court shall have the witnesses examined separately and apart from each other. (Amended 1965, No. 194, § 10, operative February 1, 1967; 1973, No. 249 (Adj. Sess.), § 54, eff. April 9, 1974; 2009, No. 154, § 238.)

§ 6607. Disclosure of confidential records; notice to prosecution

When a defendant seeks access to a victim's school records, or to any other records of a victim that are by law confidential, the defendant shall provide written notice to the prosecutor that the records have been requested prior to the service of any subpoena requesting the records. (Added 2007, No. 40, § 11.)

Subchapter 2: Uniform Act To Secure The Attendance Of Witnesses From Without The State In Criminal Cases

§ 6641. Definitions

As used in this subchapter, "action" shall include any proceeding or investigation by a grand jury commenced or about to be commenced, or any action, prosecution or proceeding; "witness" shall include a person whose testimony is desired in any such action; and the word "state" shall include any territory of the United States and District of Columbia.

§ 6642. Summoning witnesses in this State to testify in another state

If a judge of a court of record in any state which by its laws has made provision for commanding persons within that state to attend and testify in an action in this State, certifies under the seal of such court that there is an action pending in that court, that a person being within this State is a material witness in the action, and that his or her presence will be required for a specified number of days, upon presentation of the certificate to any Superior judge in the unit in which the person is, the judge shall fix a time and place for a hearing in the unit and shall notify the witness by an order stating the purpose of the hearing and directing him or her to appear therefor at a time and place certain. (Amended 1965, No. 194, § 10, operative February 1, 1967; 2009, No. 154 (Adj. Sess.), § 110.)

§ 6643. Hearing and summons

If at such hearing the judge determines that the witness is material and necessary, that it will not cause undue hardship to the witness to be compelled to attend and testify in such action in the other state, and that the laws of the state in which such action is pending will give to him or her protection from arrest and the service of civil and criminal process, he or she shall issue a summons, with a copy of the certificate attached, directing the witness to attend and testify in the court where the action is pending at a time and place specified in the summons. In such hearing the certificate shall be prima facie evidence of all the facts stated therein.

§ 6644. Arrest and delivery

If such certificate recommends that the witness be taken into immediate custody and delivered to an officer of the requesting state to ensure his or her attendance in the requesting state, such judge may direct, in lieu of notification of the hearing, that such witness be forthwith brought before him or her for such hearing. If at such hearing the judge is satisfied as to the desirability of such custody and delivery, for which determination the certificate shall be prima facie proof of such desirability, he or she may order, in lieu of issuing subpoena or summons, that such witness be taken forthwith into custody and delivered to an officer of the requesting state; provided, however, that a witness so taken into custody may enter into recognizance for such attendance as provided in section 6605 of this title.

§ 6645. Penalties

If the witness, who is summoned as provided in section 6643 of this title, after being paid or tendered by some properly authorized person the sum of 10 cents a mile for each mile and $10.00 for each day that he or she is required to travel and attend as a witness, fails without good cause to attend and testify as directed in the summons, he or she shall be imprisoned not more than two years or fined not more than $1,000.00, or both.

§ 6646. Witness from another state summoned to testify in this State

If a person in any state which by its laws has made provision for commanding persons within its borders to attend and testify in an action in this State is a material witness in an action pending in a court of record in this State, a Superior judge may issue a certificate under the seal of the court stating these facts and specifying the number of days the witness will be required. The certificate may include a recommendation that the witness be taken into immediate custody and delivered to an officer of this State to ensure his or her attendance in this State. The certificate shall be presented to a judge of a court of record of the state in which the witness is found. (Amended 1965, No. 194, § 10, operative February 1, 1967; 2009, No. 154 (Adj. Sess.), § 111.)

§ 6647. Fees and penalties

If the witness is summoned to attend and testify in this State, he or she shall be tendered the sum of 10 cents a mile for each mile by the ordinary traveled route to and from the court where such action is pending and $10.00 a day for each day that he or she is required to travel and attend as a witness. The witness fee shall be paid by the party who sought the attendance of the witness. A witness who has appeared in accordance with the provisions of the summons shall not be required to remain within this State a longer period of time than the period mentioned in the certificate, unless ordered by the court. If such witness, after coming into this State, fails without good cause to attend and testify as directed in the summons, he or she shall be punished in the manner provided for in section 6645 of this title. (Amended 1991, No. 245 (Adj. Sess.), § 94(d).)

§ 6648. Exemption from arrest and service of process

(a) If a person comes into this State in obedience to a summons directing him or her to attend and testify in such action in this State, he or she shall not, while in this State pursuant to such summons, be subject to arrest or the service of process, civil or criminal, in connection with matters that arose before his or her entrance under the summons.

(b) If a person passes through this State while going to another state in obedience to a summons to attend and testify in such action in that state or while returning therefrom, he or she shall not while so passing through this State be subject to arrest or the service of process, civil or criminal, in connection with matters that arose before his or her entrance into this State under the summons.

§ 6649. Uniform interpretation

This subchapter shall be so interpreted and construed as to effectuate its general purpose to make uniform the law of the states which enact it.

Subchapter 3: Depositions

§§ 6681-6684. Repealed. 1973, No. 118, § 25, eff. Oct. 1, 1973.

Subchapter 4: Depositions And Discovery

§§ 6721-6727. Repealed. 1973, No. 118, § 25, eff. Oct. 1, 1973.

Chapter 221: Judgment, Sentence, And Execution

Subchapter 1: Generally

§ 7001. Conviction by court having jurisdiction

A person shall not be punished for an offense unless he or she is convicted thereof in a court having jurisdiction of the cause and the person.

§ 7002. Conviction to be by plea, verdict, or judgment

A person shall not be punished for an offense unless by confession of his or her guilt in open court, or by admitting the truth of the charge against him or her by his or her plea or demurrer, or by the verdict of a jury accepted by the court and recorded, or by the judgment of a Criminal Division of the Superior Court when the respondent waives trial by jury. (Amended 1965, No. 194, § 10, operative February 1, 1967; 1973, No. 249 (Adj. Sess.), § 55, eff. April 9, 1974; 2009, No. 154, § 238.)

§ 7003. Repealed. 1973, No. 118, § 25, eff. Oct. 1, 1973.

§ 7004. Record of convictions; report to Commissioner of Public Safety

In all cases of felony or misdemeanor in which a conviction or plea of guilty is had in their respective courts, clerks of the Superior Court shall forthwith forward to the Commissioner of Public Safety, on quadruplicate forms to be furnished by him or her, for file in the identification and records division of the Department of Public Safety, a certified report of the conviction, together with the sentence and any other facts that may be required by the Commissioner. A fee of $0.50 for such certified report shall be allowed by the Commissioner of Finance and Management in settlement of the accounts of such courts. (Amended 1959, No. 329 (Adj. Sess.), § 8; 1965, No. 194, § 10, operative February 1, 1967; 1973, No. 193 (Adj. Sess.), § 3, eff. April 9, 1974; 1973, No. 249 (Adj. Sess.), § 56, eff. April 9, 1974; 2009, No. 154 (Adj. Sess.), § 112.)

§ 7005. Repealed. 1963, No. 83.

§ 7006. Repealed. 1999, No. 4, § 7.

Subchapter 2: Sentence And Commitment

§ 7030. Sentencing alternatives

(a) In determining which of the following should be ordered, the court shall consider the nature and circumstances of the crime, the history and character of the defendant, the need for treatment, and the risk to self, others, and the community at large presented by the defendant:

(1) A deferred sentence pursuant to section 7041 of this title.

(2) Referral to a community reparative board pursuant to 28 V.S.A. chapter 12 in the case of an offender who has pled guilty to a nonviolent felony, a nonviolent misdemeanor, or a misdemeanor that does not involve the subject areas prohibited for referral to a community justice center under 24 V.S.A. § 1967. Referral to a community reparative board pursuant to this subdivision does not require the court to place the offender on probation. The offender shall return to court for further sentencing if the reparative board does not accept the case or if the offender fails to complete the reparative board program to the satisfaction of the board in a time deemed reasonable by the board.

(3) Probation pursuant to 28 V.S.A. § 205.

(4) Supervised community sentence pursuant to 28 V.S.A. § 352.

(5) Sentence of imprisonment.

(b) When ordering a sentence of probation, the court may require participation in the Restorative Justice Program established by 28 V.S.A. chapter 12 as a condition of the sentence. (Added 1989, No. 291 (Adj. Sess.), § 2; amended 1999, No. 148 (Adj. Sess.), § 61, eff. May 24, 2000; 2009, No. 146 (Adj. Sess.), § D11.)

§ 7031. Form of sentences; maximum and minimum terms

(a) When a respondent is sentenced to any term of imprisonment, other than for life, the court imposing the sentence shall not fix the term of imprisonment, unless the term is definitely fixed by statute, but shall establish a maximum and may establish a minimum term for which the respondent may be held in imprisonment. The maximum term shall not be more than the longest term fixed by law for the offense of which the respondent is convicted, and the minimum term shall be not less than the shortest term fixed by law for the offense. If the court suspends a portion of the sentence, the unsuspended portion of the sentence shall be the minimum term of sentence solely for the purpose of any reductions of term for good behavior as set forth in 28 V.S.A. § 811. A sentence shall not be considered fixed as long as the maximum and minimum terms are not identical.

(b) The sentence of imprisonment of any person convicted of an offense shall commence to run from the date on which the person is received at the correctional facility for service of the sentence. The court shall give the person credit toward service of his or her sentence for any days spent in custody as follows:

(1) The period of credit for concurrent and consecutive sentences shall include all days served from the date of arraignment or the date of the earliest detention for the offense, whichever occurs first, and end on the date of the sentencing. Only a single credit shall be awarded in cases of consecutive sentences, and no credit for one period of time shall be applied to a later period.

(2) In sentencing a violation of probation, the court shall give the person credit for any days spent in custody from the time the violation is filed or the person is detained on the violation, whichever occurs first, until the violation is sentenced. In a case in which probation is revoked and the person is ordered to serve the underlying sentence, the person shall receive credit for all time previously served in connection with the offense.

(3) A defendant who has received pre-adjudication treatment in a residential setting for a substance use disorder after the charge has been filed shall earn a reduction of one day in the offender's minimum and maximum sentence for each day that the offender receives the inpatient treatment.

(c) If any such person is committed to a jail or other place of detention to await transportation to the place at which his or her sentence is to be served, his or her sentence shall commence to run from the date on which he or she is received at the jail or the place of detention.

(d) A person who receives a zero minimum sentence for a conviction of a nonviolent misdemeanor or nonviolent felony as defined in 28 V.S.A. § 301 shall report to probation and parole as directed by the court and begin to serve the sentence in the community immediately, unless the person is serving a prior sentence at the time. (Amended 1969, No. 182 (Adj. Sess.), § 1; 1971, No. 199 (Adj. Sess.), § 5; 1973, No. 36, § 1, eff. date, see note set out below; 1999, No. 127 (Adj. Sess.), § 3; 2011, No. 41, § 2, eff. May 20, 2011; 2013, No. 4, § 1, eff. April 3, 2013; 2019, No. 56, § 4, eff. June 10, 2019.)

§ 7032. Consecutive sentences

(a) If a person who has been sentenced to a term or terms of imprisonment is convicted of another offense punishable by imprisonment before he or she has been discharged from the former sentence or sentences, the court may sentence him or her to an additional term of imprisonment and shall specify whether this additional term shall be served concurrent with or consecutive to the prior sentence or sentences.

(b) In any case where a person is convicted of two or more offenses punishable by imprisonment and is sentenced for more than one of these offenses, he or she may be sentenced to as many terms as there are offenses of which he or she is convicted. When such multiple sentences are imposed they shall run concurrent with or consecutive to each other as the court determines at the time of sentencing and each shall run from its respective date of commitment after sentence. When such multiple sentences are in addition to a prior sentence or sentences from which the person has not yet been discharged, they shall run concurrently with or consecutive to any prior sentence or sentences as the court shall determine at the time of sentencing.

(c) In all cases where multiple or additional sentences have been or are imposed, the term or terms of imprisonment under those sentences shall be determined in accordance with the following definitions:

(1) When terms run concurrently, the shorter minimum terms merge in and are satisfied by serving the longest minimum and the shorter maximum terms merge in and are satisfied by discharge of the longest maximum term.

(2) When terms run consecutively, the minimum terms are added to arrive at an aggregate minimum to be served equal to the sum of all minimum terms and the maximum terms are added to arrive at an aggregate maximum equal to the sum of all maximum terms. A person shall serve no more time on consecutive minimum sentences than the sum of the minimum terms, regardless of whether the sentences are imposed on the same or different dates. If a person has served a minimum term and subsequently incurs another criminal charge, the time the person spends in custody awaiting disposition of the new charge shall count toward the minimum term of the new sentence, if one is imposed. This subdivision shall not require the Department of Corrections to release a person from incarceration to

community supervision at the person's minimum term. (Amended 1971, No. 199 (Adj. Sess.), § 6; 2013, No. 4, § 2, eff. April 3, 2013.)

§ 7033. Commitment for different offenses on one mittimus

When a person is convicted before the same court of different offenses, upon all of which he or she is lawfully sentenced to imprisonment, he or she may be committed for all of such offenses upon one mittimus, and the mittimus shall recite the sentence in each case, and contain an order that unless all fines are paid before the expiration of the term or terms of imprisonment, such person shall be imprisoned as provided when a fine only is imposed. Such a term of imprisonment for nonpayment of a fine shall be served consecutive to the previous term or terms to which the respondent is sentenced. (Amended 1969, No. 131, § 3, eff. April 23, 1969; 1971, No. 199 (Adj. Sess.), § 7.)

§ 7034. Repealed. 2009, No. 154 (Adj. Sess.), § 113.

§ 7035. Commitment on more than one mittimus; length of sentence

The Commissioner of Corrections shall hold an inmate committed to his or her custody on one or more than one mittimus for the term or terms contained therein, and the inmate shall have the same right of lessening a term of imprisonment by payment of fines as is provided in other cases. (Amended 1969, No. 131, § 4, eff. April 23, 1969; 1971, No. 199 (Adj. Sess.), § 8.)

§§ 7036-7038. Repealed. 1971, No. 199 (Adj. Sess.), § 22.

§ 7039. Manner of committing to jail

When a prisoner is committed to jail on criminal process, the commitment shall be in the manner prescribed for commitments on civil process.

§ 7040. Repealed. 1971, No. 199 (Adj. Sess.), § 22.

§ 7041. Deferred sentence

(a) Upon an adjudication of guilt and after the filing of a presentence investigation report, the court may defer sentencing and place the respondent on probation upon such terms and conditions as it may require if a written agreement concerning the deferring of sentence is entered into between the State's Attorney and the respondent and filed with the clerk of the court.

(b) Notwithstanding subsection (a) of this section, the court may defer sentencing and place the respondent on probation without a written agreement between the State's Attorney and the respondent if the following conditions are met:

(1) [Repealed.]

(2) the crime for which the respondent is being sentenced is not a listed crime as defined in subdivision 5301(7) of this title;

(3) the court orders a presentence investigation in accordance with the procedures set forth in V.R.C.P. Rule 32, unless the State's Attorney agrees to waive the presentence investigation;

(4) the court permits the victim to submit a written or oral statement concerning the consideration of deferment of sentence;

(5) the court reviews the presentence investigation and the victim's impact statement with the parties; and

(6) the court determines that deferring sentence is in the interests of justice.

(c) Notwithstanding subsections (a) and (b) of this section, the court may not defer a sentence for a violation of section 3253a (aggravated sexual assault of a child, section 2602 (lewd and lascivious conduct with a child unless the victim and the defendant were within five years of age and the act was consensual), 3252(c) (sexual assault of a child under 16 unless the victim and the defendant were within five years of age and the act was consensual), 3252(d) or (e) (sexual assault of a child), 3253(a)(8) (aggravated sexual assault), or 3253a (aggravated sexual assault of a child) of this title.

(d) Entry of deferment of sentence shall constitute an appealable judgment for purposes of appeal in accordance with 12 V.S.A. § 2383 and V.R.A.P. Rule 3. Except as otherwise provided, entry of deferment of sentence shall constitute imposition of sentence solely for the purpose of sentence review in accordance with section 7042 of this title. The court may impose sentence at any time if the respondent violates the conditions of the deferred sentence during the period of deferment.

(e) Upon violation of the terms of probation or of the deferred sentence agreement, the court shall impose sentence. Upon fulfillment of the terms of probation and of the deferred sentence agreement, the court shall strike the adjudication of guilt and discharge the respondent. Except as provided in subsection (h) of this section, the record of the criminal proceedings shall be expunged upon the discharge of the respondent from probation, absent a finding of good cause by the court. The court shall issue an order to expunge all records and files related to the arrest, citation, investigation, charge, adjudication of guilt, criminal proceedings, and probation related to the deferred sentence. Copies of the order shall be sent to each agency, department, or official named therein. Thereafter, the court, law enforcement officers, agencies, and departments shall reply to any request for information that no record exists with respect to such person upon inquiry in the matter. Notwithstanding this subsection, the record shall not be expunged until restitution has been paid in full.

(f) A deferred sentence imposed under subsection (a) or (b) of this section may include a restitution order issued pursuant to section 7043 of this title. Nonpayment of restitution shall not constitute grounds for imposition of the underlying sentence.

(g) [Repealed.]

(h) The Vermont Crime Information Center shall retain a special index of deferred sentences for sex offenses that require registration pursuant to subchapter 3 of chapter 167 of this title. This index shall only list the name and date of birth of the subject of the expunged files and records, the offense for which the subject was convicted, and the docket number of the proceeding that was the subject of the expungement. The special index shall be confidential and may be accessed only by the director of the Vermont Crime Information Center and a designated clerical staffperson for the purpose of providing information to the Department of Corrections in the preparation of a presentence investigation in accordance with 28 V.S.A. §§ 204 and 204a. (Added 1971, No. 239 (Adj. Sess.); amended 2001, No. 134 (Adj. Sess.), § 2; 2003, No. 57, § 5, eff. July 1, 2004; 2005, No. 63, § 9; 2005, No. 198 (Adj. Sess.), § 3, eff. Sept. 1, 2006; 2009, No. 1, §§ 33, 33b, eff. July 1, 2014; 2009, No. 58, §§ 9, 26, 27; 2019, No. 77, § 18, eff. June 19, 2019.)

§ 7042. Sentence review

(a) Any court imposing a sentence under the authority of this title, within 90 days of the imposition of that sentence, or within 90 days after entry of any order or judgment of the Supreme Court upholding a judgment of conviction, may upon its own initiative or motion of the defendant, reduce the sentence.

(b) A State's Attorney or the Attorney General, within seven business days of the imposition of a sentence, may file with the sentencing judge a motion to increase, reduce, or otherwise modify the sentence. This motion shall set forth reasons why the sentence should be altered. After hearing, the court may confirm, increase, reduce, or otherwise modify the sentence.

(c) After a motion is filed under subsection (b) of this section, a defendant's time for filing an appeal under 12 V.S.A. § 2383 shall commence to run upon entry of a final order under subsection (b). (Added 1977, No. 251 (Adj. Sess.); amended 1981, No. 223 (Adj. Sess.), § 12; 2017, No. 11, § 29.)

§ 7043. Restitution

(a)(1) Restitution shall be considered in every case in which a victim of a crime, as defined in subdivision 5301(4) of this title, has suffered a material loss.

(2) For purposes of this section, "material loss" means uninsured property loss, uninsured out-of-pocket monetary loss, uninsured lost wages, and uninsured medical expenses.

(3) In cases where restitution is ordered to the victim as a result of a human trafficking conviction under chapter 60 of this title, "material loss" shall also mean:

(A) attorney's fees and costs; and

(B) the greater of either:

(i) the gross income or value of the labor performed for the offender by the victim; or

(ii) the value of the labor performed by the victim as guaranteed by the minimum wage and overtime provisions of 21 V.S.A. § 385.

(b)(1) When ordered, restitution may include:

(A) return of property wrongfully taken from the victim;

(B) cash, credit card, or installment payments paid to the Restitution Unit; or

(C) payments in kind, if acceptable to the victim.

(2) In the event of a victim's crime-related death, the court may, at the request of the Restitution Unit, direct the Unit to pay up to $10,000.00 from the Restitution Fund to the victim's estate to cover future uninsured material losses caused by the death.

(c) Restitution hearing.

(1) Unless the amount of restitution is agreed to by the parties at the time of sentencing, the court shall set the matter for a restitution hearing.

(2) Prior to the date of the hearing, the prosecuting attorney shall provide the defendant with a statement of the amount of restitution claimed together with copies of bills that support the claim for

restitution. If any amount of the restitution claim has been paid by the Victims Compensation Fund, the prosecuting attorney shall provide the defendant with copies of bills submitted by the Victims Compensation Board pursuant to section 5358a of this title.

(3) Absent consent of the victim, medical and mental health records submitted to the Victims Compensation Board shall not be discoverable for the purposes of restitution except by order of the court. If the defendant files a motion to view copies of such records, the prosecuting attorney shall file the records with the court under seal. The court shall conduct an in camera review of the records to determine what records, if any, are relevant to the parties' dispute with respect to restitution. If the court orders disclosure of the documents, the court shall issue a protective order defining the extent of dissemination of the documents to any person other than the defendant, the defendant's attorney, and the prosecuting attorney.

(d) In awarding restitution, the court shall make findings with respect to:

(1) The total amount of the material loss incurred by the victim. If sufficient documentation of the material loss is not available at the time of sentencing, the court shall set a hearing on the issue, and notice thereof shall be provided to the offender.

(2) The offender's current ability to pay restitution, based on all financial information available to the court, including information provided by the offender.

(e)(1) An order of restitution shall establish the amount of the material loss incurred by the victim, which shall be the restitution judgment order. In the event the offender is unable to pay the restitution judgment order at the time of sentencing, the court shall establish a restitution payment schedule for the offender based upon the offender's current and reasonably foreseeable ability to pay, subject to modification under subsection (l) of this section. Notwithstanding 12 V.S.A. chapter 113 or any other provision of law, interest shall not accrue on a restitution judgment.

(2)(A) Every order of restitution shall:

(i) include the offender's name, address, telephone number, and Social Security number, provided that the Social Security number is redacted pursuant to the Vermont Rules for Public Access to Court Records;

(ii) include the name, address, and telephone number of the offender's employer; and

(iii) require the offender, until his or her restitution obligation is satisfied, to notify the Restitution Unit within 30 days if the offender's address, telephone number, or employment changes, including providing the name, address, and telephone number of each new employer.

(B) [Repealed.]

(3) An order of restitution may require the offender to pay restitution for an offense for which the offender was not convicted if the offender knowingly and voluntarily executes a plea agreement that provides that the offender pay restitution for that offense. A copy of the plea agreement shall be attached to the restitution order.

(f)(1) If not paid at the time of sentencing, restitution may be ordered as a condition of probation, supervised community sentence, furlough, preapproved furlough, or parole if the convicted person is sentenced to preapproved furlough, probation, or supervised community sentence, or is sentenced to imprisonment and later placed on parole. A person shall not be placed on probation solely for purposes of paying restitution. An offender may not be charged with a violation of probation, furlough, or parole for nonpayment of a restitution obligation incurred after July 1, 2004.

(2) The Department of Corrections shall work collaboratively with the Restitution Unit to assist with the collection of restitution. The Department shall provide the Restitution Unit with information about the location and employment status of the offender.

(g)(1) When restitution is requested but not ordered, the court shall set forth on the record its reasons for not ordering restitution.

(2)(A) If restitution was not requested at the time of sentencing as the result of an error by the State, or if expenses arose after the entry of a restitution order, the victim may request restitution payable from the Restitution Fund. Restitution paid under this subdivision shall be payable from the Restitution Fund and shall not be payable by the offender. If the restitution is for expenses that arose after the entry of a restitution order, the restitution shall be capped at $1,000.00.

(B) A request under this subdivision shall be filed with the Restitution Unit within one year after the imposition of sentence or the entry of the restitution order.

(h) Restitution ordered under this section shall not preclude a person from pursuing an independent civil action for all claims not covered by the restitution order.

(i)(1) The court shall transmit a copy of a restitution order and the plea agreement, if any, to the Restitution Unit, which shall make payment to the victim in accordance with section 5363 of this title.

(2) To the extent that the Victims Compensation Board has made payment to or on behalf of the victim in accordance with chapter 167 of this title, restitution, if imposed, shall be paid to the Restitution Unit, which shall make payment to the Victims Compensation Fund.

(j) The Restitution Unit may bring an action, including a small claims procedure, on a form approved by the Court Administrator, to enforce a restitution judgment order entered by the Criminal Division of the Superior Court. The action shall be brought against the offender in the Civil Division of the Superior Court of the unit where the offender resides or in the unit where the order was issued. In an action under this subsection, a restitution order issued by the Criminal Division of the Superior Court shall be enforceable in the Civil Division of the Superior Court or in a small claims procedure in the same manner as a civil judgment. Superior and Small Claims Court filing fees shall be waived for an action brought under this subsection.

(k) All restitution payments shall be made to the Restitution Unit, with the exception of restitution relating to a conviction for welfare fraud ordered under this section and recouped by the Economic Services Division. The Economic Services Division shall provide the Restitution Unit with a monthly report of all restitution collected through recoupment. This subsection shall have no effect upon the collection or recoupment of restitution ordered under Title 33.

(l) The sentencing court may modify the payment schedule of a restitution order if, upon motion by the Restitution Unit or the offender, the court finds that modification is warranted by a substantial change in circumstances.

(m)(1) After an enforcement action is filed pursuant to subsection (j) of this section, any further proceedings related to the action shall be heard in the court where it was filed. The court shall set the matter for hearing and shall provide notice to the Restitution Unit, the victim, and the offender. Upon filing of a motion for financial disclosure, the court may order the offender to appear at the hearing and disclose assets and liabilities and produce any documents the court deems relevant.

(2) If the court determines the offender has failed to comply with the restitution order, the court may take any action the court deems necessary to ensure the offender will make the required restitution payment, including:

(A) amending the payment schedule of the restitution order;

(B) ordering, in compliance with the procedures required in Rule 4.1 of the Vermont Rules of Civil Procedure, the disclosure, attachment, and sale of assets and accounts owned by the offender;

(C) ordering trustee process against the offender's wages; or

(D) ordering the suspension of any recreational licenses owned by the offender.

(3) If the court finds that the offender has an ability to pay and willfully refuses to do so, the offender may be subject to civil contempt proceedings under 12 V.S.A. chapter 5.

(n)(1) Any monies owed by the State to an offender who is under a restitution order, including Vermont Lottery winnings, unclaimed property, and tax refunds, shall be used to discharge the restitution order to the full extent of the unpaid total financial losses, regardless of the payment schedule established by the courts.

(2) The Office of the Treasurer shall, prior to delivery or payment of unclaimed property valued at $50.00 or more to a claimant pursuant to 27 V.S.A. § 1255, determine whether the claimant has an outstanding restitution order.

(A) The Restitution Unit shall inform the Treasurer of persons with outstanding restitution orders. Each person subject to such an order shall be identified by name and Social Security or federal identification number.

(B) If any such claimant owes restitution, the Restitution Unit, after notice to the owner, may request and the Treasurer shall transfer unclaimed property of such owner valued at $50.00 or more to the Restitution Unit to be applied to the amount of restitution owed. The notice shall advise the owner of the action being taken and, if he or she is not the person liable under the Restitution Judgment Order, the right to appeal the setoff; or advise the owner if the underlying conviction was vacated or is under appeal.

(3) When an offender is entitled to a tax refund, any restitution owed by the offender shall be withheld from the refund pursuant to 32 V.S.A. chapter 151, subchapter 12.

(4)(A) For all Vermont Lottery games, the Commissioner of Liquor and Lottery shall, before issuing prize money of $500.00 or more to a winner, determine whether the winner has an outstanding restitution order. If the winner owes restitution, the Commissioner of Liquor and Lottery shall withhold the entire amount of restitution owed and pay it to the Restitution Unit. The remainder of the winnings, if any, shall be sent to the winner. The winner shall be notified by the Restitution Unit of the offset prior to payment to the victim and given a period not to exceed 20 days to contest the accuracy of the information.

(B) The Restitution Unit shall inform the Commissioner of Liquor and Lottery of persons with outstanding restitution orders upon request. Each person subject to such an order shall be identified by name, address, and Social Security number.

(C) If a Vermont Lottery winner has an outstanding restitution order and an outstanding child support order, the Lottery winnings shall be offset first pursuant to 15 V.S.A. § 792 by the amount of child support owed, and second pursuant to this subsection by the amount of restitution owed. The remainder of the winnings, if any, shall be sent to the winner.

(5) Unless otherwise provided, monies paid under this subsection shall be paid directly to the Restitution Unit.

(o) After restitution is ordered and prior to sentencing, the court shall order the offender to provide the court with full financial disclosure on a form approved by the Court Administrator. The disclosure of an offender aged 18 or older shall include copies of the offender's most recent State and federal tax returns. The court shall provide copies of the form and the tax returns to the Restitution Unit.

(p) An obligation to pay restitution is part of a criminal sentence and is:

(1) nondischargeable in the U.S. Bankruptcy Court to the maximum extent provided under 11 U.S.C. §§ 523 and 1328;

(2) not subject to any statute of limitations; and

(3) not subject to the renewal of judgment requirements of 12 V.S.A. § 506.

(q) A transfer of property made with the intent to avoid a restitution obligation shall be deemed a fraudulent conveyance for purposes of 9 V.S.A. chapter 57, and the Restitution Unit shall be entitled to the remedies of creditors provided under 9 V.S.A. § 2291. (Added 1983, No. 229 (Adj. Sess.), § 3; amended 1989, No. 291 (Adj. Sess.), § 3; 1993, No. 169 (Adj. Sess.), § 2, eff. June 3, 1993; 1997, No. 148 (Adj. Sess.), § 63, eff. April 29, 1998; 2001, No. 134 (Adj. Sess.), § 3; 2003, No. 57, § 6, eff. July 1, 2004; 2003, No. 92 (Adj. Sess.), § 5; 2005, No. 51, § 5; 2005, No. 162 (Adj. Sess.), § 3, eff. Jan. 1, 2007; 2007, No. 40, § 6; 2009, No. 154 (Adj. Sess.), § 114; 2011, No. 55, §§ 7, 14, 15; 2011, No. 145 (Adj. Sess.), § 5; 2011, No. 145 (Adj. Sess.), § 7, eff. May 15, 2012; 2013, No. 34, § 9; 2013, No. 126 (Adj. Sess.), § 3; 2015, No. 96 (Adj. Sess.), § 1; 2019, No. 73, § 23.)

§ 7043a. Licenses or governmental contracts

(a) As used in this section, "license" means any license, certification, or registration issued by an agency to conduct a trade or business, including a license to practice a profession or occupation, or a license required to engage in recreational activities, including a license to hunt, fish, or trap.

(b) Every applicant for a license shall sign a statement that the applicant is in good standing with respect to any restitution order. A license may not be issued or renewed without such a statement.

(c) For the purposes of this section, a person is in good standing with respect to any restitution order if:

(1) 60 days or fewer have elapsed since the date a restitution judgment was issued;

(2) the person is in compliance with a repayment plan approved by the restitution unit; or

(3) the person is in compliance with a court-ordered restitution judgment order. (Added 2007, No. 51, § 12, eff. Jan. 1, 2008.)

§ 7044. Sentence calculation; notice to defendant

(a) Within 30 days after sentencing in all cases where the court imposes a sentence which includes a period of incarceration to be served, the Commissioner of Corrections shall provide to the court and the Office of the Defender General a calculation of the potential shortest and longest lengths of time the defendant may be incarcerated taking into account the provisions for reductions of term pursuant to 28 V.S.A. § 811 based on the sentence or sentences the defendant is serving, and the effect of any credit for time served as ordered by the court pursuant to 13 V.S.A. § 7031. The Commissioner's calculation shall be a public record.

(b) In all cases where the court imposes a sentence that includes a period of incarceration to be served, the Department of Corrections shall provide the defendant with a copy and explanation of the sentence calculation made pursuant to subsection (a) of this section. (Added 1995, No. 50, § 3; amended 2009, No. 58, § 16.)

§ 7045. Life without parole sentence prohibited for persons under 18 years of age

A court shall not sentence a person to life imprisonment without the possibility of parole if the person was under 18 years of age at the time of the commission of the offense. (Added 2015, No. 22, § 1, eff. May 14, 2015.)

Subchapter 3: Execution Of Death Sentence

§ 7101. Sentence and warrant

In pronouncing sentence of death upon a person who is convicted of a capital crime, the court shall appoint a week within which the sentence shall be executed. At the time of such sentence, the court shall order a warrant to be issued by the clerk, under the seal of the court for the county in which such sentence is passed, to be directed to the Commissioner of Corrections, stating the conviction and sentence and commanding him or her to cause execution to be done in accordance with the provisions of such sentence, upon a day within the week so appointed. At the same time, the clerk shall transmit to the sheriff of the county in which such sentence is passed a mittimus directing him or her to deliver the body of such person to the Commissioner of Corrections and deliver to him or her a true and attested copy of such mittimus, the original of which shall be returned by the sheriff to the court from which issued. Unless a reprieve is granted or the inmate is pardoned, the sentence of death shall be executed by the Commissioner of Corrections, or by a person acting under his or her direction, within the week appointed by the court. If a reprieve is granted, the sentence of death shall be executed within the week beginning on the day next after the day on which the term of respite expires, and such sentence shall be executed on such day within such week as the Commissioner elects. Previous announcement thereof shall not be made, except to such persons as are to be present. (Amended 1971, No. 199 (Adj. Sess.), § 9.)

§ 7102. Pardon

If such inmate is pardoned by the Governor, the Governor shall forthwith issue his or her warrant to the Commissioner of Corrections superseding the original warrant provided for in section 7101 of this title. (Amended 1971, No. 199 (Adj. Sess.), § 10.)

§ 7103. Place of execution

The sentence of death shall be carried into effect at a place designated by the Commissioner of Corrections. (Amended 1971, No. 199 (Adj. Sess.), § 11.)

§ 7104. Manner of confinement

When the sentence of death is imposed, the court shall sentence, at the same time, the respondent to the custody of the Commissioner of Corrections until the time of execution. (Amended 1971, No. 199 (Adj. Sess.), § 12.)

§ 7105. Persons present at execution

There shall be present at the execution of the sentence of death, the Commissioner of Corrections or in case of his or her disability, the keeper, the person who is to perform the execution and his or her assistant, such persons as the Commissioner shall designate, and two physicians approved by the Commissioner. The physicians present shall be the legal witnesses of the execution. There may also be present the sheriff of the county in which the condemned was convicted or one of his or her deputies approved by him or her, such clergyman as the condemned may desire, and not more than three other persons to be selected by the Commissioner. There shall be paid to the person actually performing the execution and to his or her assistant such sums for services and expenses as the Commissioner shall approve. (Amended 1971, No. 199 (Adj. Sess.), § 13.)

§ 7106. Manner of execution

The punishment of death shall be inflicted by causing to pass through the body of the convict a current of electricity of sufficient intensity to cause death, and the application of such current shall be continued until such convict is dead.

§ 7107. Returns of Commissioner

When the Commissioner of Corrections inflicts the punishment of death upon an inmate, in obedience to a warrant as aforesaid, he or she shall forthwith return a copy thereof with his or her doings thereon to the Office of the Secretary of State, and shall forthwith return the original warrant with his or her doings thereon to the court from which it was issued. The clerk thereof shall subjoin to the record of the sentence a brief abstract of the Commissioner's return upon such warrant. (Amended 1971, No. 199 (Adj. Sess.), § 14.)

Subchapter 4: Petition For Review

§ 7131. Prisoner in custody under sentence

A prisoner who is in custody under sentence of a court and claims the right to be released upon the ground that the sentence was imposed in violation of the constitution or laws of the United States, or of the State of Vermont, or that the court was without jurisdiction to impose the sentence, or that the sentence was in excess of the maximum authorized by law, or is otherwise subject to collateral attack, may at any time move the Superior Court of the county where the sentence was imposed to vacate, set aside or correct the sentence. However, the Superior or District judge who presided when the original sentence was imposed shall not hear the application. (Added 1966, No. 41 (Sp. Sess.), § 1(a), eff. March 12, 1966; 1973, No. 193 (Adj. Sess.), § 3, eff. April 9, 1974.)

§ 7132. Contents of motion

The motion may be informal, but shall identify the offense, the date of sentencing, and the alleged violation or defect in the sentence. (Added 1966, No. 41 (Sp. Sess.), § 1(b), eff. March 12, 1966.)

§ 7133. Notice and hearing

Unless the motion and the files and records of the case conclusively show that the prisoner is entitled to no relief, the court shall cause notice thereof to be served upon the State's Attorney and Attorney General, grant a prompt hearing thereon, determine the issues and make findings of fact and conclusions of law with respect thereto. The court may entertain and decide the motion without requiring the production of the prisoner at the hearing but the prisoner may attend if he or she so requests. If the court finds that the judgment was made without jurisdiction, or that the sentence imposed was not authorized by law or is otherwise open to collateral attack, or that there has been such a denial or infringement of the constitutional rights of the prisoner as to make the judgment vulnerable to collateral attack, it shall vacate and set the judgment aside and shall discharge the prisoner or resentence him or her or grant a new trial or correct the sentence as may appear appropriate. (Added 1966, No. 41 (Sp. Sess.), § 1(c), eff. March 12, 1966.)

§ 7134. Successive motions

The court is not required to entertain a second or successive motion for similar relief on behalf of the same prisoner. (Added 1966, No. 41 (Sp. Sess.), § 1(d), eff. March 12, 1966.)

§ 7135. Appeals

An appeal may be taken to the Supreme Court from the order entered on the motion. (Added 1966, No. 41 (Sp. Sess.), § 1(e), eff. March 12, 1966.)

§ 7136. Priority of procedure

An application for a writ of habeas corpus in behalf of a prisoner entitled to move for relief under sections 7131-7135 of this title, shall not be entertained if it appears that the applicant has failed to apply for relief under this subchapter and 12 V.S.A. §§ 3953 and 3957 or that the court has denied him or her relief, unless it also appears that the remedy by motion is inadequate or ineffective to test the legality of his or her detention. (Added 1966, No. 41 (Sp. Sess.), § 2, eff. March 12, 1966.)

§ 7137. Assignment of counsel

The court may appoint counsel if the prisoner is unable financially to employ counsel, and may order that all necessary costs and expenses incident to the matter, including court costs, stenographic services, printing, and reasonable compensation for legal services, be paid by the State from the appropriation to the court where the sentence was imposed. On appeal, the Supreme Court may make a similar order. (Added 1966, No. 41 (Sp. Sess.), § 3, eff. March 12, 1966.)

Chapter 223: Fines, Costs, And Penalties

Subchapter 1: Collection Of Fines, Costs, Penalties, And Forfeitures

§ 7171. Collection by complaint, information, or indictment

(a) Fines, forfeitures, and penalties incurred or imposed by statute may be recovered by complaint, information, or indictment, unless some other mode of recovery is specially provided.

(b) The Court Administrator is authorized to contract with private collection agencies for collection of penalties, fines, surcharges, court costs, and any other assessment authorized by law incurred or imposed by statute on persons who fail to pay, at or after time of judgment, after notice that failure to pay the debt will result in the debt being referred to a collection agency and that the debtor will be liable for the collection agency's fee. The Court Administrator may agree to pay collection agencies a fee based on a fixed rate for services rendered or a percentage of the amount actually collected by such agencies and remitted to the state. The debtor shall be liable for the collection agency's fee, in addition to the judgment amount. The collection agency shall deduct its fee from the collected amount and remit the balance to the judiciary. All collection agency fees shall be governed by the contract with the Court Administrator and shall be clearly disclosed in all notices sent by the collection agency to the debtor. (Amended 1985, No. 266 (Adj. Sess.), § 7, eff. June 4, 1986; 2007, No. 51, § 4; 2009, No. 4, § 117, eff. April 29, 2009.)

§ 7172. Liability of person fined; security; imprisonment

(a) A person fined for the breach of a penal law or other offense shall pay such fine or give sufficient security for the same, or shall be imprisoned by order of the court before which the trial is had, as provided in such case, or be liable to have his or her estate sold therefor.

(b) Cost of prosecution shall not be taxed against a respondent in any criminal cause. (Amended 1969, No. 131, § 5, eff. April 23, 1969.)

§ 7173. Mittimus against property of respondent

A mittimus issued by a court for the collection of a penalty, and fine in criminal prosecutions, in the discretion of such court, in addition to the prescribed form, may be issued against the goods, chattels, or lands of the respondent in the form in which executions are issued. Such mittimus may be levied upon the goods, chattels, or lands of the respondent, and the same sold in satisfaction thereof as in the sale of personal property or real estate upon execution. (Amended 1969, No. 131, § 6, eff. April 23, 1969.)

§§ 7174-7177. Repealed. 1969, No. 131, § 36, eff. April 23, 1969.

§ 7178. Suspension of fines

A Superior judge, in his or her discretion, may suspend all or any part of the fine assessed against a respondent. (Amended 1969, No. 131, § 7, eff. April 23, 1969; 1969, No. 222 (Adj. Sess.), § 4; 1973, No. 249 (Adj. Sess.), § 57, eff. April 9, 1974; 2009, No. 154 (Adj. Sess.), § 115.)

Subchapter 2: Imprisonment In Lieu Of Payment Of Fines And Costs

§ 7179. Fines not dischargeable in bankruptcy

A criminal fine owed to the State shall be nondischargeable, to the maximum extent provided under 11 U.S.C. § 523, in the U.S. Bankruptcy Court and shall not be subject to a statute of limitations. (Added 2001, No. 134 (Adj. Sess.), § 4, eff. June 13, 2002; amended 2009, No. 146 (Adj. Sess.), § D3.)

§ 7180. Remedies for failure to pay fines, costs, surcharges, and penalties

(a) As used in this section:

(1) "Amount due" means all financial assessments, including penalties, fines, surcharges, court costs, and any other assessments imposed by statute as part of a sentence for a criminal conviction.

(2) "Designated collection agency" means a collection agency designated by the Court Administrator pursuant to subsection 7171(b) of this title.

(3) "Designated credit bureau" means a credit bureau designated by the Court Administrator or the Court Administrator's designee.

(b) Collection of amount due. If an amount due remains unpaid for 75 days after the court provides the defendant with a notice of judgment, the court may refer the matter to a designated collection agency or initiate civil contempt proceedings pursuant to this section.

(c) Civil contempt proceeding.

(1) Notice of hearing. The court shall provide notice by first-class mail sent to the defendant's last known address that a contempt hearing will be held pursuant to this subsection, and that failure to appear at the contempt hearing may result in the sanctions listed in subdivision (2) of this subsection.

(2) Failure to appear. If the defendant fails to appear at the contempt hearing, the court may direct the clerk to:

(A) Cause the matter to be reported to one or more designated credit bureaus.

(B) Issue a judicial summons ordering the defendant to appear in district court.

(C) Issue an arrest warrant if the defendant fails to appear in response to the judicial summons. The arrest warrant shall be limited to arrest during court hours only and order that the defendant be brought immediately to court.

(3) Hearing. The hearing shall be conducted in a summary manner. The court shall examine the defendant and any other witnesses and may require the defendant to produce documents relevant to the defendant's ability to pay the amount due. Evidence is admissible if it is of a type commonly relied upon by a reasonably prudent person in the conduct of his or her affairs. The Vermont Rules of Evidence shall not apply except that the rules related to privilege shall apply. The State shall not be a party except with the permission of the court. The defendant may be represented by counsel at the defendant's own expense.

(4) Contempt.

(A) The court may conclude that the defendant is in contempt if the court finds that:

(i) the defendant knew or reasonably should have known that he or she owed the amount due;

(ii) the defendant had the ability to pay all or any portion of the amount due; and

(iii) the defendant failed to pay all or any portion of the amount due.

(B) If the court concludes that the defendant is in contempt, the court may:

(i) Order payment of the amount due on a specific date.

(ii) Assess an additional penalty not to exceed ten percent of the amount due.

(iii) Direct that the matter be reported to one or more designated credit bureaus. The Court Administrator or the Court Administrator's designee is authorized to contract with one or more credit bureaus for the purpose of reporting information about unpaid Judicial Bureau judgments.

(iv) Refer to Small Claims Court for the purpose of issuing writs of attachment for property and trustee process pursuant to 12 V.S.A. § 5534. Filing fees shall be waived in such cases.

(v) Sentence the defendant to serve a term of imprisonment on furlough to participate in a program supervised by the Department of Corrections pursuant to 28 V.S.A. § 808(a) that provides reparation to the community in the form of supervised work activities. For each day the defendant participates in supervised work activities, the defendant shall be given credit against the amount owed at the hourly rate for minimum wage. A defendant who is determined by the Department of Corrections to be ineligible for the preapproved furlough supervised work program may be ordered by the court to serve a sentence in a correctional facility, in which event the defendant shall be given credit against the amount owed for every day served at a rate determined by the court.

(C) If the court concludes that the defendant is not in contempt because the defendant does not have the ability to pay the amount due, the court may:

(i) suspend all or any part of the amount due in the interests of justice, except that the court may not waive surcharges imposed pursuant to section 7282 of this title;

(ii) order the defendant to participate in the Restorative Justice Program conducted by a community reparative board and direct the reparative board to determine an appropriate amount of community service to be performed in lieu of all or part of the amount due.

(d) For purposes of civil contempt proceedings, the venue shall be statewide.

(e) Notwithstanding 32 V.S.A. § 502, the Court Administrator is authorized to contract with a third party to collect fines, penalties, and fees by credit card, debit card, charge card, prepaid card, stored value card, and direct bank account withdrawals or transfers, as authorized by 32 V.S.A. § 583, and to add on and collect or charge against collections a processing charge in an amount approved by the Court Administrator.

(f)(1) A defendant who is not incarcerated may file a motion to convert all or part of a traffic offense fine to community service. The court may grant the motion if the defendant establishes that he or she has made a good faith effort to pay the fine but is unable to do so. A fine converted to community service pursuant to this subsection shall not be considered a modification of sentence and shall not be subject to the time limits of Vermont Rule of Criminal Procedure 35.

(2) Community service performed pursuant to a motion granted under this subsection shall be:

(A) credited against outstanding fines at the then-existing rate of the Vermont minimum wage:

(B) monitored by Diversion, a restorative justice panel of a community justice center, or a similar entity approved by the court, that shall report on the defendant's compliance status to the court;

(C) performed in the county where the offense occurred.

(3) A conversion of a fine to community service under this subsection:

(A) shall not apply to surcharges, court costs, or other assessments;

(B) shall be in addition to the contempt procedures applicable under this section. (Added 2009, No. 146 (Adj. Sess.), § D3; amended 2015, No. 58, § E.204.6, eff. June 11, 2015.)

§§ 7221-7225. Repealed. 2009, No. 146 (Adj. Sess.), § D3.

Subchapter 3: Treasury Entitled To Fines And Costs And Liable For Costs
§ 7251. Municipalities; payment to and liability of
(a) Fines, forfeitures, and penalties, imposed by the District or Superior court or by the Judicial Bureau for violation of a village, town, or city ordinance shall be paid to the village, town, or city, respectively, except for a $12.50 administrative charge for each case which shall be retained by the State.

(b) Fines, forfeitures, and penalties imposed by the Judicial Bureau for all speeding traffic violations under 23 V.S.A. chapter 13, subchapter 8 entitled "speed restrictions" on State highways and for height and width violations under 23 V.S.A. § 1431 and length violations under 23 V.S.A. § 1432 on town highways resulting from the enforcement by towns within the jurisdiction of the town shall be paid to the town by the formula set forth in subsection (c) of this section except for the administrative charge according to the provisions of subsection (a) of this section which shall be retained by the State. The enforcement by towns shall be by a town law enforcement officer or a law enforcement officer by contract with the town. Such law enforcement officer shall be certified according to the provisions of 20 V.S.A. § 2358. Nothing in this section shall be construed to limit the jurisdiction of a certified law enforcement officer. The revenue that is collected by the State pursuant to enforcement of this section by a town shall be distributed annually during the first quarter of the fiscal year immediately following the fiscal year in which the fines, forfeitures, and penalties are collected.

(c) The allocation of revenue to the towns under the formula shall be updated annually by the State Court Administrator and shall provide that the revenue be distributed to those towns whose law enforcement efforts on State highways and town highways as specifically set forth in subsection (b) of this section have resulted in the imposition of the fines, forfeitures, and penalties for all speeding traffic violations under 23 V.S.A. chapter 13, subchapter 8 entitled "speed restrictions" and for height and width violations under 23 V.S.A. § 1431 and length violations under 23 V.S.A. § 1432 provided that no town may receive more than five percent of the total revenue in any given year. The formula used for distribution shall reflect the percentage of a town's law enforcement expenditures as it relates to the town's total municipal taxing effort. The town's total municipal taxing effort shall be determined by subtracting the town's school taxes assessed from the total taxes assessed as provided each year in the annual report of the division of property valuation and review by the Vermont Department of Taxes. By July 31 of each year, the local legislative body of any town that had law enforcement efforts resulting in the imposition of fines, forfeitures, and penalties and that wishes to participate shall submit to the Court Administrator the total amount of the funds spent for law enforcement in the most recently completed town fiscal year.

(d) Fines, forfeitures, and penalties imposed by the Judicial Bureau for violations of subdivisions 352(3), (4), and (9) of this title, relating to animal cruelty that result from the enforcement by villages, towns, and cities within their jurisdiction shall be paid to the respective village, town, or city, except for a $12.50 administrative charge for each violation that shall be retained by the State. The enforcement by villages, towns, and cities shall be by a local law enforcement officer or a law enforcement officer by contract with the village, town, or city. Such law enforcement officer shall be certified according to the provisions of 20 V.S.A. § 2358. (Amended 1973, No. 249 (Adj. Sess.), § 58, eff. April 9, 1974; 1975, No. 227 (Adj. Sess.), § 4; 1989, No. 109, § 7; 1993, No. 237 (Adj. Sess.), § 7, eff. Nov. 1, 1994; 1995, No. 77 (Adj. Sess.), § 6, eff. March 21, 1996; 1995, No. 133 (Adj. Sess.), § 1; 1997, No. 46, §§ 8, 9; 1997, No. 121 (Adj. Sess.), § 30; 2001, No. 149 (Adj. Sess.), § 74, eff. June 27, 2002; 2007, No. 51, § 21.)

§ 7252. Fines and penalties payable to State

All fines, forfeitures, and penalties received by the District or Superior court or by the Judicial Bureau, except as provided in section 7251 of this title, shall belong and be paid to the State, except for a $12.50 administrative charge for each offense or violation where a fine or penalty is assessed. The administrative charge shall be deposited in the Court Technology Special Fund established pursuant to 4 V.S.A. § 27. (Amended 1969, No. 131, § 14, eff. April 23, 1969; 2007, No. 65, § 62.)

§ 7253. Payment of costs by State

The costs of prosecution for the breach of a penal law or other offense, except as provided in section 7251 of this title, shall be paid out of the treasury of the State.

§ 7254. Unorganized towns and gores

Unless otherwise disposed of by law, fines, forfeitures, and penalties imposed on a person residing in an unorganized town or gore, shall belong and be paid to the State. (Amended 1969, No. 131, § 15, eff. April 23, 1969.)

§ 7255. Exceptions where respondent committed in default of payment

When the penalty is wholly or partly by fine payable to the treasurer of a county, town, or village, if the respondent is committed in default of payment, the fine shall be payable to the State, and the costs shall be paid from the State treasury as in other cases where the costs are paid by the State. (Amended 1969, No. 131, § 23, eff. April 23, 1969.)

§ 7256. Repealed. 1969, No. 302 (Adj. Sess.), § 5, eff. April 10, 1970.

§§ 7257, 7258. Repealed. 1973, No. 249 (Adj. Sess.), § 111, eff. April 9, 1974.

§ 7259. Private prosecutors- Liability for and right to costs

When a person other than an informing officer, becomes a prosecutor, he or she shall enter his or her name and place of residence at the foot of the complaint, information or indictment, and shall be liable to pay costs on such prosecution, and, on conviction, may receive costs.

§ 7260. Recognizance to respondent

The prosecutor shall, before a warrant issues for the arrest of the respondent, enter into a recognizance with surety to the respondent, conditioned to prosecute to effect, or, on failure thereof, to pay the costs adjudged to the respondent.

§ 7261. Prosecutor to advance fees

The prosecutor shall advance the fees and incur the expenses of prosecution in the same manner as in civil causes, and no treasury shall be liable for the same.

§ 7262. Travel expenses

(a) Any person extradited to the State of Vermont on the basis of one or more criminal offenses alleged to have been committed in the State of Vermont against whom all charges are subsequently dismissed, either by the State's Attorney or the Attorney General due to insufficient evidence or by the court on the basis of the State's failure to establish a prima facie case, may be compensated for travel-related expenses necessary to return to the place from which the person was extradited.

(b) The court shall hear the defendant's request for travel-related expenses, as related to subsection (a) of this section, as soon as possible after dismissal and may order that such payment be made forthwith as the court in its discretion deems appropriate.

(c) Payments so ordered shall be made from the amount appropriated to the Attorney General for extraditions. (Added 1981, No. 74.)

Subchapter 4: Assessment And Collection Of Additional Surcharges

§ 7281. Repealed. 2011, No. 63, § E.221.2.

§ 7282. Surcharge

(a) In addition to any penalty or fine imposed by the court or Judicial Bureau for a criminal offense or any civil penalty imposed for a traffic violation, including any violation of a fish and wildlife statute or regulation, violation of a motor vehicle statute, or violation of any local ordinance relating to the operation of a motor vehicle, except violations relating to seat belts and child restraints and ordinances relating to parking violations, the clerk of the court or Judicial Bureau shall levy an additional surcharge of:

(1) $5.00 for any offense or violation committed prior to June 1, 1990.

(2) $8.00 for any offense or violation committed after May 31, 1990, but before July 1, 1991, of which $3.00 shall be deposited into a special fund account to be known as the Victim' Compensation Fund.

(3) $10.00 for any offense or violation committed after June 30, 1991, but before July 1, 1993, of which $5.00 shall be deposited into a special fund account to be known as the Victims Compensation Fund.

(4) $17.50 for any offense or violation committed after June 30, 1993, but before July 1, 2001, of which $12.50 shall be deposited into a special fund account to be known as the Victims Compensation Fund.

(5) $20.50 for any offense or violation committed after June 30, 2001, but before July 1, 2003, of which $13.50 shall be deposited into a special fund account to be known as the Victims Compensation Fund.

(6) For any offense or violation committed after June 30, 2003, but before July 1, 2005, $21.00, of which $13.75 shall be deposited into the Victims Compensation Special Fund.

(7) For any offense or violation committed after June 30, 2005, but before July 1, 2006, $22.00, of which $14.75 shall be deposited into the Victims Compensation Special Fund.

(8)(A) For any offense or violation committed after June 30, 2006, but before July 1, 2008, $26.00, of which $18.75 shall be deposited in the Victims Compensation Special Fund.

(B) For any offense or violation committed after June 30, 2008, but before July 1, 2009, $36.00, of which $28.75 shall be deposited in the Victims' Compensation Special Fund.

(C) For any offense or violation committed after June 30, 2009, but before July 1, 2013, $41.00, of which $23.75 shall be deposited in the Victims Compensation Special Fund created by section 5359 of this title, and of which $10.00 shall be deposited in the Domestic and Sexual Violence Special Fund created by section 5360 of this title.

(D) For any offense or violation committed after June 30, 2013, $47.00, of which $29.75 shall be deposited in the Victims Compensation Special Fund created by section 5359 of this title, and of which $10.00 shall be deposited in the Domestic and Sexual Violence Special Fund created by section 5360 of this title.

(9) For any offense or violation committed after June 30, 2003, an amount equal to 15 percent of the fine imposed for the offense, rounded upward to the nearest whole dollar, which shall be deposited into the Crime Victims' Restitution Special Fund established by section 5363 of this title.

(b) The surcharges imposed by this section shall not be waived by the court.

(c) SUI surcharge. In addition to any penalty or fine imposed by the court or Judicial Bureau for a criminal offense committed after July 1, 2009, the clerk of the court or Judicial Bureau shall levy an additional surcharge of $100.00 to be deposited in the General Fund, in support of the Specialized Investigative Unit Grants Board created in 24 V.S.A. § 1940(c), and used to pay for the costs of Specialized Investigative Units. (Added 1985, No. 182 (Adj. Sess.), § 1; amended 1989, No. 109, § 9; 1989, No. 214 (Adj. Sess.), § 3, eff. May 31, 1990; 1993, No. 88, § 1; 2001, No. 65, § 4; 2003, No. 57, § 7, eff. June 4, 2003; 2005, No. 72, § 23; 2005, No. 202 (Adj. Sess.), § 23; 2007, No. 40, § 9, eff. July 1, 2012; 2007, No. 174 (Adj. Sess.), § 20; 2009, No. 47, § 12, eff. July 1, 2012; 2011, No. 63, § E.221.3; 2011, No. 162 (Adj. Sess.), § E.220.2; 2013, No. 72, § 12.)

§ 7283. Repealed. 2011, No. 63, § E.221.4.

Chapter 225: New Trials

§§ 7301-7304. Repealed. 1973, No. 118, § 25, eff. Oct. 1, 1973.

Chapter 227: Appeals To Supreme Court

§ 7401. Appeal

In criminal actions or proceedings, the defendant may appeal to the Supreme Court as of right all questions of law involved in any judgment of conviction and in any other order or judgment as to which the State has appealed, provided that if the State fails to perfect or prosecute such appeal, the appeal of the defendant shall not be heard. (Amended 1973, No. 118, § 20, eff. Oct. 1, 1973; 1973, No. 193 (Adj. Sess.), § 3, eff. April 9, 1974; 2009, No. 154 (Adj. Sess.), § 116.)

§ 7402. Repealed. 1973, No. 118, § 25, eff. Oct. 1, 1973.

§ 7403. Appeal by the State

(a) In a prosecution for a misdemeanor, questions of law decided against the State shall be allowed and placed upon the record before final judgment. The court may pass the same to the Supreme Court before final judgment. The Supreme Court shall hear and determine the questions and render final judgment thereon, or remand the cause for further trial or other proceedings, as justice and the State of the cause may require.

(b) In a prosecution for a felony, the State shall be allowed to appeal to the Supreme Court any decision, judgment, or order dismissing an indictment or information as to one or more counts.

(c) In a prosecution for a felony, the State shall be allowed to appeal to the Supreme Court from a decision or order:

(1) granting a motion to suppress evidence;

2) granting a motion to have confessions declared inadmissible; or

(3) granting or refusing to grant other relief where the effect is to impede seriously, although not to foreclose completely, continuation of the prosecution.

(d) In making this appeal, the attorney for the State must certify to the court that the appeal is not taken for purpose of delay and that:

(1) the evidence suppressed or declared inadmissible is substantial proof of a fact material in a proceeding; or

(2) the relief to be sought upon appeal is necessary to avoid seriously impeding such proceeding.

(e) The appeal in all cases shall be taken within seven business days after the decision, judgment, or order has been rendered. In cases where the defendant is detained for lack of bail, he or she shall be released pending the appeal upon such conditions as the court shall order unless bail is denied as provided in the Vermont Constitution or in other pending cases. Such appeals shall take precedence on the docket over all cases and shall be assigned for hearing or argument at the earliest practicable date and expedited in every way. (Amended 1965, No. 194, § 10, eff. February 1, 1967; 1981, No. 223 (Adj. Sess.), § 13; 2009, No. 154 (Adj. Sess.), § 117; 2017, No. 11, § 30.)

§ 7404. Repealed. 1973, No. 118, § 25, eff. Oct. 1, 1973.

§ 7405. Bail forfeited in Supreme Court

When a respondent forfeits his or her bail after conviction in a District or Superior Court and after going at large upon bail for his or her appearance before the Supreme Court, the Supreme Court shall render judgment that the bonds are forfeited, adjudge that the respondent has waived his or her exceptions and order the cause to be remanded to the court for sentence or such further proceedings as the law requires. (Amended 1965, No. 194, § 10, operative February 1, 1967; 1973, No. 193 (Adj. Sess.), § 3, eff. April 9, 1974.)

§ 7406. Repealed. 1973, No. 118, § 25, eff. Oct. 1, 1973.

Chapter 229: Bail And Recognizances

§ 7551. Imposition of bail, secured appearance bonds, and appearance bonds

(a) Bonds; generally. A bond given by a person charged with a criminal offense or by a witness in a criminal prosecution under section 6605 of this title, conditioned for the appearance of the person or witness before the court in cases where the offense is punishable by fine or imprisonment, and in appealed cases, shall be taken to the Criminal Division of the Superior Court where the prosecution is pending and shall remain binding upon parties until discharged by the court or until sentencing. The person or witness shall appear at all required court proceedings.

(b) Limitation on imposition of bail, secured appearance bonds, and appearance bonds.

(1) Except as provided in subdivision (2) of this subsection, no bail, secured appearance bond, or appearance bond may be imposed:

(A) at the initial appearance of a person charged with a misdemeanor if the person was cited for the offense in accordance with Rule 3 of the Vermont Rules of Criminal Procedure; or

(B) at the initial appearance or upon the temporary release pursuant to Rule 5(b) of the Vermont Rules of Criminal Procedure of a person charged with a violation of a misdemeanor offense that is eligible for expungement pursuant to subdivision 7601(4)(A) of this title.

(2) In the event the court finds that imposing bail is necessary to mitigate the risk of flight from prosecution for a person charged with a violation of a misdemeanor offense that is eligible for expungement pursuant to subdivision 7601(4)(A) of this title, the court may impose bail in a maximum amount of $200.00.

(3) This subsection shall not be construed to restrict the court's ability to impose conditions on such persons to reasonably mitigate the risk of flight from prosecution or to reasonably protect the public in accordance with section 7554 of this title. (Amended 2001, No. 124 (Adj. Sess.), § 1, eff. June 5, 2002; amended 2017, No. 62, § 1; 2017, No. 164 (Adj. Sess.), § 1.)

§ 7552. Repealed. 2001, No. 124 (Adj. Sess.), § 13, eff. June 5, 2002.

§ 7553. Release in cases punishable by life imprisonment

A person charged with an offense punishable by life imprisonment when the evidence of guilt is great may be held without bail. If the evidence of guilt is not great, the person shall be bailable in accordance with section 7554 of this title. (Added 1987, No. 102, § 1; amended 1993, No. 143 (Adj. Sess.), § 1.)

§ 7553a. Acts of violence; denial of release on bail

A person charged with an offense that is a felony, an element of which involves an act of violence against another person, may be held without bail when the evidence of guilt is great and the court finds, based upon clear and convincing evidence, that the person's release poses a substantial threat of physical violence to any person and that no condition or combination of conditions of release will reasonably prevent the physical violence. (Added 1993, No. 143 (Adj. Sess.), § 2.)

§ 7553b. Right to speedy trial if bail is denied

(a) Except in the case of an offense punishable by death or life imprisonment, if a person is held without bail prior to trial, the trial of the person shall be commenced not more than 60 days after bail is denied.

(b) If the trial is not commenced within 60 days and the delay is not attributable to the defense, the court shall immediately schedule a bail hearing and shall set bail for the person. (Added 1993, No. 143 (Adj. Sess.), § 3.)

§ 7554. Release prior to trial

(a) Release; conditions of release. Any person charged with an offense, other than a person held without bail under section 7553 or 7553a of this title, shall at his or her appearance before a judicial officer be ordered released pending trial in accordance with this section.

(1) The defendant shall be ordered released on personal recognizance or upon the execution of an unsecured appearance bond in an amount specified by the judicial officer unless the judicial officer determines that such a release will not reasonably mitigate the risk of flight from prosecution as required. In determining whether the defendant presents a risk of flight from prosecution, the judicial officer shall consider, in addition to any other factors, the seriousness of the offense charged and the number of offenses with which the person is charged. If the officer determines that the defendant presents a risk of flight from prosecution, the officer shall, either in lieu of or in addition to the methods of release in this section, impose the least restrictive of the following conditions or the least restrictive combination of the following conditions that will reasonably mitigate the risk of flight of the defendant as required:

(A) Place the defendant in the custody of a designated person or organization agreeing to supervise him or her if the defendant is charged with an offense that is not a nonviolent misdemeanor or nonviolent felony as defined in 28 V.S.A. § 301.

(B) Place restrictions on the travel or association of the defendant during the period of release.

(C) Require the defendant to participate in an alcohol or drug treatment program. The judicial officer shall take into consideration the defendant's ability to comply with an order of treatment and the availability of treatment resources.

(D) Upon consideration of the defendant's financial means, require the execution of a secured appearance bond in a specified amount and the deposit with the clerk of the court, in cash or other security as directed, of a sum not to exceed 10 percent of the amount of the bond, such deposit to be returned upon the appearance of the defendant as required.

(E) Upon consideration of the defendant's financial means, require the execution of a surety bond with sufficient solvent sureties, or the deposit of cash in lieu thereof.

(F) Impose any other condition found reasonably necessary to mitigate the risk of flight as required, including a condition requiring that the defendant return to custody after specified hours.

(G) Place the defendant in a program of community-based electronic monitoring in accordance with section 7554d of this title.

(2) If the judicial officer determines that conditions of release imposed to mitigate the risk of flight will not reasonably protect the public, the judicial officer may impose in addition the least restrictive of the following conditions or the least restrictive combination of the following conditions that will reasonably ensure protection of the public:

(A) Place the defendant in the custody of a designated person or organization agreeing to supervise him or her if the defendant is charged with an offense that is not a nonviolent misdemeanor or nonviolent felony as defined in 28 V.S.A. § 301.

(B) Place restrictions on the travel, association, or place of abode of the defendant during the period of release.

(C) Require the defendant to participate in an alcohol or drug treatment program. The judicial officer shall take into consideration the defendant's ability to comply with an order of treatment and the availability of treatment resources.

(D) Impose any other condition found reasonably necessary to protect the public, except that a physically restrictive condition may only be imposed in extraordinary circumstances.

(E) Suspend the officer's duties in whole or in part if the defendant is a State, county, or municipal officer charged with violating section 2537 of this title and the court finds that it is necessary to protect the public.

(F) Place the defendant in a program of community-based electronic monitoring in accordance with section 7554d of this title.

(3) A judicial officer may order that a defendant not harass or contact or cause to be harassed or contacted a victim or potential witness. This order shall take effect immediately, regardless of whether the defendant is incarcerated or released.

(b) Judicial considerations in imposing conditions of release. In determining which conditions of release to impose:

(1) In subdivision (a)(1) of this section, the judicial officer, on the basis of available information, shall take into account the nature and circumstances of the offense charged; the weight of the evidence against the accused; the accused's employment; financial resources, including the accused's ability to

post bail; the accused's character and mental condition; the accused's length of residence in the community; and the accused's record of appearance at court proceedings or of flight to avoid prosecution or failure to appear at court proceedings.

(2) In subdivision (a)(2) of this section, the judicial officer, on the basis of available information, shall take into account the nature and circumstances of the offense charged; the weight of the evidence against the accused; and the accused's family ties, employment, character and mental condition, length of residence in the community, record of convictions, and record of appearance at court proceedings or of flight to avoid prosecution or failure to appear at court proceedings. Recent history of actual violence or threats of violence may be considered by the judicial officer as bearing on the character and mental condition of the accused.

(c) Order. A judicial officer authorizing the release of a person under this section shall issue an appropriate order containing a statement of the conditions imposed, if any; shall inform such person of the penalties applicable to violations of the conditions of release; and shall advise him or her that a warrant for his or her arrest will be issued immediately upon any such violation.

(d) Review of conditions.

(1) A person for whom conditions of release are imposed and who is detained as a result of his or her inability to meet the conditions of release or who is ordered released on a condition that he or she return to custody after specified hours, or the State, following a material change in circumstances, shall, within 48 hours following application, be entitled to have the conditions reviewed by a judge in the court having original jurisdiction over the offense charged. A party applying for review shall be given the opportunity for a hearing. Unless the conditions of release are amended as requested, the judge shall set forth in writing or orally on the record a reasonable basis for continuing the conditions imposed. In the event that a judge in the court having original jurisdiction over the offense charged is not available, any Superior judge may review such conditions.

(2) A person for whom conditions of release are imposed shall, within five working days following application, be entitled to have the conditions reviewed by a judge in the court having original jurisdiction over the offense charged. A person applying for review shall be given the opportunity for a hearing. Unless the conditions of release are amended as requested, the judge shall set forth in writing or orally on the record a reasonable basis for continuing the conditions imposed. In the event that a judge in the court having original jurisdiction over the offense charged is not available, any Superior judge may review such conditions.

(e) Amendment of order. A judicial officer ordering the release of a person on any condition specified in this section may at any time amend the order to impose additional or different conditions of release, provided that the provisions of subsection (d) of this section shall apply.

(f) Definition. The term "judicial officer" as used in this section and section 7556 of this title shall mean a clerk of a Superior Court or a Superior Court judge.

(g) Admissibility of evidence. Information stated in, or offered in connection with, any order entered pursuant to this section need not conform to the rules pertaining to the admissibility of evidence in a court of law.

(h) Forfeiture. Nothing contained in this section shall be construed to prevent the disposition of any case or class of cases by forfeiture of collateral security if such disposition is authorized by the court.

(i) Forms. The Court Administrator shall establish forms for appearance bonds, secured appearance bonds, surety bonds, and for use in the posting of bail. Each form shall include the following information:

(1) The bond or bail may be forfeited in the event that the defendant or witness fails to appear at any required court proceeding.

(2) The surety or person posting bond or bail has the right to be released from the obligations under the bond or bail agreement upon written application to the judicial officer and detention of the defendant or witness.

(3) The bond will continue through sentencing in the event that bail is continued after final adjudication.

(j) Juveniles. Any juvenile between 14 and 16 years of age who is charged with a listed crime as defined in subdivision 5301(7) of this title shall appear before a judicial officer and be ordered released pending trial in accordance with this section within 24 hours following the juvenile's arrest. (Added 1967, No. 337 (Adj. Sess.), § 4; amended 1969, No. 125, § 12; 1973, No. 193 (Adj. Sess.), § 3, eff. April 9, 1974; 1987, No. 102, § 2; 1989, No. 293 (Adj. Sess.), § 1; 1993, No. 143 (Adj. Sess.), § 4; 2001, No. 124 (Adj. Sess.), § 2, eff. June 5, 2002; 2003, No. 73 (Adj. Sess.), § 6, eff. March 1, 2004; 2005, No. 63, § 10; 2005, No. 193 (Adj. Sess.), § 10; 2007, No. 108 (Adj. Sess.), § 1; 2007, No. 169 (Adj. Sess.), § 2; 2009, No. 154 (Adj. Sess.), § 118; 2015, No. 43, § 2; 2015, No. 125 (Adj. Sess.), § 1; 2015, No. 153 (Adj. Sess.), § 18; 2017, No. 164 (Adj. Sess.), § 3.)

§ 7554a. Approval of fidelity companies and agents; duty of Court Administrator

The Court Administrator, after consultation with the Commissioner of Financial Regulation, may approve an entity that is licensed or authorized under the provisions of 8 V.S.A. chapter 111, and any agent who is licensed under the provisions of 8 V.S.A. chapter 131, to act as a surety, or on behalf of a surety, in this State to execute a bond in the form established by the Court Administrator under subsection 7554(i) of this title, or post bail as required as a condition of release, and if so approved, the entity or agent shall not need to be approved by any court, judicial officer, or any other person. (Added 1993, No. 233 (Adj. Sess.), § 83, eff. June 21, 1994; amended 1995, No. 180 (Adj. Sess.), § 38(a); 2001, No. 124 (Adj. Sess.), § 3, eff. June 5, 2002; 2011, No. 78 (Adj. Sess.), § 2, eff. April 2, 2012.)

§ 7554b. Home detention program

(a) Definition. As used in this section, "home detention" means a program of confinement and supervision that restricts a defendant to a preapproved residence continuously, except for authorized absences, and is enforced by appropriate means of surveillance and electronic monitoring by the Department of Corrections. The court may authorize scheduled absences such as for work, school, or treatment. Any changes in the schedule shall be solely at the discretion of the Department of Corrections. A defendant who is on home detention shall remain in the custody of the Commissioner of Corrections with conditions set by the court.

(b) Procedure. At the request of the court, the Department of Corrections, or the defendant, the status of a defendant who is detained pretrial in a correctional facility for inability to pay bail after bail has been set by the court may be reviewed by the court to determine whether the defendant is appropriate for home detention. The review shall be scheduled upon the court's receipt of a report from the Department determining that the proposed residence is suitable for the use of electronic monitoring. A defendant held without bail pursuant to section 7553 or 7553a of this title shall not be eligible for release to the Home Detention Program on or after June 1, 2018. At arraignment or after a hearing, the court may order that the defendant be released to the Home Detention Program, provided that the court finds placing the defendant on home detention will reasonably assure his or her appearance in court when required and the proposed residence is appropriate for home detention. In making such a determination, the court shall consider:

(1) the nature of the offense with which the defendant is charged;

(2) the defendant's prior convictions, history of violence, medical and mental health needs, history of supervision, and risk of flight; and

(3) any risk or undue burden to other persons who reside at the proposed residence or risk to third parties or to public safety that may result from such placement.

(c) Failure to comply. The Department of Corrections may revoke a defendant's home detention status for an unauthorized absence or failure to comply with any other condition of the Program and shall return the defendant to a correctional facility.

(d) Credit for time served. A defendant shall receive credit for a sentence of imprisonment for time served in the Home Detention Program. (Added 2009, No. 146 (Adj. Sess.), § D4; amended 2017, No. 62, § 11; 2017, No. 164 (Adj. Sess.), § 7.)

§ 7554c. Pretrial risk assessments; needs screenings

(a)(1) The objective of a pretrial risk assessment is to provide information to the court for the purpose of determining whether a person presents a risk of nonappearance or a risk of re-offense so the court can make an appropriate order concerning bail and conditions of pretrial release. The assessment shall not assess victim safety or risk of lethality in domestic assaults.

(2) The objective of a pretrial needs screening is to obtain a preliminary indication of whether a person has a substantial substance abuse or mental health issue that would warrant a subsequent court order for a more detailed clinical assessment.

(3) Participation in a risk assessment or needs screening pursuant to this section does not create any entitlement for the assessed or screened person.

(b)(1) Except as provided in subdivision (2) of this subsection, a person who is arrested, lodged, and unable to post bail within 24 hours of lodging shall be offered a risk assessment and, if deemed appropriate by the pretrial services coordinator, a needs screening prior to arraignment.

(2) A person charged with an offense for which registration as a sex offender is required pursuant to chapter 167, subchapter 3 of this title or an offense punishable by a term of life imprisonment shall not be eligible under this section.

(3) Participation in risk assessment or needs screening shall be voluntary and a person's refusal to participate shall not result in any criminal legal liability to the person.

(4) In the event an assessment or screening cannot be obtained prior to arraignment, the risk assessment and needs screening shall be conducted as soon as practicable.

(5) A person who qualifies pursuant to subdivision (1) of this subsection and who has an additional pending charge or a violation of probation shall not be excluded from being offered a risk assessment or needs screening unless the other charge is a listed crime.

(6) Any person charged with a criminal offense or who is the subject of a youthful offender petition pursuant to 33 V.S.A. § 5280, except those persons identified in subdivision (2) of this subsection, may choose to engage with a pretrial services coordinator.

(c) The results of the risk assessment and needs screening shall be provided to the person and his or her attorney, the prosecutor, and the court. Pretrial services coordinators may share information only within the limitations of subsection (e) of this section.

(d)(1) At arraignment, the court may order a person to do the following:

(A) meet with a pretrial services coordinator on a schedule set by the court;

(B) participate in a needs screening with a pretrial services coordinator; and

(C) participate in a clinical assessment by a substance abuse or mental health treatment provider and follow the recommendations of the provider.

(2) The court may order the person to engage in pretrial services. Pretrial services may include the pretrial services coordinator:

(A) supporting the person in meeting conditions of release imposed by the court, including the condition to appear for judicial proceedings; and

(B) connecting the person with community-based treatment programs, rehabilitative services, recovery supports, and restorative justice programs.

(3) If possible, the court shall set the date and time for the clinical assessment at arraignment. In the alternative, the pretrial services coordinator shall coordinate the date, time, and location of the clinical assessment and advise the court, the person and his or her attorney, and the prosecutor.

(4) An order authorized in subdivision (1) or (2) of this subsection shall be in addition to any conditions of release permitted by law and shall not limit the court in any way. Failure to comply with a court order authorized by subdivision (1) or (2) of this subsection shall not constitute a violation of section 7559 of this title.

(5) This section shall not be construed to limit a court's authority to impose conditions pursuant to section 7554 of this title.

(e)(1) Information obtained from the person during the risk assessment or needs screening shall be exempt from public inspection and copying under the Public Records Act and, except as provided in subdivision (2) of this subsection, only may be used for determining bail, conditions of release, and appropriate programming for the person in the pending case. The information a pretrial services coordinator may report is limited to whether a risk assessment indicates risk of nonappearance, whether further substance use assessment or treatment is indicated, whether mental health assessment or treatment is indicated, whether a person participated in a clinical assessment, and whether further engagement with pretrial services is recommended, unless the person provides written permission to release additional information. Information related to the present offense directly or indirectly derived from the risk assessment, needs screening, or other conversation with the pretrial services coordinator shall not be used against the person in the person's criminal or juvenile case for any purpose, including impeachment or cross-examination. However, the fact of participation or nonparticipation in risk assessment or needs screening may be used in subsequent proceedings. The immunity provisions of this subsection apply only to the use and derivative use of information gained as a proximate result of the risk assessment, needs screening, or other conversation with the pretrial services coordinator.

(2) The person shall retain all of his or her due process rights throughout the risk assessment and needs screening process and may release his or her records at his or her discretion.

(3) All records of information obtained during risk assessment or needs screening shall be stored in a manner making them accessible only to the Director of Pretrial Services and pretrial service coordinators for a period of three years, after which the records shall be maintained as required by sections 117 and 218 of this title and any other State law. The Director of Pretrial Services shall be responsible for the destruction of records when ordered by the court.

(f) The Attorney General's Office shall:

(1) contract for or otherwise provide the pretrial services described in this section, including performance of risk assessments, needs screenings, and pretrial monitoring services, and

(2) develop pretrial services outcomes following the designated State of Vermont performance accountability framework and, in consultation with the Department of State's Attorneys and Sheriffs, the Office of the Defender General, the Center for Crime Victim Services, and the Judiciary, report annually on or before December 1 to the General Assembly on services provided and outcome indicators. (Added 2013, No. 179 (Adj. Sess.), § C.339.1; 2013, No. 195 (Adj. Sess.), § 2, eff. Jan. 1, 2015; amended 2015, No. 12, § 2, eff. May 1, 2015; 2015, No. 140 (Adj. Sess.), § 1, eff. May 25, 2016; 2017, No. 61, § 3; 2019, No. 77, § 19, eff. June 19, 2019.)

§ 7554d. Electronic Monitoring Pilot Program

(a)(1) The Windham County Sheriff's Office (WCSO) shall establish and manage a two-year electronic monitoring pilot program in Windham County for the purpose of supervising persons ordered to be under electronic monitoring as a condition of release or in addition to or in lieu of the imposition of bail pursuant to section 7554 of this title. The program shall be a part of an integrated community incarceration program and shall provide 24-hours-a-day, seven-days-a-week electronic monitoring with supervision and immediate response.

(2) For purposes of this program, if electronic monitoring is ordered by the court pursuant to section 7554 of this title, the court shall use the following criteria for determining whether electronic monitoring is appropriate:

(A) the nature of the offense with which the defendant is charged;

(B) the defendant's prior convictions, history of violence, medical and mental health needs, history of supervision, and risk of flight; and

(C) any risk or undue burden to other persons who reside at the proposed residence or risk to third parties or to public safety that may result from the placement.

(3) The WCSO shall establish written policies and procedures for the electronic monitoring program, shall provide progress reports on the development of the policies and procedures to the Justice Oversight Committee, and shall submit the final policies and procedures to the Committee for approval on or before June 30, 2016.

(b) The goal of the pilot program is to assist policymakers in determining whether electronically monitored home detention and home confinement can be utilized for pretrial detention and as a post-adjudication option to reduce recidivism, to improve public safety, and to save valuable bed space for detainees and inmates who, without an electronic monitoring program, would otherwise be lodged in a correctional facility. Additional benefits may include reducing transportation costs, increasing detainee access to services, reducing case resolution time, and determining if the program can be replicated statewide.

(c) The WCSO shall work with the Crime Research Group (CRG) for design and evaluation assistance. The program shall be evaluated by CRG to determine if the stated goals have been attained, the cost and savings of the program, identifying what goals or objective were not met and if not, what could be changed to meet the goals and objectives to ensure program success. The Joint Fiscal Office shall contract with the CRG to provide design and evaluation services.

(d)(1) The WCSO is authorized to enter into written agreements with the sheriffs of other counties permitting those counties to participate in the pilot program subject to the policies and procedures established by the WCSO under this section. At least one of the agreements shall be between the WCSO and a county with a significant population.

(2) The purpose of expanding the electronic monitoring program to other counties under this subsection is to increase the number of participants to a level sufficient to permit evaluation of whether the program is meeting the bed savings and other goals identified in subsection (b) of this section.

(e) The Department of Corrections shall enter into a memorandum of understanding with the Department of State's Attorneys and Sheriffs for oversight and funding of the electronic monitoring program established by this section. The memorandum shall establish processes for:

(1) transmitting funding for the electronic monitoring program from the Department of Corrections to the Department of State's Attorneys and Sheriffs for purposes of allocation to the sheriff's departments participating in the program; and

(2) maintaining oversight of the electronic monitoring program to ensure that it complies with the requirements of this section and the policies and procedures established by the WCSO pursuant to subdivision (a)(3) of this section.

(f) The pilot program shall be in effect from July 1, 2014 through June 30, 2018. (Added 2013, No. 179 (Adj. Sess.), § E.339.1; amended 2015, No. 125 (Adj. Sess.), § 2, eff. May 23, 2016.)

§ 7555. Repealed. 1967, No. 337 (Adj. Sess.), § 6.

§ 7555a. Legislative findings

The General Assembly finds:

(1) During the 1991-2 and the 1993-4 sessions, the General Assembly adopted Proposal 7, which proposed to amend section 40 of Chapter II of the Vermont Constitution to allow a judge to order a person charged with a felony involving an act of violence to be held without bail when the evidence of guilt is great and the court finds by clear and convincing evidence

(A) that the person's release poses a substantial threat of physical violence to any person; and

(B) that no condition of release will reasonably prevent the physical violence.

(2) On November 8, 1994, the voters of the State of Vermont approved Proposal 7.

(3) On December 13, 1994, the Governor certified the amendment thereby making it effective on that date.

(4) As amended, section 40 of Chapter II of the Vermont Constitution provides that if a judge orders a person held without bail, that person is entitled to a review de novo by a single Justice of the Supreme Court forthwith.

(5) Given the unique nature of the trial court hearing which can result in the accused being denied bail, in passing Proposal 7, and its enabling legislation, H.589, the General Assembly intended to provide the accused with a second evidentiary hearing by a single Justice without regard to the record compiled before the trial court. However, in the case of State v. Madison, No. 95-046 (1995), the Vermont Supreme Court held that the term "review de novo" as it is used in section 40 of Chapter II of the Vermont Constitution and in H.589 does not require the single Justice to conduct a second evidentiary hearing and that the Legislature should have used the term "hearing de novo" if it intended a second, independent evidentiary hearing.

(6) Proposal 7 substantially increased the court's authority prior to trial and conviction to incarcerate persons accused of certain offenses. It was the intent of the General Assembly to balance this increased judicial authority with increased due process for the accused person. That increased due process was intended to be in the form of a new and independent evidentiary hearing.

(7) In certain respects, the Vermont Constitution is not a grant of power to the Legislature, but is a limitation on its general powers. Section 40(2) of Chapter II establishes the minimum required due process for an accused, but the General Assembly may require greater due process.

(8) It was the clear and unequivocal intent of the General Assembly that a person who is denied bail and is incarcerated prior to trial under the authority of section 40(2) of Chapter II be entitled to a second full evidentiary hearing by a single Justice.

(9) In order to implement the intent of the General Assembly, subsection 7556(d) of this title is amended to make it clear and unequivocal that a person who is denied bail under the authority of section 40(2) of

Chapter II is entitled to a second full evidentiary hearing by a single Justice. Such a hearing is intended to be in addition to but not in conflict with the constitutionally required minimum due process established by Proposal 7. (Added 1995, No. 170 (Adj. Sess.), § 24a, eff. May 15, 1996.)

§ 7556. Appeal from conditions of release

(a) A person who is detained, or whose release on a condition requiring him or her to return to custody after specified hours is continued, after review of his or her application pursuant to subsection 7554(d) or (e) of this title by a judicial officer, other than a judge of the court having original jurisdiction over the offense with which he or she is charged or a Justice of the Supreme Court, may move the court having original jurisdiction over the offense with which he or she is charged to amend the order. The motion shall be determined promptly.

(b) When a person is detained after a court denies a motion under subsection (a) of this section or when conditions of release have been imposed or amended by the judge of the court having original jurisdiction over the offense charged, an appeal may be taken to a single Justice of the Supreme Court who may hear the matter or at his or her discretion refer it to the entire Supreme Court for hearing. No further appeal may lie from the ruling of a single Justice in matters to which this subsection applies. Any order so appealed shall be affirmed if it is supported by the proceedings below. If the order is not supported, the Supreme Court or single Justice hearing the matter may remand the case for a further hearing or may, with or without additional evidence, order the person released. The appeal shall be determined forthwith.

(c) When a person is released, with or without bail or other conditions of release, an appeal may be taken by the State to a single Justice of the Supreme Court who may hear the matter or at his or her discretion refer it to the entire Supreme Court for hearing. No further appeal may lie from the ruling of a single Justice in matters to which this subsection applies. Any order so appealed shall be affirmed if it is supported by the proceedings below. If the order is not supported, the Supreme Court or single Justice hearing the matter may remand the case for a further hearing or may, with or without additional evidence, modify or vacate the order. The appeal shall be determined forthwith.

(d) A person held without bail under section 7553a of this title prior to trial shall be entitled to an independent, second evidentiary hearing on the merits of the denial of bail, which shall be a hearing de novo by a single Justice of the Supreme Court forthwith. Pursuant to 4 V.S.A. § 22 the Chief Justice may appoint and assign a retired justice or judge with his or her consent or a Superior judge or District judge to a special assignment on the Supreme Court to conduct that de novo hearing. Such hearing de novo shall be an entirely new evidentiary hearing without regard to the record compiled before the trial court; except, the parties may stipulate to the admission of portions of the trial court record.

(e) A person held without bail prior to trial shall be entitled to review of that determination by a panel of three Supreme Court Justices within seven business days after bail is denied. (Added 1967, No. 337 (Adj. Sess.), § 5; amended 1977, No. 235 (Adj. Sess.), § 7; 1981, No. 223 (Adj. Sess.), § 14; 1993, No. 143 (Adj. Sess.), § 5; 1995, No. 170 (Adj. Sess.), § 24b, eff. May 15, 1996; 2017, No. 11, § 31.)

§ 7557. Bail upon postponement of trial

When a District or Superior court postpones the trial of a criminal case or the examination of a person charged with a criminal offense, the court may impose the least restrictive conditions or combination of conditions permitted under subdivision 7554(a)(1) of this title which will reasonably assure the person's appearance before the court on the day to which the trial or examination is postponed. (Amended 1965, No. 194, § 10, operative February 1, 1967; 1973, No. 249 (Adj. Sess.), § 59, eff. April 9, 1974; 2001, No. 124 (Adj. Sess.), § 4, eff. June 5, 2002.)

§ 7558. Repealed. 1973, No. 118, § 25, eff. Oct. 1, 1973.

§ 7559. Release; designation; sanctions

(a) The officer in charge of a facility under the control of the department of corrections, county jail or a local lockup shall discharge any person held by him or her upon receipt of an order for release issued by a judicial officer pursuant to section 7554 of this title, accompanied by the full amount of any bond or cash bail fixed by the judicial officer. The officer in charge, or a person designated by the Court Administrator, shall issue a receipt for such bond or cash bail, and shall account for and turn over such bond or cash bail to the court having jurisdiction.

(b) The Court Administrator shall designate persons to set bail for any person under arrest prior to arraignment when the offense charged provides for a penalty of less than two years imprisonment or a fine of less than $1,000.00 or both. Such persons designated by the Court Administrator shall be considered judicial officers for the purposes of sections 7554 and 7556 of this title.

(c) Any person who is designated by the Court Administrator under subsection (b) of this section, may refuse the designation by so notifying the Court Administrator in writing within seven days of the designation.

(d) A person who has been released pursuant to section 7554 of this title with or without bail on condition that he or she appear at a specified time and place in connection with a prosecution for an offense and who without just cause fails to appear shall be imprisoned not more than two years or fined not more than $5,000.00, or both.

(e) The State's Attorney may commence a prosecution for criminal contempt under Rule 42 of the Vermont Rules of Criminal Procedure against a person who violates a condition of release imposed under section 7554 of this title The maximum penalty that may be imposed under this subsection shall be a fine of $1,000.00 or imprisonment for six months, or both. Upon commencement of a prosecution for criminal contempt, the court shall review, in accordance with section 7554 of this title, and may continue or modify conditions of release or terminate release of the person.

(f) Notwithstanding Rule 3 of the Vermont Rules of Criminal Procedure, a law enforcement officer may arrest a person without a warrant when the officer has probable cause to believe the person without just cause has failed to appear at a specified time and place in connection with a prosecution for an offense or has violated a condition of release relating to a restriction on travel or a condition of release that he or she not directly contact, harass, or cause to be harassed a victim or potential witness. (Amended 1971, No. 99; 1973, No. 118, § 21, eff. Oct. 1, 1973; 1971, No. 99; 1973, No. 118, § 21, eff. Oct. 1, 1973; 1973, No. 249 (Adj. Sess.), § 60, eff. April 9, 1974; 1981, No. 223 (Adj. Sess.), § 15; 1987, No. 102, § 3.)

§ 7560. Repealed. 2001, No. 124 (Adj. Sess.), § 13, eff. June 5, 2002.

§ 7560a. Failure to appear; forfeiture of bond; proceedings

(a) If a person who has been released on a secured or unsecured appearance bond or a surety bond fails to appear in court as required:

(1) The court may:

(A) issue a warrant for the arrest of the person; and

(B) upon hearing and notice thereof to the bailor or surety, forfeit any bail posted on the person.

(2)(A) The State's Attorney may file a motion to forfeit the amount of the bond against the surety in the Civil or Criminal Division of the Superior Court where the bond was executed.

(B) A motion filed under this subdivision shall:

(i) include a copy of the bond;

(ii) state the facts upon which the motion is based; and

(iii) be served upon the surety.

(b) The surety may respond to a motion to forfeit a bond. Responses must be served within 14 days of service of the motion.

(c) Upon notice to the parties, the court shall schedule a hearing on a motion to forfeit a bond. The court shall order the surety to produce the principal at the hearing.

(d) If the court finds that the surety has violated the terms of the bond by failing to produce the principal at the hearing or at any other court appearance at which the principal was required to appear, the court shall grant the motion to forfeit the bond. The court may, on motion, or on its own motion, adjust the amount of the forfeiture and order the forfeiture of all or part of the bond amount to the State.

(e) If a surety fails to comply with a forfeiture order issued under subsection (d) of this section, the Attorney General may commence proceedings to enforce the order and collect the forfeited amount.

(f) No bond may be forfeited, in whole or in part, for violation of any condition of release other than a condition that the principal appear in court as required.

(g)(1) Service and filing under this section shall be pursuant to Rule 49 of the Vermont Rules of Criminal Procedure.

(2) Computation of time under this section shall be pursuant to Rule 45 of the Vermont Rules of Criminal Procedure. (Added 2001, No. 124 (Adj. Sess.), § 5, eff. June 5, 2002; amended 2009, No. 154 (Adj. Sess.), § 119; 2017, No. 11, § 32.)

§ 7561. Repealed. 1973, No. 118, § 25, eff. Oct. 1, 1973.

§ 7562. Relief of bail- warrant to arrest and commit

If a surety or a person who has posted bail wishes to surrender the principal in discharge of the person's obligations under the bond or bail agreement, the person may apply in writing to a judicial officer, as defined in subsection 7554(f) of this title, for a warrant to apprehend and detain the principal. The court shall, absent good cause shown, thereupon issue such warrant, and on detention of the principal, the person's obligation under the bond or bail agreement shall be discharged. (Amended 2001, No. 124 (Adj. Sess.), § 6, eff. June 5, 2002.)

§ 7563. Execution of warrant; expenses

(a) On receipt of a warrant issued under section 7562 of this title with respect to a person charged with a criminal offense, and tender of fees provided for by law, an officer shall apprehend and detain the defendant, and leave with the officer in charge of the facility a copy of the warrant, with his or her return thereon. The expense of arrest and transport of the defendant to the facility shall be paid by the person applying for the warrant.

(b) On receipt of a warrant issued under section 7562 of this title with respect to a witness in a criminal prosecution, and tender of fees provided for by law, an officer shall apprehend the witness and deliver him or her to the court for disposition. (Amended 2001, No. 124 (Adj. Sess.), § 7, eff. June 5, 2002.)

§ 7564. Fees

Fees for the arrest and detention shall be the same as for the service of other process. If there is dispute about the amount of fees, it shall be submitted to the court which issued the warrant, and its decision shall be final. (Amended 2001, No. 124 (Adj. Sess.), § 8, eff. June 5, 2002.)

§§ 7565-7569. Repealed. 2001, No. 124 (Adj. Sess.), § 13, eff. June 5, 2002.

§ 7570. Power of court to return forfeited security

A surety may file a motion requesting the return of forfeited bail, bond or any other security at any time after the order of forfeiture is entered. The court shall set the motion for hearing and provide notice thereof to the surety and the state's attorney. If the court finds the interests of justice would be served by returning all or part of the security, the court may grant the motion and return as much of the security as it deems equitable under the circumstances. (Amended 2001, No. 124 (Adj. Sess.), § 9, eff. June 5, 2002.)

§§ 7571, 7572. Repealed. 2001, No. 124 (Adj. Sess.), § 13, eff. June 5, 2002.

§ 7573. Peace bonds

The Criminal Division of the Superior Court may order a person who is arrested for a criminal offense to find sureties that he or she will keep the peace, when it is necessary, and may order the person detained until he or she complies. The Court Administrator shall establish a form for peace bonds that includes notification that the surety has the right to be released from the obligations under the bond upon written application to the judicial officer and detention of the defendant. (Amended 1965, No. 194, § 10, operative February 1, 1967; 1973, No. 249 (Adj. Sess.), § 63, eff. April 9, 1974; 2001, No. 124 (Adj. Sess.), § 10, eff. June 5, 2002; 2009, No. 154, § 238.)

§ 7574. Release in cases after conviction

Upon an adjudication of guilt, the trial judge shall review the terms and conditions of release and may terminate them or may continue or alter them pending sentence or pending notice of appeal or the expiration of the time allowed for filing notice of appeal. In making such review, the judge shall consider the factors set forth in subsection 7554(b) of this title, as well as the defendant's conduct during the trial and the fact of conviction. Any denial of or change in the terms of release shall be reviewable in the manner provided in sections 7554 and 7556 of this title for pretrial release. (Added 1987, No. 102, § 4.)

§ 7575. Revocation of the right to bail

The right to bail may be revoked entirely if the judicial officer finds that the accused has:

(1) intimidated or harassed a victim, potential witness, juror, or judicial officer in violation of a condition of release; or

(2) repeatedly violated conditions of release in a manner that impedes the prosecution of the accused; or

(3) violated a condition or conditions of release that constitute a threat to the integrity of the judicial system; or

(4) without just cause, failed to appear at a specified time and place ordered by a judicial officer; or

(5) in violation of a condition of release, been charged with a felony or a crime against a person or an offense similar to the underlying charge, for which, after hearing, probable cause is found. (Added 1989, No. 293 (Adj. Sess.), § 2; amended 2017, No. 164 (Adj. Sess.), § 4.)

§ 7576. Definitions

As used in this chapter:

(1) "Appearance bond" means a written agreement that allows a person charged with a criminal offense to be released if the person pledges to pay the court a specified amount in the event the person fails to appear at a court proceeding.

(2) "Bail" means any security, including cash, pledged to the court to ensure that a person charged with a criminal offense will appear at future court proceedings.

(3) "Clinical assessment" means the procedures, to be conducted after a client has been screened, by which a licensed or otherwise approved counselor identifies and evaluates an individual's strengths, weaknesses, problems, and needs for the development of a treatment plan.

(4) "Needs screening" means a preliminary systematic procedure to evaluate the likelihood that an individual has a substance abuse or a mental health condition.

(5) "Risk assessment" means a pretrial assessment that is designed to be predictive of a person's failure to appear in court and risk of violating pretrial conditions of release with a new alleged offense.

(6) "Secured appearance bond" means a written agreement which allows a person charged with a criminal offense to be released if:

(A) the person pledges to pay the court a specified amount in the event that the person fails to appear at a court proceeding; and

(B) a portion of the bond is paid to the court prior to release.

(7) "Surety" means:

(A) a person who agrees to be responsible for guaranteeing the appearance in court of a person charged with a criminal offense; or

(B) a person who agrees to be responsible for guaranteeing that another person complies with the conditions of a peace bond under section 7573 of this title.

(8) "Surety bond" means a written agreement, in a form established by the Court Administrator, under which a surety guarantees the appearance in court of a person charged with a criminal offense, and pledges to pay the court a specified amount if the person fails to appear.

(9) "Flight from prosecution" means any action or behavior undertaken by a person charged with a criminal offense to avoid court proceedings. (Added 2001, No. 124 (Adj. Sess.), § 11, eff. June 5, 2002; amended 2015, No. 12, § 1, eff. May 1, 2015; 2017, No. 164 (Adj. Sess.), § 5.)

Chapter 230: Expungement And Sealing Of Criminal History Records

§ 7601. Definitions

As used in this chapter:

(1) "Court" means the Criminal Division of the Superior Court.

(2) "Criminal history record" means all information documenting an individual's contact with the criminal justice system, including data regarding identification, arrest or citation, arraignment, judicial disposition, custody, and supervision.

(3) "Predicate offense" means a criminal offense that can be used to enhance a sentence levied for a later conviction and includes operating a vehicle under the influence of alcohol or other substance in violation of 23 V.S.A. § 1201, domestic assault in violation of section 1042 of this title, and stalking in violation of section 1062 of this title. "Predicate offense" shall not include misdemeanor possession of cannabis, a disorderly conduct offense under section 1026 of this title, or possession of a controlled substance in violation of 18 V.S.A. § 4230(a), 4231(a), 4232(a), 4233(a), 4234(a), 4234a(a), 4234b(a), 4235(b), or 4235a(a).

(4) "Qualifying crime" means:

(A) a misdemeanor offense that is not:

(i) a listed crime as defined in subdivision 5301(7) of this title;

(ii) an offense involving sexual exploitation of children in violation of chapter 64 of this title;

(iii) an offense involving violation of a protection order in violation of section 1030 of this title;

(iv) prostitution as defined in section 2632 of this title, or prohibited conduct under section 2601a of this title; or

(v) a predicate offense;

(B) a violation of subsection 3701(a) of this title related to criminal mischief;

(C) a violation of section 2501 of this title related to grand larceny;

(D) a violation of section 1201 of this title related to burglary, excluding any burglary into an occupied dwelling, as defined in subdivision 1201(b)(2) of this title;

(E) a violation of 18 V.S.A. § 4223 related to fraud or deceit;

(F) a violation of section 1802 of this title related to uttering a forged or counterfeited instrument;

(G) a violation of 18 V.S.A. § 4230(a) related to possession and cultivation of cannabis;

(H) a violation of 18 V.S.A. § 4231(a) related to possession of cocaine;

(I) a violation of 18 V.S.A. § 4232(a) related to possession of LSD;

(J) a violation of 18 V.S.A. § 4233(a) related to possession of heroin;

(K) a violation of 18 V.S.A. § 4234(a) related to possession of depressant, stimulant, and narcotic drugs;

(L) a violation of 18 V.S.A. § 4234a(a) related to possession of methamphetamine;

(M) a violation of 18 V.S.A. § 4234b(a) related to possession of ephedrine and pseudoephedrine;

(N) a violation of 18 V.S.A. § 4235(b) related to possession of hallucinogenic drugs;

(O) a violation of 18 V.S.A. § 4235a(a) related to possession of ecstasy; or

(P) any offense for which a person has been granted an unconditional pardon from the Governor. (Added 2011, No. 131 (Adj. Sess.), § 1; amended 2013, No. 76, § 8; 2015, No. 36, § 1, eff. May 26, 2015; 2017, No. 57, § 3; 2017, No. 83, § 161(3); 2019, No. 32, § 2; 2019, No. 167 (Adj. Sess.), § 33, eff. Oct. 7, 2020.)

§ 7602. Expungement and sealing of record, postconviction; procedure

(a)(1) A person may file a petition with the court requesting expungement or sealing of the criminal history record related to the conviction if:

(A) the person was convicted of a qualifying crime or qualifying crimes arising out of the same incident or occurrence;

(B) the person was convicted of an offense for which the underlying conduct is no longer prohibited by law or designated as a criminal offense;

(C) pursuant to the conditions set forth in subsection (g) of this section, the person was convicted of a violation of 23 V.S.A. § 1201(a) related to operating under the influence of alcohol or other substance, excluding a violation of that section resulting in serious bodily injury or death to any person other than the operator, or related to operating a school bus with a blood alcohol concentration of 0.02 or more or operating a commercial vehicle with a blood alcohol concentration of 0.04 or more; or

(D) pursuant to the conditions set forth in subsection (h) of this section, the person was convicted under 1201(c)(3)(A) of a violation of subdivision 1201(a) of this title related to burglary when the person was 25 years of age or younger, and the person did not carry a dangerous or deadly weapon during commission of the offense.

(2) The State's Attorney or Attorney General shall be the respondent in the matter.

(3) The court shall grant the petition without hearing if the petitioner and the respondent stipulate to the granting of the petition. The respondent shall file the stipulation with the court, and the court shall issue the petitioner an order of expungement and provide notice of the order in accordance with this section.

(4) This section shall not apply to an individual licensed as a commercial driver pursuant to 23 V.S.A. chapter 39 seeking to seal or expunge a record of a conviction for a felony offense committed in a motor vehicle as defined in 23 V.S.A. § 4.

(b)(1) The court shall grant the petition and order that the criminal history record be expunged pursuant to section 7606 of this title if the following conditions are met:

(A) At least five years have elapsed since the date on which the person successfully completed the terms and conditions of the sentence for the conviction, or if the person has successfully completed the terms and conditions of an indeterminate term of probation that commenced at least five years previously.

(B) The person has not been convicted of a crime arising out of a new incident or occurrence since the person was convicted for the qualifying crime.

(C) Any restitution and surcharges ordered by the court have been paid in full, provided that payment of surcharges shall not be required if the surcharges have been waived by the court pursuant to section 7282 of this title.

(D) The court finds that expungement of the criminal history record serves the interests of justice.

(2) The court shall grant the petition and order that all or part of the criminal history record be sealed pursuant to section 7607 of this title if the conditions of subdivisions (1)(A), (B), and (C) of this subsection are met and the court finds that:

(A) sealing the criminal history record better serves the interests of justice than expungement; and

(B) the person committed the qualifying crime after reaching 19 years of age.

(c)(1) The court shall grant the petition and order that the criminal history record be expunged pursuant to section 7606 of this title if the following conditions are met:

(A) At least 10 years have elapsed since the date on which the person successfully completed the terms and conditions of the sentence for the conviction.

(B) The person has not been convicted of a felony arising out of a new incident or occurrence in the last seven years.

(C) The person has not been convicted of a misdemeanor during the past five years.

(D) Any restitution and surcharges ordered by the court for any crime of which the person has been convicted has been paid in full, provided that payment of surcharges shall not be required if the surcharges have been waived by the court pursuant to section 7282 of this title.

(E) After considering the particular nature of any subsequent offense, the court finds that expungement of the criminal history record for the qualifying crime serves the interests of justice.

(2) The court shall grant the petition and order that all or part of the criminal history record be sealed pursuant to section 7607 of this title if the conditions of subdivisions (1)(A), (B), (C), and (D) of this subsection are met and the court finds that:

(A) sealing the criminal history record better serves the interests of justice than expungement; and

(B) the person committed the qualifying crime after reaching 19 years of age.

(d) For petitions filed pursuant to subdivision (a)(1)(B) of this section, unless the court finds that expungement would not be in the interests of justice, the court shall grant the petition and order that the criminal history record be expunged in accordance with section 7606 of this title if the following conditions are met:

(1) The petitioner has completed any sentence or supervision for the offense.

(2) Any restitution and surcharges ordered by the court have been paid in full, provided that payment of surcharges shall not be required if the surcharges have been waived by the court pursuant to section 7282 of this title.

(e) For petitions filed pursuant to subdivision (a)(1)(B) of this section for a conviction for possession of a regulated drug under 18 V.S.A. chapter 84, subchapter 1 in an amount that is no longer prohibited by law or for which criminal sanctions have been removed:

(1) The petitioner shall bear the burden of establishing that his or her conviction was based on possessing an amount of regulated drug that is no longer prohibited by law or for which criminal sanctions have been removed.

(2) There shall be a rebuttable presumption that the amount of the regulated drug specified in the affidavit of probable cause associated with the petitioner's conviction was the amount possessed by the petitioner.

(f) Prior to granting an expungement or sealing under this section for petitions filed pursuant to subdivision 7601(4)(D) of this title, the court shall make a finding that the conduct underlying the conviction under section 1201 of this title did not constitute a burglary into an occupied dwelling, as defined in subdivision 1201(b)(2) of this title. The petitioner shall bear the burden of establishing this fact.

(g) For petitions filed pursuant to subdivision (a)(1)(C) of this section, only petitions to seal may be considered or granted by the court. This subsection shall not apply to an individual licensed as a commercial driver pursuant to 23 V.S.A. chapter 39. Unless the court finds that sealing would not be in the interests of justice, the court shall grant the petition and order that the criminal history record be sealed in accordance with section 7607 of this title if the following conditions are met:

(1) At least 10 years have elapsed since the date on which the person successfully completed the terms and conditions of the sentence for the conviction, or if the person has successfully completed the terms and conditions of an indeterminate term of probation that commenced at least 10 years previously.

(2) At the time of the filing of the petition:

(A) the person has only one conviction of a violation of 23 V.S.A. § 1201, which shall be construed in accordance with 23 V.S.A. § 1211; and

(B) the person has not been convicted of a crime arising out of a new incident or occurrence since the person was convicted of a violation of 23 V.S.A. § 1201(a).

(3) Any restitution ordered by the court has been paid in full.

(4) The court finds that sealing of the criminal history record serves the interests of justice.

(h) For petitions filed pursuant to subdivision (a)(1)(D) of this section, unless the court finds that expungement or sealing would not be in the interests of justice, the court shall grant the petition and order that the criminal history record be expunged or sealed in accordance with section 7606 or 7607 of this title if the following conditions are met:

(1) At least 15 years have elapsed since the date on which the person successfully completed the terms and conditions of the sentence for the conviction, or the person has successfully completed the terms and conditions of an indeterminate term of probation that commenced at least 15 years previously.

(2) The person has not been convicted of a crime arising out of a new incident or occurrence since the person was convicted of a violation of subdivision 1201(c)(3)(A) of this title.

(3) Any restitution ordered by the court has been paid in full.

(4) The court finds that expungement or sealing of the criminal history record serves the interests of justice. (Added 2011, No. 131 (Adj. Sess.), § 1; amended 2015, No. 36, § 2, eff. May 26, 2015; 2017, No. 57, § 4; 2017, No. 178 (Adj. Sess.), § 1; 2019, No. 32, § 3, eff. Oct. 1, 2019; 2019, No. 167 (Adj. Sess.), § 13, eff. Oct. 7, 2020.)

§ 7603. Expungement and sealing of record, no conviction; procedure

(a) Unless either party objects in the interests of justice, the court shall issue an order sealing the criminal history record related to the citation or arrest of a person:

(1) within 60 days after the final disposition of the case if:

(A) the court does not make a determination of probable cause at the time of arraignment; or

(B) the charge is dismissed before trial without prejudice; or

(2) at any time if the prosecuting attorney and the defendant stipulate that the court may grant the petition to seal the record.

(b) If a party objects to sealing or expunging a record pursuant to this section, the court shall schedule a hearing to determine if sealing or expunging the record serves the interests of justice. The defendant and the prosecuting attorney shall be the only parties in the matter.

(c), (d) [Repealed.]

(e) Unless either party objects in the interests of justice, the court shall issue an order expunging a criminal history record related to the citation or arrest of a person:

(1) within 60 days after the final disposition of the case if:

(A) the defendant is acquitted of the charges; or

(B) the charge is dismissed with prejudice;

(2) at any time if the prosecuting attorney and the defendant stipulate that the court may grant the petition to expunge the record.

(f) Unless either party objects in the interests of justice, the court shall issue an order to expunge a record sealed pursuant to subsection (a) or (g) of this section eight years after the date on which the record was sealed.

(g) A person may file a petition with the court requesting sealing or expungement of a criminal history record related to the citation or arrest of the person at any time. The court shall grant the petition and issue an order sealing or expunging the record if it finds that sealing or expunging the record serves the interests of justice, or if the parties stipulate to sealing or expungement of the record.

(h) The court may expunge any records that were sealed pursuant to this section prior to July 1, 2018 unless the State's Attorney's office that prosecuted the case objects. Thirty days prior to expunging a record pursuant to this subsection, the court shall provide to the State's Attorney's office that prosecuted the case written notice of its intent to expunge the record. (Added 2011, No. 131 (Adj. Sess.), § 1; amended 2017, No. 178 (Adj. Sess.), § 2; 2019, No. 32, § 4.)

§ 7604. New charge

If a person is charged with a criminal offense after he or she has filed a petition for expungement pursuant to this chapter, the court shall not act on the petition until disposition of the new charge. (Added 2011, No. 131 (Adj. Sess.), § 1.)

§ 7605. Denial of petition

If a petition for expungement is denied by the court pursuant to this chapter, no further petition shall be brought for at least two years, unless a shorter duration is authorized by the court. (Added 2011, No. 131 (Adj. Sess.), § 1; amended 2017, No. 57, § 5.)

§ 7606. Effect of expungement

(a) Order and notice. Upon finding that the requirements for expungement have been met, the court shall issue an order that shall include provisions that its effect is to annul the record of the arrest, conviction, and sentence and that such person shall be treated in all respects as if he or she had never been arrested, convicted, or sentenced for the offense. The court shall provide notice of the expungement to the respondent, Vermont Crime Information Center (VCIC), the arresting agency, and any other entity that may have a record related to the order to expunge. The VCIC shall provide notice of the expungement to the Federal Bureau of Investigation's National Crime Information Center.

(b) Effect.

(1) Upon entry of an expungement order, the order shall be legally effective immediately and the person whose record is expunged shall be treated in all respects as if he or she had never been arrested, convicted, or sentenced for the offense.

(2) In any application for employment, license, or civil right or privilege or in an appearance as a witness in any proceeding or hearing, a person may be required to answer questions about a previous criminal history record only with respect to arrests or convictions that have not been expunged.

(3) The response to an inquiry from any person regarding an expunged record shall be that "NO CRIMINAL RECORD EXISTS."

(4) Nothing in this section shall affect any right of the person whose record has been expunged to rely on it as a bar to any subsequent proceedings for the same offense.

(c) Process.

(1) The court shall remove the expunged offense from any accessible database that it maintains.

(2) Until all charges on a docket are expunged, the case file shall remain publicly accessible.

(3) When all charges on a docket have been expunged, the case file shall be destroyed pursuant to policies established by the Court Administrator.

(d) Special index.

(1) The court shall keep a special index of cases that have been expunged together with the expungement order. The index shall list only the name of the person convicted of the offense, his or her date of birth, the docket number, and the criminal offense that was the subject of the expungement.

(2) The special index and related documents specified in subdivision (1) of this subsection shall be confidential and shall be physically and electronically segregated in a manner that ensures confidentiality and that limits access to authorized persons.

(3) Inspection of the expungement order may be permitted only upon petition by the person who is the subject of the case. The Chief Superior Judge may permit special access to the index and the documents for research purposes pursuant to the rules for public access to court records.

(4) [Repealed].

(5) The Court Administrator shall establish policies for implementing this subsection. (Added 2011, No. 131 (Adj. Sess.), § 1; amended 2015, No. 133 (Adj. Sess.), § 2a, eff. May 25, 2016; 2017, No. 57, § 6; 2017, No. 178 (Adj. Sess.), § 3; 2017, No. 201 (Adj. Sess.), § 3; 2019, No. 32, § 5.)

§ 7607. Effect of sealing

(a) Order and notice. Upon entry of an order to seal, the order shall be legally effective immediately and the person whose record is sealed shall be treated in all respects as if he or she had never been arrested, convicted, or sentenced for the offense and that its effect is to annul the record of arrest, conviction, and sentence. The court shall provide notice of the sealing to the respondent, Vermont Crime Information Center (VCIC), the arresting agency, and any other entity that may have a record related to the order to seal. The VCIC shall provide notice of the sealing to the Federal Bureau of Investigation's National Crime Information Center.

(b) Effect.

(1) Except as provided in subdivision (c) of this section, upon entry of a sealing order, the order shall be legally effective immediately and the person whose record is sealed shall be treated in all respects as if he or she had never been arrested, convicted, or sentenced for the offense.

(2) In any application for employment, license, or civil right or privilege or in an appearance as a witness in any proceeding or hearing, a person may be required to answer questions about a previous criminal history record only with respect to arrests or convictions that have not been sealed.

(3) The response to an inquiry from any member of the public regarding a sealed record shall be that "NO CRIMINAL RECORD EXISTS."

(c) Exceptions. Notwithstanding any other provision of law or a sealing order:

(1) An entity that possesses a sealed record may continue to use it for any litigation or claim arising out of the same incident or occurrence or involving the same defendant.

(2) A criminal justice agency as defined in 20 V.S.A. § 2056a may use the criminal history record sealed in accordance with section 7602 or 7603 of this title without limitation for criminal justice purposes as defined in 20 V.S.A. § 2056a. A sealed record of a prior violation of 23 V.S.A. § 1201(a) shall be admissible as a predicate offense for the purpose of imposing an enhanced penalty for a subsequent violation of that section, in accordance with the provisions of 23 V.S.A. § 1210.

(d) Process.

(1) The court shall bar viewing of the sealed offense in any accessible database that it maintains.

(2) Until all charges on a docket have been sealed, the case file shall remain publicly accessible.

(3) When all charges on a docket have been sealed, the case file shall become exempt from public access.

(e) Special index.

(1) The court shall keep a special index of cases that have been sealed together with the sealing order. The index shall list only the name of the person convicted of the offense, his or her date of birth, the docket number, and the criminal offense that was the subject of the sealing.

(2) The special index and related documents specified in subdivision (1) of this subsection shall be confidential and shall be physically and electronically segregated in a manner that ensures confidentiality and that limits access to authorized persons.

(3) Except as provided in subsection (c) of this section, inspection of the sealing order may be permitted only upon petition by the person who is the subject of the case. The Chief Superior Judge may permit special access to the index and the documents for research purposes pursuant to the rules for public access to court records.

(4) The Court Administrator shall establish policies for implementing this subsection. (Added 2011, No. 131 (Adj. Sess.), § 1; amended 2015, No. 133 (Adj. Sess.), § 2b, eff. May 25, 2016; 2019, No. 32, § 6.)

§ 7608. Victims

(a) At the time a petition is filed pursuant to this chapter, the respondent shall give notice of the petition to any victim of the offense who is known to the respondent. The victim shall have the right to offer the respondent a statement prior to any stipulation or to offer the court a statement. The disposition of the petition shall not be unnecessarily delayed pending receipt of a victim's statement. The respondent's inability to locate a victim after a reasonable effort has been made shall not be a bar to granting a petition.

(b) As used in this section, "reasonable effort" means attempting to contact the victim by first-class mail at the victim's last known address and by telephone at the victim's last known phone number. (Added 2011, No. 131 (Adj. Sess.), § 1.)

§ 7609. Expungement of criminal history records of an individual 18-21 years of age

(a) Procedure. Except as provided in subsection (b) of this section, the record of the criminal proceedings for an individual who was 18-21 years of age at the time the individual committed a qualifying crime shall be expunged within 30 days after the date on which the individual successfully completed the terms and conditions of the sentence for the conviction of the qualifying crime, absent a finding of good cause by the court. The court shall issue an order to expunge all records and files related to the arrest, citation, investigation, charge, adjudication of guilt, criminal proceedings, and probation related to the sentence. A copy of the order shall be sent to each agency, department, or official named in the order. Thereafter, the court, law enforcement officers, agencies, and departments shall reply to any request for information that no record exists with respect to such individual. Notwithstanding this subsection, the record shall not be expunged until restitution and surcharges have been paid in full, provided that payment of surcharges shall not be required if the surcharges have been waived by the court pursuant to section 7282 of this title.

(b) Exceptions.

(1) A criminal record that includes both qualifying and nonqualifying offenses shall not be eligible for expungement pursuant to this section.

(2) The Vermont Crime Information Center shall retain a special index of sentences for sex offenses that require registration pursuant to chapter 167, subchapter 3 of this title. This index shall only list the name and date of birth of the subject of the expunged files and records, the offense for which the subject was convicted, and the docket number of the proceeding that was the subject of the expungement. The special index shall be confidential and shall be accessed only by the Director of the Vermont Crime Information Center and an individual designated for the purpose of providing information to the Department of Corrections in the preparation of a presentence investigation in accordance with 28 V.S.A. §§ 204 and 204a.

(c) Petitions. An individual who was 18-21 years of age at the time the individual committed a qualifying crime may file a petition with the court requesting expungement of the criminal history record related to the qualifying crime after 30 days have elapsed since the individual completed the terms and conditions for the sentence for the qualifying crime. The court shall grant the petition and issue an order sealing or expunging the record if it finds that sealing or expunging the record serves the interests of justice. (Added 2017, No. 201 (Adj. Sess.), § 2; amended 2019, No. 167 (Adj. Sess.), § 14, eff. Oct. 7, 2020.)

§ 7610. Criminal history record sealing special fund

There is established the Criminal History Record Sealing Special Fund, which shall be managed in accordance with 32 V.S.A. chapter 7, subchapter 5. Fees collected pursuant to 32 V.S.A. § 1431(e) for the filing of a petition to seal a criminal history record of a violation of 23 V.S.A. § 1201(a) shall be deposited into and credited to this Fund. This Fund shall be available to the Office of the Court Administrator, the Department of State's Attorneys and Sheriffs, the Department of Motor Vehicles, and the Vermont Crime Information Center to offset the administrative costs of sealing such records. Balances in the Fund at the end of the fiscal year shall be carried forward and remain in the Fund. (Added 2019, No. 32, § 7.)

Chapter 231: Uniform Collateral Consequences Of Conviction

§ 8001. Short title

This chapter may be cited as the Uniform Collateral Consequences of Conviction Act. (Added 2013, No. 181 (Adj. Sess.), § 1, eff. Jan. 1, 2016.)

§ 8002. Definitions

As used in this chapter:

(1) "Collateral consequence" means a mandatory sanction or a discretionary disqualification.

(2) "Conviction" includes an adjudication for delinquency for purposes of this chapter only, unless otherwise specified. "Convicted" has a corresponding meaning.

(3) "Court" means the Criminal Division of the Superior Court.

(4) "Decision-maker" means the State acting through a department, agency, officer, or instrumentality, including a political subdivision, educational institution, board, or commission, or its employees or a government contractor, including a subcontractor, made subject to this chapter by contract, by law other than this chapter, or by ordinance.

(5) "Discretionary disqualification" means a penalty, disability, or disadvantage that an administrative agency, governmental official, or court in a civil proceeding is authorized, but not required, to impose on an individual on grounds relating to the individual's conviction of an offense. Discretionary disqualifications do not encompass charging decisions, such as the imposition of pre-charge diversion or intervention programs.

(6) "Mandatory sanction" means a penalty, disability, or disadvantage imposed on an individual as a result of the individual's conviction of an offense which applies by operation of law whether or not the penalty, disability, or disadvantage is included in the judgment or sentence. The term does not include imprisonment, probation, parole, supervised release, forfeiture, restitution, fine, assessment, or costs of prosecution.

(7) "Offense" means a felony, misdemeanor, or delinquent act under the laws of this State, another state, or the United States.

(8) "Incarceration" means confinement in jail or prison.

(9) "State" means a state of the U.S., the District of Columbia, Puerto Rico, the United States Virgin Islands, or any territory or insular possession subject to the jurisdiction of the United States. (Added 2013, No. 181 (Adj. Sess.), § 1, eff. Jan. 1, 2016.)

§ 8003. Limitation on scope

(a) This chapter does not provide a basis for:

(1) invalidating a plea, conviction, or sentence;

(2) a cause of action for money damages;

(3) a claim for relief from or defense to the application of a collateral consequence based on a failure to comply with this chapter; or

(4) seeking relief from a collateral consequence imposed by another state or the United States or a subdivision, agency, or instrumentality thereof, unless the law of such jurisdiction provides for such relief.

(b) This chapter shall not affect:

(1) the duty an individual's attorney owes to the individual;

(2) a claim or right of a victim of an offense; or

(3) a right or remedy under law other than this chapter available to an individual convicted of an offense. (Added 2013, No. 181 (Adj. Sess.), § 1, eff. Jan. 1, 2016.)

§ 8004. Identification, collection, and publication of laws regarding collateral consequences

(a)(1) The Attorney General shall:

(A) identify or cause to be identified any provision in this State's Constitution, statutes, and administrative rules which imposes a mandatory sanction or authorizes the imposition of a discretionary disqualification and any provision of law that may afford relief from a collateral consequence;

(B) prepare or compile from available sources a collection of citations to, and the text or short descriptions of, the provisions identified under subdivision (a)(1)(A) of this section not later than January 1, 2016; and

(C) update the collection provided under subdivision (B) of this subdivision (1) annually by January 1.

(2) In complying with subdivision (a)(1) of this section, the Attorney General may rely on or incorporate the summary of this State's mandatory sanctions, discretionary disqualifications, and relief provisions prepared by the National Institute of Justice described in Section 510 of the Court Security Improvement Act of 2007, Pub. L. No. 110-177, § 510, 121 Stat. 2534 (2008) as it exists and as it may be amended.

(b) The Attorney General shall include or cause to be included the following statements in a prominent manner at the beginning of the collection required by subsection (a) of this section:

(1) This collection has not been enacted into law and does not have the force of law.

(2) An error or omission in this collection or any reference work cited in this collection is not a reason for invalidating a plea, conviction, or sentence or for not imposing a mandatory sanction or authorizing a discretionary disqualification.

(3) The laws of other jurisdictions that impose additional mandatory sanctions and authorize additional discretionary disqualifications are not included in this collection.

(4) This collection does not include any law or other provision regarding the imposition of or relief from a mandatory sanction or a discretionary disqualification enacted or adopted after [insert date the collection was prepared or last updated].

(c) The Attorney General shall publish or cause to be published the collection prepared and updated as required by subsection (a) of this section.

(d) The Attorney General shall publish or cause to be published as part of the collection the title and Internet address, if available, of the most recent collection of:

(1) the collateral consequences imposed by federal law; and

(2) any provision of federal law that may afford relief from a collateral consequence.

(e) An agency that adopts a rule pursuant to 3 V.S.A. §§ 836-844 that implicates collateral consequences to a conviction shall forward a copy of the rule to the Attorney General. (Added 2013, No. 181 (Adj. Sess.), § 1, eff. Jan. 1, 2016.)

§ 8005. Notice of collateral consequences and eligibility for expungement in pretrial proceeding

(a) When an individual receives formal notice that the individual is charged with an offense, the court shall provide either oral or written notice substantially similar to the following to be communicated to the individual:

(1) If you plead guilty or are convicted of an offense, you may suffer additional legal consequences beyond jail or prison, home confinement, probation, and fines. These consequences may include:

(A) being unable to get or keep some licenses, permits, or jobs;

(B) being unable to get or keep benefits such as public housing or education;

(C) receiving a harsher sentence if you are convicted of another offense in the future;

(D) having the government take your property;

(E) being unable to serve in the military or on a jury;

(F) being unable to possess a firearm; and

(G) being unable to exercise your right to vote if you move to another state.

(2) If you are not a U.S. citizen, a guilty plea or conviction may also result in your deportation, removal, exclusion from admission to the United States, or denial of citizenship.

(3) The law may provide ways to obtain some relief from these consequences.

(4) Further information about the consequences of conviction is available on the Internet at http://legislature.vermont.gov/statutes/chapter/13/231.

(b) Before the court accepts a plea of guilty or nolo contendere from an individual, the court shall:

(1) confirm that the individual received the notice required by subsection (a) of this section and had an opportunity to discuss the notice with counsel, if represented, and understands that there may be collateral consequences to a conviction; and

(2) provide written notice, as part of a written plea agreement or through another form, of the following:

(A) that collateral consequences may apply because of the conviction;

(B) the Internet address of the collection of laws published under this chapter;

(C) that there may be ways to obtain relief from collateral consequences;

(D) that the conviction may be eligible for expungement or sealing pursuant to section 7602 of this title;

(E) contact information for government or nonprofit agencies, groups, or organizations, if any, offering assistance to individuals seeking relief from collateral consequences; and

(F) that conviction of a crime in this State does not prohibit an individual from voting in this State. (Added 2013, No. 181 (Adj. Sess.), § 1, eff. Jan. 1, 2016; amended 2017, No. 57, § 1.)

§ 8006. Notice of collateral consequences and eligibility for expungement upon release

(a) Prior to the completion of a sentence, an individual in the custody of the Commissioner of Corrections shall be given written notice of the following:

(1) that collateral consequences may apply because of the conviction;

(2) the Internet address of the collection of laws published under this chapter;

(3) that there may be ways to obtain relief from collateral consequences;

(4) that the conviction may be eligible for expungement or sealing pursuant to section 7602 of this title;

(5) contact information for government or nonprofit agencies, groups, or organizations, if any, offering assistance to individuals seeking relief from collateral consequences; and

(6) that conviction of a crime in this State does not prohibit an individual from voting in this State.

(b) For persons sentenced to incarceration, the notice shall be provided not more than 30 days and at least 10 days before completion of the sentence. If the sentence is for a term of less than 30 days then notice shall be provided when the sentence is completed.

(c) For persons receiving a sentence involving community supervision, such as probation, furlough, home confinement, conditional reentry, or parole, the notice shall be provided by the Department of Corrections in keeping with its mission of ensuring rehabilitation and public safety.

(d) For persons receiving a penalty involving a fine only, the court shall, at the time of the judgment, provide either oral or written notice that the conviction may be eligible for expungement or sealing pursuant to section 7602 of this title. (Added 2013, No. 181 (Adj. Sess.), § 1, eff. Jan. 1, 2016; amended 2017, No. 57, § 2.)

§ 8007. Authorization required for mandatory sanction; ambiguity

(a) A mandatory sanction may be imposed only by statute or ordinance or by a rule adopted in the manner provided in 3 V.S.A. §§ 836-844. A law or rule shall impose unambiguously a collateral consequence in order for a court to impose a collateral consequence.

(b) A law creating a collateral consequence that is ambiguous as to whether it imposes an automatic mandatory sanction or whether it authorizes a decision-maker to disqualify a person based upon his or her conviction shall be construed as authorizing a discretionary disqualification. (Added 2013, No. 181 (Adj. Sess.), § 1, eff. Jan. 1, 2016.)

§ 8008. Decision to disqualify

In deciding whether to impose a discretionary disqualification, a decision-maker shall undertake an individualized assessment to determine whether the benefit or opportunity at issue should be denied the individual. In making that decision, the decision-maker may consider, if substantially related to the benefit or opportunity at issue, the particular facts and circumstances involved in the offense and the essential elements of the offense. A conviction itself may not be considered except as having established the elements of the offense. The decision-maker shall also consider other relevant information, including the effect on third parties of granting the benefit or opportunity and whether the individual has been granted relief such as an order of limited relief or a certificate of restoration of rights. (Added 2013, No. 181 (Adj. Sess.), § 1, eff. Jan. 1, 2016.)

§ 8009. Effect of conviction by another state or the United States; relieved or pardoned conviction

(a) For purposes of authorizing or imposing a collateral consequence in this State, a conviction of an offense in a court of another state or the United States is deemed a conviction of the offense in this State with the same elements. If there is no offense in this State with the same elements, the conviction is deemed a conviction of the most serious offense in this State which is established by the elements of the offense. A misdemeanor in the jurisdiction of conviction may not be deemed a felony in this State, and an offense lesser than a misdemeanor in the jurisdiction of conviction may not be deemed a conviction of a felony or misdemeanor in this State.

(b) For purposes of authorizing or imposing a collateral consequence in this State, a juvenile adjudication in another state or the United States may not be deemed a conviction of a felony, misdemeanor, or offense lesser than a misdemeanor in this State, but may be deemed a juvenile adjudication for the delinquent act in this State with the same elements. If there is no delinquent act in this State with the same elements, the juvenile adjudication is deemed an adjudication of the most serious delinquent act in this State which is established by the elements of the offense.

(c) A conviction that is reversed, overturned, or otherwise vacated by a court of competent jurisdiction of this State, another state, or the United States on grounds other than rehabilitation or good behavior may not serve as the basis for authorizing or imposing a collateral consequence in this State.

(d) A pardon issued by another state or the United States has the same effect for purposes of authorizing, imposing, and relieving a collateral consequence in this State as it has in the issuing jurisdiction.

(e) A conviction that has been relieved by expungement, sealing, annulment, set-aside, or vacation by a court of competent jurisdiction of another state or the United States on grounds of rehabilitation or good behavior, or for which civil rights are restored pursuant to statute, has the same effect for purposes of authorizing or imposing collateral consequences in this State as it has in the jurisdiction of conviction. However, such relief or restoration of civil rights does not relieve collateral consequences applicable under the law of this State for which relief could not be granted under section 8012 of this title or for which relief was expressly withheld by the court order or by the law of the jurisdiction that relieved the conviction. An individual convicted in another jurisdiction may seek relief under section 8010 or 8011 of this title from any collateral consequence for which relief was not granted in the issuing jurisdiction, other than those listed in section 8012 of this title, and the court shall consider that the conviction was relieved or civil rights restored in deciding whether to issue an order of limited relief or certificate of restoration of rights.

(f) A charge or prosecution in any jurisdiction which has been finally terminated without a conviction and imposition of sentence based on successful participation in a deferred adjudication or diversion program may not serve as the basis for authorizing or imposing a collateral consequence in this State. This subsection does not affect the validity of any restriction or condition imposed by law as part of participation in the deferred adjudication or diversion program, before or after the termination of the charge or prosecution. (Added 2013, No. 181 (Adj. Sess.), § 1, eff. Jan. 1, 2016.)

§ 8010. Order of limited relief

(a) An individual convicted of an offense may petition for an order of limited relief from one or more mandatory sanctions related to employment, education, housing, public benefits, or occupational licensing. The individual seeking an order of relief shall provide the prosecutor's office with notice of his or her petition. After notice, the petition may be presented to the sentencing court at or before sentencing or to the Superior Court at any time after sentencing. If the petition is filed prior to sentencing, it shall be treated as a motion in the criminal case. If the petition is filed after sentencing, it shall be treated as a post-judgment motion.

(b) Except as otherwise provided in section 8012 of this title, the court may issue an order of limited relief relieving one or more of the mandatory sanctions described in this chapter if, after reviewing the petition, the individual's criminal history record, any filing by a victim under section 8014 of this title, and any other relevant evidence, it finds the individual has established by a preponderance of the evidence that:

(1) granting the petition will materially assist the individual in obtaining or maintaining employment, education, housing, public benefits, or occupational licensing;

(2) the individual has substantial need for the relief requested in order to live a law-abiding life; and

(3) granting the petition would not pose an unreasonable risk to the safety or welfare of the public or any individual.

(c) The order of limited relief shall specify:

(1) the mandatory sanction from which relief is granted; and

(2) any restriction imposed pursuant to subsections 8013(a) and (b) of this title.

(d) An order of limited relief relieves a mandatory sanction to the extent provided in the order.

(e) If a mandatory sanction has been relieved pursuant to this section, a decision-maker may consider the conduct underlying a conviction as provided in subsection 8008 of this title. (Added 2013, No. 181 (Adj. Sess.), § 1, eff. Jan. 1, 2016.)

§ 8011. Certificate of restoration of rights

(a) An individual convicted of an offense may petition the court for a certificate of restoration of rights relieving mandatory sanctions not sooner than five years after the individual's most recent conviction of a felony or misdemeanor in any jurisdiction, or not sooner than five years after the individual's release from incarceration pursuant to a criminal sentence in any jurisdiction, whichever is later. The individual seeking restoration of rights shall provide the prosecutor's office with notice of his or her petition.

(b) Except as otherwise provided in section 8012 of this title, the court may issue a certificate of restoration of rights if, after reviewing the petition, the individual's criminal history, any filing by a victim under section 8015 of this title or a prosecuting attorney, and any other relevant evidence, it finds the individual has established by a preponderance of the evidence that:

(1) the individual is engaged in or seeking to engage in a lawful occupation or activity, including employment, training, education, or rehabilitative programs, or the individual otherwise has a lawful source of support;

(2) the individual is not in violation of the terms of any criminal sentence or that any failure to comply is justified, excused, involuntary, or insubstantial;

(3) a criminal charge is not pending against the individual; and

(4) granting the petition would not pose an unreasonable risk to the safety or welfare of the public or to any individual.

(c) A certificate of restoration of rights must specify any restriction imposed and mandatory sanction from which relief has not been granted under section 8013 of this title.

(d) A certificate of restoration of rights relieves all mandatory sanctions, except those listed in section 8012 of this title and any others specifically excluded in the certificate.

(e) If a mandatory sanction has been relieved pursuant to this section, a decision-maker may consider the conduct underlying a conviction as provided in section 8008 of this title. (Added 2013, No. 181 (Adj. Sess.), § 1, eff. Jan. 1, 2016.)

§ 8012. Discretionary disqualifications and mandatory sanctions not subject to order of limited relief or certificate of restoration of rights

(a) An order of limited relief or certificate of restoration of rights may not be issued to relieve the following mandatory sanctions:

(1) requirements imposed by chapter 167, subchapter 3 of this title (sex offender registration; law enforcement notification);

(2) a motor vehicle license suspension, revocation, limitation, or ineligibility pursuant to Title 23 for which restoration or relief is available; or

(3) ineligibility for employment by law enforcement agencies, including the Office of the Attorney General, State's Attorney, police departments, sheriff's departments, State Police, or the Department of Corrections.

(b) An order of limited relief or certificate of restoration of rights may not be issued to relieve a discretionary disqualification or mandatory sanction imposed due to:

(1) a conviction of a listed crime as defined in section 5301 of this title; or

(2) a conviction of trafficking of regulated drugs pursuant to 18 V.S.A. chapter 84. (Added 2013, No. 181 (Adj. Sess.), § 1, eff. Jan. 1, 2016.)

§ 8013. Issuance, modification, and revocation of order of limited relief and certificate of restoration of rights

(a) When a petition is filed under section 8010 or 8011 of this title, including a petition for enlargement of an existing order of limited relief or certificate of restoration of rights, the court shall notify the office that prosecuted the offense giving rise to the collateral consequence from which relief is sought and, if the conviction was not obtained in a court of this State, the Attorney General. The court may issue an order or certificate subject to restriction or condition.

(b) The court may restrict an order of limited relief or certificate of restoration of rights if it finds just cause by a preponderance of the evidence. Just cause includes subsequent conviction of a related felony in this State or of an offense in another jurisdiction that is deemed a felony in this State. An order of restriction may be issued:

(1) on motion of the court, the prosecuting attorney who obtained the conviction, or a government agency designated by that prosecutor;

(2) after notice to the individual and any prosecutor that has appeared in the matter; and

(3) after a hearing if requested by the individual or the prosecutor that made the motion or any prosecutor that has appeared in the matter.

(c) The court shall order any test, report, investigation, or disclosure by the individual it reasonably believes necessary to its decision to issue or modify an order of limited relief or certificate of restoration of rights. If there are material disputed issues of fact or law, the individual and any prosecutor notified under subsection (a) of this section or another prosecutorial agency designated by a prosecutor notified under subsection (a) of this section may submit evidence and be heard on those issues.

(d) A criminal history record as defined in 20 V.S.A. § 2056a and a criminal conviction record as defined in 20 V.S.A. § 2056c shall include issuance and modification of orders and certificates.

(e) The court may adopt rules for application, determination, modification, and revocation of orders of limited relief and certificates of restoration of rights.

(f) If the court grants in part or denies a petition under section 8010 or 8011 of this title, the court may order that the person not petition for relief for that particular offense under either section for a period not to exceed five years. (Added 2013, No. 181 (Adj. Sess.), § 1, eff. Jan. 1, 2016.)

§ 8014. Reliance on order or certificate as evidence of due care

In a judicial or administrative proceeding alleging negligence or other fault, an order of limited relief or a certificate of restoration of rights may be introduced as evidence of a person's due care in hiring, retaining, licensing, leasing to, admitting to a school or program, or otherwise transacting business or engaging in activity with the individual to whom the order was issued, if the person knew of the order or certificate at the time of the alleged negligence or other fault. (Added 2013, No. 181 (Adj. Sess.), § 1, eff. Jan. 1, 2016.)

§ 8015. Victim's rights

A victim of an offense may participate in a proceeding for issuance of an order of limited relief or a certificate of restoration of rights in the same manner as at a sentencing proceeding pursuant to section 5321 of this title to the extent permitted by rules adopted by the court. (Added 2013, No. 181 (Adj. Sess.), § 1, eff. Jan. 1, 2016.)

§ 8016. Uniformity of application and construction

In applying and construing this uniform act, consideration must be given to the need to promote uniformity of the law with respect to its subject matter among states that enact it. (Added 2013, No. 181 (Adj. Sess.), § 1, eff. Jan. 1, 2016.)

§ 8017. Savings and transitional provisions

(a) This chapter applies to collateral consequences whenever enacted or imposed, unless the law creating the collateral consequence expressly states that this chapter does not apply.

(b) This chapter does not invalidate the imposition of a mandatory sanction on an individual before July 1, 2014, but a mandatory sanction validly imposed before July 1, 2014 may be the subject of relief under this chapter. (Added 2013, No. 181 (Adj. Sess.), § 1, eff. Jan. 1, 2016.)

Chapter 232: Vermont Electronic Communication Privacy Act

§ 8101. Definitions

As used in this chapter:

(1) "Adverse result" means:

(A) danger to the life or physical safety of an individual;

(B) flight from prosecution;

(C) destruction of or tampering with evidence;

(D) intimidation of potential witnesses; or

(E) serious jeopardy to an investigation or undue delay of a trial.

(2) "Electronic communication" means the transfer of signs, signals, writings, images, sounds, data, or intelligence of any nature in whole or in part by a wire, a radio, electromagnetic, photoelectric, or photo-optical system.

(3) "Electronic communication service" means a service that provides to its subscribers or users the ability to send or receive electronic communications, including a service that acts as an intermediary in the transmission of electronic communications, or stores protected user information.

(4) "Electronic device" means a device that stores, generates, or transmits information in electronic form.

(5) "Government entity" means a department or agency of the State or a political subdivision thereof, or an individual acting for or on behalf of the State or a political subdivision thereof.

(6) "Law enforcement officer" means:

(A) a law enforcement officer certified at Level II or Level III pursuant to 20 V.S.A. § 2358;

(B) the Attorney General;

(C) an Assistant Attorney General;

(D) a State's Attorney; or

(E) a Deputy State's Attorney

(7) "Lawful user" means a person or entity who lawfully subscribes to or uses an electronic communication service, whether or not a fee is charged.

(8) "Protected user information" means electronic communication content, including the subject line of e-mails, cellular tower-based location data, GPS or GPS-derived location data, the contents of files entrusted by a user to an electronic communication service pursuant to a contractual relationship for the storage of the files whether or not a fee is charged, data memorializing the content of information accessed or viewed by a user, and any other data for which a reasonable expectation of privacy exists.

(9) "Service provider" means a person or entity offering an electronic communication service.

(10) "Specific consent" means consent provided directly to the government entity seeking information, including when the government entity is the addressee or intended recipient or a member of the intended audience of an electronic communication. Specific consent does not require that the originator of a communication have actual knowledge that an addressee, intended recipient, or member of the specific audience is a government entity.

(11) "Subscriber information" means the name, names of additional account users, account number, billing address, physical address, e-mail address, telephone number, payment method, record of services used, and record of duration of service provided or kept by a service provider regarding a user or account. (Added 2015, No. 169 (Adj. Sess.), § 5, eff. Oct. 1, 2016.)

§ 8102. Limitations on compelled production of electronic information

(a) Except as provided in this section, a law enforcement officer shall not compel the production of or access to protected user information from a service provider.

(b) A law enforcement officer may compel the production of or access to protected user information from a service provider:

(1) pursuant to a warrant;

(2) pursuant to a judicially recognized exception to the warrant requirement;

(3) with the specific consent of a lawful user of the electronic communication service;

(4) if a law enforcement officer, in good faith, believes that an emergency involving danger of death or serious bodily injury to any person requires access to the electronic device information without delay; or

(5) except where prohibited by State or federal law, if the device is seized from an inmate's possession or found in an area of a correctional facility, jail, or lock-up under the jurisdiction of the Department of Corrections, a sheriff, or a court to which inmates have access and the device is not in the possession of an individual and the device is not known or believed to be in the possession of an authorized visitor.

(c) A law enforcement officer may compel the production of or access to information kept by a service provider other than protected user information:

(1) pursuant to a subpoena issued by a judicial officer, who shall issue the subpoena upon a finding that:

(A) there is reasonable cause to believe that an offense has been committed; and

(B) the information sought is relevant to the offense or appears reasonably calculated to lead to discovery of evidence of the alleged offense;

(2) pursuant to a subpoena issued by a grand jury;

(3) pursuant to a court order issued by a judicial officer upon a finding that the information sought is reasonably related to a pending investigation or pending case; or

(4) for any of the reasons listed in subdivisions (b)(1)-(3) of this section.

(d) A warrant issued for protected user information shall comply with the following requirements:

(1) The warrant shall describe with particularity the information to be seized by specifying the time periods covered and, as appropriate and reasonable, the target individuals or accounts, the applications or services covered, and the types of information sought.

(2)(A) The warrant shall require that any information obtained through execution of the warrant that is unrelated to the warrant's objective not be subject to further review, use, or disclosure without a court order.

(B) A court shall issue an order for review, use, or disclosure of information obtained pursuant to subdivision (A) of this subdivision (2) if it finds there is probable cause to believe that:

(i) the information is relevant to an active investigation;

(ii) the information constitutes evidence of a criminal offense; or

(iii) review, use, or disclosure of the information is required by State or federal law.

(e) A warrant or subpoena directed to a service provider shall be accompanied by an order requiring the service provider to verify the authenticity of electronic information that it produces by providing an affidavit that complies with the requirements of Rule 902(11) or 902(12) of the Vermont Rules of Evidence.

(f) A service provider may voluntarily disclose information other than protected user information when that disclosure is not otherwise prohibited by State or federal law.

(g) If a law enforcement officer receives information voluntarily provided pursuant to subsection (f) of this section, the officer shall destroy the information within 90 days unless any of the following circumstances apply:

(1) A law enforcement officer has or obtains the specific consent of the sender or recipient of the electronic communications about which information was disclosed.

(2) A law enforcement officer obtains a court order authorizing the retention of the information. A court shall issue a retention order upon a finding that the conditions justifying the initial voluntary disclosure persist. The order shall authorize the retention of the information only for as long as:

(A) the conditions justifying the initial voluntary disclosure persist; or

(B) there is probable cause to believe that the information constitutes evidence of the commission of a crime.

(3) A law enforcement officer reasonably believes that the information relates to an investigation into child exploitation and the information is retained as part of a multiagency database used in the investigation of similar offenses and related crimes.

(h) If a law enforcement officer obtains electronic information without a warrant under subdivision (b)(4) of this section because of an emergency involving danger of death or serious bodily injury to a person that requires access to the electronic information without delay, the officer shall, within five days after obtaining the information, apply for a warrant or order authorizing obtaining the electronic information or a motion seeking approval of the emergency disclosures. The application or motion shall set forth the facts giving rise to the emergency and shall, if applicable, include a request supported by a sworn affidavit for an order delaying notification under subdivision 8103(b)(1) of this section. The court shall promptly rule on the application or motion. If the court finds that the facts did not give rise to an emergency or denies the motion or application on any other ground, the court shall order the immediate destruction of all information obtained, and immediate notification pursuant to subsection 8103(a) of this title if it has not already been provided.

(i) This section does not limit the existing authority of a law enforcement officer to use legal process to do any of the following:

(1) require an originator, addressee, or intended recipient of an electronic communication to disclose any protected user information associated with that communication;

(2) require an entity that provides electronic communications services to its officers, directors, employees, or agents for the purpose of carrying out their duties to disclose protected user information associated with an electronic communication to or from an officer, director, employee, or agent of the entity; or

(3) require a service provider to provide subscriber information.

(j) A service provider shall not be subject to civil or criminal liability for producing or providing access to information in good faith reliance on the provisions of this section. This subsection shall not apply to gross negligence, recklessness, or intentional misconduct by the service provider. (Added 2015, No. 169 (Adj. Sess.), § 5, eff. Oct. 1, 2016.)

§ 8103. Notice to user or subscriber

(a) Except as otherwise provided in this section, a law enforcement officer who executes a warrant or obtains electronic information in an emergency pursuant to subdivision 8102(b)(4) of this section shall serve upon, or deliver to by registered or first-class mail, electronic mail, or other means reasonably calculated to be effective, the identified targets of the warrant or emergency request a notice that informs the recipient that information about the recipient has been compelled or requested, and, if there was an emergency request, states with reasonable specificity the nature of the government action relative to which the information is sought. The notice shall include a copy of the warrant if a warrant was obtained. The notice shall be served, mailed, or delivered by reliable electronic means contemporaneously with the execution of the warrant, or, in the case of an emergency, within three days after obtaining the electronic information.

(b)(1) When a warrant is sought or electronic information is obtained in an emergency under subdivision 8102(b)(4) of this title, the law enforcement officer may submit a request supported by a sworn affidavit for an order delaying the notification required by subsection (a) of this section and prohibiting any party providing information from notifying any other party that information has been sought. The court shall issue the order if it determines that there is reason to believe that notification may have an adverse result. The delay shall not exceed the period of time for which the court finds there is reason to believe that the notification may have the adverse result, and in no event shall the delay exceed 90 days.

(2) The court may grant additional extensions of the delay for periods of up to 90 days each on the same grounds as provided for in subdivision (1) of this subsection.

(3) When the delayed notification period expires, a law enforcement officer shall serve upon, or deliver to by registered or first-class mail, electronic mail, or reliable electronic means to the identified targets of the warrant:

(A) the order for delayed notification;

(B) a document that includes the information described in subsection (a) of this section; and

(C) a copy of all electronic information obtained or a summary of that information, including, at a minimum:

(i) the number and types of records disclosed;

(ii) the date and time when the earliest and latest records were created; and

(iii) a copy of the motion seeking delayed notification.

(c) If there is no identified target of a warrant or emergency request at the time of its issuance, the government entity shall submit to the Department of Public Safety within three days of the execution of the warrant or issuance of the request all of the information required by subsection (a) of this section. If an order delaying notice is issued pursuant to subsection (b) of this section, the law enforcement officer shall submit to the Department upon the expiration of the delayed notification period all of the information required in subdivision (b)(3) of this section. The Department shall publish all reports required by this subsection on its Internet website within 90 days of receipt. The Department shall redact names and other identifying information from the reports.

(d) Except as otherwise provided in this section, nothing in this chapter shall prohibit or limit a service provider or any other party from disclosing information about any request or demand for electronic information.

(e) For purposes of this chapter, a warrant served upon a service provider is deemed to have been executed no later than five days after the information or data compelled by the warrant has been produced by the service provider to a law enforcement officer. (Added 2015, No. 169 (Adj. Sess.), § 5, eff. Oct. 1, 2016.)

§ 8104. Exclusive remedies for a violation of this chapter

(a) A defendant in a trial, hearing, or proceeding may move to suppress electronic information obtained or retained in violation of the U.S. Constitution, the Vermont Constitution, or this chapter.

(b) A defendant in a trial, hearing, or proceeding shall not move to suppress electronic information on the ground that Vermont lacks personal jurisdiction over a service provider, or on the ground that the constitutional or statutory privacy rights of an individual other than the defendant were violated.

(c) A service provider who receives a subpoena issued pursuant to this chapter may file a motion to quash the subpoena. The motion shall be filed in the court that issued the subpoena before the expiration of the time period for production of the information. The court shall hear and decide the motion as soon as practicable. Consent to additional time to comply with process under section 8106 of this title does not extend the date by which a service provider shall seek relief under this subsection. (Added 2015, No. 169 (Adj. Sess.), § 5, eff. Oct. 1, 2016.)

§ 8105. Execution of warrant for information kept by service provider

A warrant issued under this chapter may be addressed to any Vermont law enforcement officer. The officer shall serve the warrant upon the service provider, the service provider's registered agent, or, if the service provider has no registered agent in the State, upon the Office of Secretary of State in accordance with 12 V.S.A. §§ 851-858. If the service provider consents, the warrant may be served via U.S. mail, courier service, express delivery service, facsimile, electronic mail, an Internet-based portal maintained by the service provider, or other reliable electronic means. The physical presence of the law enforcement officer at the place of service or at the service provider's repository of data shall not be required. (Added 2015, No. 169 (Adj. Sess.), § 5, eff. Oct. 1, 2016.)

§ 8106. Service provider's response to warrant

(a) The service provider shall produce the items listed in the warrant within 30 days unless the court orders a shorter period for good cause shown, in which case the court may order the service provider to produce the items listed in the warrant within 72 hours. The items shall be produced in a manner and format that permits them to be searched by the law enforcement officer.

(b) This section shall not be construed to limit the authority of a law enforcement officer under existing law to search personally for and locate items or data on the premises of a Vermont service provider.

(c) As used in this section, "good cause" includes an investigation into a homicide, kidnapping, unlawful restraint, custodial interference, felony punishable by life imprisonment, or offense related to child exploitation. (Added 2015, No. 169 (Adj. Sess.), § 5, eff. Oct. 1, 2016.)

§ 8107. Criminal process issued by Vermont court; reciprocity

(a) Criminal process, including subpoenas, search warrants, and other court orders issued pursuant to this chapter, may be served and executed upon any service provider within or outside the State, provided the service provider has contact with Vermont sufficient to support personal jurisdiction over it by this State. Notwithstanding any other provision in this chapter, only a service provider may challenge legal process, or the admissibility of evidence obtained pursuant to it, on the ground that Vermont lacks personal jurisdiction over it.

(b) This section shall not be construed to limit the authority of a court to issue criminal process under any other provision of law.

(c) A service provider incorporated, domiciled, or with a principal place of business in Vermont that has been properly served with criminal process issued by a court of competent jurisdiction in another state, commonwealth, territory, or political subdivision thereof shall comply with the legal process as though it had been issued by a court of competent jurisdiction in this State. (Added 2015, No. 169 (Adj. Sess.), § 5, eff. Oct. 1, 2016.)

§ 8108. Real time interception of information prohibited

A law enforcement officer shall not use a device that via radio or other electromagnetic wireless signal intercepts in real time from a user's device a transmission of communication content, real time cellular tower-derived location information, or real time GPS-derived location information, except for purposes of locating and apprehending a fugitive for whom an arrest warrant has been issued. This section shall not be construed to prevent a law enforcement officer from obtaining information from an electronic communication service as otherwise permitted by law. (Added 2015, No. 169 (Adj. Sess.), § 5, eff. Oct. 1, 2016.)